SIMILAR BUT DIFFERENT
BELL BEAKERS IN EUROPE

Sidestone Press

SIMILAR BUT DIFFERENT
BELL BEAKERS IN EUROPE

Edited by
Janusz Czebreszuk

In memory of Humphrey Case

Reviewers:
Prof. Lech Czerniak Ph. D.
Prof. Aleksander Kośko Ph. D.
Prof. Lech Krzyżaniak Ph. D.

Assistant editor:
Patrycja Silska

© 2004, 2014 The Individual Authors

First edition 2004, published by Adam Mickiewicz University, Poland

Second edition 2014, published by Sidestone Press, Leiden
     www.sidestone.com

ISBN 978-90-8890-222-2

Layout: Zbigniew Bartkowiak

Photograph cover & design: Bell Beaker from National Museum of Antiquities, Leiden (The Netherlands); e1911-9.13-14 found in mound D at Uddelermeer, Apeldoorn, height 20cm; photo & design by Karsten Wentink

Contents

Janusz Czebreszuk
    Introduction 7

General point of view

Humphrey Case
    Beakers and the Beaker Culture 11

Marc Vander Linden
    Polythetic networks, coherent people: a new historical hypothesis
    for the Bell Beaker phenomenon 35

Laura Salanova
    The frontiers inside the western Bell Beaker block 63

Robin Furestier
    Bell Beaker lithic industry: a rediscover paradise? 77

Bell Beakers common ware

Christian Strahm
    Die Glockenbecher-Phänomen aus der Sicht der Komplementär-
    -Keramik 101

Marie Besse
    Bell Beaker common ware during the third Millennium BC in Europe 127

Valentina Leonini
    La ceramique domestique du Campaniforme de l'Italie Centrale et
    Septentionale 149

Regional point of view

Alex Gibson
    Burials and Beakers: seeing beneath the veneer in late Neolithic
    Britain 173

Olivier Lemercier
    Historical model of setting and spreading out of the Bell Beaker
    culture in Mediterranean France 193

Lucia Sarti
    L'epicampaniforme en Italie Centrale: stratigraphies, datations
    radiometriques, productions lithiques et ceramiques 205

Janusz Czebreszuk
    Bell Beakers: an outline of present stage of research 223

Preface

Janusz Czebreszuk

The proposal from Sidestone Press to reprint the book, *Similar but Different. Bell Beakers in Europe,* came as a surprise. Contemporary scholarship, succumbing to the overwhelming 'pressure of novelty' typical of our culture, quickly forgets about older studies. From this point of view, the 10 years that have passed since the first edition was published (let me remind the readers: the book was originally brought out by the Adam Mickiewicz University Press in Poznań in 2004) is a long time. However, I still receive e-mails from various people and bookshops asking for *Similar but Different…*, which shows that it continues to be in demand. The study also continues to be cited as can be seen from *The Oxford Handbook of the European Bronze Age* (eds. H. Fokkens, A. Harding) published in 2013.

It is beyond question that certain claims made in *Similar but Different…*, have become somewhat dated. Still, I believe that the crucial claims have remained valid. One is the setting of discussion perspectives on the phenomenon of Bell Beakers. On the one hand, they cover theoretically-oriented general issues (looking for similarities), and, on the other, clearly local (regional) ones centred on facts (usually bringing out differences). In this context I would like to emphasize the importance of Chapter 2 (Bell Beakers common ware). It discusses issues that fall between these two extremes (here: concretized in so-called common ware) and is a product of the need to combine both perspectives (general and local) into a single explanatory model in the form of 'a medium-range theory'. This need has not been sufficiently satisfied yet. For the study of Bell Beakers thus far has yet to help us understand what drove their development nor has it revealed how the above culture as a driving force was implanted in specific regions.

What does not vary, arguably, is the fact that the rise of Bell Beakers in no place radically impedes the development of earlier groups: Bell Beakers only enrich the spectrum of cultural states in a region. They are always connected to special objects, in particular those made from materials coming 'from afar' and having a prestigious value. Such issues though, as the way 'Beaker' traits are manifested in archaeological finds (more in graves than in settlements or vice versa), vary from region to region. The same is true for the length of time 'Beaker' traits manifested themselves in a region or their intensity of cultural interaction. All this makes the 'reading' of Bell Beakers productive only when it confronts a general knowledge of the subject with detailed data from specific regions. All this can still be found in *Similar but Different…*

I shared the news of a possible reprint of the book with its authors, who – after an initial surprise – agreed to the re-publication of their texts. Some of them, however, decided to add short postscripts to their chapters accompanied by bibliographical supplements. Among them are Marie Besse, Alex Gibson and Olivier Lemercier.

It is a wish of all of us (the editor, authors and publisher) to dedicate this reprint to the memory of Humphrey Case, one of the authors of *Similar but Different…* who is no longer with us. His great oeuvre on which we draw to this very day, his extensive knowledge which he willingly shared with others and his absorbing mind which searched for new ideas until the very end shall remain a benchmark for us.

J. Czebreszuk,
Rokietnica 3.10.2013

M. Besse

The analysis of the common ware of the Bell Beaker culture I carried out in 2003 at the level of the phenomenon, permitted to highlight the various influences stemming from the pre-Bell Beaker substratum within the process of establishment of the Bell Beaker culture. New questions raised and diversified approaches were developed. In this perspective, we have analysed the absolute chronology of the Bell Beaker based on critical review of the associations between radiocarbon dates and common ware (PIGUET / BESSE 2009). It appeared that the significance of the local Neolithic background had different weight according to the regions. We therefore aimed at understanding, for each region, the role of individuals – bearers of the Bell Beaker culture – their possible migrations and their various origins.

Jocelyne Desideri obtained her PhD degree in 2007 from the University of Geneva. In her thesis she investigated the non-metric dental traits of individuals stemming from the Final Neolithic, the Bell Beaker period and the Early Bronze Age by improving this method using strontium isotope analyses in order to evaluate the significance of individual migration (DESIDERI / BESSE 2010; DESIDERI *et al.* 2010; DESIDERI 2011). The use of natural resources was advanced in order to interpret the migration of individuals and the diffusion of the Bell Beaker culture.

In her doctoral thesis, completed in 2008 at the University of Geneva, Florence Cattin has analysed the copper sources, the minerals on the one hand and the metal artefacts dated to the Final Neolithic and the Bell Beaker culture on the other (CATTIN *et al.* 2011). Since that time, we are continuously working on a holistic approach to the Bell Beaker culture, weighting the relative significance of the different factors with the aim of explaining the technical, economic, social and cultural aspects of the Bell Beaker societies during the third millennium before the Current Era (BESSE 2012).

Bibliografia

BESSE M. 2012. Prehistory of the Upper Rhône Valley: from Neanderthals to Modern Humans. *Archives des Sciences* 65: 229-236.

CATTIN F./ GUÈNETTE-BECK B./ CURDY P./ MEISSER N./ ANSERMET S./ HOFMANN B./ KÜNDIG R./ HUBERT V./ WÖRLE M./ HAMETNER K./ GÜNTHER D./ WICHSER A./ ULRICH A./ VILLA I.M./ BESSE M. 2011. Provenance of Early Bronze Age metal artefacts in Western Switzerland using elemental and lead isotopic compositions and their possible relation with copper minerals of the nearby Valais. *Journal of Archaeological Science*, 38, 1221-1233.

DESIDERI J. 2011. When Beakers Met Bell Beakers. An analysis of dental remains. *British Archaeological Reports, International Series* 2292. Oxford: Archaeopress.

DESIDERI J./ BESSE M. 2010. Swiss Bell Beaker population dynamics: eastern or southern influences? *Archaeological and Anthropological Sciences,* 2, 157-173.

DESIDERI J./ PRICE D./ BURTON J./ FULLAGAR P./ BESSE M. 2010. Mobility evidence during the Bell Beaker period in Western Switzerland through strontium isotope study. Annual Meeting of the American Association of Physical Anthropology (79; April 2010; Albuquerque, New Mexico : abstracts). *American Journal of Physical Anthropology,* 141, Suppl. 50, 93.

PIGUET M./ BESSE M. 2009. Chronology and Bell Beaker common ware, *Radiocarbon,* 51, 2, 817-830.

A. Gibson

My article was published in 2004 and written earlier. It documented a theme that I was researching and was intended to illustrate that much of the perceived Beaker burial practice (crouched, accompanied inhumation below a round barrow) was already familiar to Neolithic populations and that many Beakers are associated with other burial forms (multiple, disarticulated, partial, cremated) all of which have their antecedents in the Neolithic. Since 2004, however, extensive radiocarbon dates have shown that the chronology is much longer than previously anticipated. The burial practices which are found in Beaker times in fact relate to the middle Neolithic (3600-2900 cal BC) rather than the later (3000-2400 cal BC). With this chronological hiatus, comes the problem of continuity. It can now be seen that in the middle Neolithic there is a variety of burial customs and funerary monuments. In the later Neolithic, burial tends to be almost exclusively by cremation. In the early Beaker period (2500-2200 cal BC) there is a distinctive Beaker burial package with continental similarities but also with local nuances. By the late Beaker period (2200-1800 cal BC) there is a resurgence of the variety of burial practices familiar from the middle Neolithic. These are also associated with ceramic and artifact forms and materials and with monument types that also owe their influence to that period. This then seems to represent a resurrection of tradition rather than a continuum.

O. Lemercier

The doctoral thesis behind this short text was published in 2004 with a first documentary basis about the Beaker in the south-east of France (LEMERCIER 2004). Since then, studies have been extended to the Mediterranean France between the Alps and the Pyrenees with more than 580 sites. The chronological sequence of three sets (early Beaker phase - maritime and geometric dotted styles, middle Beaker phase – Rhodano-Provençal and Pyrenean groups and late Beaker phase - Barbed Wire ware) has been specified (LEMERCIER *et al.* in press) and the Rhodano-Provençal group has been the subject of a specific study (LEMERCIER / FURESTIER 2009). The theoretical model: Phenomenon (foreign installation, first contacts) and Cultural (acculturation of local cultures and creation of new entities) remains valid regionally (LEMERCIER 2012a; 2012b). Several studies have been conducted on the burial data (LEMRCIER / TCHÈRÈMISSINOFF 2011) and the late phase and Barbed Wire ceramic in the Bronze Age transition showing a strong local tradition and new impulses (VITAL / CONVERTINI & LEMERCIER 2012). Today's documentary work is extended to the whole of France with more than 1,500 sites have yielded Beaker remains. A Beaker atlas is currently in project.

Bibliografia

LEMERCIER O. 2004. *Les Campaniformes dans le sud-est de la France*, Lattes : Publications de l'UMR 154 du CNRS / ADAL, 2004, 515 p. (Monographies d'Archéologie Méditerranéenne n°18).

LEMERCIER O. 2012a. Interpreting the Beaker phenomenon in Mediterranean France: an Iron Age analogy, *Antiquity,* 86, 311, 2012, 131-143.

LEMERCIER O. 2012b. The Mediterranean France Beakers Transition, In: FOKKENS H./ NICOLIS F. (eds.): *Background to Beakers. Inquiries into the regional cultural background to the Bell Beaker complex*. Leiden: Sidestone Press, 81-119.

LEMERCIER O./ FURESTIER R. 2009. Après les « vrais campaniformes »: Le Rhodano-Provençal dans le sud-est de la France, In: Collectif : *De Méditerranée et d'ailleurs, Mélanges offerts à Jean Guilaine,* Toulouse: Archives d'Ecologie Préhistorique, 2009, 391-402.

LEMERCIER O./ FURESTIER R./ GADBOIS-LANGEVIN R./ SCHULZ PAULSSON B. In press. Chronologie et périodisation des campaniformes en France méditerranéenne, In: *Chronologie de la Préhistoire récente dans le sud de la France* : *Acquis* 1992-2012 / *Actualité de la recherche. Actes des 10e Rencontres Méridionales de Préhistoire Récente* (Ajaccio, 18-20 octobre 2012).

LEMERCIER O./ TCHEREMISSINOFF Y. 2011. Du Néolithique final au Bronze ancien: les sepultures individuelles campaniformes dans le sud de la France, In: SALANOVA L./ TCHEREMISSINOFF Y. (eds.): *Les sepultures individuelles campaniformes en France, Gallia Préhistoire Supplément* XLI, Paris : CNRS, 177-194.

VITAL J./ CONVERTINI F./ LEMERCIER O. (eds.) 2012. Composantes culturelles et premières productions céramiques du Bronze ancien dans le sud-est de la France. Résultats du Projet Collectif de Recherche 1999-2009, *British Archaeological Reports, International Series* 2446, Oxford : Archaeopress.

Similar but Different. Bell Beakers in Europe
Czebreszuk J. (ed.)
Poznań 2004

INTRODUCTION

Janusz Czebreszuk (Poznań, Poland)

Paradoxically enough, Bell Beakers can be said to be the most contemporary phenomenon in Europe's prehistory. A look on a map is enough. They spread across most of the continent, from the Atlantic as far as the Vistula and the middle Danube, which roughly corresponds with the territory of the European Union now. In this context I would like to share with the readers a personal reflection. It frequently happens that when I talk to colleagues who work on Bell Beakers in different parts of Europe we quickly relate to each other: we know what each of us is talking about in spite of the fact that we are not always of the same mind. When I later read papers written by the same people, I am overwhelmed by quite different emotions. I read the papers and what I find in them is not quite the Bell Beakers that we have recently discussed. Why is that so? One thing is absolutely clear: Bell Beakers are a question that does not make life easier for the archaeologists who work on them, at least for the present author. Every researcher working on Bell Beakers has his/her own intuition of the phenomenon, but when it comes to expressing their intuitions in terms of a systematic description, troubles begin. As always, one could give many reasons for this state of affairs. I believe, however, that the true 'mystery' of Bell Beakers lies in dialectic between the general or supraregional and the particular or local. Cannot the same be said about the discussion on contemporary Europe and the role of the European Union in it?

The present book faithfully mirrors the temperature and major issues of the discussion concerning Bell Beakers, which is currently held among archaeologists. The issues touch three main areas. The first and the most general comprises new proposals in the search for the genesis and development dynamics of Bell Beakers (cf. papers by H. Case, M. Vander Linden, L. Salanova i R. Furestier). On the other extreme, we have the exploration of different regional shades of Bell Beakers (cf. papers by A. Gibson, O. Lemercier i L. Sarti). In between, lies the most peculiar area of Bell Beakers where the universal meets the particular. In this area, the discussion currently concerns the much-debated question of the so-called accompanying ceramics (cf. papers by Ch. Strahm, M. Besse i V. Leonini).

The publishing of this volume would not have been possible without the support from many people, in particular from my home Adam Mickiewicz University in Poznań and the Poznań Prehistoric Society. I would like to express special thanks to the Vice Rector, Prof. Bronisław Marciniak, Ph.D., the Dean of the Historical Faculty, Prof. Danuta Minta-Tworzowska, Ph.D., and the Director of the Institute of Prehistory, Prof. Hanna Kóčka-Krenz, Ph.D., for their financial support of this publication. Furthermore, I thank the President of the Poznań Prehistoric Society, Dr. Jacek Kabaciński, for making up the budget of this project.

Janusz Czebreszuk
Rokietnica, April 4th, 2004

General Point of View

Similar but Different. Bell Beakers in Europe
Czebreszuk J. (ed.)
Poznań 2004

BEAKERS AND THE BEAKER CULTURE

Humphrey Case (Oxford, Great Britain)

Summary

This contribution argues that potters at the Tagus estuary developed the Maritime Bell Beaker by around the turn of the first and second quarters of the 3rd millennium BC. - following local tradition and inspired both by knowledge of African pottery and of early Single Grave pottery to the north.

The Maritime beaker become in turn, during the second quarter, the inspiration for various pottery styles which spread out over the Iberian peninsula, and for variously related or similar styles which were evolved thence in Atlantic and southern France; and, by the mid 3rd millennium, for Bell Beaker styles which were developed in northern and central Europe, Britain, Ireland, and the Mediterranean islands.

It is argued that the Bell Beaker was part of an archaeological culture of beaker - tanged copper knife - wristguard - projectile head - a culture likewise of Iberian origin, which became recurrent in burials throughout the beaker world, and which represented a symbolical hunting equipment, which not only honoured the ancestors but ensured their protection for the living.

Beakers

Chronology

Radiocarbon chronology is applied in this contribution in probabilistic quarter millennium spans, thus: - second quarter of the 3rd millennium, around the mid 3rd millennium, third quarter of the 3rd millennium, and so on. This summary procedure (justified in CASE 1995a, 14-15) is adopted with the intention of providing solutions, which are both meaningful and more likely than not to be correct, when making as much use as possible of available results, taking account of the uncertainties of radiocarbon dating both in sampling and other procedures.

Thus, for example, the Single Grave / Corded Ware period in northwest Europe is assessed in two phases: an early phase from the first quarter of the 3rd millennium BC, and a later phase from within the second quarter and persisting into the third quarter (CASE 1993, 248).

Typology and chronology:
an Iberian origin for the Bell Beaker

For more than a quarter of a century, the conclusions of LANTING / VAN DER WAALS (1976), that the Bell Beaker was part of a continuous sequence of development at the Lower Rhine from late Single Grave / Corded Ware pottery, provided the basis for the so-called Dutch model. This model asserting that the Lower Rhine was the European point of origin of Bell Beaker pottery was adopted by many scholars and provided a fundamental and valuable framework for international research.

Continuing work on associations and radiocarbon chronology (DRENTH / LANTING 1991; LANTING / VAN DER PLIGHT 1999/2000; DRENTH / HOGESTIJN 2001) has confirmed and refined the LANTING / VAN DER WAALS chronology for the Lower Rhine: that early Single Grave pottery was first in use in the first quarter of the second millenium BC; that AOO beakers (hybrid Single Grave / Bell Beaker types in my view) were evolved within the second quarter; and that the earliest Bell Beakers appeared around the middle of the 3rd millennium BC or early in its third quarter, partly overlapping with the AOO types in a late Single Grave contexts.

However, research reported at the Riva del Garda Colloquium 1998 (HARRISON / MARTÍN 2001; MÜLLER / VAN WILLIGEN 2001) or published shortly afterwards (BAILLY / SALANOVA 1998) argued that radiocarbon results , while not conrradicting the LANTING/ VAN DER WAALS sequence at the Lower Rhine (VAN DER BEEK / FOKKENS 2001), showed that Bell Beakers (including Maritime types) were earlier in Atlantic and southwest Europe than at the Lower Rhine or indeed elsewhere in Europe - stretching back to the turn of the first and second quarters of the 3rd millennium BC and thus partly overlapping with early Single Grave pottery to the north. This favours arguments that the various Lower Rhenish AOO types, occuring both in graves and in Late Single Grave settlement assemblages, do not represent a systemic production but rather are hybrids, being the earliest efforts by Single Grave potters to render a type of pottery which had become familiar in the Atlantic west -a familiarity emphasised by the recurrent association of AOO types with Grand-Pressigny flint (*e.g.* Fig. 3, no. 2); and that the Lower Rhenish Maritimes are later more accurate versions of this Atlantic type (CASE 1993, 248; 1995a, 18).

The exceptionally large numbers of beakers of the Maritime group in Atlantic and southwest Europe (especially in Estremadura and other regions around the Tagus estuary: HARRISON 1977, 12; SALANOVA 2000a) compared with elsewhere in Europe (including the Lower Rhine where they are comparatively rare – and marginal (DRENTH / HOGESTIJN 2001, 312) additionally supports arguments not only that the Maritime beaker inspired Bell Beaker development in Iberia (HARRISON / MARTÍN 2001), but that it had a similar role more or less all over the beaker world.

An Iberian homeland; the Tagus estuary

The Iberian peninsula would not be a surprising point of origin for the Bell Beaker; it was above all a major region where action was afoot in Chalcolithic Europe west of the Rhine and Alps - with its rather numerous and sometimes intricate walled enclosures (especially the *castros* around the accessible and environmentally attractive Tagus estuary: HARRISON 1977, 24-25); with its very numerous and sometimes spectacular tombs (cave, pit, cist, rock-cut and monumental, drystone and megalithic); and with its extensive settlement evidence; and exceptionally rich assemblages of material culture from which complex exchange-patterns can be inferred.

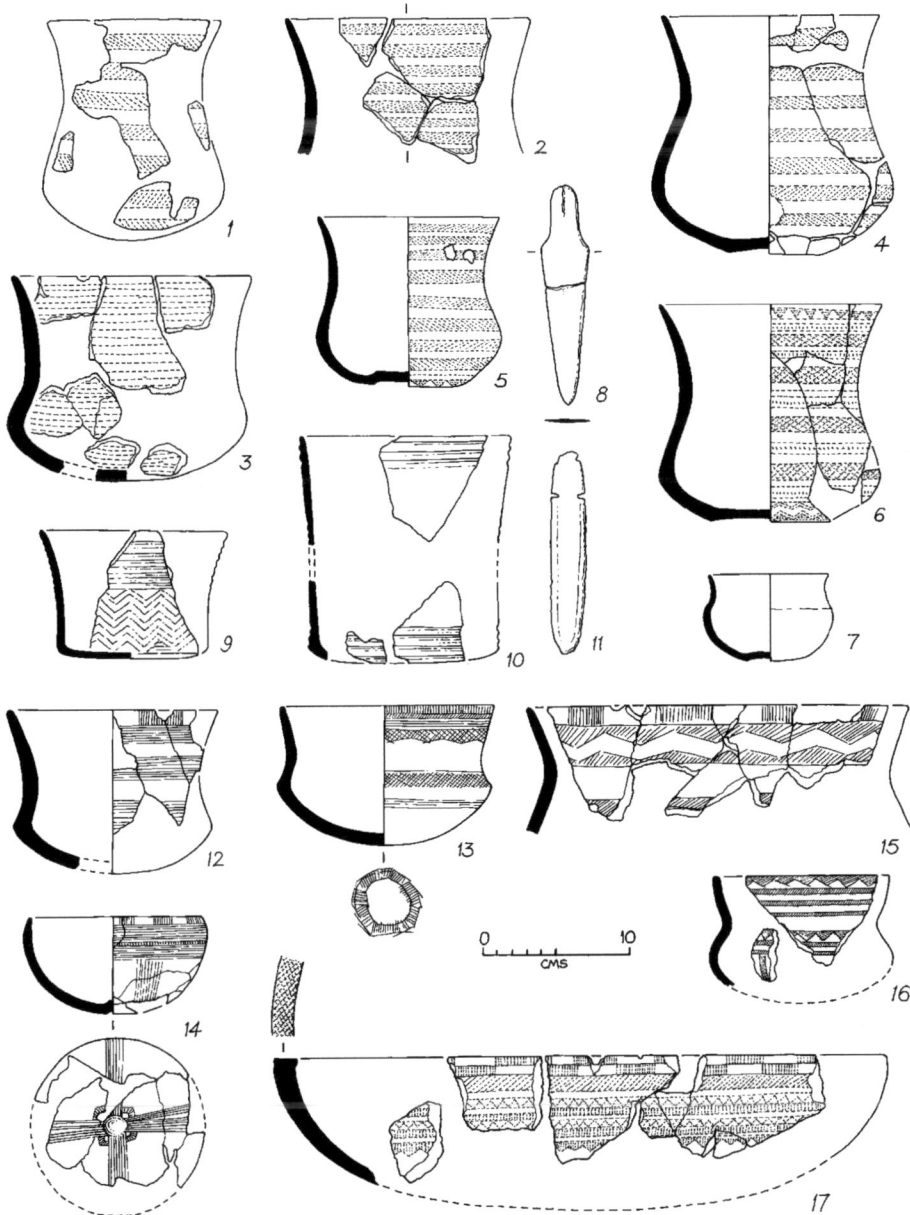

Fig. 1. Maritime beakers: *no. 1*, Zambujal, Estremadura; *no. 2*, House 2, Penha Verde, Sintra; no. *4*, Barrow 242, Veiga dos Mouros, La Coruña. Linear-zoned beaker: *no. 3*, House 2, Penha Verde, Sintra. *Puntillado geométrico* beakers and associations: *nos. 5-8*, Arenero de Miguel Ruiz, Madrid (quartzite core not illustrated). *Copos* and copper knife: *nos. 9-11*, Vila Nova de San Pedro, Estremadura. Palmela style pottery: *nos. 12-14*, Cova da Moura, Torres Vedras; *15*, Montes Claros, Lisbon; *nos. 16, 17*, Tomb IV, Alapraia, Cascais. *No. 1*, after KUNST 1995b, 2001; *2-8, 12-15*, after HARRISON 1977; *9-10*, after DO PAÇO 1959; *11*, after JALHAY / DO PAÇO 1945; *16, 17*, after DO PAÇO 1955.

A pre-Dutch model hypothesis (proposed in BLANCE 1961 and further reviewed in detail in HARRISON 1977, 44-48) was that the Maritime beaker (*e.g.* Fig. 1, nos. 1, 2, 4) was invented by potters around the Tagus estuary. Harrison's summary conclusion was that this „would be neither an unusual nor improbable development" (*op. cit.*, 47) and radiocarbon dating gives it a new edge.

A local contribution to the Maritime style

The argument is that Maritime beakers were invented by potters working in the tradition of the fine ware pots or *copos* (Fig. 1, nos. 9, 10: *e.g.* Do PAÇO 1959, Figs. 4-6: KUNST 1987; 1995a, Taf. 13b, c; 1995b, Fig. 4b) of the late 4th to early 3rd millennium pre- Bell Beaker phase of the Portuguese Chalcolithic (Vila de San Pedro 1 = VNSP 1). Like Maritime beakers in various ways, *copos* show oxidised firing, fine slips, flaring and sharp outlines and rounded bases, and decoration which includes linear zonal patterns and many motifs (including verticality) common to subsequent Bell Beaker developments (Do PAÇO 1959, Figs. 4-6; KUNST 2001, Fig. 1; HARRISON 1977, Fig. 25, rows 3-7, *passim*).

Such initiative by potters in the most inventive region of Chalcolithic western Europe is consistent with stratification. Evidence at Rotura, Setubal, Estremadura (summarised in KUNST 1995a, 148) appears to indicate that *copos* died out before beakers appeared, but pottery analyses at Zambujal, Torres Vedras, Estremadura (KUNST 1995a) show overlap with the Maritime beaker from the first and second quarter of the 3rd millennium BC (radiocarbon results for phases 2 and 3 listed in HARRISON/ MARTÍN 2001, Fig. 7). At these two enclosures and at Leceia, Oeiras, Estremadura (CARDOSO 1994, 1997a, 1997b, 2000, 2001), the later Chalcolithic phase (VNSP 2) is characterised by incised or grooved so-called Acacia-leaf pottery (*e.g.* CARDOSO 1994, Figs. 121-126). This pottery appears pre- Maritime beaker at Zambujal (KUNST 1995a) but with very substantial overlap, and radiocarbon results at Leceia (summarised CARDOSO 1977 a, 26-27) suggest that it was contemporary with *evolved* Bell Beaker pottery (with the Palmela style and incised elements) in the second quarter of the 3rd millennium BC and possibly from the turn of the first and second quarters. At Leceia, beaker pottery including Maritime and evolved sherds (CARDOSO 2001, Fig. 10) was stratified in superficial levels; but two beaker-associated house sites were on the margins of the occupied area and have been dated respectively to the turn of the first and second quarters (with of Maritime and evolved elements: CARDOSO 2001, Fig. 9) and to the mid 3rd millennium BC (with the Palmela style: *loc. cit*, Fig. 7; and radiocarbon results Table 1). I take the evidence at these long-occupied sites to show regional variations, and bearing in mind residuality to suggest that *copos* may have gone out of fashion quite rapidly when Bell Beakers came in, despite apparent overlap. But what were the other elements of the new style?

Non-local contributions: Africa and the north

One non-local element was zonal notched decoration, which is absolutely characteristic of Portuguese Maritime group beakers (with a substantial proportion of it produced by shell-impressions: SALANOVA 2000b, 184, Fig. 113). But notched decoration is virtually absent from VNSP 1. I suggest that this fashion was acquired by potters around the Tagus estuary through contacts with north Africa. VNSP 1 connections in that direction have often been inferred through the acquisition of ostrich shell and ivory. Chronological relationships are far from precise, but zonal notched (comb) impressions are a conspicuous feature of Atlantic northwest Moroccan Late Neolithic pottery: for example at the 4th millennium inhumation cemeteries at El Kiffen and Skhirat, and elsewhere (Daugas 2002, 145-153; information J-P. Daugas). At the cemetery at Rouazi, Skhirat, south of Rabat, small pots and bracelets of ivory and ostrich shell beads occurred, and pottery shapes included bowls and sub-beaker forms; incised decoration was also represented and red-slipped wares were prominent and at least pot was cord-impressed. Although the origin of the Bell Beaker was at the Tagus estuary, I take it that a major decorative inspiration came from north Africa, where copper metallurgy may already have been in progress in the fourth millennium BC (Daugas 2002, 154). The Bell Beaker, being of Portuguese origin, was itself intrusive in the north African sequence (*loc. cit.*, 153): at least two significant concentrations of Maritime beakers of Portuguese affinity in coastal Morocco appear to show such continuing contacts; and a wristguard and Palmela points in Morocco (Harrison 1977, 41-42) should be similarly explained.

Finally, I suggest that the basic beaker shape itself - with tripartite division of the pot into neck, belly, and base in contrast to the bipartite structure of the *copos* (*cf.* Fig. 1, nos. 1, 2, 4 with nos. 9, 10) - came from knowledge of and admiration for Single Grave / Corded Ware beakers to the north[1]. Such contacts with the Single Grave / Corded Ware world to the north would have been *via* the Atlantic fringe along routes familiar earlier in the Neolithic (Cunliffe 2001 for communications in the Atlantic area from prehistoric to early historic times). These 3rd millennium contacts imply minor movements of people in seasonal explorations, west and south from the Single Grave / Corded Ware frontier around the Rhine and north and east from the Tagus estuary, promoting exchanges of information and the transmission of ideas; and not the implausibly large-scale migrations of the so-called invasionist models for this period; or the largely disproved notions of similar movements of pottery around Europe like pieces on a chessboard.

Evidence for such early contacts has tended to be indirect (Case 1995a, 18-19); but more direct evidence of contact between the Corded Ware world and northeast Spain before or around the mid 3rd millennium has come with the wooden mortuary house of Single Grave / Corded affinity (cf. Hvass 1992) at Tres Montes, Navarre, with at least one inhumation burial with Maritime and Cord-zoned-Maritime beakers (Fig. 3, no. 9) both represented (Andrés / Garcia Sesma 1998; summary and radiocarbon results in Harrison / Martín 2001).

---

[1] The flattened bases of some Maritimes might also suggest knowledge of Corded Ware, although the recurrent omphalos and ring bases cannot be derived from that direction. Local experiments? Or perhaps showing some distant knowledge of metal vessels in east Mediterranean regions?

The Maritime beaker as a prototype

The Tagus potters thus produced an exceptionally striking and symbolically charged artefact - representing a fusion of the crafts of two continents and of widespread regions. Typically it has overall horizontal bands of directionally opposed oblique hatching (Fig. 1, nos.1, 2, 4), the visual impact of which would have been all the stronger if one allows for the possibility that these bands on some of the finer reddish or reddish-brown pots were embellished with paler coloured or white filling to produce strongly contrasting stripes (HÁJEK 1966, Pl. 11, nos. 1 & 2 for possible reconstructions of evolved central European types).

The Maritime group: variations on a prototype

It should not be surprising that such a striking pot was widely imitated; and versions of it recur in grave and non-grave associations more or less throughout the peninsula and significantly on the Moroccan coast - although they were overwhelmingly concentrated at the Tagus estuary (HARRISON 1977, Fig. 1). Nor should it be surprising that the Tagus potters rapidly produced variations in notch-impressed motifs which also became widespread, including unidirectionally hatched banding and banding embellished with minor geometrical figures (*e.g.* at Zambujal: KUNST 1987, Figs. 47, 48, nos. S1-14, S16-22, S25, 26), leading to the more complex motifs of the so-called *puntillado geométrico* (*e.g.* Fig. 1, nos. 5, 6 on the Spanish Meseta). Another rarer variant was overall notched linear decoration (so-called all-over-ornamented: Fig. 1, no. 3) - held however not to be primeval at Zambujal (KUNST 1987, 105, 125-127)[2]. Such variations occur at the Tagus estuary in varying proportions (SALANOVA 2000a, 400-402) and similarly occur elsewhere in settlement contexts in the peninsula (*e.g.* Moncín, Zaragoza, HARRISON / MORENO LÓPEZ / LEGGE 1994; Cerro de la Virgén, Granada, layer II A 1 and with more evolved beaker elements (SCHÜLE / PELLICER, Fig. 8). Similarly they recur in graves, for example the Maritime prototype alone (Veiga dos Mouros, La Coruña; Calvazi d'Amposta, I and II, Tarragona: HARRISON 1977, Figs. 67, 88) and in combinations of variants in single graves (*e.g.* in the Madrid region Fig. 1, nos. 5, 6, Arenero de Miguel Ruiz; and Entretérminos (*op.cit.* Fig. 75) and in megalithic associations (*e.g.* Canada Honda G, Seville: LEISNER / LEISNER 1943, Pl. 67, no. 21).

This family of pots (prototype and variants) is referred to here as the *Maritime Group,* and was long-lasting: radiocarbon results are from around the turn of the first and second quarters of the 3rd millennium BC at the Tagus estuary (*e.g.* Zambujal; HARRISON / MARTÍN 2001, Fig. 7) to the mid millennium (Tres Montes, Navarre; *loc. cit.*) or third quarter (in southern Spain; CASE 1987, 116; HARRISON / MARTÍN 2001, Fig. 9).

In Portugal and elsewhere the Maritime group can be considered as part of a fine ware complex including shouldered (Fig. 1, no. 7 in the Madrid area) and to some extent hemispherical bowls (HARRISON 1977, 13-17; and as at Moncín, Zaragoza,

---

2 This variant and the opposed - banded prototype comprise the *standard* as defined in SALANOVA 2000a; also 2000b, *passim.*

HARRISON / MORENO LÓPEZ / LEGGE 1994); and at Moncín at least the associated undecorated pottery seems similar to that of the local Chalcolithic.

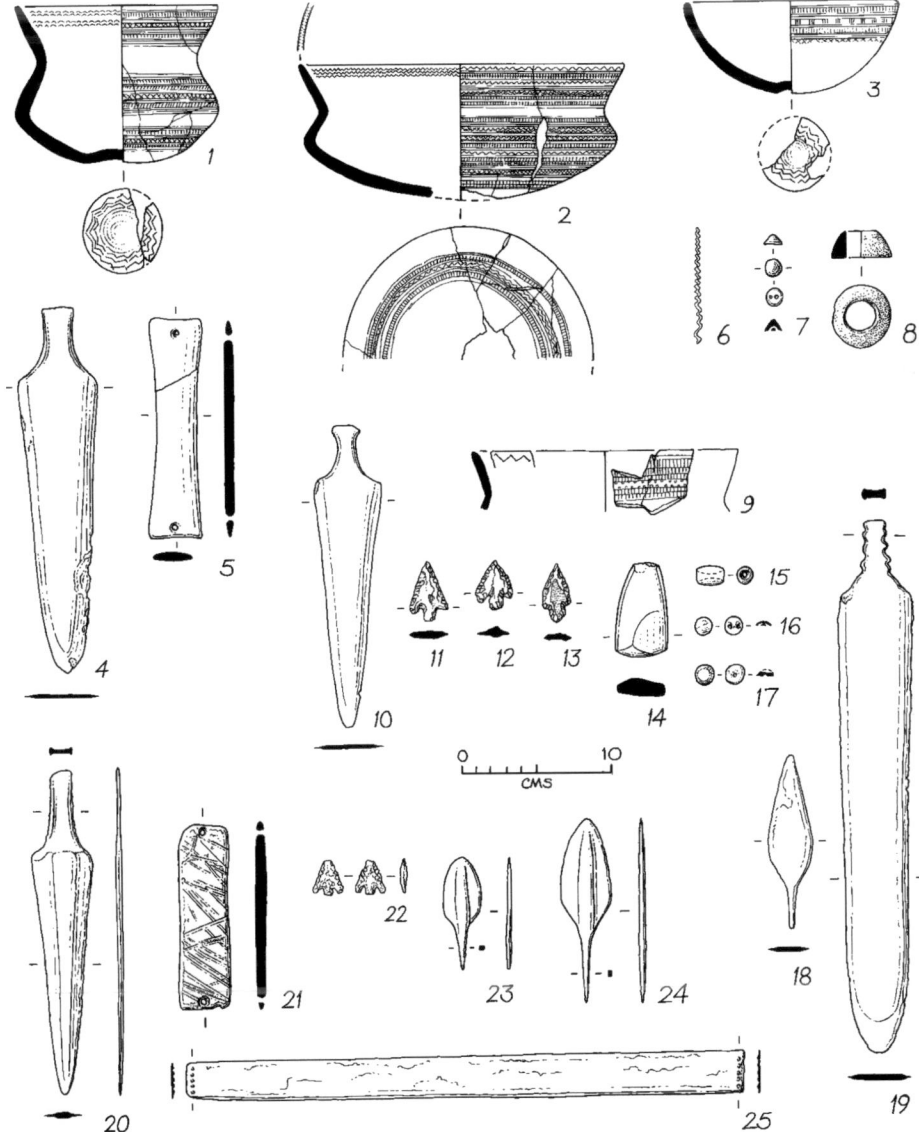

Fig. 2. Ciempozuelos style beakers and associations: *Nos. 1-8*, El Pago de la Peña, Zamora; *9-17*, San Martín de La Guardia, Alava (eleven other bone V-buttons not illustrated); *18, 19*, Cerro de San Miguel, Burgos; *20-25*, Fuente Olmedo. Valladolid (three pots comparable to *nos. 1-3*, and ten other Palmela points not illustrated). *Nos. 4, 10, 18-20, 23, 24*: copper. *Nos. 5, 8, 14, 15, 21*: stone. *No. 22*: flint. *Nos. 6, 25*: gold. *Nos. 16, 17*: bone. *Nos. 1-8*, after HARRISON 1977 and GARRIDO-PENA 2000; *9-17*, after HARRISON 1977; *18-25*, after GARRIDO-PENA 2000.

Evolution from the Maritime Group: some regional developments within the peninsula

The Maritime style may have persisted rather strongly more or less unaltered in northern Portugal and Galicia along the Atlantic sea-ways (Fig. 1, no. 4: SALANOVA 2000a, 402; COLLIGA 2001), but generally and elsewhere highly individualistic regional styles were relatively rapidly produced under the inspiration of the Maritime style, and (as implied in HARRISON / MARTÍN 2001), before or around the mid 3rd millennium. Prominent among such were the Ciempozuelos style of central, eastern and southeastern Spain (*e.g.* Fig. 2, nos. 1-3, 9: HARRISON / MARTÍN 2001, map Fig. 6; radiocarbon results from Atalyuela, Rioja, *loc. cit.*, Fig. 7) and the Palmela style of the Lisbon estuary (*e.g.* Fig. 2, nos. 12-17: radiocarbon results, HARRISON / MARTÍN 2001, *loc. cit.*).

These styles show varied ranges of sizes and forms, with beakers recurrently in a minority compared with more or less similarly decorated bowls (conspicuously with strongly developed decorated rims in the Palmela style (*e.g.* Fig.1, no. 17: DO PAÇO 1955, Figs. 46-53), and cups and dishes, and some pedestal forms also in the Palmela style. Rounded bases are everywhere recurrent. Some standardisation of pottery grave offerings is apparent in the Ciempozuelos style (GARRIDO-PENA 1997, 195-196. Recalling Corded Ware practice?). As in Maritime group association at Moncín, the undecorated pottery associated with these styles in non-grave contexts (*e.g.* at El Ventorro, Madrid; HARRISON 1977, 60-61) seems similar to that of the local pre-beaker Chalcolithic. (Cordons under the rim as recurrent north of the peninsula seem rare).

Decorative characteristics of these regional developments

These are threefold:

(1) An *extended* repertoire of incision (*e.g.* Fig. 1, nos. 12-16; 2, nos. 1-3), grooving and jabs with the primeval notched impressions generally much less frequent.

(2) *Elaboration* of horizontal geometrical motifs, positive and reserved (*e.g.* Fig. 1, no. 15), developing from those of the Maritime group: triangles, chevrons and variants, lozenges, chequer and ladder patterns and criss-cross (*e.g.* Fig. 1, nos. 12-17 and Ciempozuelos style: GARRIDO-PENA 2000, Figs. 46, 47) and some verticality (*e.g.* Fig. 1, nos. 14, 16 and *op. cit.* Pl. 30, no. 6). Some of these motifs can be seen in the Portuguese Acacia-leaf pottery (especially incised chevrons) and even in the decorative schemes of the *copos* and may show widespread shared traditions in textiles (HARRISON 1977, 45-47).

(3) A *rearrangement* of zoning: the regular alternating decorative/plain zonation fell seriously out of fashion, and the decorative zones were separated by more prominent plain zones (*e.g.* Fig. 1, nos. 12, 13; 2, no. 1) or were shunted together into broad bands (*e.g.* Fig. 1, no. 17; 2, no. 2)- recurrently so broad as to virtually cover more or less the whole exterior of the vessel[3]. A narrow band of inner rim decoration is characteristic of the Ciempozuelos style (Fig. 2, nos. 1, 2, 9).

Beaker dispersal beyond the Iberian peninsular

The adoption of the Bell Beaker beyond Iberia and throughout its European range proceeded generally following a similar pattern to that within the peninsula: an initial minor presence generally of the Maritime group (or more or less closely similar versions of it, and sometimes cord-impressed variants, p. 11) in graves rather than settlements; rapidly followed by strongly regional developments in shape, decoration and repertoire in beakers and associated pottery, in abundance in graves and settlements, showing various contributions from the local pre-beaker Neolithic and with derivatives of the Maritime persisting to some extent -and with decoration following numerous variations on the threefold pattern described above. Briefly, some examples: - In the French Pyrenees and Languedoc-Rousillion (SALANOVA 2000b, 108-123) and Provence (LEMERCIER 1998a; 2002) this process may have begun in the second quarter, more or less synchronous with developments in the Iberian peninsula. The same may have been true of the north Italian mainland (a problematical area, MÜLLER / VAN WILLIGEN 2001, 65) but may have been delayed until the mid millennium (NICOLIS 2001, 220, not before 2500 BC)[4]; and a mid millennium starting date may apply to some at least of the Mediterranean islands (*e.g.* the Balearics (WALDREN 1997).

Elsewhere a starting date around the mid 3rd millennium seems widespread, for example; by the Swiss Lakes (with Maritime type contemporary with late Corded Ware; EBERSHWEILER / GROSS-KLEE 1999); at the Lower Rhine (with its general sequence, Maritime - Locally Developed - Veluwe; LANTING / VAN DER WAALS 1976); in Ireland (CASE 1995a) and Britain (CASE 1993; 2001). A similar process can be seen in the Upper Danube basin (HEYD 2000), where, as in the Middle Elbe region (MÜLLER 1999, Ab. 18), it may have been delayed until early in the third quarter of the 3rd millennium (HEYD 2000, 472-473) but where one result from Marktbergel 7, Bavaria (NADLER 1997) appears to indicate a start before the mid millennium; the equivalently dated sample Ua-10410 from Cham ZG - Oberwil, central Switzerland (GNEPF / HÄMMERLE / HOCHULI 1998, 76) may be residual. Beaker representation in south Scandinavia seems to date from the third quarter (VANKILDE 2001).

An exception to this process of development from Maritime or similarly austere variants to regional diversity is seen in Brittany, which shows a pattern similar to that seen on a smaller scale across the Bay of Biscay in Galicia, with an unusual predominance (especially in south Finistère and the Morbihan) of the Maritime group and its fairly close variants (SALANOVA 2000b, 35-54), thein distribution extending to the Channel Islands (*op. cit.*, 54-68). How early this process began remains to

---

3   Variations of this kind were noted by VAN DER WAALS / GLASBERGEN 1955: *e.g.* „zone contraction" in discussing Dutch Locally Developed beakers, and broad bands in the case of the Veluwe beakers.

4   A date around the mid 3rd millennium seems possible for the south grave at S. Cristina, Brescia (NICOLIS 2001, 209, 210, 212 and references), with CZM type beaker and associated wooden mortuary structure recalling Tres Montes, Navarre (page 6, above). Also the east-west burial orientation at S. Cristina and the rare axe association recall Corded Ware burial practice.

be seen, but it would not be surprising if it were before the mid 3rd millennium (as radiocarbon results from Les Fouillages, Guernsey suggest: KINNES 1988, 17).

In the early stages, the general trend of change will have been northwards and eastwards - for example, upstream in the Rhône corridor (as LEMERCIER recognises: 2002, 637) rather than downstream as generally held.

Finally, we must recognise that these regional developments imposed themselves one on the other to produce complex webs of affinity (*e.g.* in Ireland: CASE 1995a, 20-21), and remind ourselves that these pan-European changes will have been imposed in varying degrees on local pottery styles. And we should also bear in mind that eventually more than the adoption of a few exotic pots (mainly for burial) was involved (for instance at Alle, Noir Bois, Jura, some 60-80% of sherds from settlement middens came from beakers or large beaker-shaped jars: OTHENIN-GIRARD 1998, Fig. 6. *cf.* also CASE 1995b, Fig. 6.4).

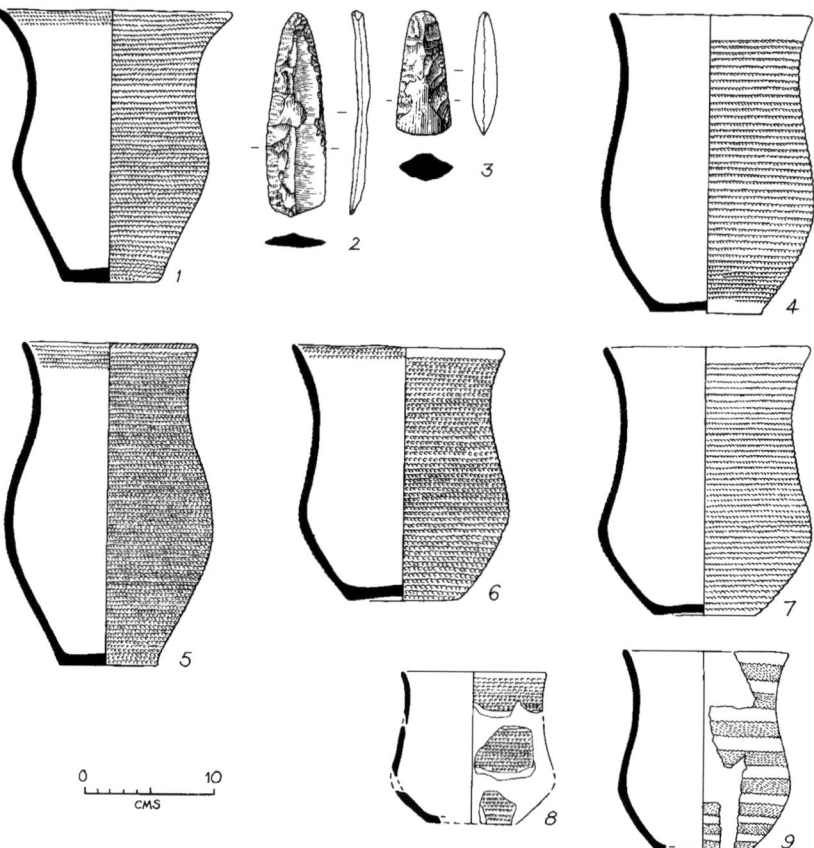

Fig.3. 2IIb beakers and associations: *Nos. 1-3*, Hünxe- Hamweg grave A (*2*, Grand-Pressigny flint; *3*, other flint); *4*, Mellem; *5*, Jablines, Seine- et-Marne (Grand-Pressigny knife unillustrated). Other cord-impressed beakers: *Nos.6*, Bathgate, West Lothian; *7*, Poses, Eure; *8*, Treille, Aude. CZM beaker: *No. 9*, Tres Montes, Navarre. *Nos. 1-4*, after LANTING / VAN DER WAALS 1976; *5, 8*, after SALANOVA 2000b; *7*, after BILLARD / PENNA 1995; *9*, after HARRISON / MARTÍN 2001.

All-over-corded beakers (AOC) and cord-zoned Maritimes (CZM)

Where then stands the all-over-corded variant, often assumed to have been primeval in European Bell Beaker development?

First of all, we must confront the hybrid type 2IIb at the Lower Rhine, of the second quarter of the 3rd millennium BC. These rather localised later Single Grave pots, which occur both in settlements (GINKEL / HOGESTIJN 1997; HOGESTIJN 1997) and graves, are of two kinds: those with narrow base, flaring rims and comparatively high shoulders (e.g. Fig. 3, no. 1; and LANTING / VAN DER WAALS 1976, Figs. 11, 12, 14, 17 right) and those with likewise slender but more flowing profiles (e.g. Fig. 3, no. 4; and loc. cit., Figs. 15, 18 and possibly 13). Both these kinds show a skewed distribution beyond the Lower Rhine: little or no presence northwards (where P47, ring-ditch 201, Radley, Oxfordshire, CLEAL 1999, 204, is a possible example); hardly any to the west where one from Jablines, Seine-et-Marne (Fig. 3, no. 5), which like some of the Dutch pots was associated with a knife of Grand-Pressigny flint (e.g. Fig. 3, no. 2), is a good example of the slender type (SALANOVA 2000b, 324, no. 108); but examples, and others comparable to Lower Rhenish hybrid types, recur southwards, upstream in the Middle Rhine region (e.g BANTELMANN 1982, Pls. 1, no. 31; 2, no. 751; 4, no. 174 A).

However, in western Europe generally we are concerned with a more numerous and quite widespread squatter AOC type, with proportions closer to the Maritime group, for instance: Bathgate, West Lothian (Fig. 3, no. 6) or St. Andrews, Fife (CLARKE 1970, Fig. 6); Poses, Eure (Fig. 3, no. 7; BILLARD / PENA 1995, 290, Fig. 12); Treille, Aude (Fig. 3, no. 8; SALANOVA 2000b, 357, no. 151); Filomena, Catalonia (HARRISON 1977, Fig. 87, nos. 1750, 1751); and with the generally similarly proportioned CZM type itself (e.g. Fig. 3, no. 9; Tres Montes, Navarre: HARRISON / MARTÍN 2001, Fig. 3, no. 3).

When and where did these more numerous and quite widespread variants originate? Beaker pottery with corded decoration is virtually absent from Portugal and uncommon in Spain where its distribution is emphatically northern and central (OTERO 1997, Fig. 6), which argues against AOC and CZM being part of a primeval template (contra HARRISON / MARTÍN 2001) - although it cannot altogether be ruled out that CZM owes something to early Single Grave / Corded Ware pottery where corded decoration was prevalent. If AOC beakers are to be related however to the Lower Rhenish 2IIb, which seems very plausible, they should be seen as secondary developments - although early in origin, say second quarter of the third millennium. At Moncín, the CZM variant was primeval alongside the Maritime type (HARRISON / MORENO LÓPEZ / LEGGE 1994); but the contexts of some early dates quoted for AOC in MÜLLER / VAN WILLIGEN 2001, Fig. 3 (GAR-12408, MC-491, Beta-90622) are of uncertain relevance (cf. GUILAINE / CLAUSTRE / LEMERCIER / SABATIER 2001, 254; COLLIGA 2001, 158, 159, footnote 3). These cord-impressed variants were by no means invariably early, and the AOC type persisted late: at Tres Montes, Navarre, the CZM type was deposited around the mid millennium (HARRISON / MARTÍN 2001, Fig. 7); but in Britain the AOC type persisted through the third and fourth quarters (CASE 1993, 260) and survived as late at the Middle Rhine (Tückelhausen, Hesse; SCHRÖTER / WAMSER 1979/80).

These widespread, conspicuous but generally minority variants may have been innovations in several major regions more or less contemporaneously. Corded decoration is much more frequent in the Languedoc- Rousillon (*e.g.* Fig. 3, no. 8) than elsewhere in western France (SALANOVA 2000b, 121; a possible secondary source for south-east France, LEMERCIER 2002, 637). It is a comparatively minor element in Brittany (SALANOVA 2000b, Fig. 21); but settlement scatters with a substantial proportion of cord impressions are a north British feature (CASE 1993; 2001: Group C). Inner rim decoration (*e.g.* Fig. 3, no. 6) which AOC shares with Lower Rhenish 2IIb (*e.g.* Fig. 3, no. 1) is recurrent in the Spanish Ciempozuelos style (*e.g.* Fig. 2, nos. 1, 2, 9), but also in British Late Neolithic Grooved Ware!

The spread of information and ideas

Finally, all these developments in potting are potentially explainable by exchanges of information in seasonal gatherings and movements (longer range by men, shorter and more frequent by women: discussed in CASE 1998, 408-410), but procurement distances were not great even for important associations (cf. stone for wristguards in northwest Bohemia: TUREK 1998, 109). Movements of this kind, to and from, would have been an essential requirement in a pattern of small and dispersed settlements, of the kind apparently recurrent throughout the beaker world, for example as at Moncín, Zaragoza (HARRISON / MORENO LÓPEZ / LEGGE 1994); and the evidence from Britain and Ireland is consistent with such a pattern (CASE in preparation), as is that in my view from Molenaarsgraaf, western Netherlands (LOUWE KOOIJMANS 1974, 194 ff), Myrhøj, Jutland (JENSEN 1972) and Alle, Bois Noir, Jura (OTHENIN-GIRARD 1998); and a comparatively dense distribution such as at Liptice II, Bohemia (TUREK 1998, 110) or at Cortaillod / sur les Rochettes Est (VON BURG pers. infor.) could be explainable by settlement drift.

However, some apparently very limited transport of pottery was involved: for example a few Maritime beakers in Brittany have fabrics containing exogenous rocks (SALANOVA 2000b, 35 and references). And some unidirectional movements of people seem very likely; PRICE / GRUPE / SCHRÖTER 1998 saw no evidence for mass migration in central Europe in the beaker period, but considered that approaching a quarter of the population might have been be short-distance migrants (also DESIDERI / EIDES in press, for evidence from western Switzerland). Some movements of people carrying gifts or as marriage partners seems very plausible – or as exponents of craft practices other than potting, as seen in the detailed similarity of tanged copper knives throughout the beaker world (p. 13) or in the prevalence in settlement contexts of so-called thumbnail scrapers. And population movement could explain some abrupt interventions at earlier ritual monuments (*e.g.* Petit-Chasseur, Sion, Valais, GALLAY 1976, 281–282; and in the Languedoc, DUBAY 2001), and to some limited extent could explain development generally, say in south-east France (LEMERCIER 2002).

The Beaker Culture

Culture is an ambiguous term, enigmatic with several potential meanings. However it is plain enough that the Bell Beaker was a component of a rich and varied culture - not only in a fairly unspecialised sense of that term as used by the general

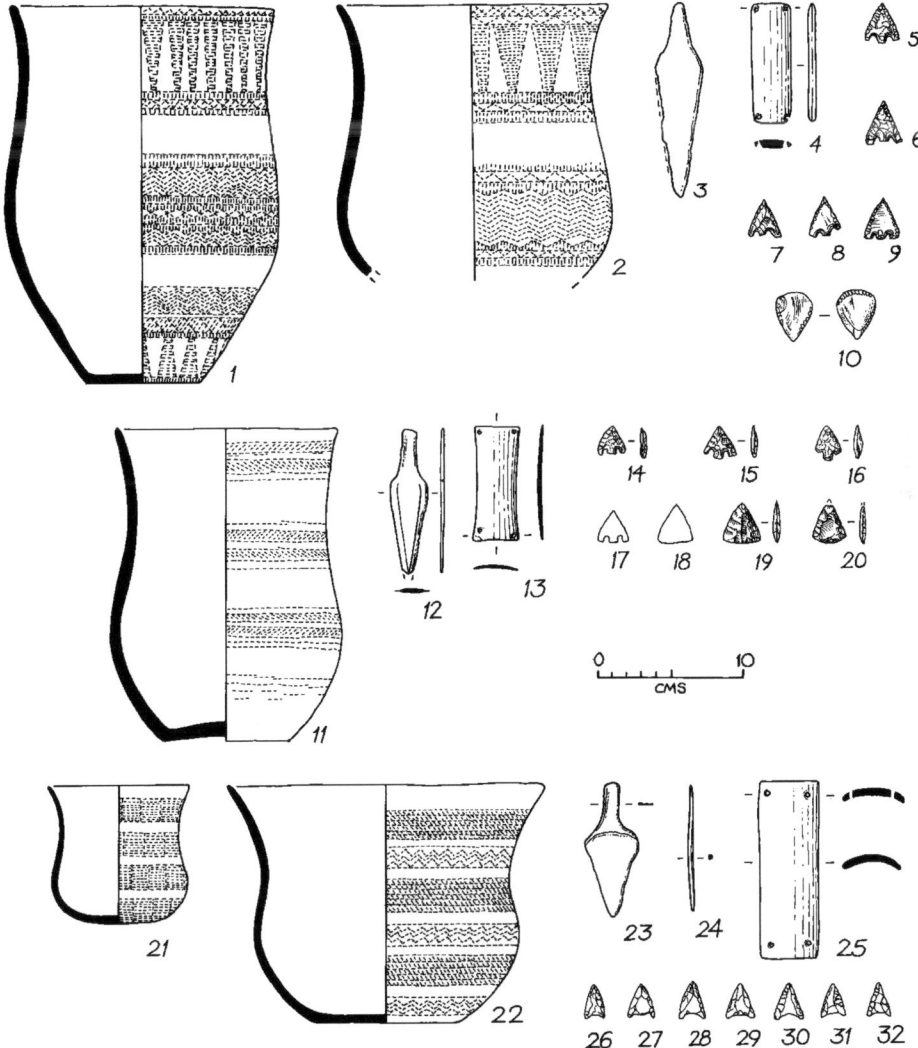

Fig. 4. *Nos. 1-10*, Aremberg, Nord; *nos. 11-20*, Ede- Ginkelse Heide; *nos. 21-32*, Smolín - 1-13/51. *Nos. 3, 12, 23, 24*, copper; *4, 13, 25*, stone; *5-10, 14-20, 26-32*, flint. *Nos. 1-10*, after SALANOVA 2000b and reference; *11-20*, after LANTING / VAN DER WAALS 1976; *21-32*, after DVOŘAK / MATEJICOVÁ / PEŠKA / RAKOVSKÝ 1996.

public, but also as employed in more specialised contexts by historians, sociologists, social anthropologists, etc.

Take for instance the major kinds of burial practice associated with the Maritime and regional pottery styles in the Iberian peninsula, major categories of which like the pottery continue earlier Chalcolithic traditions (as summarised in HARRISON / MARTÍN 2001) and are reflected largely throughout the beaker world, especially:- single-grave burial; individual and multiple burials in earlier collective tombs and monuments (but including burial in one massive monument possibly specially built: Cańada de Carrascal, Seville; LEISNER / LEISNER 1943, Pl. 62; HARRISON 1977, 69); also cave and ossuary burials.

However, the term *Beaker Culture* has been discredited through becoming intertwined with the invasionist model. This has tended to obscure the existence of a culture in a strictly archaeological sense: in the virtually pan-European complex of associations of beaker - tanged copper knife - stone wristguard - piercing arrowhead or other projectile (Figs. 4 and 5, *passim)*. The individual components of this complex (its archery element emphasised by the central European bow pendants) are present in varying degrees throughout the Bell Beaker's geographical range. Recurrent as burial associations, on rare occasions they are present in full panoply and also over a major segment of the beaker world, for instance: - in Ciempozuelos association on the Spanish Meseta, Mejorada del Campo II and Fuente Olmedo (*e.g.* Fig. 2, nos. 20-24: GARRIDO-PENA 2000, Pls. 49, 98, Table 1); in southern Britain, Roundway 8 near Avebury (*e.g.* Fig. 5, nos. 13 – 17: CASE 1998, Fig. 2, nos. 13-17), Winterslow JSS1, Wilts (CLARKE / COWIE / FOXON 1985, Pl. 4.4) and a recently discovered burial near Stonehenge (information Andrew Fitzpatrick); in north coastal France, Aremberg, Nord (Fig. 4, nos. 1-10: SALANOVA 2000b, 331, nos.122 and references); at the Lower Rhine, Ede-Ginkelse Heide (Fig. 4, nos. 11 – 20: LANTING / VAN DER WAALS 1976, Fig. 25) and Luntersche Heide (BUTLER / VAN DER WAALS 1966, 53, Fig. 7)[5]; in the Upper Danube Basin, Trieching 1 and the typologically later Altenmarkt 3, grave 5 (HEYD 2000, taf. 83, 84); in Moravia, Smolín 1-13/51 (Fig. 4, nos. 21-32: DVOŘÁK / MATĚJIČOVÁ / PEŠKA / RAKOVSKÝ 1996, 40, Taf. 53); and a recently excavated burial in the Czech Republic (information Jan Turek).

Partial burial associations are more numerous still and also widespread. If for example one takes wristguard and arrowhead/or other projectile as symbolically interchangeable in representing archery, the list can be expanded by including as examples: El Pago de La Peña, Zamora (Fig. 2, nos. 1-8; GARRIDO-PENA 2000, Pl. 102, Table 1); S. Martin de La Guardia (Fig. 2, nos. 9-17) and Mejorada del Campo I (HARRISON 1977, Figs. 74, 76); Dolmen de Penker, Finistère (L'HELGOUAC'H 1984, Fig. 2, nos. 8-10); Mere 6a, Wilts and Dorchester XII, Oxon and Barnack, Cambs (Fig. 5, nos. 8-12, 18-25), Driffield C38, Yorks (CASE 2001, Fig. 6, nos. 1-5) and Gemeinlebern verf. 2071, Lower Austria (NEUGEBAUER / NEUGEBAUER 1993/1994, Abb. 4; HEYD 2000, Taf. 106). And a flint blade or knife could be interchangeable with a copper one and another pot for a beaker (*e.g.* DVOŘÁK / MATĚJIČOVÁ / PEŠKA / RAKOVSKÝ 1996, 33-34, 60, Taf. 42).

This Bell Beaker grave association is in strong contrast to its Corded Ware equivalent of battleaxe - axe - knife - beaker - arrowhead, and has Atlantic affinities. Trieching 1 (HEYD 2000, Taf. 83) with its beaker comparatively little evolved from the Maritime group, its two-hole wristguard and barbed-and-tanged arrowhead, has a strong Atlantic flavour; similarly the two-hole wristguard from Mere 6a

---

5   And also apparently Lunteren, Luntese Berg (VAN DER WAALS 1976, 60, no. 51) to which however a radiocarbon result around the turn of the third and fourth quarters of the 3rd millennium may not apply (*loc. cit.*, 41).

(Fig. 5, no.12) and the barbed-and- tanged arrowhead from Roundway 8 (Fig. 5, no. 17); similar wristguards from Lunterse Heide and Gemeinlebern and similar arrowheads from Aremberg (Fig. 4, nos. 5-9), Ede-Ginkelse Heide (Fig. 4, nos. 14-17) and Lunteren 1. All these are essentially Atlantic types in Bell Beaker association (as noted in CASE 1995a, 19, 23-24). Can these Atlantic affinities be focussed more clearly?

Tanged copper knives

(Figs. 2, nos. 4, 10, 19, 20; 4, nos. 3, 12, 23; 5, nos. 9, 14, 19, 23)

These so-called West European knives are widespread in the beaker world and numerous in Iberian contexts (e.g. Portugal: HARRISON 1977, 51. Spanish Meseta: GARRIDO-PENA 2000, 179-184), and I take them to be an Iberian innovation. HARRISON (1974, 85) saw no major technological discontinuity between VNSP and beaker-associated metallurgy. Two-edged copper knives with linguate blades (e.g. Fig. 1, no. 11) like some West European knives (e.g. Fig. 2, nos. 4, 19; also less markedly, Fig. 5, nos, 9, 14, 19) are a feature of Iberian pre-beaker copper industries (HARRISON 1974, Fig. 111, nos. 16, 17; DELIBES DE CASTRO / FERNANDEZ MANZANO / HERRÁN MARTINEZ 1998, Fig. 6, nos. 10, 13)[6]. These earlier Chalcolithic knives (and one such has been reported in Maritime beaker association: (Calvari d'Amposta 1, Catalonia: HARRISON 1977, Fig. 88) typically have notched hafting attachments (Fig. 1, no. 11) and sometimes lozenge blade sections; and midrib sections are known (Alcala 3, Algarve: LEISNER / LEISNER 1943, pl. 79, nos. 5-9 alongside the type without midrib, nos. 14-17). In my view, beaker innovations were to replace the notches as hafting aids with hammered flanges to the tang (e.g. Fig. 2, nos. 4, 10, 19, 20; possibly influenced by flanged axe technology to the east?) and substitute grooved blade sections (Fig. 2, nos. 4, 10, 19) of potentially razor-like sharpness (CASE 1953 on British knives) - features which spread throughout the beaker world (e.g. Fig. 5, nos. 9, 14, flanges no. 19, grooves no. 23; Fig. 4, no. 12, flanges no. 23). Such knives recur in Ciempozuelos contexts (e.g. Pago de la Peña, Zamora, HARRISON 1977, Fig. 69; other examples GARRIDO-PENA 2000) and probably occur in Palmela context (HARRISON 1977, Fig. 42), but also in Maritime Group associations (single-grave Arenera de Miguel Ruiz, Madrid, HARRISON 1977, Fig. 77; individual burial in collective tomb, Cañada del Carrascal, Seville, LEISNER / LEISNER 1943, Taf. 62, 67) and in later Maritime but pre-Ciempozuelos context at Montefrio, Granada (ARRIBAS / MOLINA 1980. Phase IV). The type was recorded in the later Chalcolithic (presumably second quarter of the 3rd millennium) phase at Leceia, Lisbon region (so exhibited at the Museum of the Câmara Municipal de Oeiras), and around the turn of the 3rd and 2nd millennia at Fuente Olmedo on the Meseta (GARRIDO-PENA 2000, 197, Pl. 98). In short, these knifes

---

[6] Copper awls also occur in pre-beaker industries (DELIBES DE CASTRO / FERNÁNDEZ MANZANO/ HERRÁN MARTÍNEZ 1998, Fig. 6; HARRISON / MARTÍN 2001, Fig. 10, but the rectangular-sectioned type, which is recurrent in a pan-European context (e.g. Figs. 4, no. 24; 5, no.3), seems to be a Bell Beaker innovation: in Maritime associations possibly (Cañada Honda de Gandul G, Seville, LEISNER / LEISNER 1943, Taf. 67, 1 no. 17; S. Pedro do Estoril, Lisbon area, HARRISON 1977, 110) and in later associations (e.g. Grutas de Cascais, Lisbon area, op. cit., Fig. 42); but apparently early in Morocco (DAUGAS 2002, 154).

were a recurrent, long-lasting feature in the peninsula and their emergence there before the mid 3rd millennium is a strong possibility[7]. The fashion for them may have spread rapidly with the Bell Beaker. A radiocarbon result (MÜLLER 1999, 80) from the well-known Corded Ware / Bell Beaker grave at Bleckendorf, Harz region (MATTHIAS 1968, 9ff, Taf. 5) suggests a date before the mid millennium, which however is out of line with other Bell Beaker dates in the Middle Elbe region (MÜLLER 1999, Abb. 18). A date around the turn of the third and fourth quarters is indicated at Chilbolton, Hants (KINNES 1994).

Stone wristguards

(Figs 2, nos. 5, 21; 4, nos. 4, 13, 25; 5, nos. 12, 16, 21, 24)

I take stone wristguards to be symbolical, durable but comparatively expensive and impractical representations of hide or leather ones. Representations of this kind are conspicuous in pre-beaker Portuguese Chalcolithic contexts (*e.g.* stone sandals, hafted adzes or hoes, so-called „pine cones" (LEISNER 1965, Taf. 69, nos.5, 6; 30, nos. 16; 31, no. 37). Added inspiration may have come from the decorative stone plaques among the cult furniture of the Chalcolithic Alentjo culture, represented strongly in tombs in the Lisbon region (*e.g.* Praia das Maças, Sintra: LEISNER / ZBYSZEWSKI / DA VIEGA FERREIRA 1969, Pl. D); occasionally undecorated stone plaques bored like wristguards appear associated (LEISNER / LEISNER 1959, Taf. 5, no.4; 34, 5, no. 4). Chronological overlap seems at first sight improbable; but a strong attraction to the earlier tombs is seen in secondary Beaker period burial deposits in tombs in the Lisbon region, during the course of which the earlier and spectacular cult paraphernalia will surely have been revealed.

Stone wristguards are quite widespread in Iberia and Atlantic Europe and present in Morocco. Those with two opposed holes are characteristic of Atlantic Europe (Fig. 2, nos. 5, 21), where four-holed types are rare. The converse is true for central Europe (Fig. 4, no. 25); both types occur in Ireland, Britain and at the Lower Rhine (CASE 1995a, 23). The earliest dated European wristguard (four-hole) is mid 3rd millennium at Cova de Frare, Barcelona (MARTÍN / GUILAINE / THOMMERET 1981). The two-hole type was in Palmela association in the Lisbon region (HARRISON 1977, 49 and possibly Figs. 42, 66) and in Ciempozuelos context at Cerro de la Virgen, Granada (SCHÜLE / PELLICER 1966, Fig. 19, no.1) and recurrently on the Meseta (GARRIDO-PENA 2000, 188-190), where dated around the turn of the 3rd and 2nd millennia at Fuente Olmedo. Stone wristguards were long-lasting like the tanged knives, and their strong presence in Argaric contexts from the fourth quarter of the 3rd millennium emphases their power as a symbol. A gold sheet or foil example from Vila Nova de Cerveira (National Museum, Belem), a piece comparable in splendour to the diadem or bracelet from Fuente Olmedo (Fig. 2, no. 25; GARRIDO-PENA 2000, Fig. 98), appears

---

[7] Occurrences in southern France - in Maritime group context at La Balance, Vaucluse (SALANOVA 2000b, 378, Fig. 102) and a notched-and-rivet-tanged apparently transitional type in CZM association at La Fare, Forcalquier, Alpes- de- Haute- Provence (LEMERCIER 1998b, 35) - may have been as early.

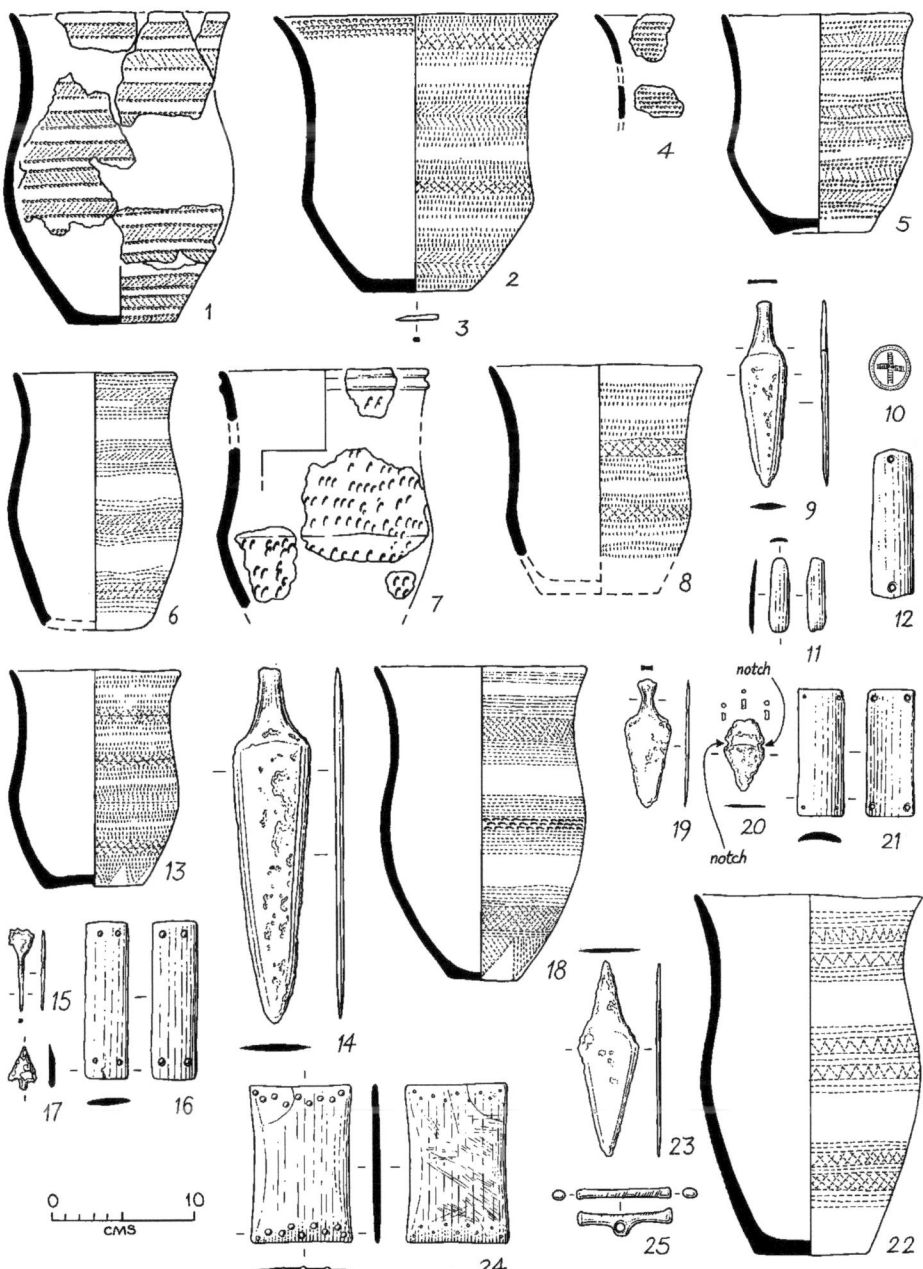

Fig. 5. Beakers and associations. *No. 1*, Wilsford cum Lake 54, Wilts; *nos. 2, 3*, Thickthorn 163a, Dorset; *nos. 4, 5*, Stanton Harcourt II/2, Oxon; *nos. 6,7*, Dean Bottom, Wilts; *8–12*, Mere 6a, Wilts; *13–17*, Roundway 8, Wilts; *18–21*, Dorchester XII, Oxon; *22–25*, Barnack, Cambs. Nos. *9, 14, 15, 19, 23* and probably *3*, copper; *no. 20* (rivet), bronze; *nos. 12, 16, 21, 24*, slate or other rock; *no. 17*, flint; *no. 25*, bone or ivory; *no. 10, 24* (wristguard mounts), gold. After Case 2001.

a skeuomorph of north European stone wristguards with multiple rivet caps (cf. in copper or bronze, Driffield C38, Yorks, CASE 1998, Fig. 3 nos. 1–5; also gold at Barnack, Cambs, here Fig. 5, no. 24). But significantly the Vila Nova de Cerveira specimen has only two attachment holes; its pin-prick decoration recalls that on a gold fragment from Cañada de Carrascal (LEISNER / LEISNER 1943, Pl. 67, in cf. Palmela association).

Piercing flint arrowheads

(Figs. 2, nos. 11-13, 22; 4, nos. 5-9, 14-17, 26-32; 5, no 17).

These are highly important associations of the Iberian pre-beaker Chalcolithic, especially the hollow-based examples of spectacular variety in VNSP 1 (DO PAÇO / COSTA ARTHUR 1952, Fig. 14), with examples in possible Maritime beaker association (Cañada Honda de Gandul G, Carmona: LEISNER / LEISNER 1943, Taf. 67). But the lozenge and tanged types are also widespread (in pre-beaker Alemtejo culture association at Praia das Maças and Casainhos, Sintra: LEISNER / ZBYSZEWSKI / DA VEIGA FERREIRA 1969, Pls. C, 1-81; F, 57-59; P, 35-59, 61, 67). I take these to be models for the barbed-and-tanged type which itself appears in pre-beaker association (Los Pozas, Zamora: DELIBES DO CASTRO / FERNÁNDEZ MANZANO / HARRÁN MARTÍNEZ 1998, Fig. 2); in Ciempozuelos association at San Martin de la Guardia, Alava (Fig. 2, nos. 11-13; HARRISON 1977, Fig. 74), and at Atalayuela, Rioja (HARRISON 1988, Fig. 2) before the mid 3rd millennium and at Fuente Olmedo, Valladolid (Fig. 2, no. 22; GARRIDO-PENA 2000, Fig. 98) around the turn of the 3rd and 2nd millennia; and was most characteristic of beaker associations in Atlantic Europe northwards - in contrast to the hollow-based type characteristic of central Europe (Fig. 4, nos. 26-32).

Palmela points

(Fig. 2, nos. 18, 23, 24)

However, the most conspicuous projectile heads in Iberian Bell Beaker associations are the well-known copper Palmela points. These may have been modelled on pre-beaker lozenge or tanged flint arrowheads, but only a minority (some 15%) can perhaps seriously be considered as arrowheads, the remainder appearing too heavy (cf. a sample from the Meseta in GARRIDO-PENA 2000, Fig. 84 with a sample of nearly 400 English and Irish flint arrowheads in GREEN 1980, 209, Table II.24) and as a group they are probably best taken as javelins. Present more or less throughout the peninsula, with a major concentration in the Tagus estuary area and with outliers in coastal north Morocco (HARRISON 1977, Fig. 24), they diminish in frequency in Atlantic and elsewhere in Mediterranean Europe (ROUSSOT-LARROQUE 1994, map 6). Probably to be associated with the Palmela beaker complex in the Lisbon area (HARRISON 1977, Fig. 24; CARDOSO 2001, 149-151), they are well represented in Ciempozuelos contexts on the Meseta (e.g. Fuente Olmedo, Valladolid: GARRIDO-PENA 2000, Fig. 98, nos. 7-17), occurring in association with tanged knives (with which they share hollow.ground edges) and wristguards (e.g. op. cit., 62, Table 1). In short, although the type continues in Argaric associations, it can be taken as an integral part of the Bell Beaker culture complex under discussion here.

Ancestors and the otherworld

This survey has emphasised three important aspects of the beaker - tanged copper knife - wristguard - projectile head complex: - its Iberian origin, its pan- European extent and its persistence. With pre-beaker roots in the Iberian peninsula, it became focussed there before or around the mid 3rd millennium and spread thence more or less throughout the beaker world, reaching central Europe in the third quarter. In its Iberian homeland it persisted until the end of the millennium.

A fourth important aspect is that it is a burial association. These aspects together point to a strong significance in ethos and mythology. Bell Beaker burial practice has recently been reviewed (CASE in press; and complementary views in GIBSON, this volume). Briefly, those burials surviving in the record cannot by their frequencies be those of complete communities but must represent a selection - presumably from members of elite groups: comprising men, women and some children. Their grave goods as a whole are not functional but symbolical. This is seen not only in their recurrently incomplete (Fig. 5, nos. 1, 5), broken or damaged state (Fig. 5, nos. 21, 24, 19, 20) or worn down and resharpened (possibly Fig. 5, no. 23), but also in their functional inappropriateness. For example, stone is not a very practical material for a wristguard especially when embellished with gold (*e.g.* Fig. 5, no. 24). As for the beaker itself, insular and continental evidence from both burial and non-burial contexts together indicate that it had pluralistic roles within a range of both special and everyday pottery (CASE 1995b). But what we are concerned with here is its symbolical significance as forming part of a complex of burial associations.

What then was the significance of this complex of burial associations in the context of *culture,* as that term is broadly used by anthropologists, historians and the public at large? I suggest that it represents a symbolical hunting equipment - and for the hunting of big game, such as the horse, the wild ox, red deer, the wild pig[8], mankind and perhaps monsters of the spirit world - the projectiles to wound the quarry and wind it until it dropped, the knife to give the *coup-de grâce* by cutting its throat, and the beaker from which to drink its blood. Thus, equipment redolent of a stylish existence, conducive to competitive display, exemplifying courage, endurance and cunning, and the power of the ancestors to protect the living from malevolence from the spirit world - a power which only they (and only some among them) fully possessed. The burial record suggests these attributes and duties fell normally to men[9], as members of what I interpret to be privileged kinship groups of men, women and children entitled to exceptional burial and entrusted to serve the living in the Otherworld, in various roles as seen over the whole range of their burial offerings.

Warborough 2002

---

8   Boar's tusks are quite frequent central European grave goods and occur similarly elsewhere.

9   Not necessarily the elders or men. A man aged 35-40 has indeed been provisionally identified at the recently discovered Stonehenge burial; but a man of 18 was identified at Fuente Olmedo (GARRIDO-PENA 2000, 59) and a woman at a recently excavated burial of similar kind in the Czech Republic (information Jan Turek), and no burial was recorded at Smolín 1-13/5.

Acknowledgments

I am grateful to Richard Harrison for valued comment and much sharing of information; and for much information to João Cardoso, J-P. Daugas, Andrew Fitzpatrick, Rafael Garrido-Pena and Jean Guilaine; and to Volker Heyd, Olivier Lemercier, Laure Salanova, Jan Turek, Zita van der Beek and other members of the organisation *Archéologie et gobelets*; and to numerous other colleagues at the Colloquium *Bell Beakers Today*.

References

ANDRÉS T. / GARCIA M.L. / SESMA J. 1998. El sepulchro calcolítico de Tres Montes (Las Bárdenas Reales), Navarra. In: DE BALBIN BERHMANN R. / BUÉNO RAMIREZ P. (eds), *II Congresso de Arquelogia Peninsular (Zamora 1966) II*, 301 – 308.

ARRIBAS A. / MOLINA F. 1980. Nuevas Apportaciones al Inicio de la Metalurgia en la Peninsular Iberica. El Poblado de los Castillejos de Montefrio (Granada). In: RYAN M. (ed.), *The Origins of Metallurgy in Atlantic Europe*. Dublin, 7-34.

BAILLY Y.M. / SALANOVA L. 2000. Les dates radiocarbones du Campaniforme en Europe occidentale: analyse critique des principales se» ujes des dates. *Actes du Colleque „CIA Archéologie"*. *Memoires de la Sociéte Préhistorique Française* 26, 219-224.

BANTELMANN N. 1982. *Endneolithische Funde in rheinisch-wesfälischen Raum*. Neumünster.

BEEK Z. VAN DER / FOKKENS H. 2001. 24 years after Oberried: the „Dutch Model" reconsidered. In: NICOLIS F. (ed.), *Bell Beakers Today: Pottery, people, culture, symbols in prehistoric Europe*. Trento, 301-308.

BILLARD C. / PENNA B. 1995. Les sites de Poses „Les quatre chemins" et „La plaine de Poses" (Eure): Transition Néolithique moyen-récent et Campaniforme. *Revue archéologique de l'Ouest*, supplement 7, 273-291.

BLANCE B. 1961. *The origin and development of the Bronze Age in the Iberian Peninsular*. PhD thesis, University of Edinburgh.

BUTLER J.J. / VAN DER WAALS J. D. 1966. Bell Beakers and Early Metal-Working in the Netherlands. *Palaeohistoria* 12, 41-139.

CARDOSO J. L. 1994. *Leceia 1983-1993, Oeiras*. (Estudios Arqueológicas de Oeiras).

1997a. *O povoado de Leceia (Deiras)*. Lisbon.

1997b. Génese, Apogeu e Declínio des Fortifiçiônes calcolíthícas da Estremadura. *Zephyrus* 50, 249-261.

2000. The Fortified Site of Leceia (Oeiras) in the Context of the Chalcolithic in Portuguese Estremadura. *Oxford Journal of Archaeology* 19 (2), 37-55.

2001. Le phénomène campaniforme dans les basses vallées du Tage et du Sado (Portugal). In: NICOLIS F. (ed.), *Bell Beakers Today; Pottery, people, culture, symbols in prehistoric Europe*. Trento, 139-154.

CASE H.J. 1953. The Mere, Roundway and Winterslow Beaker Culture knives. *Wiltshire Archaeological and Natural History Magazine* 55, 135-138.

1987. Postscript: Oxford International West Mediterranean Bell Beaker Conference. In: WALDREN W.H. / KENNARD R.C. (eds.), *Bell Beakers of the Western Mediterranean*. Oxford, 115-127.

1993. Beakers: Deconstruction and After. *Proceedings of the Prehistoric Society* 59, 241-268.

1995a. Irish Beakers in their European Context. In: WADDELL J. / SHEE TWOHIG E. (eds.) *Ireland in the Bronze Age*. Dublin, 14-29.

1995b. Beakers; loosening a stereotype. In: KINNES I. / VARNDELL G. (eds.), *„Unbaked Urns of Rudely Shape"*. Oxford, 55-67.

1998. Ou en sont les Campaniformes de l'autre côté de la Manche? *Bulletin de la Société Préhistorique Française* 95, 403-411.

2001. The Beaker Culture in Britain and Ireland: Groups, European Contacts and Chronology. In: NICOLIS F. (ed.), *Bell Beakers Today: Pottery, people, culture, symbols in prehistoric Europe*. Trento, 361-377.

in press. Beaker burial in Britain and Ireland: a role for the dead. Coloquium: *Les sépultures du Néolithique final et du Bronze ancien, 2700-2000 avant J.-C. (Sion 2001)*.

in prep. *The Beaker Culture in Britain and Ireland and its continental connections.*

CLARKE D.L. 1970. *Beaker Pottery of Great Britain and Ireland*. Cambridge.

CLARKE D.V. / COWIE T.G. / FOXON A. 1985. *Symbols of Power at the time of Stonehenge*. Edinburgh.

CLEAL R.M.J. 1999 (1993). Prehistoric Pottery. In: BARCLAY A. / HALPIN C. (eds), *Excavations at Barrow Hills, Radley Oxfordshire: volume 1, The Neolithic and Bronze Age Monument Complex*. Oxford, 195-210.

COLLIGA A.M. 2001. État de la question du Campaniforme dans le contexte culturel Chalcolithique du Nord-est de la péninsule Ibérique. In: NICOLIS F. (ed.), *Bell Beakers Today: Pottery, people, culture, symbols in prehistoric Europe*. Trento, 155-171.

CUNLIFFE B. 2001. *Facing the Ocean: the Atlantic and its peoples*. Oxford.

DAUGAS J-P. 2002. Le Néolithique du Maroc: pour un modèle d'évolution chronologique et culturelle. *Bulletin d' Archéologie Marocaine* 19, 135-156.

DELIBES DE CASTRO G. / FERNÁNDEZ MANZANO J. / HARRÁN MARTÍNEZ J.I. 1998. La métallurgie de l'Age du Cuivre dans le nord du plateau espagnol: charactéristiques des coulées et systèmes de production. In: MORDANT C. / PERNOT M. / RYCHNER V. (eds.), *L'atelier du bronzier en Europe du XXe au VIIIe siècle avant nôtre ère*. Paris.

DESIDERI J. / EIDES S. in press. L'apport de la morphologie cranienne et dentaire sur la question de peuplement campaniforme en Suisse occidentale sous forme de l' analyse logiciste. Colloquium: *Les sépultures du Néolithique final et du Bronze ancien, 2700-2000 avant J.-C. (Sion 2001)*.

DO PAÇO A. 1955. *Necrópole de Alapraia*. Separata dos Anais 6. Lisbon.

1959. Castro de Vila Nova de S. Pedro. XI. Nota sobre un tipo de cerámica del estrato Vila Nova I. *Ampurias* 21, 252-260.

DO PAÇO A. / COSTA ARTHUR M. de L. 1952. Castro de Vila Nova de S. Pedro. Campanha de Escavações (1951), *Broteria* 54, 5-25.

DRENTH E. / HOGESTIJN W.J.H. 2001. The Bell Beaker Culture in the Netherlands; the state of research in 1998. In: NICOLIS F. (ed.) *Bell Beakers Today: Pottery, people, culture, symbols in prehistoric Europe*. Trento, 309-332.

DRENTH E. / LANTING A.E. 1991. Die Chronologie der Einzelgrabkultur in die Niederlanden. In: STRAHM C. (ed), *Internationales Symposion: Die kontintaleuropoäischen Gruppen der Kultur mit Schnurkeramik. Zusammenfassungen: die Chronologie der regionalen Gruppen*. Freiburg i. Br., 103-114.

DUBAY H., in press. *Les Peiriéres à Villedubert (Aude), France: une sépulture collective campaniforme bâtie sur les ruines d'un dolmen*. Colloquium: *Les sépultures du Néolithique final et du Bronze ancien, 2700-2000 avant J.-C. (Sion 2001)*.

DVOŘÁK P. / MATĚJIČOVÁ A. / PEŠKA J. / RAKOVSKÝ I. 1996. *Graberfelder der Glockenbecherkultur in Mähren II.* Brno-Olomouc.

EBERSCHWELER B. with contribution by GROSS-KLEE E. 1999. Die jüngsten endneolithischen Ufer siedlungen am Zürichsee. *Jahrbuch der Schweizerischen Gesellschaft für Ur- und Frühgeschichte* 82, 39-64.

GALLAY A. 1976. The position of the Bell-Beaker civilisation in the chronoogical sequence of Petit-Chasseur, Sion, Valais, Switzerland. In: LANTING J.N. / VAN DER WAALS J.D. (eds), *Glockenbechersymposion Oberried.* Bossum, 279-306.

GARRIDO-PENA R. 1997. Bell Beakers in the Southern Meseta of the Iberian Peninsula: socio-economic context and new data. *Oxford Journal of Archaeology* 16(2), 187-209.

GARRIDO-PENA R. 2000. *El Campaniforme en la Meseta Central de la Península Ibérica.* Oxford.

GINKEL E. VAN / HOGESTIJN W.J.H. 1997. *Bekermensen aan Zee* (ROB Noord-Holland), esp. pp. 93-117.

GNEPF U. / HÄMMERLE S. / HOCHULI S. 1998. New Bell Beaker finds from central Switzerland. In: BENZ M. / VAN WILLIGEN S. (eds), *Some New Approaches to the Bell Beaker „Phenomenom": Lost Paradise?* Oxford, 73-79.

GREEN H.S. 1980. *The Flint Arrowheads of the British Isles.* Oxford.

GUILAINE J. / CLAUSTRE F. / LEMERCIER O. / SABATIER P. 2001. Campaniformes et environment en France méditerranéene. In: NICOLIS F. (ed.), *Bell Beakers Today: Pottery, people, culture, symbols in prehistoric Europe.* Trento, 229-275.

HÁJEK L. 1966. Die älteste Phase der Glockenbecherkultur in Böhmen und Mähren. *Pamatky Archeologické* 57, 210-241.

HARRISON R.J. 1974. A reconsideration of the Iberian background to Beaker metallurgy. *Palaeohistoria* 16, 63-105.

HARRISON R.J. 1977. *The Bell Beaker Cultures of Spain and Portugal (Harvard).*

HARRISON R.J. 1988. Bell Beakers in Spain and Portugal: working with radiocarbon dates in the 3rd millennium B.C. *Antiquity* 62, 464-472.

HARRISON R.J./ MARTÍN A. M. 2001. Bell Beakers and social complexity in Central Spain. In: NICOLIS F. (ed.), *Bell Beakers Today: Pottery, people, culture, symbols in prehistoric Europe.* Trento, 111-124.

HARRISON R. J. / MORENO LÓPEZ C. / LEGGE A. J. 1994. *Moncín: Un Poplado de la Edad del Bronce, Zaragoza.* Zaragoza.

HEYD V. 2000. *Die Spätkupferzeit in Süddeutschland.* Bonn.

HOGESTIJN J.H.W. 1997. Enkele resultaten van het archeologische onderzoek op twee woonplaatsen van de Enkelgrafcultuur bij Winkel in de Groetpolder. In: HALLEWAS D.P. / SCHEEPSTRA G.H. / WOLTERING P.J. (eds), *Dynamisch Landschap.* Van Gorcum, 27-45.

HVASS L. 1992. Die Einzelgrabkultur in Jütland, Dänemark. In: BUCHVALDEK M. / STRAHM C. (eds), *Die kontinentaleuropäischen Gruppen der Kultur mit Schnurkeramik.* Prague, 221-228.

JALHAY E. / DO PAÇO A. 1945. El Castro de Vilanova de San Pedro. *Actas y Memorias de la Sociedad Española de Anthropología, Etnografía y Prehistoria* 20, 5-93.

JENSEN J.A. 1972. *Bopladsen Myrhøj, 3 hustomter med klokkebaegerkeramik. Kuml 1972,* 61-122.

KINNES I. A. 1988. Megaliths in Action: Some Aspects of the Neolithic Period in the Channel Islands. *Archaeological Journal* 145, 13-59.

1994. *British Bronze Age Metalwork, A 17-30: Beaker and Early Bronze Age Grave Groups.* London.

KUNST M. 1987. *Zambojd: Glockenbecher und Kerbblattverzierte Keramik aus dem Grabungen 1964 bis 1973.* Madrider Beiträge 5 (Mainz).

1995a. Zylindrische Gefässe, Kerbblattverzierung und Glockenbecher in Zambujal (Portugal). *Madrider Mitteilungen* 36, 136-149.

1995b. Cerâmica do Zambujal - novos resultados para a cronologia da cerâmica calcolítica. In: KUNST M. (ed.), *Origens, Estruturas e Relaçōes Culturas Calcolíticas da Península Ibérica*. Torres Vedras, 21-29.

2001. Invasion? Fashion? Social Rank? Consideration concerning the Bell Beaker phenomenom in Copper Age fortifications of the Iberian peninsula. In: NICOLIS F. (ed.), *Bell Beakers Today: Pottery, people, culture, symbols in prehistoric Europe*. Trento, 81-90.

LANTING J.N. / VAN DER PLICHT J. 1999/2000. De ^{14}C - chronologie van de Niederlandse Pre- en Protohistorie. III: Neolithikum. *Palaeohistoria* 41/42, 1-110.

LANTING J.N. / VAN DER WAALS J.D. 1976. Beaker Culture relationships in the Lower Rhine Basin. In: LANTING J.N. / VAN DER WAALS J. D. (eds), *Glockenbechersymposion: Oberried 1974*. Bossum, 1-80.

LEISNER G. / LEISNER V. 1943. *Die Megalithgräber der Iberischen Halbinsel: Der Süden*. Berlin.

1959. Die *Megalithgräber der Iberischen Halbinsel: Der Westen*. Berlin.

LEISNER V. 1965. *Die Megalithgräber der Iberischen Halbinsel: Der Westen*. Berlin.

LEISNER V. / ZBYSZEWSKI G. / DA VEIGA FERREIRA O. 1969. *Les monuments préhistoriques de Praia das Mãças et de Casainhos*. Lisbon.

LEMERCIER O. 1998a. Phénomène, culture et tradition: status et rôles du Campaniforme au IIIe millénnaire dans le Sud-Est de la France. *Bulletin de la Société Préhistorique Française* 95, 365-382.

1998b. La Campaniforme dans la moyenne et basse vallée du Rhône. *Archeologia, hors-serie* no. 9, 30-35.

2002. Le Campaniforme dans le sud-est de la France: De l'Archéologie á l'Histoire du troisième millennaire avant notre ère. *Bulletin de la Société Préhistorique Française* 99, 635-639 (Actualités Scientifiques).

L'HELGOUAC'H J. 1984. Le groupe Campaniforme dans le nord, le centre et l'ouest de la France. In: GUILAINE J. (ed.), *L'age du Cuivre européen*. Paris, 59-80.

LOUWE KOOIJMANS 1974. *The Rhine/Meuse Delta: Four Studies on its Prehistoric Occupation and Holocene Geology*. Leiden.

MARTÍN A. / GUILAINE J. / THOMMERET J. & Y. 1981. Estratigrafiá y Dataciones C14 del Yacimento de la „Cova de Frare" de St. Llorenç del Munt (Matadepera, Barcelona). *Zephyrus* 22/23, 101-111.

MATTHIAS W. 1968. *Kataloge zur mitteldeutschen Schnurkeramik: III, Nordharzgebiet*. Berlin.

MÜLLER J. 1999. Zur Radiokarbondatierung des Jung - bis Endneolithikums und der Frühbronzezeit im Mittelelbe - Saale Gebeit (4100-1500 v. Chr.). *Bericht der Römisch-Germanisch Kommiission* 80, 31-90.

MÜLLER J. / VAN WILLIGEN S. 2001. New radiocarbon evidence for European Bell Beakers and the consequences for the diffusion of the Bell Beaker phenomenom. In: NICOLIS F. (ed.), *Bell Beakers Today: Pottery, people, culture, symbols in prehistoric Europe*. Trento, 59-80.

NADLER M. 1997. Kein „reisig Volk von Bogenschützen" - Ein Siedlungs - Komplex der Glockenbecherkultur aus Marktbergel. *Das Archâeologisch Jahr in Bayern 1977*, 61-64.

NEUGEBAUER C. / NEUGEBAUER J.W. 1993/1994. Becherzeitliche Gräber in Gemeinlebern und Oberbierbaum, NÖ. *Mitteilungen Anthropologisches Gesellschaft Wien* 123/124, 193-219.

NICOLIS F. 2001. Some observations on the cultural setting of the Bell Beakers of Northern Italy. In: NICOLIS F. (ed.), *Bell Beakers Today: Pottery, people, culture, symbols in prehistoric Europe*. Trento, 207-227.

OTERO J. SUÁREZ 1997. Un vaso campaniforme con decoracion cordada en Galicia: a Fontenla (Moaña, Pontevedra). *Boletín Auriense* 25, 9-36.

OTHENIN-GIRARD B. 1998. A Bell Beaker settlement at Alle, Noir Bois (Jura, Switzerland). In: BENZ M. / VAN WILLIGEN S. (eds), *Some New Approaches to the Bell Beaker „Phenomenom": Lost Paradise?* Oxford, 57-71.

PRICE T.D. / GRUPE G. / SCHRÖTER P. 1998. Migration in the Bell Beaker period of central Europe. *Antiquity* 72, 405-411.

ROUSSOT-LARROQUE J. 1995. Problèmes campaniformes dans la région centre-atlantique. In: KUNST M. (ed.), *Origens, Estruturas e Relaçońes das Culturas Calcolíticas da Penísula Ibérica.* Torres Vedras, 305-328.

SALANOVA L. 2000a. Mechanismes de Diffusion des Vases Campaniformes: les liens franco-portugais. *Actas do 3º Congresso de Arquelogia Peninsular IV.* Porto, 399-409.

2000b. *La question du Campaniforme en France et dans les îsles anglo-normandes.* Paris.

SCHRÖTER P. / WAMSER L. 1979/80. Eine Etagen-Doppelbeststtung der Glockenbecherkultur von Tückelhausen, stadt Ochenfurst / Underfranken. *Fundberichte aus Hessen* 19/20, 287-325.

SCHÜLE W. / PELLICER M. 1966. EL Cerro de la Virgen (Orce) Granada I. *Excavationes Arquelogicas en España* 46, 1-66.

TUREK J. 1998. The Bell Beaker period in north-west Bohemia. In: BENZ M. / VAN WILLIGEN S. (eds.), *Some New Approaches to the Bell Beaker „Phenomenom"; Lost Paradise?* Oxford, 107-119.

VANKILDE H. 2001. Beaker Representation in the Danish Late Neolithic. In: NICOLIS F. (ed.), *Bell Beakers Today: Pottery, people, culture, symbols in prehistoric Europe.* Trento, 333-360.

WAALS J.D. VAN DER / GLASBERGEN W. 1955. Beaker types and their distribution in the Netherlands. *Palaeohistoria* 4, 5-46.

WALDREN W. 1997. The definition and direction of the Beaker Culture in the Spanish Balearic Islands; a radiocarbon survey. *Oxford Journal of Archaeology* 16 (1), 25-48.

Similar but Different. Bell Beakers in Europe
Czebreszuk J. (ed.)
Poznań 2004

POLYTHETIC NETWORKS, COHERENT PEOPLE:
A NEW HISTORICAL HYPOTHESIS FOR THE BELL BEAKER PHENOMENON

Marc M. Vander Linden (Brussels, Belgium)

Introduction

Since its definition at the turn of the XIXth and XXth century, the issue of the material variability of the Bell Beaker phenomenon — not to say culture — has been a cornerstone in the field of Beaker studies. However, crucial as it might be, this problem has, I think, never been really investigated since most scholars have developed methodological paraphernalia to avoid it. Indeed, the last decades have seen a strong tendency to define „real" Bell Beaker material culture, whilst other evidence is apprehended as a formal background that the analysis must absolutely erase. This trend finds its first expression in the prestige model initiated by David Clarke and Stephen Shennan, for whom „true" bell beakers were compartmented in a package that spread from one elite to the next (SHENNAN 1976, CLARKE 1976; see BRODIE 1994, VANDER LINDEN 2001a for extended theoretical and epistemological criticisms).

Actually, this assimilation of bell beakers to prestige items by David Clarke rests in his previous work on polythetic models (CLARKE 1968). According to him, each cultural trait must be investigated separately since, *a priori*, one should not observe any correlation with other kind of evidence:

A polythetic group is a group of entities such that each entity possesses a large number of attributes of the group, each attribute is shared by large numbers of entities and no single attribute is both sufficient and necessary to the group membership (CLARKE 1968, 36; see also MALMER 1966).

This strictly analytical approach ultimately led him to consider bell beakers as independent objects, set apart of the remaining material culture because of their putative cultural or social function. To paraphrase Binford, bell beakers became extra-cultural means of social distinction. Acting so, Clarke, Shennan and other processual-like archaeologists (*e.g.* NEUSTUPNÝ 1976) introduced a distinction in the archaeological data and relegated local elements to the sole impact of the cultural substrata, much important of course but by no means susceptible to inform us about the global dynamics of the Bell Beaker phenomenon. This peculiar perception of Bell Beaker material culture still shapes many methodologies and narratives,

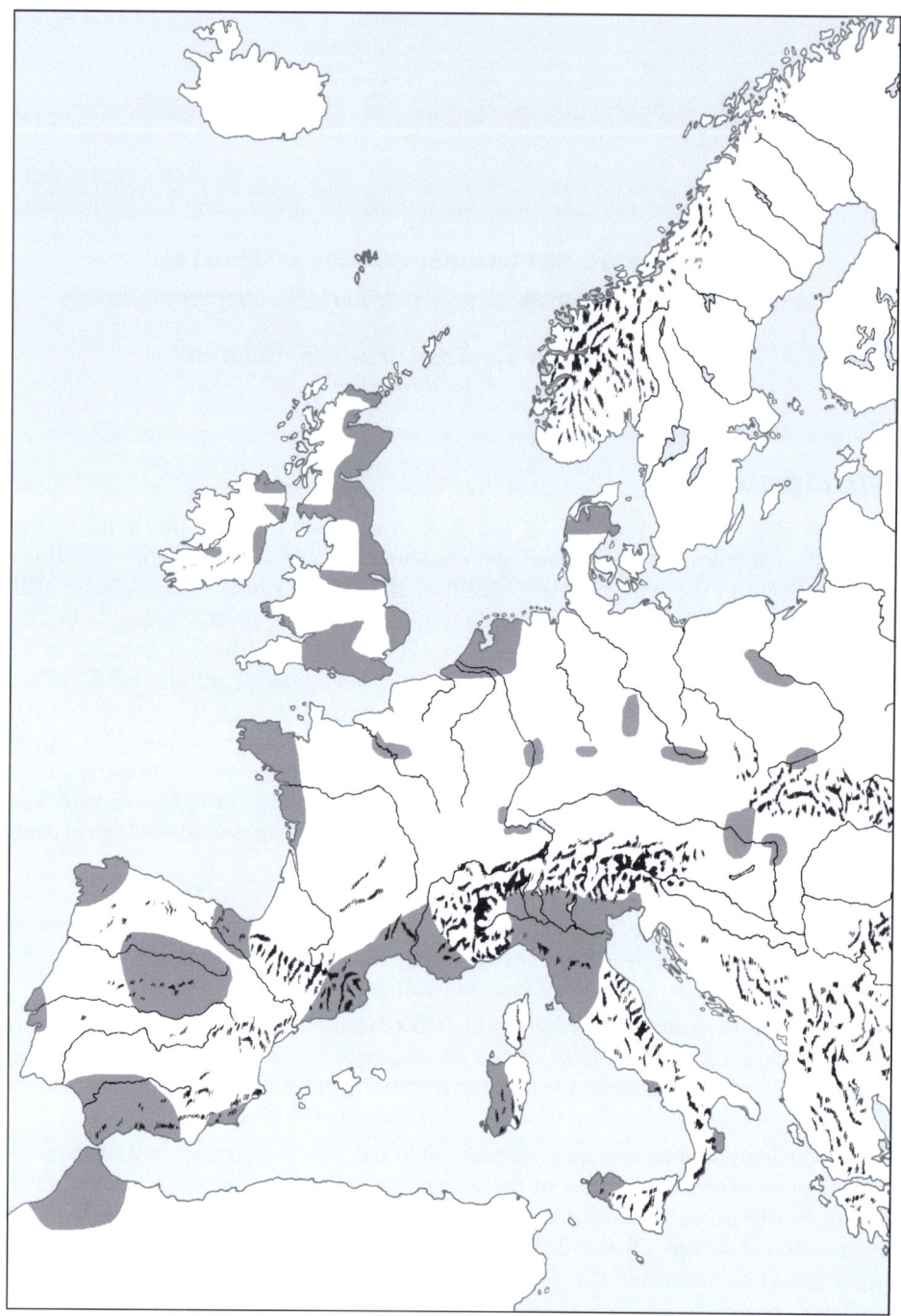

Fig. 1. General map of the Bell Beaker phenomenon.

as evidenced for instance by Laure Salanova's characterization of maritime types as a standard (SALANOVA 1997; 2000), or, by the classification adopted by Strahm and his students in their recently published *Seminar* (STRAHM 1995; BENZ *et al.* 1998a, b).

Yet, this attitude is much damageable since it implicitly assumes a ranking between cultural elements and freezes interpretation. I do not think that any correct and global reading of the Bell Beaker phenomenon will ever be reached until we focus on the recognition and understanding of few selected facets. Homogeneity and variability shape together this cultural phenomenon and give it its historical specificity in Late European Prehistory. What is thus needed is a methodological framework that allows to evaluate both dimensions of the problem at the same time, without prejudging on the potential value of the criteria taken into consideration by the analysis.

In this perspective, it is possible to re-orientate in another direction Clarke's polythetic models as, for instance, Pierre Pétrequin and his team have done in their critical re-evaluation of the Sâone-Rhône culture (PETREQUIN *et al.* 1987-1988; see also PETREQUIN 1993). Actualy, polythetic models are useless unless one tries first to evaluate the geographical nature of the various correlations and, second, to understand the cultural and social value of each investigated material or intellectual production. For instance, by confronting available data for lithics, ceramics and ornament, Pierre Pétrequin and his collaborators have re-defined the Sâone-Rhône culture as a zone of cultural transfer, a concept that better reflects the nature and multiplicity of influences of this region than the old-fashioned but still widely used concept of „archaeological culture". This methodology opens new possibilities to explore the complexity of the Bell Beaker case by acknowledging the fuzzy character of the archaeological record rather than artificially trying to impose abstract categories on it.

As part of my PhD. research (VANDER LINDEN 2001a), I have applied these principles to the entire Bell Beaker phenomenon. Indeed, although this method may potentially carried out at any scale, I have explicitly taken a broad comparative perspective in order to determine the existence — or absence — of coherent patterns that structure the construction of this huge geographical area. Several categories of evidence have been selected according to the quality or quantity of data available in the literature (ceramics, mortuary practices, architecture, exchange networks, subsistence techniques, ...). This leads to the definition of several areas that I loosely refer to as „interaction networks". Indeed, the homogeneity of each zone solely rests in the presence of a given trait which is hardly understandable if it does not express, in a way or another, the sharing of a common tradition, know-how or value. Yet, to become more efficient, an integrative dimension must be added to this overwhelmingly analytical apprehension of the archaeological record. Indeed, if it is possible to define several networks for several traits, these networks sometimes closely correspond to each other within a given area, that I will hereafter define as a region. In this perspective, a region is an homogenous area, resulting from the complementary action of several interaction networks, preferably deriving from divergent kind of evidence (for instance mortuary practices, ceramics and architecture).

As the analysis will show, the role of the cultural substrata is often primordial in the making of the Bell Beaker variability. Yet, besides punctual remarks, this particular issue will not be addressed here. Indeed, if complex processes of appropriation or rejection of the Bell Beaker phenomenon can be identified for every area, such investigation remains meaningless if one does not try to evaluate the nature of the traits that spread. To give primacy to local investigation in the conduction of the analysis is, from a strict methodological point of view, as worthless as defining the Bell Beaker phenomenon as a strictly unitary block. Nevertheless, I will privilege here the possibility to outline the global dynamics of the period, in order to set a general interpretative framework for regional investigation of modalities of appropriation by the local communities (see VANDER LINDEN 2001a, b, c, 2003).

Finally, such study bypasses both factual and evolutionist perceptions of the Bell Beaker phenomenon valorized throughout the XXth century by focusing on the underlying factors that allowed the constitution and maintenance of this cultural and/or social unity for several centuries, rather than simply subsuming these mechanisms under abstract categories like „social hierarchisation" that say nothing of the way people dealt with the construction and reproduction of their societies.

Local networks

Exchange networks

Variability is first evidenced by exchange, since there are no instances of major economic networks as known during the 5th and 4th millennia BC (e.g. PETREQUIN et al. 1997). Likewise, imports of Grand-Pressigny flint in the Low Countries abruptly stop during the AOO phase, it is with the emergence of „true" typological Bell Beaker elements (DRENTH 1989, VAN DER WAALS 1991). One could also mention the local character of pottery fabrics throughout Europe as demonstrated by numerous petrographic analyses (e.g. MILLAN / ARRIBAS 1994; PARKER / PEARSON 1995; CONVERTINI / QUERRE 1998). Albeit this list could be extended almost infinitely for every facet of material culture (for instance lithics: PAUTREAU / ROBERT 1980; JOUSSAUME 1981, 462-466; BAGOLINI / PEDROTTI 1998, 277; BAILLY et al. 1998), these few selected examples show that it is illusory to look for an economic ancestor to the Bell Beaker phenomenon and that the reasons for its partial homogeneity must not be sought in the economic sphere.

Subsistence techniques

Subsistence techniques remain, comparatively, poorly known for the Bell Beaker phenomenon. Yet, old theories that identified the spread of the Bell Beaker material culture with a pastoralist way of life cannot be sustained anymore, being on a pan-European or site-oriented scale (for instance Newgrange: MOUNT 1994). Indeed, economy often changes from one region to the next and generally reproduces former lifestyles (for instance southern France: VAQUER 1998). In other cases, changes in subsistence techniques cannot be interpreted as the by-product of a putative new Bell Beaker population but appear to be mere local readjustments (British Isles: EVANS 1990; ASHWIN 1996).

Actually, the sole element that might be completely new is the appearance and multiplication of horse bones in the archaeological record throughout the third millennium BC. However, this problem raises several difficulties, as the determination of the original area of this species or the potential subsequent way of dispersal (a complete review of the evidence is provided by Uerpmann (UERPMANN 1990; see also contributions in HÄNSEL / ZIMMER 1994). One can only suggest that the dispersal of horse may have been eased, in some cases, by the existence of the Bell Beaker network.

Funeral practices: the common element

If the founding element of the Bell Beaker „culture" remains the beaker itself, the recurrent discovery of mortuary sites points to a specific role of funeral ideology in its interpretation. In this sense, several scholars have opposed the homogeneity of central European mortuary practices to the apparent diversity of western Europe (*e.g.* HARRISON 1986; MOHEN 1988; LICHARDUS 1988). Actually, this dichotomy rests mainly in the reading given to the generalization of individual burial in central Europe and in the British Isles. This practice is seen, in a large part of contemporary Anglo-Saxon archaeological discourse, as the most probing expression of a new social order, characterized by increasing hierarchy and individualism:

the implication of the single burial might be that the end of the Neolithic saw the emergence of a kind of person 'just like us': a self-contained, decision-making entity whose exists in a state of reciprocal independence from his or her contemporaries. Now of course, this is a modern Western notion of individuality, and if we were to view later Neolithic and early Bronze Age mortuary practices in isolation, we might not be tempted to think at any such thing. But simply because corporate burial, which has been connected with a communal focus for society, declined in later Neolithic, it is easy to conclude that the new pattern was concerned with 'individuality' (THOMAS 1999, 155).

This perception is however founded on a logical error that consists to look for what mortuary practices express of the society of the living, before any investigation of the relationship between these two contexts (SHENNAN 1976; 1977; BARRETT 1990; MÜLLER 1998; but see VANDER LINDEN 2001b, in press). As long as the problem will be expressed in those terms, it is likely that it will find no solution or that all the solutions will be formulated the same way.

Alternatively, it is more interesting to apprehend mortuary practices as an integrated whole, of which purpose is to allocate a new place to the dead within the social structure, as initially expressed by Hertz (HERTZ 1907). Moreover, this „new place" does not necessarily reproduce the *social persona* of the deceased but is defined according to countless local norms related to death, after-life, conditions of death, ... (CARR 1995; LARSSON 1990; DAVID / KRAMER 2001; SCHMITT 2001). In this sense, mortuary practices do not directly inform us about past societies but illustrate how

Similar but Different. Bell Beakers in Europe

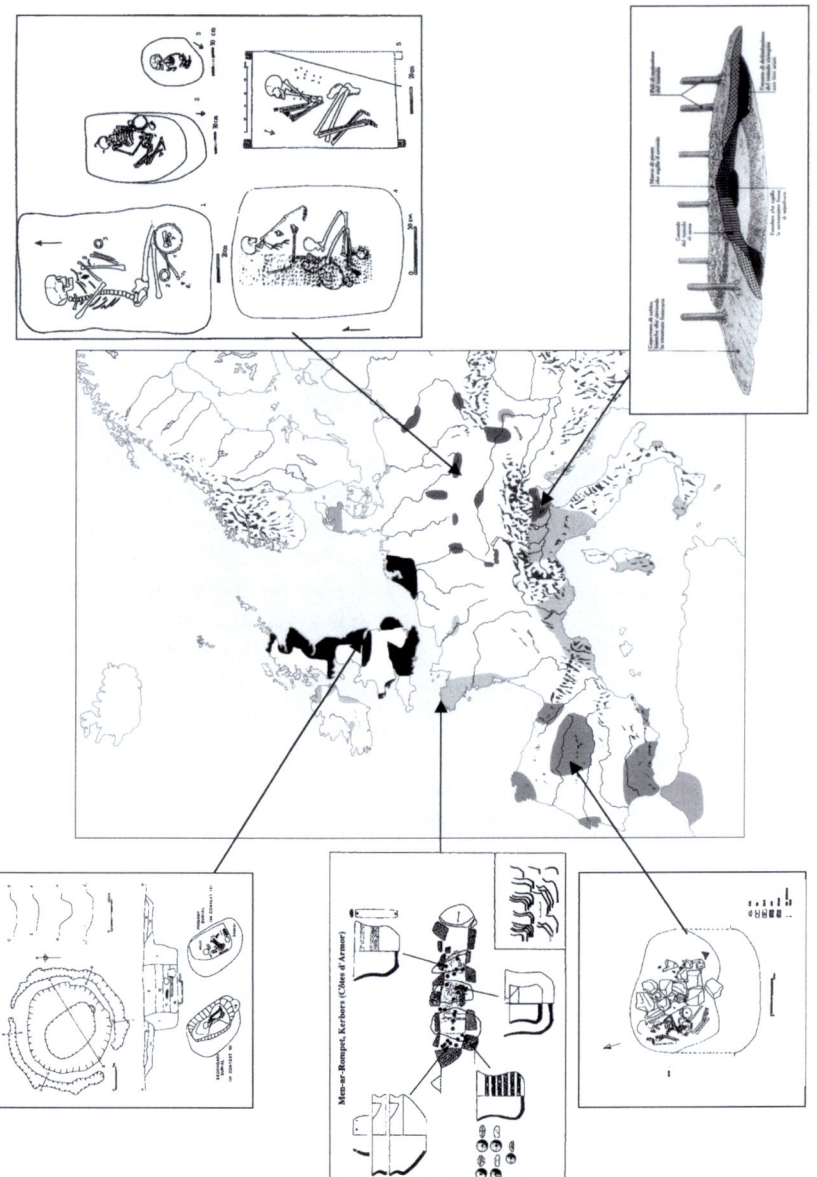

Fig. 2. Funeral practices within the Bell Beaker phenomenon. Upper left: funeral barrow of Chilbolton (Hampshire, England: after RUSSEL 1990, Fig. 2). Middle left: Bell Beaker deposit in the passage grave of Kerbors (Côtes d'Armor, France: after SALANOVA 1998, Fig. 4). Lower left: individual grave of Arenero Soto e Hijos (central Meseta, Spain: after BLASCO / RECUERO 1994, Fig. 8). Upper right: individual graves from Bohemia. 1. Prag 8-Kobylisy; 2. Knezeves I, tombe 6; 3. Knezeves I, tombe 13; 4. Brandýsek I, tombe 71; 5. Lysolaje III, tombe 16 (after HECKER 1995, Pl. 2). Lower right: reconstitution of the funeral mound of Via Bruschi (Sestio Fiorentino, Italy: after SARTI / MARTINI 1998a, Fig. 1).

people conceptualize the roles of their dead in their new community. Every practice must thus be interpreted as part of a system, and not given any preference because of putative evolutionist value as in the case of individual burial. From this point of view, one can define two major units within the Bell Beaker phenomenon, each of them being divided in smaller regional groups (Fig. 2).

In the first zone, which encompasses central Europe and the British Isles, but not Ireland, the community of the dead is elaborated thanks to a restricted set of practices that define ideal identities for the deceased (VANDER LINDEN 2001b, 2003). Such identities are built by reference to the man-woman polarity, by functional-like associations (men as warriors, women with ornaments, possible relationships between the age and sex of the dead and the size of the beaker), and by cosmological settings (men with the head to the North and women to the South in central Europe, much more regional and temporal variability in the Low Countries and the British Isles: VANDER LINDEN 2003). Wealth differences are not very important, or at least less than suggested by several scholars (e.g. REPLOGLE 1980; MÜLLER 1998). Actually, it would be quite astonishing to be faced to an absolute homogeneity according to the size and extent of the available sample. Yet, a social reading of mortuary practices is likely in some instances (correlation between grave goods and funeral architecture: DRENTH 1989; correlation between grave goods and exceptional burial procedures as in the Samborzec grave: HARRISON 1986, 54).

Beyond the anecdotic interest of these examples, other divisions occur within this area. First, funeral mounds are frequent in the British Isles and in the middle and lower basins of the Rhine, but very rare in remaining central Europe (Low Countries: LANTING / VAN DER WAALS 1976; British Isles: CLARKE 1970, BARRET 1990). Second, a symmetrical division can be done on basis of the insertion of the dead within a cosmological referential: cosmological rules are more restrictive in central Europe than in the area of the mounds (central Europe: FISCHER 1976, VANDER LINDEN 2003; Low Countries: LANTING / VAN DER WAALS 1976; British Isles: TUCKWELL 1975; MIZOGUCHI 1993). The conjunction of these two facets — loss of the visibility of the dead and use of flat grave, poor interest for cosmology in mounds — is related to the role of the cultural substrata. East, the Bell Beaker phenomenon is a reactionary discourse to Corded Ware values that is well-elaborated and suffers few exceptions to achieve its objective. In the British Isles, buildings of circular shape were common during the previous Late Neolithic, being for monuments (e.g. BRADLEY 1998) or barrows (KINNES et al. 1983), a similarity that surely eased the appropriation of Bell Beaker traits by local communities (VANDER LINDEN 2001c). This brief review of central European evidence would be incomplete if we do not mention the primacy of cremation in the Csepel group, the impact of the substrata being also evident there (KALICZ-SCHREIBER 1976).

The second major funerary network covers western Europe and Mediterranean Sea, from the Seine basin to the Gibraltar Detroit, and from the Atlantic shoreline to the Tyrrhenean Sea. In these regions, the community of the dead is no more constituted through the reiteration of restrictive practices, but solely by the insertion within the grave of specific objects as maritime beakers (e.g. SALANOVA 1997; JORGE / JORGE 1997) and, to a lesser extent, various types of weapons (daggers, Palmela points, stone wrist-guards: *e.g.* DELIBES DE CASTRO 1977; BERNABEU 1984) and ornaments (V-buttons: *e.g.* COURTIN 1974, 279-285; BERNABEU 1984; DEPALMAS *et al.* 1998, 369-370). Actually, besides the deposit of these stereotyped grave goods, the sole elements that allow to define this area are the recurrent use of megalithic graves of various architectural shape (*e.g.* TREINEN 1970; MATHERS 1984; TUSA 1998) and the multiplicity of funeral gestures (collective and secondary burial, manipulation and selection of human bones, ...: *e.g.* DUDAY 1980; LEITAO *et al.* 1984; ATZENI 1998). This systematic presence of beakers or other items of the Bell Beaker „package" does not imply an interpretive come-back to the prestige model. Instead of the social competition suggested by these hypotheses, I will insist on the enlarged capacities of social integration evidenced by other facets of material culture. For instance, in southern France and in the Iberian Peninsula, the Bell Beaker period does not mark the climax of social competition, of which every evidence disappears, but rather to the elaboration of larger cultural and, likely, social units (VANDER LINDEN 2001a).

An accurate characterization of this tradition and associated mortuary practices is complicated by the near absence of well-documented contexts (old excavations, long and complex history of megalithic monuments, ...) and, actually, only a limited amount of examples permits to assure the association between grave goods and a specific individual within graves. For instance, we may quote the possible equivalence between the estimated number of dead and the quantity of beakers found in the dolmen M XI of the megalithic cemetery of Petit-Chasseur in Sion (GALLAY / CHAIX 1984). Whatever, the volume of concerned graves and the poor variety of known elements indicate that, in this area, the becoming of a few dead is now partly conditioned by the attribution of objects that associate the deceased to a specific idealized status, strictly homologous to the identities observed in central Europe and in the British Isles.

Grave goods may well point to a — superficial? — adhesion to an unitary discourse on the deceased, the variability of other practices demonstrates that this foreign element does only concern a small fraction of the relationship towards the dead that remains conditioned, as in former local funeral traditions, by the primacy of the physical contact with the bones and by a dynamic perception of the corpse. From this point of view, the success of the Bell Beaker phenomenon is western Europe rests in its capacity to articulate, on one side, the physical relationship with the deadly remains and, on the other side, the stereotyped values given to the dead.

It is also possible to define, within this huge area, other divisions, of which individuality results of the specificity of the substrata or the nearby existence of other ideologies. The Sicilian situation is difficult to evaluate: do we have an imprecise idea of giving the dead ceramics, as suggested by the parallel development of collective grave and megalithic architecture (LEIGHTON 1999) or, beyond decorative, technical and morphological differences in pottery, has the discourse on the dead passed through? A second situation is the Iberian Peninsula. In this case, the effective presence of individual burial in the late facies does not mark, I think, the influence of the Bell Beaker ideology. On the contrary, this process appears to me as the extinction of this discourse in front of the funeral traditions of the El Argar culture that is strictly contemporary to late Bell Beaker groups that practice individual burial (on El Argar chronology: CASTRO MARTINEZ *et al.* 1996; for Andalusia: LAZARICH GONZALEZ 2000; for central Meseta: BLASCO / RECUERO 1994; for the Ferradeira horizon in southern Portugal: SCHUBART 1975).

Metallurgy

The equation posed in the first part of the XXth century between the Bell Beaker phenomenon and the first copper metallurgy appears, some fifty years after, unsustainable. This technology is, in most cases, well developed before the introduction of the Bell Beaker phenomenon that generally marks a technical regression, maybe related to difficulties to get access to copper sources (as in southern France: CONSTANTINI 1984; AMBERT / CAROZZA 1998). Thus, copper metallurgy is only native in north-western Europe, it is the Low Countries (BUTLER / VAN DER WAALS 1966), the lower Seine basin (BILLARD *et al.* 1991) and the British Isles (BUDD *et al.* 1992; O'BRIEN 1998). Data concerning production are restricted to few indications in late settlements of the lower Seine basin (site of Les Florentins: BILLARD *et al.* 1991), of the British Isles (SIMPSON 1971), to several Iberian sites (*e.g.* Zambujal: KUNST 1998; El Ventorro: HARRISON *et al.* 1975; Son Matge of which attribution to the Bell Beaker phenomenon is contested: WALDREN 1979; TOPP 1988; HOFFMAN 1995), and to the recognition of so-called „smith burials" in central Europe (MOUCHA 1989; sites of Stedten in Germany: HARRISON 1986, 32-36; see also BUTLER / VAN DER WAALS 1966).

Final products are better known and present a globally uniform character. Assemblages are always dominated by awls, ornaments, arrowheads, and mostly daggers. Some regional variants are recorded, as the famous Palmela points distributed throughout the Iberian Peninsula (*e.g.* DELIBES DE CASTRO 1977; TAVARES DA SILVA / SOARES 1998, 1022, 1025) and in western and southern France (GOMEZ / JOUSSAUME 1978; VIGNERON 1981; BEYNEIX / HUMBERT 1996). One must also note the impressive production of flat axes in Ireland (NEEDHAM 1988; O'BRIEN 1998). This preference for weapons, and more precisely for daggers, first of all concerns funeral contexts where they are found associated to men. This pattern is attested in central Europe, more guessed than proved for western Europe.

If it is common to consider these weapons as the expression of a real or ideal male warrior-like identity, it is maybe more original to note that this expression passes by the use of a highly codified symbol and not by a competing behavior as, for instance, in Late Neolithic eastern and southern France (SAINTOT 1998). The implantation of this code, shared and used by a large series of communities, also affects modes of ornament, like V-buttons, pins, or rings, that prefigure processes well-known during the Bronze Age (*e.g.* BARGE 1982, 170-175; MARECHAL *et al.* 1998; for the Bronze Age see HARDING 2000, 369-377).

Bell Beaker metallurgy thus belongs to Strahm's *Metallikum* (STRAHM 1994). These restricted elements do not tell us lots of things about the circulation of products and craftsmen, but reinforce the conclusions gained for funeral practices as the production of stereotyped weapons participates to the other restrictive gestures noticed. Moreover, this gives us a first indication that, within this ideological unity, the circulation of information and new cultural norms is greatly eased.

Ceramics

Decoration

At the most general level, all Bell Beaker productions are characterized by the superimposition of horizontal ornamental bands thanks to a restricted set of isometries (geometrical transformations that do not affect neither dimensions nor angles), especially translation and mirror symmetries. Naturally, it is possible to identify a significant series of variations within this general system. But, before investigating this dimension, it is essential to understand the reasons that underlie the permanency of this decorative structure throughout such a large geographical and temporal space as the Bell Beaker phenomenon.

This continuity cannot be reduced to the sole weight of tradition. In every case, the establishment of a Bell Beaker ceramic style does not merely concern one or several motives but a global reorganization of the decoration. So, the integration of new elements is done within the pre-existing structure (as for metopes in the Low Countries: VANDER LINDEN 1998). This coherence and the recurrence of maritime beakers in funeral contexts (as in France: SALANOVA 1998; 2000) suggest that the adjunction of horizontal bands was not anecdotal for those who used them. Albeit it is difficult, if not impossible, to ascribe this pattern a unique meaning, one must recognize its ideological value.

Since the beginnings of archaeology, pottery is the privileged trait in the definition of cultural areas. In this, classical, perspective, it is possible to define two major stylistic units. If the use of metopes does not lead to subsequent radical transformation of the general decorative structure, this is however accompanied by some innovations, like a new interest for the calculated repetition of motives and thus calculation of angles (VANDER LINDEN 1998). The geographical distribution of this trait allows to define a first stylistic area to covers the territory between the British Isles and the Csepel group in the vicinity of Budapest (Fig. 3). A second group is centered on the western Mediterranean Sea (southern France, Iberian Mediterranean shoreline, Sardinia, Sicilia). There, a common tradition can be defined on basis of the existence of vertical elements in the decorative structure, which imply a radial division of the ornamental surface (*e.g.* GILIGNY / SALANOVA 1997). One could maybe define a third group on the Atlantic shoreline (western France) since only horizontal bands are recorded there. Ceramic productions of the Estremadura, of the Basque country, of Galicia and of Meseta, with low proportions of decor with vertical structure, present an intermediary character but have nevertheless been incorporated here in the second unit.

Once more, the difficulty does not lie in the recognition of these differences but in their interpretation. Ethno-archaeological research suggests that decoration is a poor marker of social identity since decorative elements are visible at the surface of pots, at the difference of, for instance, shaping techniques. Thus, decorative elements are likely to be easily borrowed and diffused on large areas (GOSSELAIN 2000; see also BOWSER 2000). Yet, the study of decorative structure allows to partially bypass these limits (VAN BERG 1994). In this case, the recognition of stylistic simili-

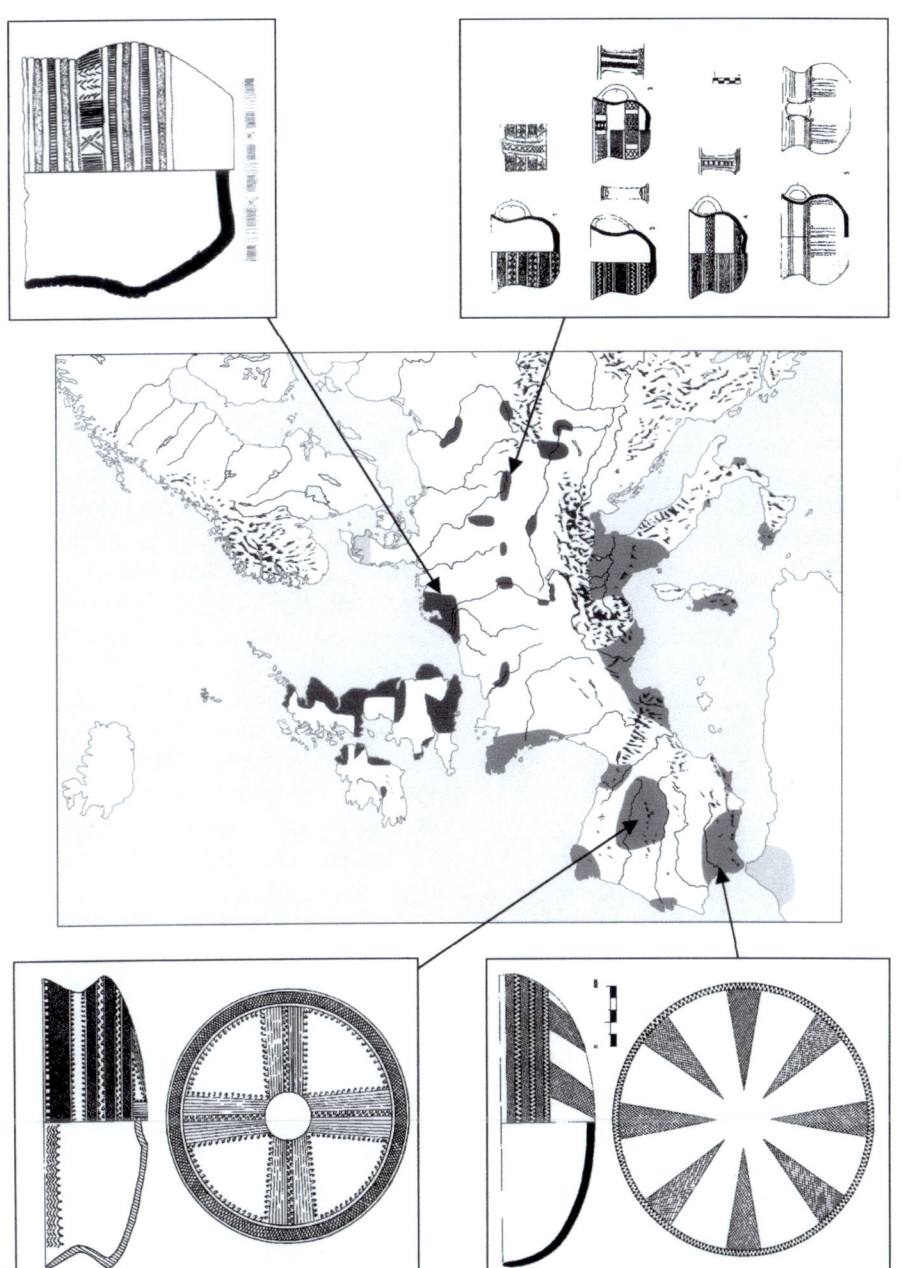

Fig. 3. Ceramic decoration within the Bell Beaker phenomenon. Upper left: Bell Beaker *cazuela* from Ciempozuelos (central Meseta, Spain: after BLASCO *et al.* 1994, Fig. 2). Lower left: pottery from El Promontori de l'Aigua Dolça i Salada (after BERNABEU 1984, Fig. 47). Upper right: Veluwe beaker from Uddelermeer (after HARRISON 1986, 23). Lower right: Bohemian Bell Beaker pots. 1. Neznámá; 2. Koštov; 3. Radovesice II; 4. Radovesice III; 5. Nechranice (after TUREK 1995, Fig. 6).

tude does not merely concern a motive, but rather precise and complex modalities applied in the disposition of decorative elements. It is likely that areas defined on this basis are to be understood in other terms than borrowing or superficial interaction, but rather like learning networks of craftsmen.

The identification of these networks is reinforced by the geographical similarity that they share with the areas defined by mortuary analysis. Indeed, metope decoration closely corresponds to the funeral area of central Europe and the British Isles. The second decorative area encompasses almost entirely the southern megalithic area, with the exception of Atlantic France that only presents horizontal ceramic decoration.

Morphology

The consideration of morphological features also leads to the definition of several interaction networks (Fig. 4). The most salient example is the central European *Begleitkeramik*, of which origins must be sought outside the Bell Beaker phenomenon itself, it is in the contemporary cultures of the Carpathian basin (MACHNIK 1991). Its frequency in funeral context in central Europe suggests that its success partially lies in its insertion with the pre-existing funeral matrix (TUREK 1998). We must also note the existence of an autonomous domestic or common ware in France, initially defined in the Sâone-Rhône axis by Gallay (GALLAY 1979; 1986; BESSE 1996). Its presence in northern Italy is subject to controversy (for instance on the site of Monte Covolo: BARFIELD 1976) but current work seems to confirm the mixed character of these assemblages (POGGIANI KELLER, personal communication, September 2001). Moreover, following Gallay (GALLAY 1979, 1986, 1997-1998), it is possible to recognize the existence of two other networks, one encompassing the lower Rhine Basin and the British Isles (LEHMANN 1965; GIBSON 1980), and a second one in the Iberian Peninsula with a high proportion of *cazuelas* and *cuencos*.

The remarks previously made on the anthropological value of decoration must be applied to morphology. Indeed, if similitude concerned a sole form, like the beaker, it would be impossible to propose any in-depth interpretation of the phenomenon (see for instance HUYSECOM 1986). In our case, the situation is different since we are dealing with relatively coherent assemblages. Moreover, if the presence of *Begleitkeramik* in southern France is only attested by two or three types, their role is essential in the constitution of ceramic assemblages of the local Early Bronze Age cultures, hence indicating that their diffusion is not the mere outcome of the success of a peculiar ceramic type (BESSE 1996).

The geographic setting of these assemblages fits well to the other facets of material culture. For instance, French common ware remains within the boundaries of the megalithic area, with the exception of the upper Rhine basin. The *cuenco* and *cazuela* complex that encompasses all Iberian groups is also enclosed within this megalithic area. Likewise, the Low Countries and the British Isles, which share a funeral specificity, evidence a close similitude in ceramic morphology.

Two major exceptions must be noted. First, northern Italy presents an intermediary status, with at the same time common ware derived from France and

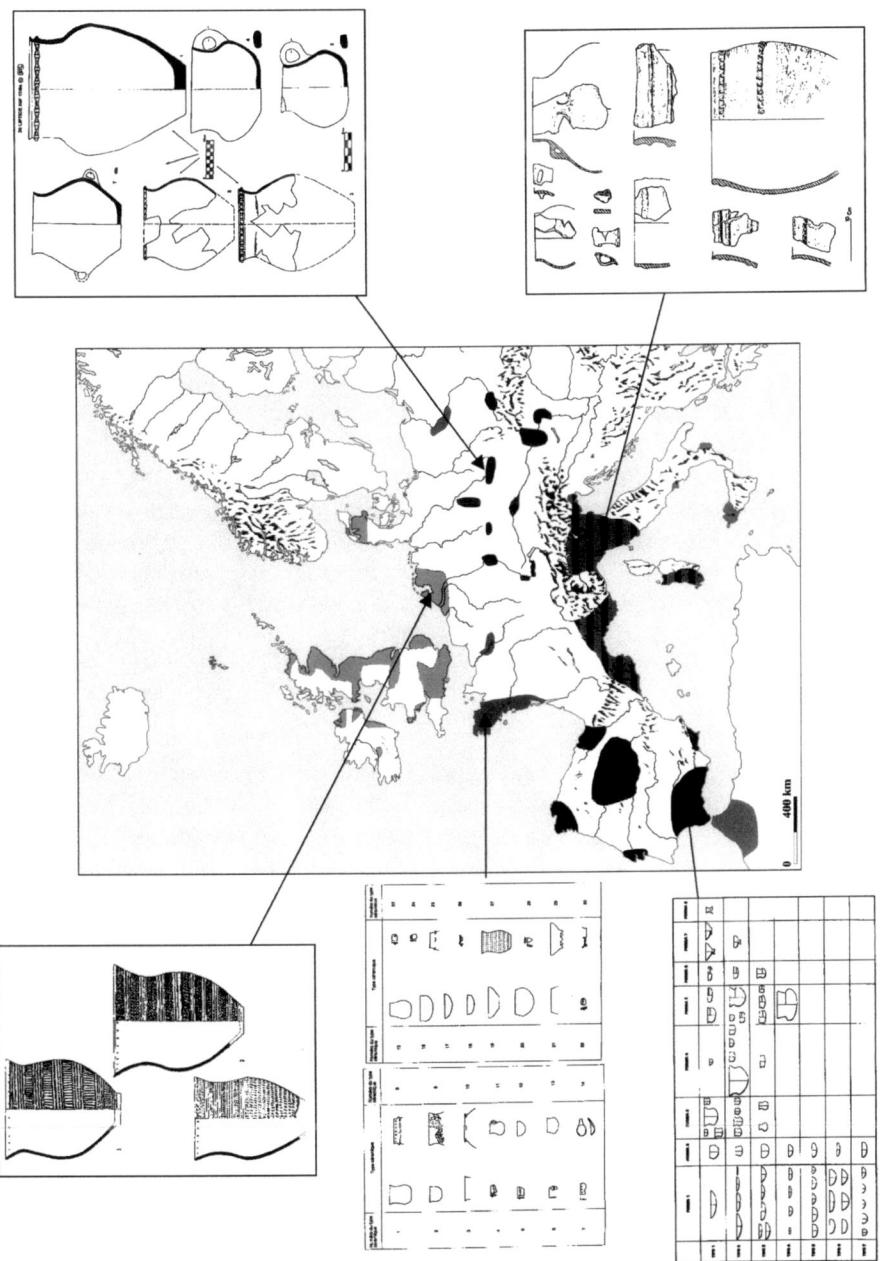

Fig. 4. Ceramic morphology within the Bell Beaker phenomenon. Upper left: *potbekers*. 1. Hanendorp; 2. Stroeër; 3. Ede (after LEHMANN 1965). Middle Left: main morphological types of French domestic ware (after BESSE 1996, Fig. 3 / 4). Lower left: main morphological types in western Andalusia. Type 1: *cazuela*. Type 2: cuenco. Type 3: beaker (*vaso*). Types 4 to 8: regional types (after LAZARICH GONZALEZ 2000, Fig. 2). Upper right: *Begleitkeramik* from Liptice II (Bohemia: after TUREK 1998, Fig. 6). Lower right: domestic ware from Monte Covolo (northern Italy: after BARFIELD 1976, Fig. 5).

Begleitkeramik. Whatever the problem of the factual identification of both assemblages, this conjunction reinforces the identification of this region as a cultural crossroad (see below). The case of *Begleitkeramik* is more complex. Indeed, its distribution in central Europe reproduces the group of flat graves with strong cosmological insertion — and also of cremation — but, for the very first time in our analysis, we are faced to a trait that bridges the funeral boundary that mid-sects the Bell Beaker phenomenon, since there is *Begleitkeramik* in northern Italy and southern France.

Technology

Numerous ethno-archaeological studies demonstrate that the *chaîne opératoire* of pottery is one of the most interesting traits in the identification of cultural traditions (see contributions in STARK 1998; GOSSELAIN 2000; LIVINGSTONE / SMITH 2000). Yet, such data are not available for the Bell Beaker phenomenon. Indeed, most researchers have focused on the characterization and identification of clay and temper in order to test the prestige model. Yet, these two facets of the *chaîne opératoire* are not the most salient elements: worldwide, potters generally use local clay available in a 7-km radius (ARNOLD 1985), while the choice of temper often results of factual interaction between craftsmen (GOSSELAIN 2000).

Settlement pattern

If, since Harrison' synthesis (HARRISON 1980, 1986), our knowledge of Bell Beaker settlement has dramatically increased thanks to new excavation or re-analysis of older data, this archaeological dimension remains poorly known (Fig. 5).

Structures are generally not well conserved, with some pits or postholes. The situation is however much different in the Tagus estuary with famous monumental sites like Zambujal or Leceia. Here, the Bell Beaker phenomenon is characterized by the reuse of previous buildings (*e.g.* Miradouro dos Capuchos: BUBNER 1979; Pico Agudo: SPINDLER 1971; Penedo: SPINDLER 1969; Pedra do Ouro: LEISNER / SCHUBART 1966; Zambujal: SANGMEISTER / SCHUBART 1972, 1981; SANGMEISTER 1976; KUNST / UERPMANN 1996; KUNST 1998). Similar processes are found in southern France, with a dry stone architecture directly borrowed from the Fontbouisse culture (for instance in Orgon, Bouches-du-Rhône: BARGE 1986). Besides this phenomenon, southern France and the Iberian Peninsula are also characterized by an impressive and exceptional diversity with caves, open air settlements, defensive implantations or sites only represented by pits or surface scatters (*e.g.* SCHÜLE 1976; BERNABEU 1984; BLASCO 1994; ALDAY RUIZ 1996; CLAUSTRE / MAZIERE 1998; LEMERCIER 1998; VAQUER *et al.* 2000).

If pits and surface scatters are current in central and northern Europe, another element characterizes settlement pattern in this region. Indeed, being in Italy (BERMOND MONTARI 1998; CREMONESI *et al.* 1998, 194; SARTI / MARTINI 1998b), in the lower Seine and Rhine basins (LOUWE KOOIJMANS 1974; BILLARD *et al.* 1991), in East England (HALL 1988; MARTIN / MURPHY 1988; HEALY / HOUSLEY 1992; ROBERTS 1998), in eastern France (BOURA 1988), in the Csepel group (KALICZ-SCHREIBER 1976; ENDRŐDI 1998) or in Bohe-

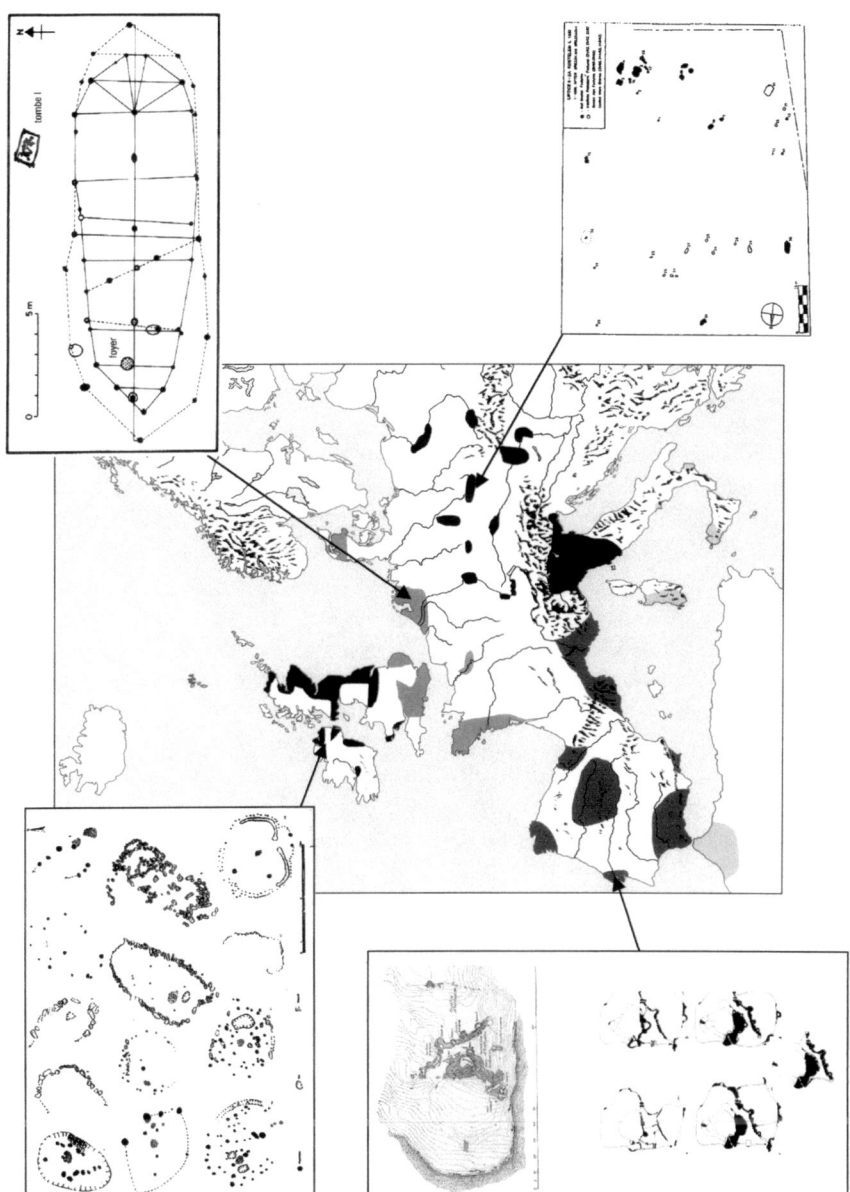

Fig. 5. Settlement pattern of the Bell Beaker phenomenon. Upper left: Bell Beaker house plans from the British Isles (1, Monknewton; Sorrisdale; 3, Lough Cur Site D house I; 4, Lough Cur site D house II; 5, Beacon Hill; 6, Lough Cur site D house III; 7, Lough Cur site C house III; 8, Northton house II; 9, Northton house I; 10, Lough Cur site C house I; 12, Rosinish; 13, Gwithian; after GIBSON 1987, fig. 1). Lower left: Zambujal Up: excavations as in 1970 (after SANGMEISTER / SCHUBART 1972, fig. 1). Low: successive building phases A: phase 1a. B: phase 2a. C: phase 3c. D: phase 4b. E: phase 5a (after KUNST 1995, Fig. 2). Upper right: house from Molenaarsgraf (Low Countries after LOUWE KOOIJMANS 1974). Lower right: plan of Liptice II (Bohemia: after TUREK 1998, Fig. 9).

mia (TUREK 1998), Bell Beaker domestic sites are often settled close to humid zones like shorelines or swamps.

Actually, poor architectural investment, or at least marked preference for techniques that have a low archaeological potential, is general to central Europe since the middle of the 4th millennium BC and corresponds to ecological constraints like the nature of available tree species (PETREQUIN / PETREQUIN 1988, 214-217; SHENNAN 1993). Furthermore, the outstanding variability of plans is also directly related to cultural substrata (long houses in Denmark: EARLE et al. 1998; BOAS 2000, see also in Scania TESCH 1993; systematic implantations along the shoreline in Atlantic France: JOUSSAUME 1970, 1981, 454-461; striking similarities between Csepel and Nagyrév houses: ENDRŐDI 1998).

These architectural differences correspond, once more, to the North-South dichotomy observed for mortuary practices, with two exceptions. First, western Atlantic France belongs to the megalithic area, albeit few individual burials are known, like the site of La Folie, near Poitiers (TCHEREMISSINOFF et al. 2000). The confusion does not so much rest in the anthropological specificity of these two facets of material culture but, I think, in the existence of two separated historic processes. On one side, the presence of beakers, most of them of maritime type, in graves corresponds to a specific way of dispersal of the Bell Beaker phenomenon. On the other side, architectural traditions underline the integration of this zone into an Atlantic cultural *koinè* that, progressively, will affect an independent historical trajectory (see below).

The second exception corresponds to northern and central Italy. Here, the close similarities of this region with central Europe give the impression of a cultural crossroad. Note that this architectural tradition will continue with the Early Bronze Age Polada culture (GUILAINE 1996).

Discussion

Only four categories of evidence are relevant to comparative work: mortuary practices, ceramic decoration and morphology, and settlement pattern. Indeed, too few data are available for pottery technology and metallurgy, whilst the strictly local character of exchange networks or subsistence techniques forbids any conclusion for our topic. Thus, on basis of these four categories, I have determined the existence of no less than 15 interaction networks within the Bell Beaker phenomenon:

1. mortuary practices: north-western Europe, central Europe, Carpathian basin, western Europe, Iberian Peninsula (Fig. 2);
2. ceramic decoration: north-western and central Europe, western Europe and Mediterranean Sea, possibly French Atlantic shoreline (Fig. 3);
3. ceramic morphology: north-western Europe, central Europe, common ware in France and northern Italy, Iberian Peninsula (Fig. 4);
4. settlement pattern: north-western and central Europe, western Mediterranean basin, late northern Atlantic *koinè* (Fig. 5).

It is noteworthy that the correlations between these interaction networks are by no means random but lead to the constitution of 5 major regions within the Bell Beaker phenomenon (Fig. 6). Albeit the frontiers are not as clear-cut as they appear on the map and may be redrawn according to the preference given to one trait in spite of another, these regions still represent focal points within the continuous variation of the Bell Beaker phenomenon and thus have a specific historical reality.

The first region lies in north-western Europe and encompasses the British Isles and the lower Rhine basin, the latter being most probably the zone of emergence of the Bell Beaker phenomenon after derivation from local Corded Ware group (Single Grave Culture or Protuding Foot Beaker: LANTING / VAN DER WAALS 1976; VANDER LINDEN 1998, 2001a). The definition of this region is based on mortuary practices (mounds and low interest in cosmology) and ceramic morphology (*potbekers*), whilst settlement pattern and ceramic decoration suggest, in a complementary perspective, strong ties with central Europe. Indeed, central Europe corresponds to the second major region, with specific mortuary practices (flat individual burials with strong cosmological reflection) and ceramic morphology (*Begleitkeramik*). Yet, the setting of the boundaries is more difficult in this case. If ceramic decoration points to contacts with north-western Europe, settlement pattern as well as *Begleitkeramik* demonstrates interactions with southerly areas like northern Italy and southern France. Moreover, I have included in this second region the Csepel group, although funerary data suggest a more peripheral position.

The third and fourth regions, respectively northern Italy[1] and Sardinia on one side, France on the other side, appear to be more complicated to define. This is no surprise because of their central geographical setting in the Bell Beaker phenomenon, which is mirrored by a variety of cultural influences. The crossroad position of the Italian group is obvious when we consider ceramic morphology, with assemblages characterized by forms deriving from both *Begleitkeramik* and French common ware. Settlement pattern rather points to northerly influences, whilst the cultural status of mortuary practices is hard to define: north-western Italy with local megalithic architecture demonstrating strong links with southern Swiss, Sardinia with continuous development of insular megalithic traditions, north-eastern Italy and region of Florence with few individual burials. On the contrary, the French group — except for the eastern territories that must be integrated to the central European region — is first of all defined on basis of funeral practices, with megalithic tombs and a multiplicity of funerary gestures usually grouped under the label „collective sepulture". Other elements are less evident to assign: common ware is well-diffused but, as previously noted, not exclusive to this territory, as *Begleitkeramik*. Ceramic decoration and settlement pattern are not really homogenous, although alternative explanations may be formulated for the last one (see below).

The definition of the last group, Iberian Peninsula, is less difficult. If ancient megalithic traditions continue during Bell Beaker times, the subsequent develop-

---

1. Southern Italy, Sicily and northern Maghreb have not been inserted in any regions because of the general deficient quality of data and because of their peripheral status evidenced, for instance, by ceramic decoration.

Similar but Different. Bell Beakers in Europe

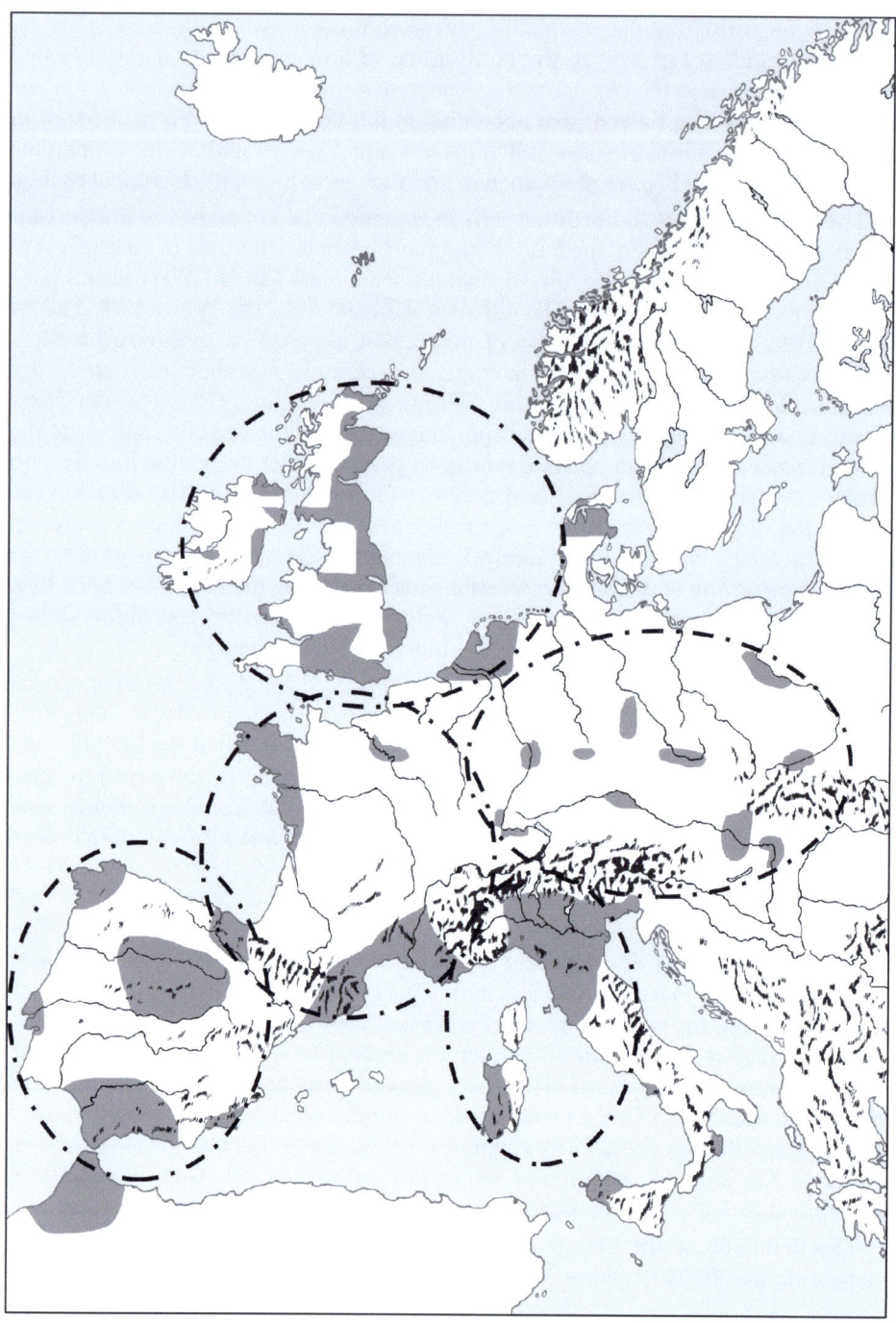

Fig. 6. Regional divisions of the Bell Beaker phenomenon as suggested by polythetic analysis.

ment of individual burial gives to this region a certain individuality. This cannot be derived from putative central European prototypes for which there are, except few non diagnostic sites (for instance La Fare in southern France or La Folie in western France: MÜLLER / LEMERCIER 1994; TCHEREMINISSOFF et al. 2000), no valid geographical intermediates. Rather than involving abstract evolutionary trends that will be expressed under the form of individual burial, I think that this element results from interactions with the El Argar culture, which begins to develop during the last quarter of the third millennium BC in south-eastern Spain. In addition, this funeral individuality corresponds to unique ceramic morphology. Ceramic decoration and settlement pattern merely underline the incorporation of this region within a larger Western Mediterranean area.

Of course, these regions remain constantly redefined throughout the development of the Bell Beaker phenomenon. For instance, northern Atlantic Europe presents a certain individuality during late phases (turn of the third and second millennium BC), as evidenced by the rise of a cultural *koinè*, defined by settlement in humid zones, an original propinquity between the physical space dedicated to the dead and the living (Molenaarsgraf: LOUWE KOOIJMANS 1974; Les Florentins: BILLARD et al. 1991; East England and Cambridgeshire: MARTIN / HALL 1988; HEALY / HOUSLEY 1992), use of local flint resources (Atlantic shoreline: JOUSSAUME 1981) and, in a few cases, instances of copper production within settlements. Likewise, the eastern side of the Bell Beaker phenomenon is characterized by processes of social fission that led to the subsequent making of new cultural groups (VANDER LINDEN 2003).

Besides the particular case of northern Italy, ceramic morphology and mortuary practices systematically appear to be the most pertinent criteria in the definition of these regions. Indeed, we have seen, at least in the case of central Europe, the weight of ecological constraints on settlement pattern, while, as suggested by ethnoarchaeological case-studies, ceramic decoration probably relies to more superficial interaction networks than ceramic morphology. Mortuary practices raise a more complex problem. Indeed, most quoted differences are regional facets (presence / absence of mounds, status of cosmology), but the logic of the funeral system remains globally unchanged, with a clear desire to assign clear-cut identities to the dead (most particularly the warrior male ideal). Supplementary elements reinforce this homogenous perception (systematic presence of maritime beakers, stereotyped metallurgical production, uniformity in ornamental modes). All these arguments indicate that the unity of the Bell Beaker phenomenon first of all rests in the success of a culturally specific funeral ideology.

Yet, this funeral unity has profound implications for the understanding of the Bell Beaker societies. Indeed, this shared funeral ideology directly leads to better interactions, from both quantitative and qualitative points of view, between individuals and communities, as evidenced by the large dispersal of all traits analyzed previously. Subsequently, we note the making and maintenance of larger social units, but, interestingly enough, without any exchange networks within or between them: diffusion and circulation only concern ideas, know-how and, first of all, individuals (see also PRICE et al. 1998).

Conclusion

Although I surely painted with an exceedingly broad brush, my purpose here was to propose a global framework within which further regional examination can be carried out, eventually leading to consequent modification of the initial hypotheses. Indeed, I think that the multiplication of new data, being from supplementary excavations or re-investigation of older data, is insufficient unless one possesses a methodological tool that allows intra- and inter-regional comparison. In this sense, it appears to be essential to place variability at the core of the Bell Beaker problem.

Besides potential methodological interest for other periods, this experiment with polythetic model first of all allows to re-evaluate the historical significance of the Bell Beaker phenomenon. Throughout this analysis, we have moved from former prestige models that stressed the individualistic and competing dimension of this phenomenon to get a more subtle perception of the underlying historical processes. Previous readings, which I assume were only derived from immediate evolutionist interpretation of individual burial, must be regarded as completely irrelevant in view of the available data. Indeed, the large dispersion of cultural traits evidenced by the Bell beaker phenomenon, which concern multiple and *a priori* non congruent facets of material of intellectual culture, and their mutual regional correspondences clearly demonstrate that this period must be set in terms of extended sociability and sharing of common traditions and values. If numerous boundaries crisscross within the Bell Beaker area, the quality of social interaction and social integration exemplified by this phenomenon finds no precedent in Later European prehistory and makes the historical uniqueness of this period.

Acknowledgments

This research is taken from my PhD. dissertation supervised by prof. Paul-Louis van Berg at the University of Brussels. Financial help was provided as a doctoral grant by the F.N.R.S. (Belgian National Fund for Scientific Research). Several people I would like to thank here have criticized and commented these ideas throughout the years: P.-L. van Berg, N. Cauwe, P. de Maret, D. Viviers, P. Pétrequin, J. Guilaine, S.Lemaitre, A. Duplouy, D. Coupé, C. Hoffmann, M.and L. Vander Linden, O. Gosselain. Nevertheless, I assume and endorse full responsibilities for everything written here.

References

ALDAY RUIZ A. 1996. *El entramado campaniforme en el País Vasco. Los datos y el desarollo del proceso historico.* Vitoria.

AMBERT P. / CAROZZA L. 1998. Origine(s) et développement de la première métallurgie française. Etat de la question. In: FRITSCH B. / MAUTE M. / MATUSCHIK I. MÜLLER J. / WOLF C. (eds), *Tradition und Innovation. Prähistorische Archäologie als historische Wissenschaft*, 149-173.

ARNOLD D. 1985. *Ceramic theory and cultural process.* Cambridge.

ASHWIN T. 1996. Neolithic and Bronze age Norfolk. *Proceedings of the Prehistoric Society* 62, 41-62.

ATZENI E., 1998. La cultura del bicchiere campaniforme in Sardegna. In: NICOLIS F. / MOTTES E. (eds), *Simbolo ed enigma. Il bicchiere campaniforme e l'Italia nella preistoria europea del III millennio a.C.*, 243-253.

BAGOLINI B. / PEDROTTI A. 1998. L'Italie septentrionale. In: GUILAINE J. (dir.), *Atlas du Néolithique européen II. L'Europe occidentale*, 233-341.

BAILLY M. / BESSE M. / GICLON J.-L. / HENON P. 1998. Le site d'habitat campaniforme de "Derrière-le-Château" à Géovreissiat et Montréal-la-Cluse (Ain): premiers résultats. In: *Rencontres Méridionales de Préhistoire récente. Deuxième session, Arles 1996*, 225-239.

BARFIELD L.H. 1976. The cultural affinities of Bell Beakers in Italy and Sicily. In: LANTING J.N. / VAN DER WAALS J.D. (eds), *Glockenbecher Symposion (Oberried 1974)*, 307-322.

BARGE H. 1982. *Les parures du Néolithique ancien au début de l'Age des Métaux en Languedoc.* Paris.

— 1986. Les cabanes campaniformes des Calades à Orgon (Bouches-du-Rhône). *Bulletin de la Société Préhistorique Française* 83, 228-230.

BARRETT J.C. 1990. The monumentality of death: the character of Early Bronze Age mortuary mounds in southern Britain. *World Archaeology* 22, 179-189.

BENZ M. / GRAMSCH A. / WIERMANN R. / VAN WILLINGEN S. 1998. Rethinking Bell Beakers. In: BENZ M. / VAN WILLINGEN S. (eds), *Some new approaches to the Bell Beaker phenomenon Lost Paradise...? Proceedings of the 2nd meeting of the „Association Archéologie et Gobelets" Feldberg (Germany), 18th-20th April 1997*, 181-191.

BENZ M. / STRAHM C. / VAN WILLINGEN S. 1998. Le Campaniforme: phénomène et culture archéologique. *Bulletin de la Société Préhistorique Française* 95, 305-314.

BERMOND MONTARI G. 1998. Gli insediamenti campaniformi di Rubiera e Sant'Ilario d'Enza. In: NICOLIS F. / MOTTES E. (dirs), *Simbolo ed enigma. Il bicchiere campaniforme e l'Italia nella preistoria europea del III millennio a.C.*, 92-94.

BERNABEU J. 1984. *El vaso campaniforme en el pais valenciano.* Valencia.

BESSE M. 1996. Types et origines potentielles de la céramique d'accompagnement du Campaniforme en France. In: MORDANT C. / GAIFFE O. (eds), *Cultures et sociétés du Bronze ancien en Europe. Actes du colloque Fondements culturels, techniques, économiques et sociaux des débuts de l'âge du Bronze. 117e Congrès national des sociétés historiques et scientifiques*, 165-180.

BEYNEIX A. / HUMBERT M. 1996. Note sur trois pointes de Palmela des environs d'Osuna (province de Séville, Espagne). *Bulletin de la Société Préhistorique Française* 92, 251-252.

BILLARD C. / CHANCEREL A. / MANTEL E. 1991. Nouveaux sites campaniformes de la basse vallée de la Seine. *Gallia Préhistoire* 33, 137-206.

BLASCO C. (ed.) 1994. *El horizonte campaniforme de la region de Madrid en el centenario de Ciempozuelos.* Madrid.

BLASCO C. / RECUERO V. 1994. Inventario general de yacimientos. In: BLASCO C. (ed.), *El horizonte campaniforme de la region de Madrid en el centenario de Ciempozuelos*, 13-46.

BLASCO C. / SANCHEZ-CAPILLA L. / CALLE J. 1994. El mundo funerario. In: BLASCO C. (ed.), *El horizonte campaniforme de la region de Madrid en el centenario de Ciempozuelos*, 75-99.

BOAS N.A. 2000. Late Neolithic and Bronze Age settlements: investigations in Djursland, Eastern Jutland. *Lunula* 8, 3-15.

BOURA F. 1988. Découverte d'un site d'habitat campaniforme à Vandières (Meurthe-et-Moselle): premiers résultats. In: *Le néolithique du nord-est de la France et des régions limitrophes. Actes du XIIIè colloque interrégional sur le Néolithique (Metz, 10, 11 et 12 octobre 1986)*, 165-172.

BOWSER B. 2000. From Pottery to Politics: An Ethnoarchaeological Study of Political Factionalism, Ethnicity, and Domestic Pottery Style in the Ecuadorian Amazon. *Journal of Archaeological Method and Theory* 7, 219-248.

BRADLEY R. 1998. *The significance of monuments. On the shaping of human experience in Neolithic and Bronze Age Europe*. London.

BRODIE N. 1994. *The Neolithic - Bronze Age transition in Britain. A critical review of some archaeological and craniological concepts*. Oxford.

BUBNER T. 1979. Die äneolithische Siedlung auf dem Miradouro dos Capuchos. *Madrider Mitteilungen* 20, 11-42.

BUDD P. / GALE D. / POLLARD A.M. / THOMAS R.G. / WILLIAMS P.A. 1992. The early development of metallurgy in the British Isles. *Antiquity* 66, 677-686.

BUTLER J.J. / VAN DER WAALS J.D. 1966. Bell Beakers and early metal-working in the Netherlands. *Palaeohistoria* 12, 41-140.

CARR C. 1995. Mortuary practices: their social, philosophical-religious, circumstancial, and physical determinants. *Journal of Archaeological Method and Theory* 2, 105-200.

CASTRO MARTINEZ P.V. / LULL V. / MILO P. 1996. *Cronologia de la Prehistoria Reciente de la Peninsula Iberica y Baleares (c. 2800-900 cal ANE)*. Oxford.

CLARKE D. 1968. *Analytical archaeology*. London.

— 1970. *Beaker pottery of Great Britain and Ireland*. Cambridge.

— 1976. The Beaker network – social and economic models. In: LANTING J.N. / VAN DER WAALS J.D. (eds), Glockenbecher Symposion (Oberried 1974), 459-477.

CLAUSTRE F. / MAZIERE F. 1998. La céramique campaniforme des Pyrénées-Orientales. *Bulletin de la Société Préhistorique Française* 95, 383-392.

CONSTANTINI G. 1984. Le Néolithique et le Chalcolithique des Grands Causses. *Gallia Préhistoire* 27, 121-210.

CONVERTINI F. / QUERRE G. 1998. Apports des études céramologiques en laboratoire à la connaissance du Campaniforme: résultats, bilan et perspectives. *Bulletin de la Société Préhistorique Française* 95, 333-341.

COURTIN J. 1974. *Le Néolithique de la Provence*. Paris.

CREMONESI G. / GRIFONI-CREMONESI R. / RADI G. / TOZZI C. / NICOLIS F. 1998. L'Italie centrale. In: GUILAINE J. (dir.), *Atlas du Néolithique européen II. L'Europe occidentale*, 165-231.

DAVID N. / KRAMER C. 2001. *Ethnoarchaeology in action*. Cambridge.

DELIBES DE CASTRO G. 1977. *El vaso campaniforme en la Meseta norte española*. Valladolid.

DEPALMAS A. / MELIS M.G. / TANDA G. 1998. La Sardaigne. In: GUILAINE J. (dir.), *Atlas du Néolithique européen II. L'Europe occidentale*, 343-394.

DRENTH E. 1989. Een onderzoek naar aspecten van de symbolische betekenis van Grand-Pressigny en Pseudo-Grand-Pressigny dolken van de Enkelgrafcultuur in Nederland In: NIKLEWICZ-HOKSE A.T.L / LAGERWERF C.A.G. (eds), *Bundel van de Steentijddag (Groningen, 1 april 1989)*, 100-121.

DUDAY H. 1980. Les rites funéraires en Languedoc au cours du troisième millénaire (quelques observations à propos de découvertes récentes). In: GUILAINE J. (ed.), *Le groupe de Véraza et la fin des temps néolithiques dans le Sud de la France et la Catalogne*, 273-282.

EARLE T. / BECH J.-H. / KRISTIANSEN K. / APERLO P. / KELERTAS K. / STEINBERG J. 1998. The political economy of Late Neolithic and early Bronze age society: the Thy archaeological project. *Norwegian Archaeological Review* 31, 1-28.

ENDRŐDI A. 1998. Results of settlement archaeology in Bell Beaker culture research in Hungary. In: BENZ M. / VAN WILLINGEN S. (eds), *Some new approaches to the Bell Beaker phenomenon Lost Paradise...? Proceedings of the 2nd meeting of the „Association Archéologie et Gobelets" Feldberg (Germany), 18th-20th April 1997*, 141-160.

EVANS J.G. 1990. Notes on some Late Neolithic and Bronze age events in long barrows ditches in southern and eastern England. *Proceedings of the Prehistoric Society* 56, 111-116.

FISCHER U. 1976. Die Dialektik der Becherkulturen. *Jahresschrift fur Mitteldeutsche Vorgeschichte* 60, 235-245.

GALLAY A. / CHAIX L. 1984. *Le site préhistorique du Petit Chasseur (Sion, Valais). 5. Le dolmen M XI.* Lausanne.

GALLAY A. 1979. Le phénomène campaniforme: une nouvelle hypothèse historique. *Archives Suisses d'Anthropologie Générale* 43, 231-258.

— 1986. Autonomie du Campaniforme rhodano-rhénan. La question de la céramique domestique. In: DEMOULE J.-P. / GUILAINE J. (dirs), *Le néolithique de la France. Hommage à Gérard Bailloud,* 431-446.

— 1997-1998. L'énigme campaniforme. Rhône-Alpes A404. L'énigmatique civilisation campaniforme. *Archéologia hors-série* 9, 14-19.

GIBSON A. 1980. Pot beakers in Britain? *Antiquity* 54, 219-221.

— 1987. Beaker domestic sites across the North Sea: a review. In: *Les relations entre le continent et les îles britanniques à l'âge du bronze. Actes du colloque de Lille dans le cadre du 22e congrès préhistorique de France. Revue archéologique de Picardie (supplément),* 7-16.

GILIGNY F. / SALANOVA L. 1997. La variabilité des corpus céramiques méridionaux au Néolithique final - Chalcolithique. *Bulletin de la Société Préhistorique Française* 94, 237-258.

GOMEZ J. / JOUSSAUME R. 1978. Analyse de deux pointes de Palmela du Centre-Ouest. *Bulletin de la Société Préhistorique Française* 75, 121-123.

GOSSELAIN O.P. 2000. Materializing identities: an African perspective. *Journal of Archaeological Method and Theory* 7, 187-217.

GUILAINE J. 1996. Le Bronze ancien en Méditerranée occidentale. In: MORDANT C. / GAIFFE O. (éds), *Cultures et sociétés du Bronze ancien en Europe. Actes du colloque Fondements culturels, techniques, économiques et sociaux des débuts de l'âge du Bronze. 117e Congrès national des sociétés historiques et scientifiques. Clermont-Ferrand 27-29 octobre 1992,* 37-68.

HALL D. 1988. Survey results in the Cambridgeshire fenland. *Antiquity* 62, 311-314.

HANSEL B. / ZIMMER S. (eds.) 1994. *Die Indogermanen und das Pferd. Akten des Internationalen interdisziplinären Kolloquiums Freie Universität Berlin, 1.-3. Juli 1992.* Budapest.

HARDING A.F. 2000. *European societies in the Bronze Age.* Cambridge.

HARRISON R.J. 1980. *The beaker folk. Copper Age archaeology in western Europe,* London.

— 1986. *L'âge du cuivre. La civilisation du vase campaniforme.* Paris.

HARRISON R. / QUERO S. / PRIEGO M.C. 1975. Beaker metallurgy in Spain. *Antiquity* 49, 273-278.

HEALY F. / HOUSLEY R. A. 1992. Nancy was not alone: human skeletons of the Early Bronze Age from the Norfolk peat fen. *Antiquity* 66, 948-955.

HECKER V. 1995. Böhmische Gruppe: Böhmen. In: STRAHM C. (dir.), *Das Glockenbecher-Phänomen. Ein Seminar,* 41-66.

HERTZ R. 1907. Contribution à une étude sur la représentation collective de la mort. *Année Sociologique* 10, 48-137.

HOFFMAN C.R. 1995. The making of material culture — the roles of metal technology in Late Prehistoric Iberia. In: LILLIOS K.T. (ed.), *The origins of complexity in Late Prehistoric Iberia,* 20-31.

HUYSECOM E. 1986. La question des bouteilles à collerette. Identification et chronologie d'un groupe méridional répandu de l'Ukraine à la Bretagne. In: *Actes du Xe Colloque interrégional sur le Néolithique. Caen, 30 septembre – 2 octobre 1983. Revue Archéologique de l'Ouest (supplément 1),* 195-215.

JORGE S.O / JORGE V. O. 1997. The Neolithic / Chalcolithic transition in Portugal. In: DIAZ-ANDREU M. / KEAY S. (eds), *The archaeology of Iberia. The dynamics of change*, 128-142.

JOUSSAUME R. 1970. Nouveau site campaniforme en Vendée. Le Marais-Girard, commune de Brétignolles. *Bulletin de la Société Préhistorique Française* 67, 243-245.

— 1981. *Le Néolithique de l'Aunis et du Poitou occidental dans son cadre atlantique.* Rennes.

KALICZ-SCHREIBER R. 1976. Die Probleme der Glockenbecherkultur in Ungarn. In: LANTING J.N. / VAN DER WAALS J.D. (eds), *Glockenbecher Symposion (Oberried 1974)*, 183-215.

KINNES I. / SCHADLA-HALL T. / CHADWICK P. / DEAN P. 1983. Duggleby Howe reconsidered. *The Archaeological Journal* 140, 83-108.

KUNST M. / UERPMANN H.-P. 1996. Zambujal (Portugal). Vorbericht über die Grabungen 1994. *Madrider Mitteilungen* 37, 10-36.

KUNST M. 1995. Central places and social complexity in the Iberian Copper Age. In: LILLIOS K.T. (ed.), *The origins of complexity in Late Prehistoric Iberia*, 32-41.

— 1998. Waren die „Schmiede" in der portugiesischen Kupferzeit gleichzeitig auch die Elite? In: FRITSCH B. / MAUTE M. / MATUSCHIK I. MÜLLER J. / WOLF C. (dirs), *Tradition und Innovation. Prähistorische Archäologie als historische Wissenschaft. Festschrift für Christian Strahm*, 541-551.

LARSSON L. 1990. Dog in fraction – symbols in actions. In: VERMEERSCH P. / VAN PEER P. (eds), *Contributions to the Mesolithic in Europe*, 153-160.

LAZARICH GONZALEZ M. 2000. Estado actual de la investigación sobre el Campaniforme en Andalucía occidental. *Madrider Mitteilungen* 41, 112-138.

LEHMANN L.T. 1965. Placing the pot beaker. *Helinium* 5, 3-31.

LEIGHTON R. 1999. *Sicily before history. An archaeological survey from the Palaeolithic to the Iron Age.* London.

LEISNER V. / SCHUBART H. 1966. Die kupferzeitliche Befestigung von Pedra do Ouro / Portugal. *Madrider Mitteilungen* 7, 9-60.

LEITAO M. / NORTH C.T. / NORTON J. / DAVEIGA FERREIRA O. / ZBYSZEWSKI G. 1984. The prehistoric burial cave at Verdelha dos Ruivos (Vialonga), Portugal. In: GUILAINE J. (dir.), *L'âge du cuivre européen. Civilisations à vases campaniformes*, 221-240.

LEMERCIER O. 1998. The Bell-Beaker Phenomenon in the southeast of France. The state of research and preliminary remarks about the TGV-excavations and some other sites of the Provence. In: BENZ M. /VAN WILLINGEN S. (eds), *Some new approaches to the Bell Beaker phenomenon Lost Paradise...? Proceedings of the 2nd meeting of the „Association Archéologie et Gobelets" Feldberg (Germany), 18th-20th April 1997*, 23-41.

LICHARDUS J. 1988. Campaniformes d'Europe centrale. In: LEROI-GOURHAN A. (dir.), *Dictionnaire de la Préhistoire*, 189.

LIVINGSTONE SMITH A. 2000. Processing clay for pottery in northern Cameroon: social and technical requirements. *Archaeometry* 42, 21-42.

LOUWE KOOIJMANS L.P. 1974. *The Rhine-Meuse delta. Four studies on its prehistoric occupation and holocene geology.* Leiden.

MACHNIK J. 1991. *The earliest Bronze Age in the Carpathian basin.* Bradford.

MALMER M.P. 1966. The correlations between definitions and interpretations of Neolithic cultures in northwestern Europe. *Palaeohistoria* 12, 373-378.

MARECHAL D. / PETREQUIN A.-M. / PETREQUIN P. / ARBOGAST R.-M. 1998. Les parures du Néolithique final à Chalain et Clairvaux. *Gallia Préhistoire* 40, 135-203.

MARTIN E. / MURPHY P. 1988. West Row Fen, Suffolk: a Bronze Age fen-edge settlement site. *Antiquity* 62, 353-358.

MATHERS C. 1984. Beyond the grave: the context and wider implications of mortuary practice in south-eastern Spain. In: BLAGG T.F.C. / JONES R.F.J. / KEAY S.J. (eds), *Papers in Iberian Archaeology*, 13-44.

MILLAN A. / ARRIBAS J.G. 1994. La ceramica: estudio tecnologico. In: BLASCO C. (ed.), *El horizonte campaniforme de la region de Madrid en el centenario de Ciempozuelos*, 117-126.

MIZOGUCHI K. 1993. Time in the reproduction of mortuary practices. *World Archaeology* 25, 223-235.

MOHEN J.-P. 1988. Campaniformes d'Europe occidentale. In: LEROI-GOURHAN A. (dir.), *Dictionnaire de la Préhistoire*, 189-190.

MOUNT C. 1994. Aspects of ritual deposition in the Late Neolithic and Beaker periods at Newgrange, Co. Meath. *Proceedings of the Prehistoric Society* 60, 433-443.

MÜLLER A. 1998. Geschlechtsspezifische Totenlage und geschlechtsspecifische Beigaben bei der Böhmisch-Märischen Gruppe bzw. Ostgruppe der Glockenbecherkultur. In: BENZ M. / VAN WILLINGEN S. (eds), *Some new approaches to the Bell Beaker phenomenon Lost Paradise...? Proceedings of the 2nd meeting of the „Association Archéologie et Gobelets" Feldberg (Germany), 18th-20th April 1997*, 121-128.

MÜLLER A. / LEMERCIER O., 1994. Le site néolithique final / chalcolithique de la Fare à Forcalquier (Alpes-de-Haute-Provence). *Bulletin de la Société Préhistorique Française* 91, 187-189.

NEEDHAM S.P. 1988. Selective deposition in the British Early Bronze Age. *World Archaeology* 20, 229-248.

NEUSTUPNY E. 1976. Paradigm lost. In: LANTING J.N. / VAN DER WAALS J.D. (eds), *Glockenbecher Symposion (Oberried 1974)*, 241-248.

O'BRIEN W. 1998. New light on Beaker metallurgy in Ireland. In: NICOLIS F. / MOTTES E. (eds), *Bell Beakers today. Pottery, people, culture, symbols in prehistoric Europe. International Colloquium. Riva del Garda (Trento, Italy). 11-16 May 1998. Abstracts*, 80-81.

PARKER PEARSON M. 1995. Southwestern Bronze Age pottery. In: KINNES I. / VARNDELL G. (eds), *„Unbaked urns of rudely shape". Essays on British and Irish pottery for Ian Longworth*, 89-100.

PAUTREAU J.-P. / ROBERT P.-P., 1980. Le gisement campaniforme des Deux Moulins au Bois-en-Ré (Charente-Maritime). *Bulletin de la Société Préhistorique Française* 77, 283-288.

PETREQUIN A.-M. / PETREQUIN P. 1988. *Le Néolithique des lacs. Préhistoire des lacs de Chalain et de Clairvaux*. Paris.

PETREQUIN P. 1993. North wind, South wind. Neolithic technical choices in the Jura Mountains, 3700-2400 BC. In: LEMONNIER P. (ed.), *Technological choices. Transformations in material cultures since the Neolithic*, 36-76.

PETREQUIN P. /CASSEN S. / CROUTSCH C. / WELLER O. 1997. Haches alpines et haches carnacéennes dans l'Europe du Ve millénaire. *Notae Praehistoricae* 17, 135-150.

PETREQUIN P. / CHASTEL J. / GILIGNY F. / PETREQUIN A.-M. / SAINTOT S. 1987-1988. Réinterprétation de la civilisation Saône-Rhône. Une approche des tendances culturelles du Néolithique final. *Gallia Préhistoire, Fouilles et Monuments archéologiques en France métropolitaine* 30, 1-89.

PRICE T.D. / GRUPE G. / SCHRÖTER P., 1998. Migration in the Bell Beaker period of central Europe. *Antiquity* 72, 405-411.

REPLOGLE B.A. 1980. Social dimensions of British and German Bell-Beakers burials: an exploratory study. *Journal of Indo-European Studies* 8, 165-199.

ROBERTS J. 1998. A contextual approach to the interpretation of the Early Bronze Age skeletons of the East Anglian Fens. *Antiquity* 72, 188-197.

RUSSEL A.D. 1990. Two Beaker burials from Chilbolton, Hampshire. *Proceedings of the Prehistoric Society* 56, 153-172.

SAINTOT S. 1998. Les armatures de flèches en silex de Chalain et de Clairvaux. *Gallia Préhistoire* 40, 204-241.

SALANOVA L. 1997. Le Campaniforme en France et dans les îles anglo-normandes: caractérisation des productions céramiques. *Bulletin de la Société Préhistorique Française* 94, 259-267.

— 1998. A long way to go... The Bell Beaker chronology in France. In: BENZ M. / VAN WILLINGEN S. (eds), *Some new approaches to the Bell beaker phenomenon Lost Paradise....? Proceedings of the 2nd meeting of the „Association Archéologie et Gobelets" Feldberg (Germany), 18th-20th April 1997*, 1-13.

— 2000. *La question du Campaniforme en France et dans les îles anglo-normandes. Productions, chronologie et rôles d'un standard céramique*. Paris.

SANGMEISTER E. 1976. Das Verhältnis der Glockenbecherkultur zu den einheimischen Kulturen der Iberischen Halbinsel. In: LANTING J.N. / VAN DER WAALS J.D. (eds), *Glockenbecher Symposion (Oberried 1974)*, 423-438.

SANGMEISTER E. / SCHUBART H. 1972. Zambujal. *Antiquity* 46, 191-197.

— 1981. *Zambujal. Die Grabungen 1964 bis 1973*. Mainz am Rhein.

SARTI L. / MARTINI F. 1998. Il tumulo di via Bruschi a Sesto Fiorentino. In: NICOLIS F. / MOTTES E. (dirs),. *Simbolo ed enigma. Il bicchiere campaniforme e l'Italia nella preistoria europea del III millennio a.C.*, 168-173.

— 1998. L'insediamento di Querciola a Sesto Fiorentino. In: NICOLIS F. / MOTTES E. (dirs), *Simbolo ed enigma. Il bicchiere campaniforme e l'Italia nella preistoria europea del III millennio a.C.*, 164-167.

SCHMITT J.-C. 2001. *Le corps, les rites, les rêves, le temps. Essais d'anthropologie médiévale*. Paris.

SCHUBART H. 1975. *Die Kultur der Bronzezeit im Südwesten der Iberischen Halbinsel*. Berlin.

SCHÜLE W. 1976. Die frühmetallzeitliche Siedlung auf dem Cerro de la Virgen in Orce (Granada). In: LANTING J.N. / VAN DER WAALS J.D. (eds), *Glockenbecher Symposion (Oberried 1974)*, 419-422.

SHENNAN S. 1976. Bell Beakers and their context in central Europe. In: LANTING J.N. /VAN DER WAALS J.D. (eds), *Glockenbecher Symposion (Oberried 1974)*, 231-239.

— 1977. The appearance of the Bell Beaker assemblage in central Europe. In: MERCER R. (ed.), *Beakers in Britain and Europe*, 51-70.

— 1993. Settlement and social change in central Europe, 3500-1500 BC. *Journal of World Prehistory* 7, 121-161.

SIMPSON D.D.A. 1971. Beaker houses and settlements in Britain. In: SIMPSON D.D.A. (ed.), *Economy and settlement in Neolithic and Early Bronze Age Britain and Europe*, 131-152.

SPINDLER K. 1971. Eine kupferzeitliche Siedlung vom Pico Agudo / Portugal. *Madrider Mitteilungen* 12, 51-71.

STARK M. (ed.) 1998. *The archaeology of social boundaries*. Washington.

STRAHM C. 1994. I grandi focolari dell'età del Rame. In: GUILAINE J. / SETTIS S. (eds), *Storia d'Europa.2-1. Preistoria è antichità*, 311-331.

STRAHM C. (Hrsg.) 1995. *Das Glockenbecher-Phänomen. Ein Seminar*. Freiburg.

TAVARES DA SILVA C. / SOARES J. 1998. Le Portugal. In: GUILAINE J. (dir.), *Atlas du Néolithique 2B. L'Europe occidentale*, 997-1050.

TCHEREMINISSOFF M. / FOUERE P. / SALANOVA L. 2000. La sépulture campaniforme de la Folie (Poitiers, Vienne): présentation préliminaire. *Internéo* 3, 161-167.

THOMAS J. 1999. *Understanding the Neolithic. A revised second edition of Rethinking the Neolithic.* London.

TOPP C. 1988. 'Incised' or 'Beaker' wares in the Balearic islands. *Bulletin of the Institute of Archaeology* 25, 67-84.

TREINEN F. 1970. Les poteries campaniformes en France. I. Typologie des poteries campaniformes françaises. II. Groupes géographiques et éléments culturels campaniformes. *Gallia Préhistoire*, 13, 53-105, 263-332.

TUCKWELL A. 1975. Patterns of burial orientation in the round barrows of East Yorkshire. *Bulletin of the Institute of Archaeology*, 12, 95-123.

TUREK J., 1995. Nálezy z období zvoncovitých pohárů povodí řeky Bíliny v severozápadních Čechách. In: *Archeologické výzkumy v severozápadnuch Čechách 1983-1992*, 123-134

    1998. The Bell Beaker period in North-West Bohemia. In: BENZ M. / VAN WILLINGEN S. (eds), *Some new approaches to the Bell beaker phenomenon Lost Paradise...? Proceedings of the 2nd meeting of the „Association Archéologie et Gobelets" Feldberg (Germany), 18th-20th April 1997*, 107-119.

TUSA S. 1998. Prospettiva mediterranea e integrità culturale del bicchiere campaniforme siciliano. In: NICOLIS F. / MOTTES E. (dirs), *Simbolo ed enigma. Il bicchiere campaniforme e l'Italia nella preistoria europea del III millennio a.C.*, 205-219.

UERPMANN H.-P. 1990. Die Domestikation des Pferdes im Chalkolithikum West- und Mitteleuropas. *Madrider Mitteilungen* 31, 109-153.

VAN BERG P.-L. 1994. *Grammaire des styles céramiques du Rubané d'Alsace.* Strasbourg.

VAN DER WAALS J.D. 1991. Silex du Grand-Pressigny aux Pays-Bas. In: *Actes du 14e colloque interrégional sur le Néolithique, Blois, 16-17-18 octobre 1987*, 193-200.

VANDER LINDEN M. 1998. La révolution spatiale du Campaniforme : essai sur les structures spatiales du Campaniforme en Europe du Nord-Ouest. In: CAUWE N. / VAN BERG P.-L. (dirs), Organisation néolithique de l'espace en Europe du Nord-Ouest. Actes du XXIIIe colloque interrégional sur le Néolithique (Bruxelles, 24-26 octobre 1997). *Anthropologie et Préhistoire. Bulletin de la Société royale belge d'Anthropologie et de Préhistoire* 109, 277-292.

    2001a. *Archéologie, complexité sociale et histoire des idées: l'espace campaniforme dans l'Europe du troisième millénaire avant notre ère*, Unpublished Ph.D. Dissertation. Brussels.

    2001b. Beer and beakers: a tentative analysis. In: GHEORGHIU D. (ed.), *Material, virtual and temporal compositions: on the relationships between objects. Papers from a session held at the European Association of Archaeologists Fifth Annual Meeting in Bournemouth 1999*, 45-51.

    2001c. Perpetuating traditions, changing ideologies. The Bell Beaker culture in the British Isles and its implication for the Indo-European problem. In: HULD M.E. / JONES-BLEY K. / DELLA VOLPE A. / ROBBINS DEXTER M. (eds), *Proceedings of the XIIth Annual UCLA Indo-European conference. Los Angeles May 26-28, 2000*, 269-286.

    2003. Competing cosmos on the relationships between Corded Ware and Bell Beaker mortuary practice. In: CZEBRESZUK J. / SZMYT M. (eds), *The Northeast Frontier of Bell Beakers. Proce of the symposium held at the Adam Mickiewicz University, Poznań (Poland), May 26-29 2002. BAR International series 1155*, 11-19.

    in press. So in Life, so in Death: British Bell Beaker Mortuary Practices as Idealised Means of Social Integration. In: VANDER LINDEN M. / NILSSON L. (eds), *Dealing with death. Papers from a session held at the European Association of Archaeologists Sixth Annual Meeting in Lisbon, September 2000.*

VAQUER J. 1998. Le midi méditerranéen de la France. In: GUILAINE J. (dir.), *Atlas du Néolithique européen II. L'Europe occidentale*, 413-500.

VAQUER J. / GANDELIN M. / MARSAC R. 2000. L'enceinte néolithique de Mourral-Millegrand à Trèbes (Aude). In: *IVes Rencontres Méridionales de Préhistoire Récente. Temps et Espace culturels. Actualité de la recherche en Préhistoire récente dans le midi. Nîmes. Carré d'Art. 28 et 29 octobre 2000. Pré-actes,* 53-55.

VIGNERON E. 1981. Eléments campaniformes de la grotte de Saint-Vérédème, Sanilhac (Gard). *Bulletin de la Société Préhistorique Française* 78, 88-96.

WALDREN W.H. 1979. A Beaker workshop area in the rock shelter of Son Matge, Mallorca. *World Archaeology* 11, 43-67.

Similar but Different. Bell Beakers in Europe
Czebreszuk J. (ed.)
Poznań 2004

THE FRONTIERS INSIDE THE WESTERN BELL BEAKER BLOCK

Laure Salanova (Nanterre, France)

The western fringe of Europe is wrongly considered as a block welded around the Bell Beaker phenomenum. The confrontation of data from north-west France and southern Portugal shows on the contrary that the Bell Beaker culture is polymorphous, not only in its composition but also in its causes and consequences. Bordered by the Atlantic ocean, these two regions do share characteristics in terms of both artefacts (stylistic convergences, diffusion from Portugal to the French Atlantic littoral of copper Palmela points) and the context of discoveries (persistence of graves of collective vocation) (SALANOVA 2000). Yet the Bell Beaker culture is expressed here in multiple facets. Through these differences, the western Bell Beaker block can be divided into a number of sub-groups, each corresponding to a distinct cultural pattern.

The contrasts in north-west France

In northern France, the Bell Beaker culture has been rather neglected by researchers, particularly in the Paris basin where data are poor. In Brittany, on the contrary, numerous finds from the megalithic graves of the southern coast aroused interest very early.

Composition of the BB set

The number of sites is greater in the west: 121 in Brittany, 73 in the Paris basin. The quantity of finds is also different from one region to the other: 725 vessels in Brittany, 119 in Normandy, less than 50 vessels in the other regions (Fig. 1). In the current state of knowledge, the Bell Beaker culture is massively concentrated on the southern littoral of Brittany, whilst in the Paris basin it is best represented along the Seine valley. These disparities can not be explained by the history of research: while the southern coast of Brittany has always attracted more archaeological attention than the northern coast, the Paris basin has been an area of intense archaeological activity for several decades now.

At the stylistic level, Breton Bell Beakers are dominated by the standardized style (hatched bands or horizontal lines as a unique theme), which represents over half

Similar but Different. Bell Beakers in Europe

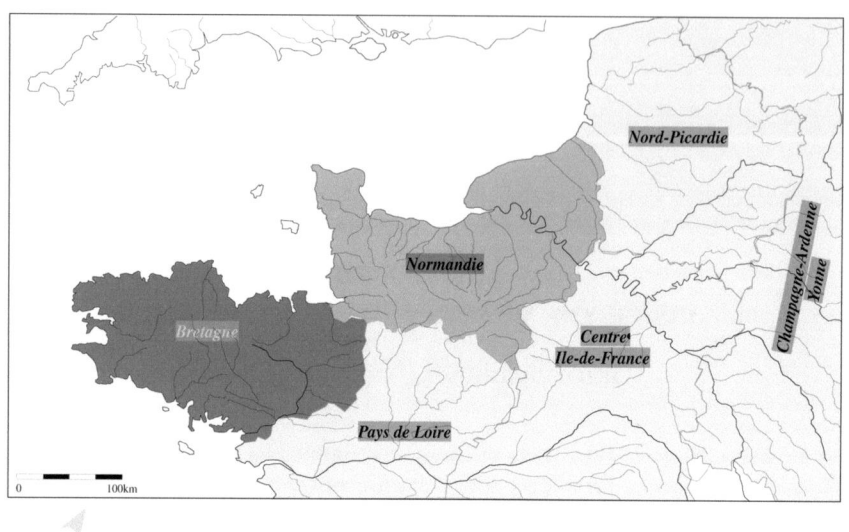

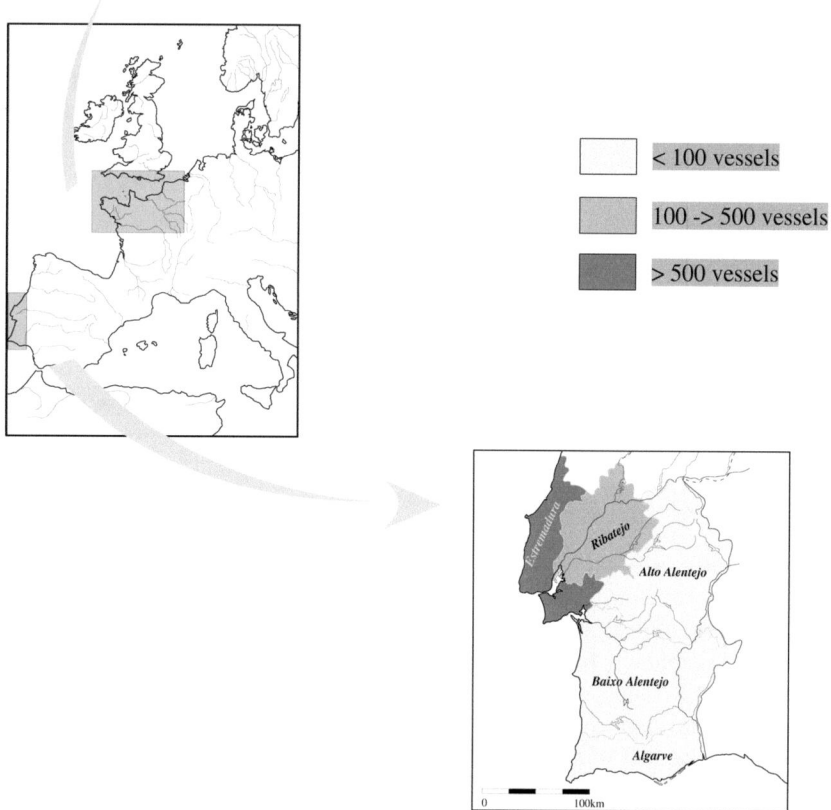

Fig. 1.   Bell Beaker distribution in the north of France and the south of Portugal.

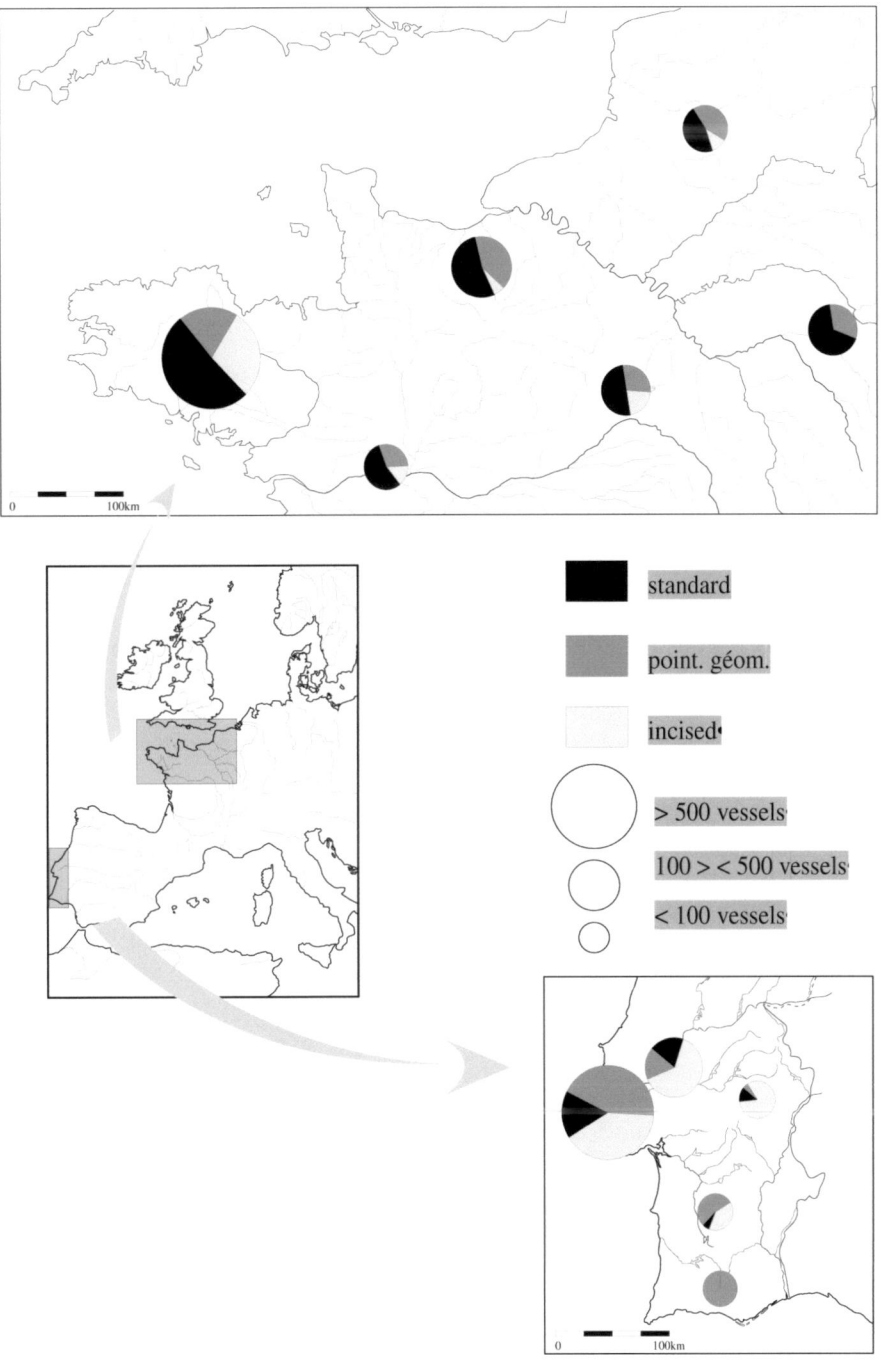

Fig. 2. Representation of Bell Beaker styles in the north of France and the south of Portugal.

the decorated vessels (Fig. 2). This high proportion explains the term „Breton monotonous style". The other styles are rare: 18% incised vessels[1] and 12% impressed-geometric (*pointillé-géométrique*) vessels. In the Paris basin, while the standardized decoration is well represented (mainly horizontal line decoration), there are numerous stylistic patterns, reflecting the variety of influences in this region.

Apart from pottery, the rest of the assemblage is very poorly represented: 5 copper daggers and 6 archer's wristguards in Brittany, 5 daggers and 6 wristguards in the Paris basin. In addition, the Paris basin has produced bone ornaments, whilst soil acidity in Brittany does not allow this kind of preservation. However, gold ornaments (strips which are curved or have perforated ends) are specific to Brittany. It is generally considered that these ornaments are made in Brittany, from alluvial gold nuggets, while copper deposits are unknown in both Brittany and the Paris basin.

The context of discoveries

Of the 121 sites with Bell Beaker finds known today in Brittany, almost all are burial contexts, 81% of which are megalithic graves. In the Paris basin, on the contrary, half the Bell Beaker material represents stray finds with no context.

Domestic sites are extremely rare throughout north-west France. The remains cover small areas and are generally unstructured and heterogeneous. As with settlements throughout the 3rd millennium B.C., our knowledge is very limited. The few known domestic sites have at least produced coarse pottery: urns with a horizontal cordon beneath the rim, large vessels with perforations just below the rim, large beakers with disorganized fingernail decoration. Certain graves contain this type of vessel, especially in Brittany (SALANOVA 1998).

In funerary context, the Bell Beaker phenomenum is complex because various types of practice co-exist. A few single graves occur in Brittany (megalithic cists), but they are much more common in the Paris basin (15 burials in pits, sometimes beneath barrows). Nevertheless, the collective tombs constructed at the beginning of the 3rd millennium continue in use and produce Bell Beaker deposits. When excavation has been sufficiently precise, one notes that these are individualized deposits, as in the small gallery-grave (*allée couverte*) of Kerbors (north Brittany) where several separate assemblages could be distinguished (Fig. 3-2), or the megalithic tomb of Gâvres (south Brittany) in which the terminal cell had been emptied and re-used as a cist (Fig. 3-1). While Bell Beaker finds are common in the Breton megalithic tombs (Fig. 4-1), they are rare in the Paris basin: out of 400 recorded monuments, only 9, all located along the Seine valley, have produced Bell Beaker material (Fig. 4-2). Nonetheless, burials in collective graves have been radiocarbon dated to the Bell Beaker horizon, although no artefacts are associated.

---

1. The proportion of incised vessels is in fact over-estimated, du to a very fragmentary assemblage from northern Brittany. This assemblage, recovered by survey, includes several hundred small sherds, for which it is impossible to count the minimum number of vessels.

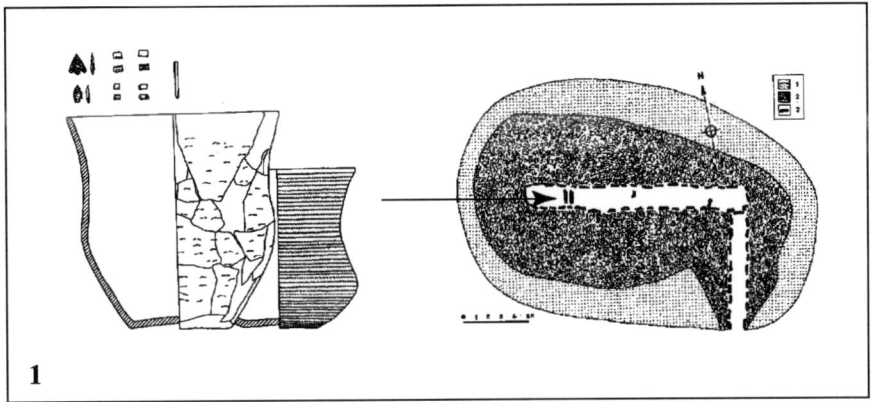

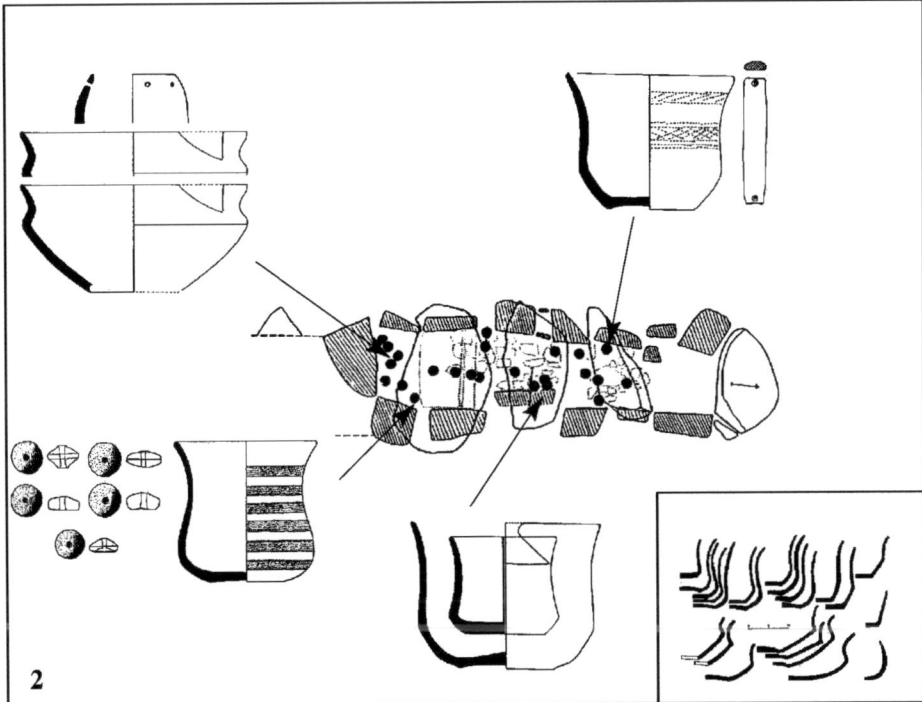

Fig. 3. Individualized Bell Beaker deposits in Breton megalithic tombs (1: Gâvres, Morbihan, after L'HELGOUACH 1976; 2: Kerbors, Côtes d'Armor, after GIOT *et al.* 1957).

In north-west France the Bell Beaker impact is thus very different. In Brittany, tombs very often produce large quantities of finds. In the Paris basin, however, burial in collective graves is still practised, but there is no link here with Bell Beakers. Furthermore, Brittany develops its own version of the maritime style, whilst no regional style emerges in the Paris basin. Styles pass through, from the

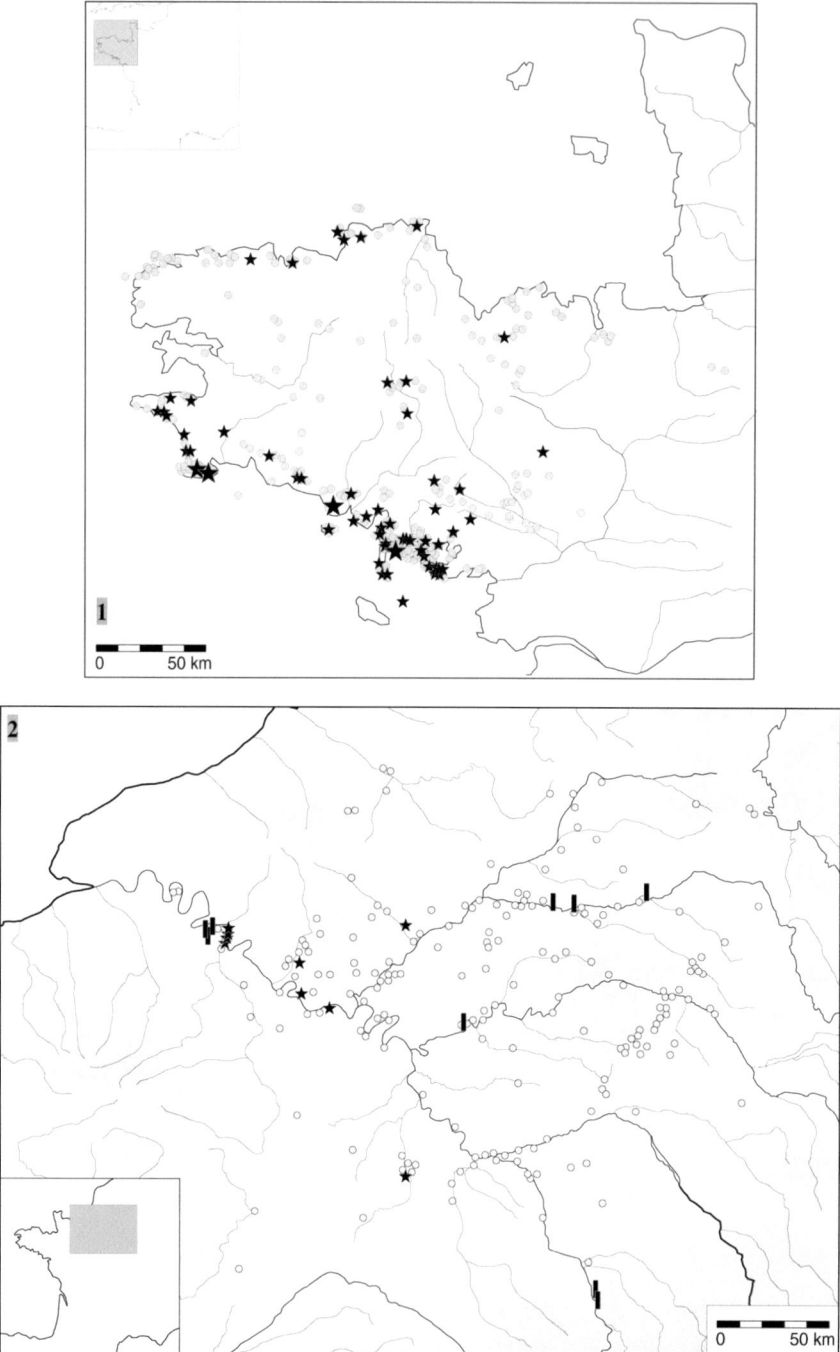

Fig. 4. Distribution of collective graves with Bell Beaker deposits (star) and without (circle), as well as Bell Beaker single burials (rectangle) in Brittany (1) and in the Paris basin (2).

west (the maritime style), east (pseudo-AOO vessels) and north (some styles similar to late English styles), but this has apparently no effect on local cultural development.

Portugal at the heart of the Bell Beaker problem in Europe

The Bell Beaker situation in southern Portugal shows the same complexity as in north-west France. The sites, 144 in total, are unevenly distributed around the Tagus estuary (Fig. 1). Once again, this distribution is not insignificant and can not be entirely attributed to the history of research.

Composition of the BB set

To this day 2500 Bell Beaker vessels have been found in Portugal. Estremadura, smaller than a French *région*, alone contains 78% of this material (about 2000 vessels), which represents one of the highest densities in Europe. The neighbouring regions, in Alentjo, are on the contrary strangely impoverished. Yet these regions have also been subject to intensive archaeological activity, since the discovery during the 20th century of several hundred megalithic graves. What is more, Alentejo is a crucial region in the 3rd millennium B.C. because the copper and hard rocks (amphibolite, schist) used at this time are extracted here and circulate as far as the littoral (CARDOSO 1999).

In addition, the Tagus estuary is not just important in quantitative terms: it also contains the greatest stylistic variety, decreasing from west to east (SALANOVA 2000). The Palmela impressed-geometric style, present on a third of the total number of south Portuguese vessels, is more frequent in the west and in the south (Baixo Alentejo, Algarve and Estremadura) (Fig. 2). The incised style, however, is more common in the east (Ribatejo and Alto Alentejo). It also represents one third of finds. Lastly, the maritime style (16% of the total) is massively concentrated in Estremadura, particularly on the fortified sites. The 291 vessels discovered in this region alone represent over one third of the maritime style vessels from the whole Iberian peninsular.

The other items of the Bell Beaker set are in fact quite rare: scarcely fifty or so artefacts for the whole of Portugal. Copper daggers and Palmela points are concentrated in Estremadura, although there are no deposits of copper ore in this region. Archer's wristguards, of which there are only about twenty in Portugal, are also more common in Estremadura, which has produced 9. Lastly, as in the Armorican massif, bone V-buttons are generally not preserved in the acid granitic soils which are widespread in Portugal.

The context of discoveries

Settlements producing Bell Beaker finds are quite numerous, but they are never pure: Bell Beaker material generally appears in the upper levels of sites occupied throughout the 3rd millennium B.C. Settlements produce small series, never more

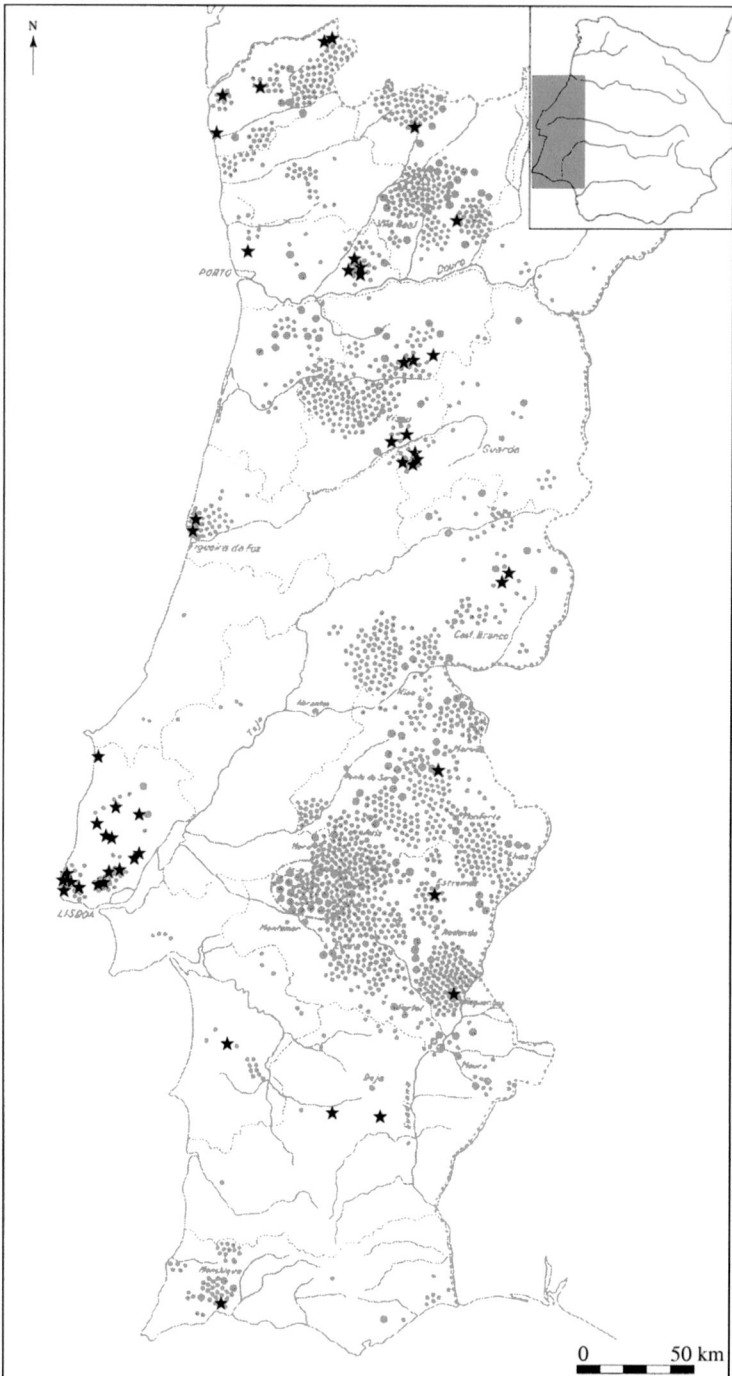

Fig. 5. Distribution of collective graves with Bell Beaker deposits (star) and without (circle) in Portugal (background map after LEISNER 1956).

than 100 vessels. Nevertheless the settlements on the Estremadura coast contain larger series, whilst Bell Beaker vessels are rare in domestic contexts in Alentejo and Algarve. Contextual data are generally insufficiently precise for determining the nature of Bell Beaker deposits in settlements. Nevertheless, when this kind of evidence is available, it turns out that Bell Beakers occur in particular features: this is the case at Zambujal (Torres Vedras) where Bell Beaker material is abundant in building V, interpreted as a metallurgical workshop (KUNST 1987), and also on the fortified site of Leceia (Oeiras), where Bell Beaker finds occurred in two stone structures („huts") built outside the enclosure (CARDOSO 1994). Overall, the low number of vessels found in settlements and their rather particular position on the site immediately suggest that a special value was attached to this material.

In tombs, the same geographical disparities can be observed. While the megalithic graves of Estremadura, and even more so the artificial caves, often produce Bell Beaker deposits, this is not the case in Alentejo (Fig. 5). Out of the hundreds of megalithic graves known in the latter region, only six contain Bell Beaker vessels. Furthermore, four of these tombs only produced undecorated beakers. No Bell Beaker single grave has been found in southern Portugal. On the contrary, as in Brittany, the deposits found in tombs with a collective vocation are individualized, although this is not always possible to identify because soil acidity has destroyed all bone remains and because of the age of most excavations. Thus in the tomb of Casas do Canal (Estremoz, Alentejo), the entrance was transformed into a cist which contained a deposit of two Bell Beaker vessels, probably associated with one person (Fig. 6-2). Likewise at Pedra Branca (Montum, Alentejo), two individualized graves were discovered in the upper level of the chamber (Fig. 6-1).

It is therefore clear that the Bell Beaker impact in southern Portugal is very different along the littoral and in the hinterland. The Estremadura region alone has produced the complete set, as well as large series, whilst in Alentejo the Bell Beaker series are rarer and smaller. In the tombs, the Alentejan vessels, often undecorated, are also less marked in cultural and symbolic terms than the classic decorated beakers of the littoral.

Conclusions

Comparison of the Portuguese and French models

At the scale of the Atlantic coast, the points in common go way beyond traditional comparisons of finds.

Firstly, the density maps for the various regions show that the Bell Beaker culture enters through the littoral, which is the area with the highest concentrations of finds, and that its presence then falls off with distance from the Atlantic ocean.

Secondly, the other artefacts that make up the „BB Set" (copper daggers, wristguards) are rare in all the regions. Furthermore, in northern France as well as southern Portugal, the raw materials used for their manufacture do not occur in the regions of high pottery density. Thus the phenomenum of Bell Beaker vessels must

Similar but Different. Bell Beakers in Europe

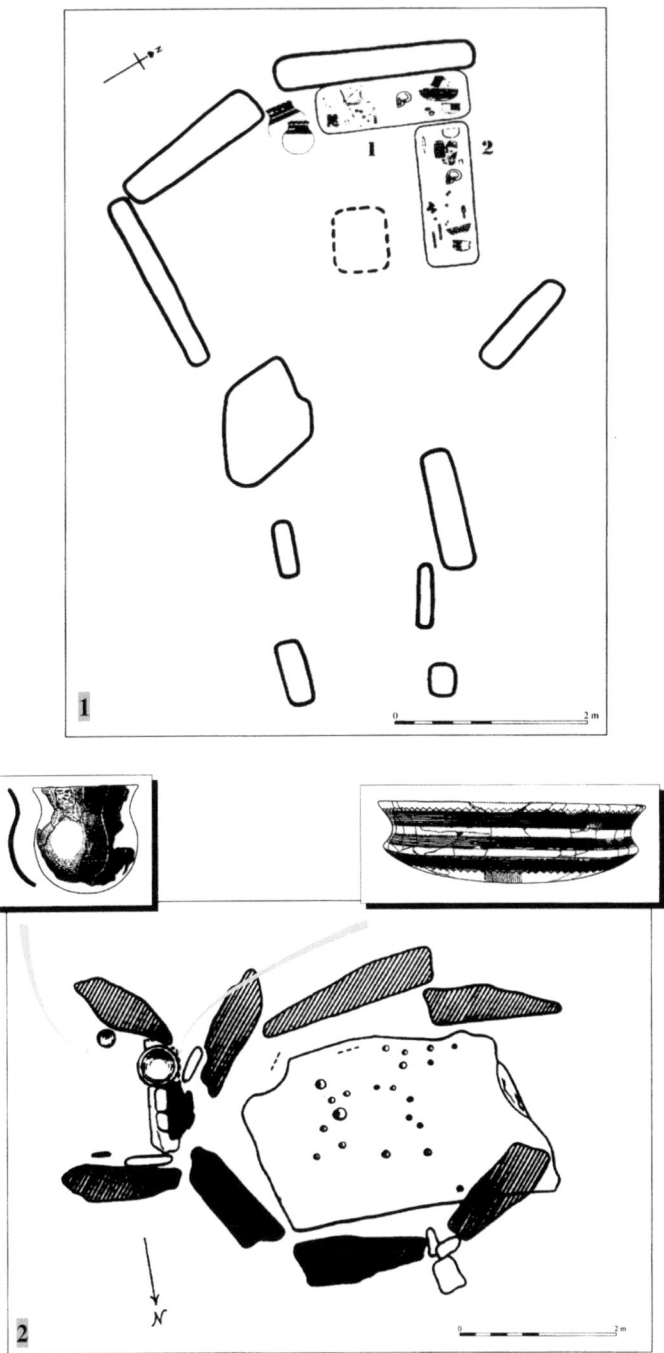

Fig. 6. Individualized Bell Beaker deposits in Portuguese megalithic graves. 1: Pedra Branca (Montum, Alentejo), after Veiga Ferreira et al. 1975; 2: Casas do Canal (Estremoz, Alentejo), after Leisner 1955.

be dissociated from the other artefacts with which they have been perhaps rather hastily linked. The classic (and rare!) Bell Beaker vessel-dagger-wristguard set comprises elements which reflect different networks.

Lastly, analysis of burial practices shows another type of influence. Whilst burial in collective graves persists all along the Atlantic coastline of Europe, the individualization of deposits increases with the Bell Beaker culture. The rate of increase is higher to the east of the zones studied: single graves in the Paris basin, clearly individualized deposits in Alentejo. We have shown elsewhere that in the Bell Beaker graves of western Europe funerary behaviour (position and orientation of the body in the grave) is identical to central Europe and the Rhine regions (SALANOVA 2003). Yet single graves and individualized deposits in collective graves produce the same assemblages. This is not therefore a chronological difference, but in fact a difference in status between the dead buried in pit graves and the dead placed in monumental, thousand-year-old chambers. The same problem of status is posed by the Portuguese settlements, which show that the Bell Beaker assemblages are spatially distinct (features which are isolated or have a particular function).

Nevertheless, beyond these points in common, the differences in representation of the Bell Beaker culture in the different regions justify division of the Atlantic Bell Beaker sphere into several sub-groups.

The frontiers of the western block

Portuguese Estremadura and Brittany share a high density of Bell Beaker vessels and a certain continuity at the end of the Neolithic (continuity in occupation of the Portuguese fortified sites with the Bell Beaker culture, persistence of collective burial in megalithic tombs or in artificial caves). Yet the Bell Beaker cultural impact is different at the beginning of the Bronze Age (Fig. 7). This period, which is little known in Estremadura, is characterized in Brittany by megalithic cists with individual deposits, then by the „Armorican Tumulus culture" (single burial in a wooden structure covered by a barrow), in which items borrowed from the Bell Beaker set appear: copper daggers, wristguards in amber or gold.

In the Paris basin too there is no break with the Bell Beaker culture; but here the assemblage is not really adopted. Foreign elements are certainly present (pseudo-AOO vessels, single graves), but they are not integrated in the local culture: they are superimposed on it. Even the beginning of the Bronze Age is not affected by the Bell Beaker trend: burial in collective graves persists.

Lastly, in Alentejo, the refusal of the Bell Beaker assemblage seems even more obvious. Here again, vessels of Atlantic appearance (maritime style) or Spanish appearance (incised style) do occur, but they remain apart from the local culture. Yet at the beginning of the Bronze Age, single graves appear in which the person is accompanied by undecorated vessels, wristguard and dagger, in the purest Bell Beaker tradition („Ferradeira horizon", SCHUBART 1971).

Beyond the material bases of the Atlantic Bell Beaker culture, we are thus dealing with four different scenarios, each of which has its own logic of development.

Similar but Different. Bell Beakers in Europe

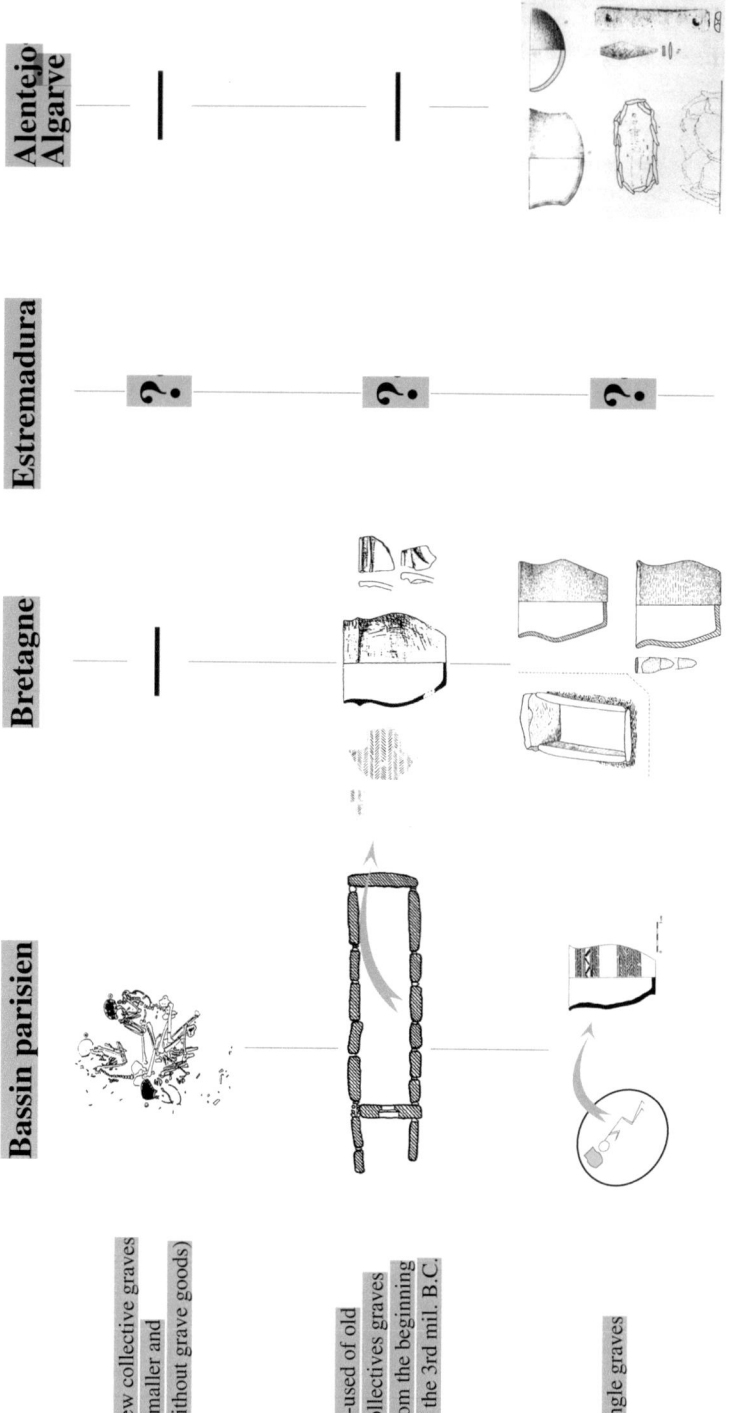

Fig. 7   Early Bronze Age burial practices in the north of France and the south of Portugal.

The causes of these differences must of course be sought in long term factors. Beyond the material wealth of each region or its position on exchange routes, the causes are related to structural problems, to the aptitude of each society to transform its culture or not. Thus in northern France, both Brittany and the Paris basin are affected by European phenomena well before the Bell Beaker period. They involve the appearance of *bouteilles à collerette* in Brittany and of perforated battle axes, in both cases originating from the east. Whilst these artefacts are not really adopted in the Paris basin, Brittany does integrate them and, with the perforated axes, even becomes a centre for diffusion due to large-scale production in south-west Brittany (GIOT *et al.* 1979). Unlike Brittany, which is particularly receptive to new ideas, the Paris basin seems to let Bell Beakers pass through as just another trend, which in any case does not upset its profoundly conservative traditions.

References

CARDOSO J. L. 1994. Leceia 1983-1993. Escavações do povoado fortificado pré-histórico. *Estudos Arqueológicos de Oeiras, n° especial.* Oeiras.

— 1999. Copper metallurgy and the importance of other raw materials in the context of chalcolithic economic intensification in portuguse Estremadura. *Journal of Iberian Archaeology* 1, 93-109.

GIOT P.R. / L'HELGOUACH J. / MONNIER J.L. 1979. *Préhistoire de la Bretagne.* Rennes.

GIOT P.R. / BRIARD J. / L'HELGOUACH J. 1957. Fouilles de l'allée couverte de Men-ar-Rompet à Kerbors. *Bulletin de la Société Préhistorique Française* 54-9, 495-515.

KUNST M. 1987. Zambujal, Glockenbecher und kerblattverzierte Keramik aus den Grabungen 1964 bis 1973. *Madrider Beiträge* 5. Mainz am Rhein.

L'HELGOUACH J. 1976. Les relations entre le groupe des vases campaniformes et les groupes néolithiques dans l'Ouest de la France. In: LANTING J.N. / VAN DER WAALS J.D. (eds), *Glockenbecher Symposion (Oberried 1974),* 439-451.

LEISNER G. / LEISNER V. 1955. *Antas na herdades do Casas de Bragança no concelho de Estremoz.* Lisboa.

LEISNER G. / LEISNER V. 1956. *Die Megalithgräber der iberischen Halbinsel. Der Westen 1.1.* Berlin.

SALANOVA L. 1998. Le statut des assemblages campaniformes en contexte funéraire: la notion de „bien de prestige". *Bulletin de la Société Préhistorique Française* 95-3, 315-326.

— 2000. Mécanismes de diffusion des vases campaniformes: les liens franco-portugais. In: JORGE V.O. (ed.), *3ᵉ Congresso de Arqueologia Peninsular (Vila Real, Portugal, 1999), vol. 4: Pré-História recente da Península ibérica, Porto,* 399-409.

SALANOVA L. 2003. Heads Nord: analysis of Bell Beaker graves in Western Europe. *Found of Iberian Archeology,* 5, 163–169.

SCHUBART H. 1971. O Horizonte de Ferradeira. Uma Cultura do Eneolítico tardío no Sul de Portugal. *Revista de Guimarães* LXXXI, 189-216.

VEIGA FERREIRA O. DA / ZBYSZEWSKI G. / LEITAO M. / NORTH C.T. / REYNOLDS DE SOUSA H. 1975. Le monument mégalithique de Pedra Branca auprès de Montum (Melides). *Communicações dos Serviços Geológicos de Portugal* LIX, 107-192.

Similar but Different. Bell Beakers in Europe
Czebreszuk J. (ed.)
Poznań 2004

BELL BEAKER LITHIC INDUSTRY:
A REDISCOVERED PARADISE?

Robin Furestier (Aix-en-Provence, France)

Summary

From the example of Southeast of France, first characterisations allow us to develop hypothesis about the value of bell beaker lithic industry as a cultural marker, and about its evolution during beaker chronology.

The southeast of France is a rich framework for the bell beaker research. More than 300 sites representing all of the ceramic stylistic phases have been registrated. A local ceramic style has been also distinguished in this area. Among these sites, more than 100 have given lithic artefacts. If all of these don't permit to study and establish a correct comparative database, more than 10 permitted to propose a first technological and typological characterisation of lithic industry.

To the typological point of view, some characteristics have been enriched. Comparing to the Later Neolithic industry, we can consider the bell beaker „tool-box" diversity falling off. The scrapers (simple and thumbnail) dominate the whole. The splintered pieces are also numerous. The side-scrapers are well represented. The arrowheads (with tang and squared-aileron, cordiformes and lancéolées) present interesting characteristics, like the lunates.

To the technological point of view, the characterisation of bell beaker production and their chaîne opératoire is more difficult. Nevertheless, it's possible to bring some specificity to the light.

About the raw material, a local provisioning is preferred and less diversity of raw material source has been observed comparing to the later Neolithic groups. A bad quality of flint results to this provisioning logic. No standardised production prevails. Flakes debitage is nearly exclusive. Most of flakes are little, short and thick. But generally, if this production seems to be privileged, all blank products are used to make tool. We can talk of an optimisation of the production.

The presence of bladelets is nearly systematic, but they're not numerous. Unfortunately, it's not possible to reconstitute their chaine operatoire. Some details of the bladelet remind the pressure technique and present sometime the heat treatment marks. They're not used as tool blank. These blades and bladelets, as specialised production (existing before beaker period), are probably not a specific beaker production, and its status among the bell beaker contexts must be studied.

This results show that a characterisation of bell beaker lithic industry is possible. Now, we have to confront the ceramic chronology proposed by Jean Guilaine and the data of lithic industry study.

The absence of data of the phase 1 (international style) prevents to differentiate the two first phases. The same limits are noticed between the regional phase (Rhodano-provençal) and the phase 4 (epicampaniforme). Nevertheless, some brought out elements authorise to propose the

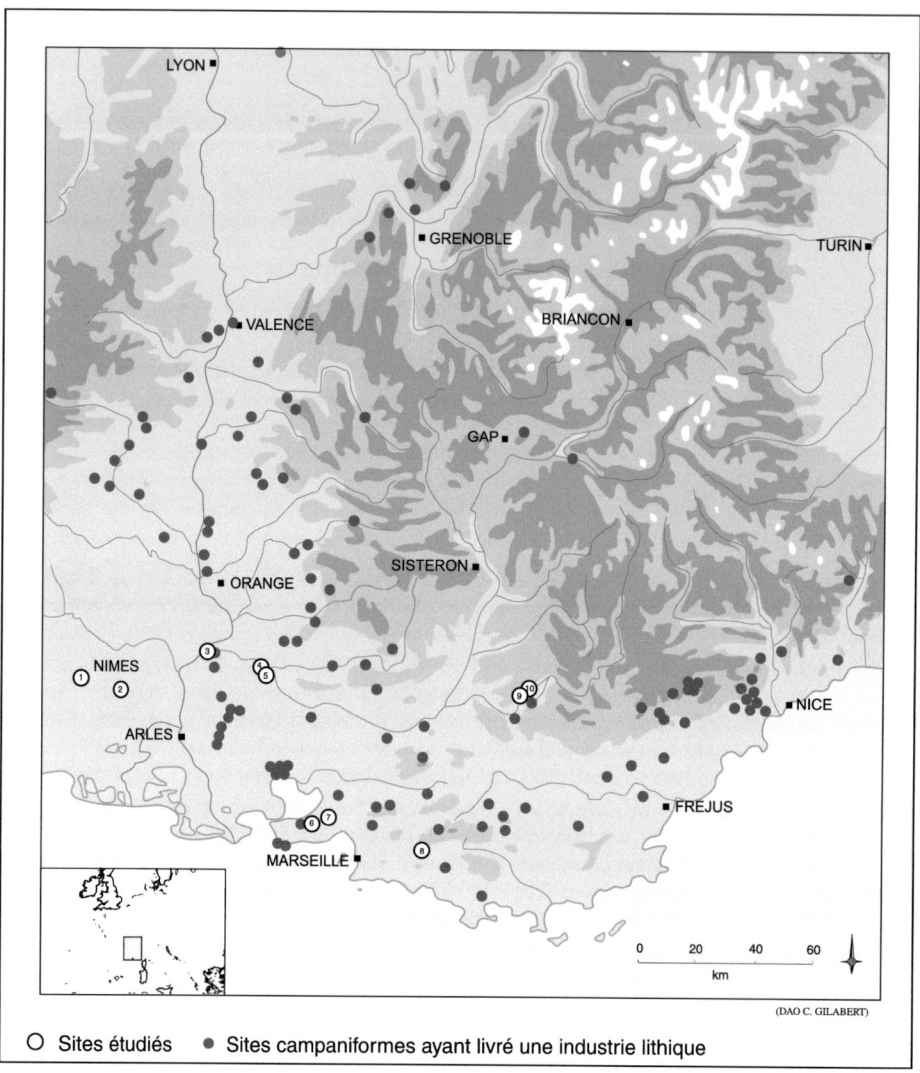

Fig. 1. Carte des sites campaniformes du sud-est de la France présentant une industrie lithique. 1. Le Mas de Vignolles IV, Nîmes (30); 2. Le Bois Sacré, Saint-Côme et Maruéjols (30); 3. La Balance, Avignon (84); 4–5. Les Calades 1 et 2, Orgon (13); 6. Le Fortin du Saut, Châteaunef-lès-Martigues (13); 7. Le Camp de Laure, Le Rove (13); 8. La Grande Baume, Gémenos (13); 9. La Grotte Murée, Montpezat (04); 10. L'Abri du Capitaine, Sainte-Croix-du-Verdon (04).

hypothesis of the separation of phase? (international-maritime-standard / pointillé géométrique) and phase? (rhodano-provençal / epicampaniforme barbelé).

In fact, it appeared easier to characterise phase? than phase? This characterisation must help us to find solutions to the evolution and diffusions problems of Bell beaker phenomenon in the southeast of France and in other countries.

Reprendre l'idée du titre de l'ouvrage de Marion BENZ et Samuel VAN WILLIGEN (1998) n'est pas seulement un pied de nez, c'est un acte militant. L'historiographie du Campaniforme pourrait devenir un chantier intéressant qui montrerait des approches peu variées du phénomène. Aussi, sans vouloir reproduire une erreur de surestimation de la valeur d'un type de vestige, il est temps de réintroduire l'industrie lithique campaniforme dans une optique de recherche plus archéologique.

Les études technologiques ont pu montrer, même pour les périodes récentes de la Préhistoire, leur intérêt dans l'élaboration de modèles culturels et dans le suivi de l'évolution de ces derniers. S'il sera peut-être bientôt temps de porter un regard critique sur les excès «techno-technologiques», il faut tenter de tirer maintenant un enseignement de cette école de technologie pour en appliquer les meilleurs aspects à l'industrie lithique campaniforme.

Pour aborder cette industrie lithique, après une première approche de ses spécificités (FURESTIER 1999 et à paraître a), une question se pose: pourquoi? Non pas «pourquoi» s'y intéresser - en tant qu'élément constitutif d'un tout, il participe à la synthèse d'un ensemble, d'un fait, archéologique. Il s'agit plutôt d'un «pourquoi l'industrie lithique est-elle considérée comme un domaine d'étude «ingrat»?».

Outre le ralentissement des recherches qu'a généré cette vision, comment comprendre le désintérêt patent manifesté à l'encontre de cette industrie? Le contraste esthétique entre céramique et lithique a déjà été évoqué (FURESTIER à paraître a) et constitue un élément de réponse, mais non «la» réponse unique. L'industrie lithique campaniforme a probablement cumulée plusieurs tares sur son cas. Mais elle pâtit surtout du syndrome de la fin. Fin de l'élément mobilier le plus important de la Préhistoire, qui coïncide avec l'apparition d'un nouvel élément promis à un avenir doré: le métal. Mais en conscience, il est peu convaincant d'envisager le remplacement de l'un par l'autre (BAILLY à paraître a). Un simple décompte du nombre d'artefacts métalliques suffit pour s'en convaincre aujourd'hui, ... et même hier.

Ce phénomène de juxtaposition des événements a précipité l'abandon des recherches sur l'industrie lithique, automatiquement qualifiée de finissante ou en cours de dégénérescence.

Comment commencer?

Un des principaux problèmes posé par l'industrie lithique campaniforme réside dans la nature archéologique même du phénomène campaniforme. En effet, rares sont les sites dits «purs», où les contextes ne présentent pas de risques de mélanges et donc d'hétérogénéité des séries disponibles. La grande majorité des sites campaniformes recensés ne livre effectivement que peu de vestiges campaniformes au milieu d'ensembles des différentes cultures du Néolithique final. Dans ces contextes, la céramique reste bien souvent le seul moyen de caractériser une présence campaniforme.

Il n'est pas question ici de donner à l'industrie lithique étudiée, une importance qu'elle n'aurait pas. Ainsi, il faut remarquer, le plus généralement, des ensembles quantitativement peu pourvus. Cet état de fait résulte d'un double constat: d'une part la diminution effective des vestiges lithiques taillés dans les ensembles disponibles, et d'autre part l'ancienneté des fouilles d'un nombre important de sites pour lesquels l'aspect esthétique de la céramique décorée a probablement primé sur le reste du mobilier jugé moins caractéristique.

Un tri important a donc été opéré pour pouvoir disposer in fine d'une base fiable, préambule nécessaire à toute caractérisation.

Dans ce cadre, le sud-est de la France montre plusieurs avantages pour ce type de démarche. D'abord, il présente plusieurs phases stylistiques campaniformes susceptibles de correspondre à une chronologie, et décrites par Jean Guilaine, avec notamment un style régional (rhodano-provençal) bien caractérisé. De plus, l'intérêt marqué depuis longtemps pour le Campaniforme de la région (COURTIN 1974) met à disposition un grand nombre de sites. Enfin, réunissant ces deux intérêts, une thèse concernant le Campaniforme de cette région est venue récemment actualiser l'ensemble des données (LEMERCIER dans ce volume). Le sud-est apparaît donc comme une région privilégiée (par son potentiel et l'investigation scientifique dont elle est l'objet) qui s'inscrit parfaitement dans le cadre des problématiques actuelles.

Ainsi, ce sont plus de trois cents sites qui ont été recensés. Parmi ceux-ci, un peu plus d'un tiers (116) ont livré des artefacts lithiques associés aux autres éléments campaniformes. Mais conséquemment aux limites énoncées plus haut, seule une dizaine de sites présente les conditions nécessaires à la caractérisation de l'industrie lithique campaniforme (Fig. 1). C'est cette base qui est utilisée (dans le cadre d'une thèse en cours[1]) comme élément de comparaison avec les autres séries connues du Campaniforme et du Néolithique final. Sans atteindre une représentativité quantitative des sites campaniformes, les sites choisis sont un bon témoin de la diversité topographique, contextuelle, et chronologique des sites connus à ce jour. Dans cette optique, j'ai notamment retenu les sites suivants:

Les Calades 1 et 2 à Orgon, Le Fortin-du-Saut à Chateauneuf-les-Martigues, La Grande Baume à Gémenos, Le Camp de Laure au Rove pour le département des Bouche-du-Rhône; La Balance à Avignon pour le Vaucluse; La Grotte Murée à Montpezat, L'abri du Capitaine à Sainte Croix-du-Verdon pour les Alpes-de-Haute-Provence; Le Mas de Vignolles IV à Nîmes et Le Bois Sacré à Saint Côme et Maruéjols pour le Gard.

Si la caractérisation n'est pas une fin en soit, elle est une étape indispensable pour retrouver le chemin du paradis perdu et apporter des éléments de réponse aux questions de diffusion et d'évolution du Campaniforme en Europe. Répondre à ces questions par le biais seul de la céramique engendrerait une vision déformée du Campaniforme. Redonner sa place à l'industrie lithique doit - au moins - améliorer la perception de ce Phénomène[2].

---

[1] «L'industrie lithique campaniforme du Sud-est de la France dans son contexte Néolithique final / Bronze ancien» sous la direction de Didier Binder (Université de Provence).

[2] Cette idée n'est pas nouvelle et a été parfaitement développée par Jean DETREY (1997, p.95).

Caractériser: du Paradis à l'enfer...

L'ambition de caractériser l'industrie lithique campaniforme n'est pas nouvelle et a déjà fait l'objet de quelques tentatives (GUILAINE 1967; COURTIN 1974). Mais là encore, des constats de «marginalité» et de «pauvreté» (ROUDIL *et al.* 1974; JOUSSAUME 1981) ont été dressés, précipitant l'abandon des recherches sur l'industrie lithique. Les points de vues développés alors ont peut-être souffert de leur époque. Sous l'impulsion de Jean Guilaine et de Jean Courtin pour la région qui nous intéresse, le Campaniforme connaît alors un renouveau certain motivé, entre autres, par la recherche de l'origine du phénomène, et par son évolution. La céramique qui s'impose comme le meilleur moyen de répondre à ces questions, propose des modèles décoratifs spécifiques qui vont permettre une subdivision chrono-typologique du Campaniforme en quatre phases stylistique (GUILAINE 1967). Les schémas développés alors (et même depuis...) sont empreints de ces modèles forts, rappelant alors la notion très décriée de «fossile directeur». La proposition de «pack» ou «set» campaniforme n'a fait que conforter cette notion. L'industrie lithique, jugée moins spécifique, n'a fait alors qu'accompagner sporadiquement les hypothèses développées à partir de la céramique.

Face à cette analyse, il ne faut pas aujourd'hui reproduire ce schéma pour l'industrie lithique en la détachant de son contexte archéologique. Mais il est nécessaire de l'isoler temporairement pour en reconnaître ses spécificités. Ses caractéristiques reconnues, elle apportera un supplément à la perception de l'ensemble du phénomène Campaniforme. L'industrie lithique campaniforme doit sortir de son image unique d'armature à pédoncule et ailerons équarris, ou à base concave pour l'Est de l'Europe.

Pour changer cette vision, la technologie apparaît certainement comme un bon moyen. Mais quelle technologie?

Malgré l'apparition de la céramique, le Néolithique a très bien su adapter le développement de la technologie lithique paléolithique à ses impératifs. Les notions d'économie des matières premières et d'économie du débitage (PERLÈS 1991) s'appliquent ainsi sans mal au Néolithique ancien et moyen. Des productions spécifiques standardisées le permettent.

Si l'industrie lithique du Néolithique final — et plus encore du Campaniforme — n'a pas fait l'objet d'études technologiques aussi poussées que pour les périodes antérieures, l'impossibilité d'appliquer les schémas d'études «classiques» y joue probablement un rôle non négligeable. Il est en effet légitime de se demander si les seuls constats d'hétérogénéité et/ou de non pertinence (cf. plus haut et BAILLY à paraître b; FURESTIER 1999) des ensembles lithiques de ces périodes justifient à eux seuls le manque d'intérêt manifesté à l'encontre des industries lithiques de la fin du Néolithique. Ce changement d'attitudes envers cet élément mobilier traduit un changement égal du statut des industries lithiques mêmes (BIRO 1991). C'est donc bien ce nouveau statut que l'étude technologique doit mettre en évidence, pour déterminer la place et le rôle de l'industrie lithique au sein même du phénomène Campaniforme.

En cela, l'approche proposée est simple: vers quels buts tendaient les productions lithiques des campaniformes? et quels moyens ont-ils mis en oeuvre pour y parvenir?

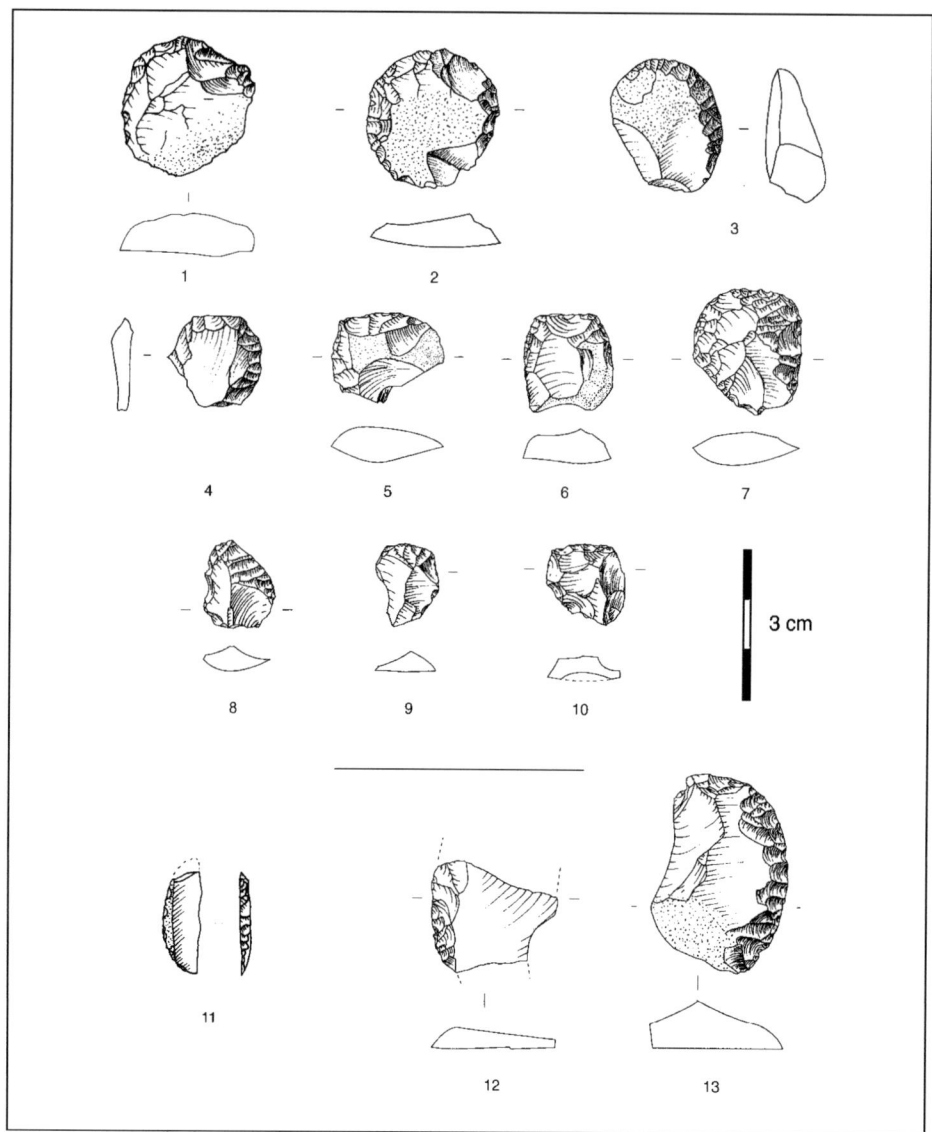

Pl. 1. Grattoirs, segment, et racloirs campaniformes (1 et 11 - Abri du Capitaine; 2-4 La Balance; 5-10, 12-13 Le Fortin du Saut).

Toute chaîne opératoire mise en oeuvre tend vers un seul but: produire des outils. Le sens donné à cette production peut varier (LEMONNIER 1991) selon le type d'outil réalisé par exemple, mais le but reste le même.

Au travers même de ces outils, le changement est déjà présent. La caisse à outils des Campaniformes se trouve très nettement réduite. La diversité encore constatée pour le début du Néolithique final est également réduite, et seuls quelques types d'outils persistent, constituant l'essentiel de l'outillage.

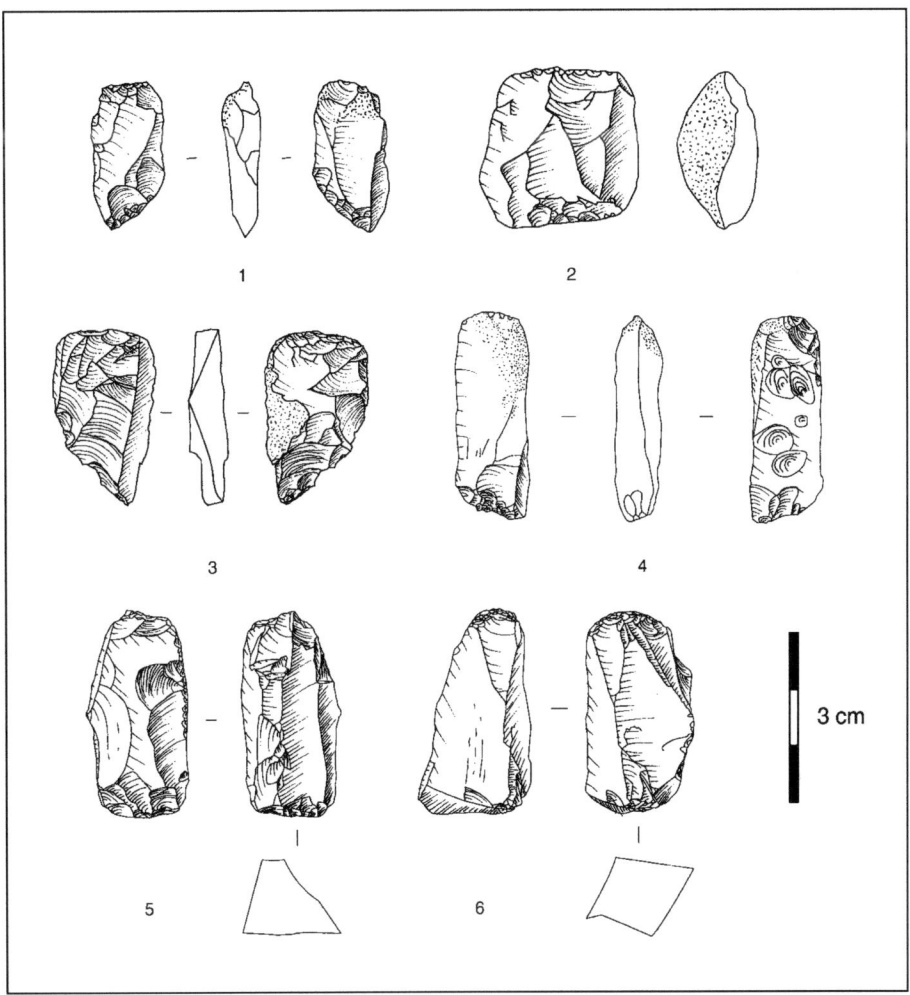

Pl. 2. Pièces esquillées campaniformes (1 – Les Juillèras; 2 – La Balance; 3 – Les Calades; 4 – Le Camp de Laure; 5–6 – Le Fortin du Saut).

La boîte à outils campaniforme

Les grattoirs (Planche 1) constituent l'outil principal. S'il en existe plusieurs types, il s'agit généralement de grattoirs simples, sur petit éclat. Les caractéristiques de la retouche ne semblent pas constituer un critère récurrent. Le plus souvent abrupte et écailleuse, elle semble être réalisée à la pierre dure, par percussion directe. Mais une grande variabilité est constatée. En revanche, le choix du support semble être plus réfléchi. Les petits éclats (3 à 5 cm) sont privilégiés. Ils sont souvent assez épais (issus de la percussion directe dure) avec une proportion remarquable d'éclats de décorticage présentant une surface corticale conséquente. Le module général semble augmenter pour l'épicampaniforme. Mais on notera toutefois que ce constat est principalement établit à partir du seul site du Camp de Laure, et qu'il reste à confirmer.

Les grattoirs unguiformes représentent le second grand type de grattoir présent dans la caisse à outils campaniforme. L'éclat est aussi le support privilégié de cet outil, mais sans caractéristiques technologiques particulières. Seule la dimension et l'aspect unguiforme prévalent, et le choix du support semble réalisé en fonction de ces impératifs.

Les pièces esquillées (Planche 2) sont le deuxième grand type d'outil des Campaniformes. Déjà remarquées pour le Jura (DETREY 1997), elles constituent une nouveauté pour le Sud-est. Cet outil à fait l'objet de nombreux articles concernant principalement sa nature et sa fonction (ESCALON DE FONTON 1969; LEBRUN-RICALENS 1989; DEWEZ 1985 pour ne citer que quelques exemples....). Sans rentrer à nouveau dans la polémique, je me contenterai d'évoquer ici la question de la différenciation des pièces esquillées, à savoir: outil ou Nucleus? Les difficultés liées à cette différenciation ont déjà été évoquées (FURESTIER à paraître b), mais de nouvelles observations permettent de faire d'autres propositions. Il semblerait donc qu'une double réponse soit envisageable, expliquant de fait les difficultés rencontrées. Ainsi, pour le Campaniforme du Sud-est, les pièces esquillées pourrait être définies comme outils et/ou nucleus. Les stigmates permettant la reconnaissance de ces pièces (BINDER 1987 par exemple) sont bien présents sur les pièces esquillées campaniformes, mais on observe plusieurs nuances à partir de leurs caractéristiques.

- Pour les éléments interprétés comme des outils, les supports sont généralement assez robustes (éclat d'entame, éclat épais, débris). Les retouches «vibrées» et fortement écaillées sont nombreuses, mais on ne distingue pas de vrais négatifs d'éclat partant des parties proximales ou distales, et témoignant d'un débitage intentionnel. Ces critères ajoutés aux dimensions quelquefois extrêmement réduites (moins de 2 cm) de certaines pièces esquillées semblent interdire l'interprétation en terme de nucleus.

- En ce qui concerne les éléments considérés comme des nucleus, les négatifs d'enlèvements apparaissent plus clairement, et un débitage spécifique sur enclume est en cours de caractérisation pour le site du Mas de Vignolles à Nîmes (Gard). Si, pour ce site, la matière première présente sous forme de galet appelle ce type de débitage (JOUSSAUME 1981; FILLION 2000), il est probable qu'un débitage d'éclat par percussion sur enclume se soit développé sur d'autres sites.

Toutefois, les pièces esquillées interprétées comme outils semblent prédominer. De plus, sur les sites campaniformes du Verdon (La Grotte Murée, et L'Abri du Jardin du Capitaine) quelques galets alluviaux ont également été exploités, sans pour autant montrer les stigmates d'un débitage sur enclume (*cf*. Planche 5, n°1).

Nous sommes peut-être ici dans un exemple caractéristique d'acculturation (Furestier à paraître a). En effet, le site du Mas de Vignolles présente une contemporanéité plus que probable avec le Fontbouisse (découverte d'un gobelet à décor mixte campaniforme / fontbouisse[3]). Or, l'industrie lithique fontbouisse de ce

---

[3]   Fouilles inédites par F. Convertini et R. Furestier qui feront l'objet d'une communication et d'un article lors des Vème Rencontres Méridionales de Préhistoire Récente à Clermont-Ferrand, Auvergne, France, Novembre 2002.

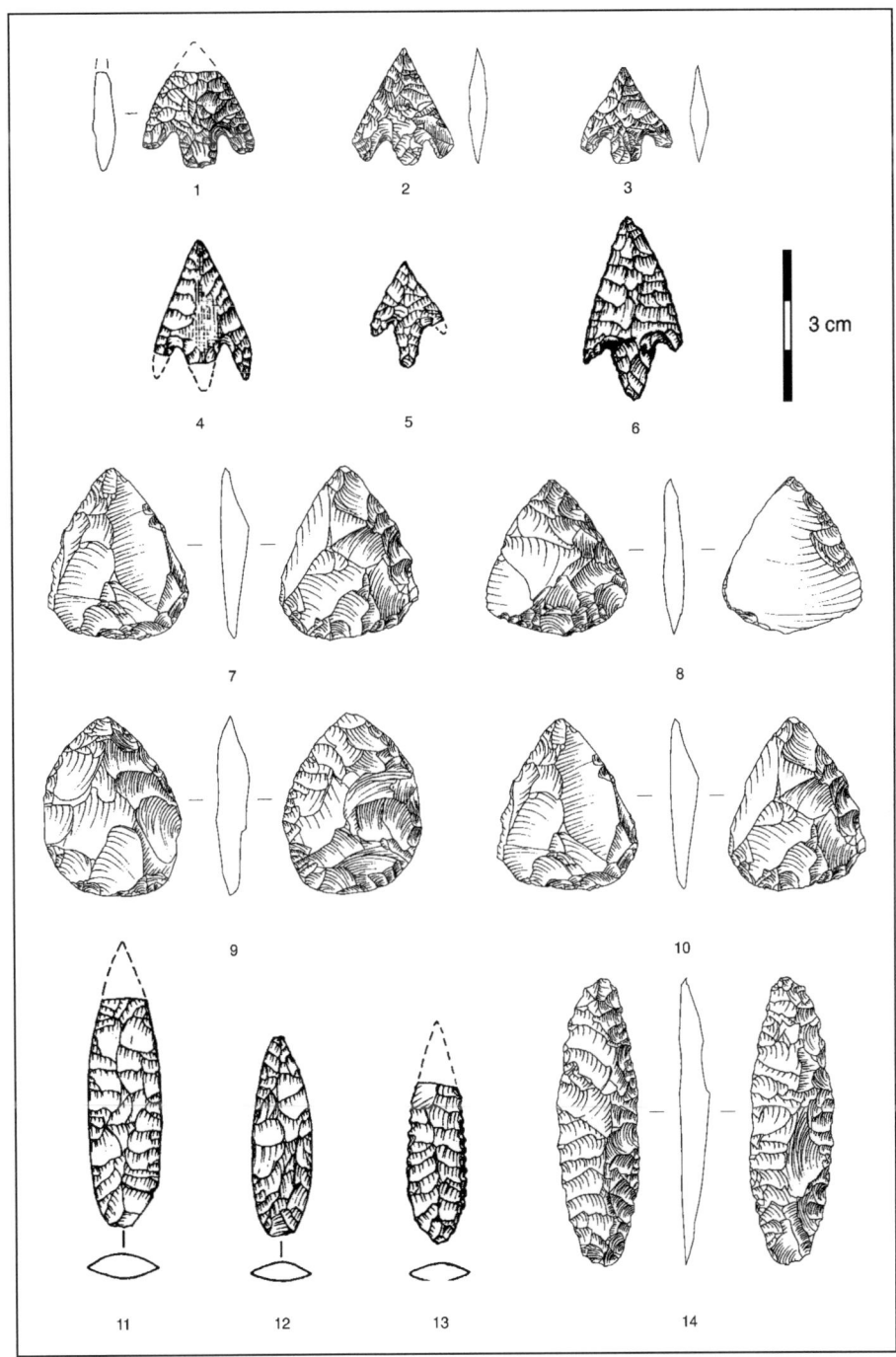

Pl. 3. Armatures campaniformes (1 - Les Calades; 2–3, 7–10, 14 - Le Fortin-du-Saut; 4, 11 - La Grotte Murèe; 5–6 - La Grande Baume; 12–13 - Abri du Capitaine) (4–6, 11–13 dessins J. Courtin).

même site semble montrer également un débitage sur enclume à partir de galets alluviaux de même provenance que ceux acquis par les campaniformes. Ce serait alors un constat d'acculturation des campaniformes de la phase régionale (rhodano-provençal) par les populations du Néolithique final local: le Fontbouisse. Les sites du Verdon, trop éloignés de l'emprise géographique de la culture fontbouisse ne subiraient pas alors leur influence.

La pièce esquillée/nucleus découverte en contexte campaniforme pourrait donc apparaître comme un témoin intéressant des relations et des échanges entre Campaniforme rhodano-provençal et Fontbouisse. Cette hypothèse qui doit être confirmée repose sur une bonne caractérisation des pièces esquillées.

Les armatures (Planche 3) sont typologiquement assez diverses. Si les armatures microlithiques ou tranchantes n'apparaissent plus, le groupe des armatures foliacées est très largement représenté. Une grande diversité est observée, mais quelques types se détachent de l'ensemble. Ainsi, les cordiformes et sub-cordiformes sont bien présentes (Les Calades, Le Fortin-du-Saut, La Balance). Les foliacées allongées ou à tendance lancéolée sont aussi observées. Elles sont moins nombreuses, mais sont présentes dans plusieurs séries étudiées. Sans disparaître, les armatures losangiques, sub-losangiques, foliacées simples, amygdaloïdes... ne sont plus récurrentes, et ne peuvent être prises en compte comme élément caractérisant. En revanche, le groupe des armatures à pédoncule et ailerons est un élément déterminant de la caractérisation de l'industrie lithique campaniforme, et d'ailleurs anciennement reconnu. Parmi ce groupe, il faut remarquer plus particulièrement les armatures à pédoncule et ailerons équarris. Si l'on fait exception des fameuses pointes de flèches armoricaines, il s'agit du seul artefact lithique exclusivement campaniforme. L'aspect prestigieux et le haut investissement technique visible de ce type de pièce à facilité sa reconnaissance et le signalement de sa présence dans les ensembles mobiliers campaniformes.

La retouche ne constitue pas un critère de distinction. L'usage du percuteur tendre en percussion directe semble privilégié, mais les possibilités de recouvrement entre les stigmates des diverses techniques de retouches ne permettent pas de catégoriser. La retouche à la pression, plus reconnaissable, a été mise en évidence. En revanche, l'aspect qualitatif de la retouche joue un rôle qui reste encore à déterminer. En effet, en ce qui concerne certaines armatures à pédoncule et ailerons équarris, et quelques grandes lancéolées, un soin particulier est apporté à la retouche (quasi exclusivement réalisée à la pression). Ce soin contraste avec le faible investissement technique constaté pour d'autres types d'armatures, mais également pour les deux types susdits. Ce contraste montre *a minima* des buts de production distincts, et probablement une différence de statut de l'objet, et/ou du tailleur...

Cette hypothèse rappelle les propositions déjà avancées de division du travail du silex en une production domestique expédiante et une production de prestige (BAILLY à paraître a et b).

Les supports choisis pour la réalisation de ces armatures (quand leur reconnaissance n'est pas interdite par une retouche couvrante) sont très majoritairement des éclats. Quelques ébauches ou armatures frustes permettent de conforter cette première observation. Aucun élément laminaire ou lamellaire ne semble avoir été utilisé.

Les segments de cercle constituent un type d'armature particulier (Planche 1 n°11). Ils bénéficient comme les armatures à pédoncule et ailerons équarris d'une reconnaissance ancienne en contexte campaniforme (et favorisée par son absence au Néolithique final non campaniforme). Leurs dimensions réduites ne permettent pas de définir systématiquement le type de support utilisé. Toutefois, éclats et lamelles (plus rarement) ont été choisis. La retouche est généralement courte, directe et abrupte, mais on peut observer quelquefois une retouche croisée.

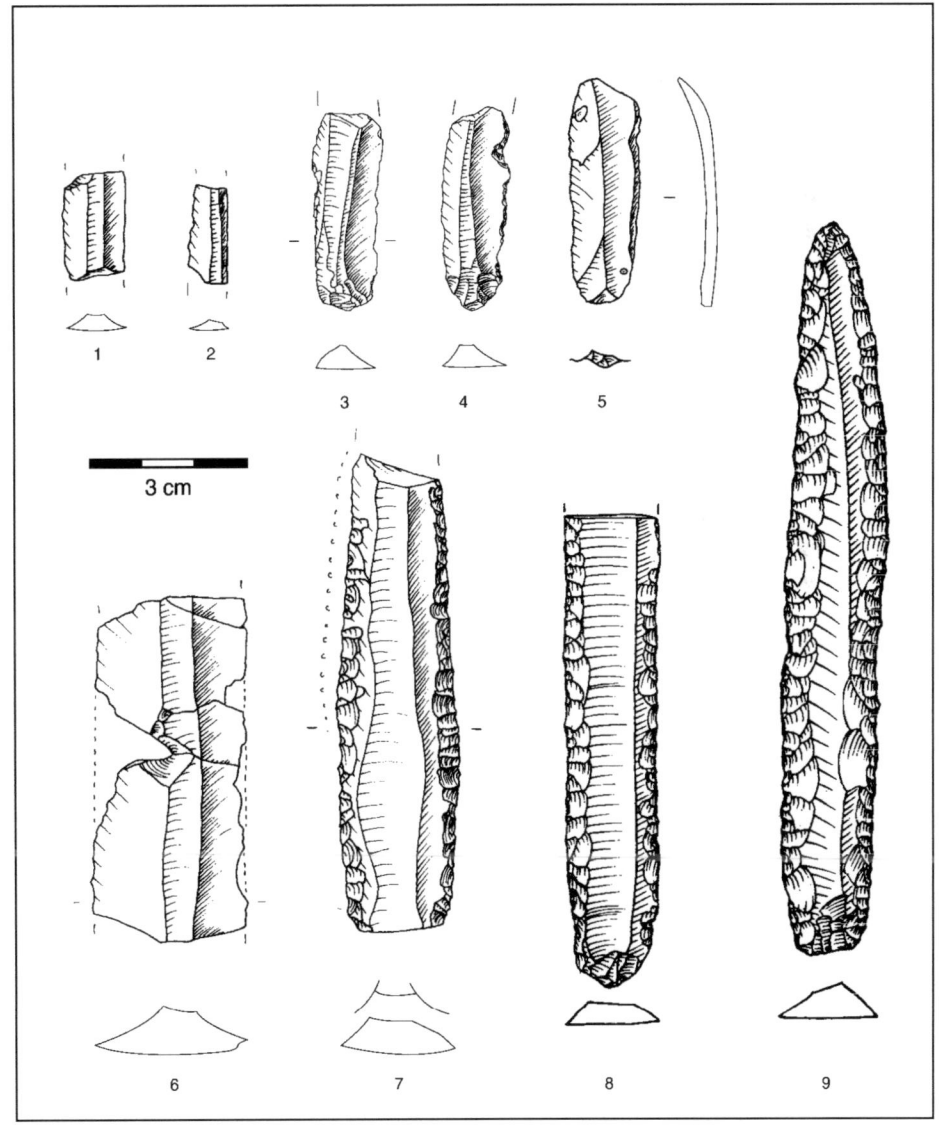

Pl. 4.   Lames et lamelles (1 - La Balance; 2, 5 - Abri du Capitaine; 3-4 - Le Fortin-du-Saut; 6-7 - La Grotte Murée; 8-9 - La Grande Baume).

L'ensemble important des pièces retouchées (pièce présentant une retouche le plus souvent marginale ou d'utilisation qu'il est impossible de classifier typologiquement) doit être cité dans cette description de l'outillage campaniforme. Il ne constitue pas en soi un élément discriminant, mais intervenant pour 30 à 50 % des pièces ayant été utilisées, il est juste de le prendre en considération d'un simple point de vue quantitatif afin de donner une meilleure image du travail du silex.

A l'instar des pièces retouchées, les autres outils observés ne sont pas discriminants des séries lithiques campaniformes. Ils constituent plutôt des tendances, accompagnant les éléments plus caractéristiques cités précédemment. Par ordre d'importance, on citera d'abord les racloirs (Planche 1 n°12 et 13). Il est remarquable qu'une partie non négligeable de ceux-ci est technologiquement très comparable aux grattoirs. L'impossibilité de déterminer clairement un front est souvent à l'origine du classement en «racloir».

Coches et surtout perçoirs apparaissent de façon assez anecdotique, et les burins sont quasiment absents.

Enfin, il faut faire état de la présence de fragments de grandes lames à bords abattus par retouche directe abrupte à semi-abrupte (Planche 4), réalisées sur silex brun rubané oligocène de la vallée du Largue (Forcalquier, Alpes-de-Haute-Provence). Ces pièces, connues pour l'ensemble du Néolithique final, doivent-elles être estimées comme un élément campaniforme caractéristique? Il s'agit d'une production particulière bien décrite (RENAULT 1998) et dont les spécificités ont assuré une diffusion sur l'ensemble du sud-est de la France (avec des exportations extrêmes vers la Suisse et le Gers), et ont assuré une présence durant toute la période Néolithique final / Bronze ancien. Cette production de ce que l'on a longtemps nommé «barres de chocolats» (COURTIN 1974 et SAUZADE 1983 entre autres...), affaire de spécialistes localisés, a probablement jouit d'un statut d'exception lui permettant une grande diffusion pour l'ensemble des groupes culturels du Néolithique final (notamment au couronnien) et une perduration jusqu'au Bronze ancien (fréquemment sous forme de «grands poignards»). La présence de ces pièces ne saurait donc caractériser l'industrie lithique campaniforme[4], et doit en cela être considérée comme un épiphénomène.

Les choix techniques (Fig. 2)

La production est conditionnée par la matière première, son état, son acquisition. Les logiques d'approvisionnement en matière première lithiques des campaniformes marque en cela un changement par rapport au Néolithique final. Le critère le plus marquant de ce changement est la place privilégiée - voire quasi exclusive - des matières premières locales. La proximité des gîtes de matières premières semble le facteur commun d'approvisionnement. La qualité n'est plus un critère discriminant

---

[4] Dès 1967, Jean Guilaine estimait d'ailleurs pour les Pyrénés françaises que ces pièces «... sont en fait assez peu spécifiques du contexte campaniforme puisqu'on les retrouve du Néolithique récent jusqu'au Bronze ancien» (GUILAINE 1967, p.67).

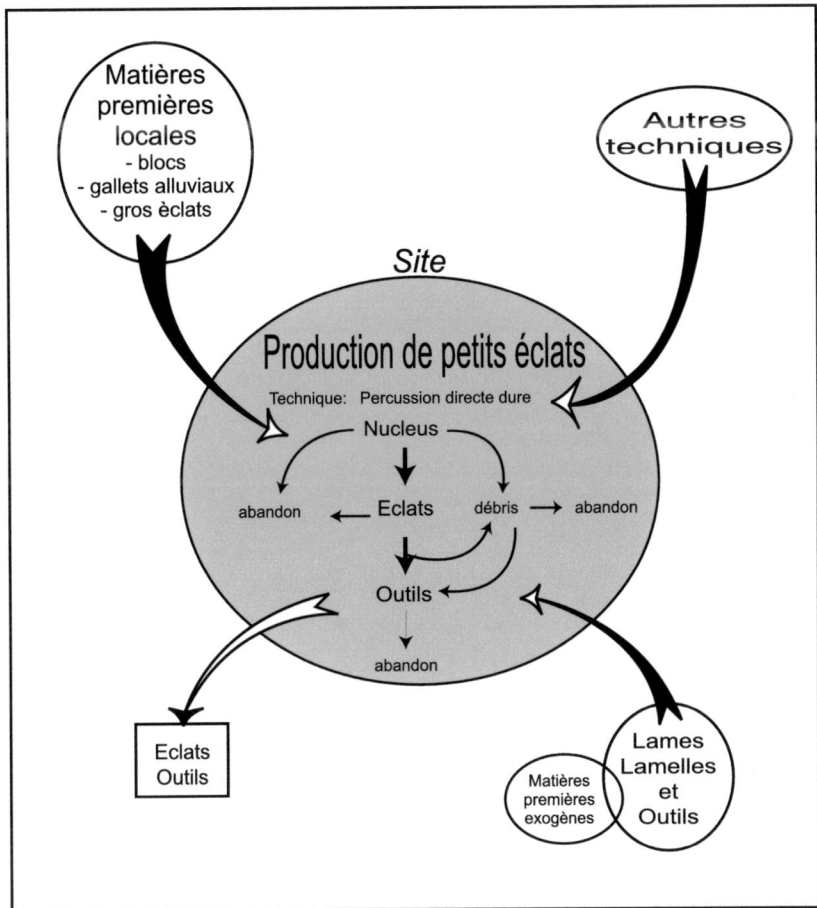

Fig. 2   Schéma synthétique de gestion des matières premières.

du choix. Ainsi, le terroir local très proche (moins de 10 km) est exploité en priorité. Les sites désavantagés par une implantation au sein de territoires pourvus de gîtes de matières premières de moyenne qualité ne montrent pas une logique d'approvisionnement différente de ceux bénéficiant au contraire de matières premières disponibles de bonne (voire très bonne) qualité. Pour certains (Les Calades par exemple) un éloignement restreint des gîtes de bonne matière première (moins de 20 km des Mont de Vaucluse) n'a pas suscité un élargissement de la sphère d'approvisionnement.

S'il est jugé «exploitable», le silex sera donc choisi. Ce constat peut être un des arguments illustrant le changement de statut de la production de l'industrie lithique campaniforme... ou tout du moins d'une partie de cette production.

Toutefois, l'acquisition de la matière première est à l'image du reste de la chaîne opératoire: simplifiée. L'éclat est le support princeps, et donc le but privilégié de la production. Mais il faut surtout produire du nombre afin de disposer d'un choix conséquent. L'essentiel des chaînes opératoires est mise en oeuvre dans cette optique.

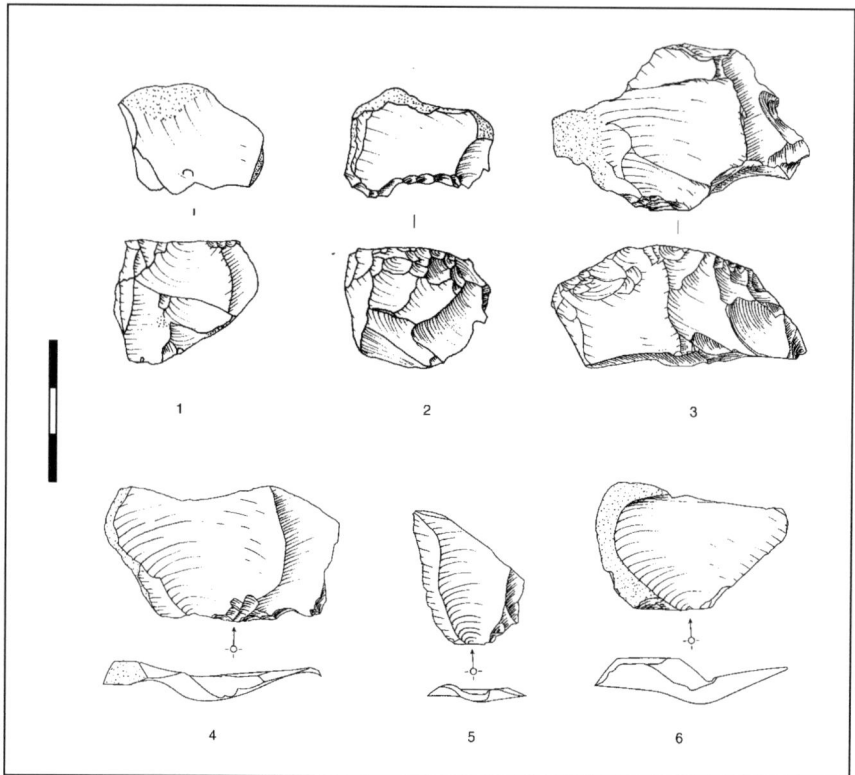

Pl. 5   Nucleus et éclats campaniformes (1 - Abri du Capitaine; 2 - La Grotte Murée; 3-6 - Le Fortin-du-Saut).

De la matière au nucleus...

S'il n'est pas encore possible de mettre clairement en évidence des chaînes opératoires distinctes par l'étude des éclats, l'examen des nucleus apporte des précisions d'ordre technologique. On remarquera ainsi trois types de nucleus qui participent du même objectif de production.
- Les nucleus sur fragment de bloc et à plan de frappe préférentiel
- Les nucleus polyédriques
- Les nucleus sur éclat.

Pour ces trois types, on relève quelques critères communs. Tout d'abord, comparé aux périodes précédentes, la réduction généralisée de l'ensemble des pièces observées apparaît clairement. S'il serait un peu excessif de voir dans cette réduction une nouvelle «microlithisation» de l'industrie lithique[5], elle constitue néanmoins un caractère remarquable, car non attribuable à l'état de la matière première

---

[5]   Il faut rappeler d'ailleurs la présence d'une industrie macrolithique en calcaire pour le site de L'Abri du Jardin du Capitaine, même s'il s'agit probablement d'un élément à distinguer de l'industrie lithique taillée sur silex, et à étudier dans sa spécificité propre.

brute. Concrètement, il en résulte des nucleus ne dépassant que rarement les 5 cm de dimensions maximales. De plus, les nucleus polyédriques peuvent représenter une phase finale de la chaîne opératoire, où les campaniformes auraient exploité l'ensemble des possibilités restantes. Les polyédriques ne seraient alors plus un type particulier de nucleus, mais un élément caractéristique d'une phase de la chaîne opératoire. Toutefois, cette hypothèse n'exclut pas définitivement la possibilité d'existence d'une chaîne opératoire spécifique préférant les angles favorables au détachement d'un éclat, à la gestion d'un plan et d'une surface de débitage uniques. Si des nucleus à plans de frappe multiples et abandonnés en cours de débitage peuvent conforter cette hypothèse, la caractérisation devient plus difficile pour les nucleus présentant un état d'exhaustion avancé.

Les techniques mises en oeuvre pour le débitage sont un autre point commun d'une majorité des nucleus. Les critères de reconnaissance du débitage à la pierre dure par percussion directe (PÉLEGRIN 2000) sont fréquemment observés sur les éclats. L'examen des négatifs d'enlèvement, des contre bulbes marqués, des cônes incipients témoignant de «ratés», ... et de l'ensemble des stigmates observables sur les nucleus permet de confirmer les déductions technologiques engendrées par l'étude des éclats.

Les spécificités des trois types de nucleus décrits se retrouvent donc essentiellement dans leurs aspects technologiques.

Pour le premier type, le plan de frappe est souvent dégagé par un enlèvement rebroussé, générant une surface lisse et un angle propres au débitage d'éclats (Planche 5). Dans ce cas, des enlèvements se développant à partir d'un autre plan de frappe peuvent être constatés, sans toutefois surpasser le caractère préférentiel du premier plan de frappe décrit.

Le second type pose donc le problème d'une spécificité qui peut être remise en cause. On notera cependant l'absence de logique réelle de débitage (caractérisée quelquefois par un débitage «aberrant» à partir d'angles quasi fermés), et la présence fréquente de ce type de nucleus parmi les séries campaniformes, ce qui constitue en soi un élément important.

Enfin, le troisième type peut montrer plusieurs caractéristiques différentes. Une chaîne opératoire optimisée de production de pièces bifaciales, avec utilisation des éclats produits par le façonnage même a déjà été décrite (FURESTIER à paraître b). Pour les autres éclats-nucleus, le but recherché est souvent difficile à déterminer. En effet, on constate fréquemment le paradoxe lié au faible avancement du débitage qui permet une bonne reconnaissance du support de départ, mais qui limite la mise en évidence des objectifs à atteindre. Il reste toutefois cette tendance d'apport de matière première sous forme d'éclats, qui devient sur le site un nucleus prêt à débiter (BINDER *et al.* à paraître).

... et du nucleus au support.

La production d'éclat est le principal facteur commun à tous les nucleus observés. Quelques caractéristiques de ces éclats ont pu être décrites. Les dimensions réduites de ces supports d'outils privilégiés sont en rapport avec celles des nucleus.

Ainsi, le module moyen se situe autour des 3 cm. De manière générale, les observations technologiques sont en accord avec celles réalisées sur les nucleus, et permettent de proposer une prédominance du débitage à la pierre dure en percussion directe. Toutefois, les possibilités de recouvrements entre les différents critères de reconnaissance des techniques de taille du silex ne permettent pas d'exclure les autres types de percussion. On remarquera notamment la présence de pièces montrant les critères caractéristiques du débitage à la pression. Mais il est probable qu'en comparaison avec la percussion directe dure, ces autres techniques apparaissent de façon plus ponctuelle.

Les surfaces supérieures des éclats montrent des négatifs d'enlèvement plus majoritairement axiaux (mais très rarement opposés), témoignant d'une prédominance d'un débitage réalisé à partir d'un plan de frappe préférentiel. Il faut noter une tendance au débitage d'éclat parfaitement dans l'axe de l'éclat précédent. La morphologie particulière des éclats qui en résulte est fréquemment observée (planche 5). Toutefois, ce type d'éclat ne semble pas particulièrement recherché en tant que support d'outil. Mais un prélèvement de certains de ces supports est toujours possible, et on notera à cet égard la rareté des remontages les concernant.

Hormis le cas des grandes lames retouchées en silex oligocène évoqué plus haut, il faut s'attarder sur la découverte de quelques fragments de lamelles dans les séries étudiées (Planche 4, n°1 à 5). Cette production est présente sous forme de produits finis, et aucun autre élément de ces chaînes opératoires n'a été découvert en contexte campaniforme. Ces pièces dont plusieurs montrent les stigmates caractéristiques du débitage à la pression (quelquefois sur silex chauffé), posent les questions de leur origine, de leur arrivée sur les sites, et de leur contemporanéité au reste de la production. Sans développer ces problèmes déjà évoqués (FURESTIER à paraître b), on constatera ici que la présence, même restreinte (souvent moins de dix pièces), de ces pièces au sein des séries étudiées est systématique. Il ne s'agit donc pas d'un phénomène anecdotique.

Proposer un schéma

Si une caractérisation est possible, elle ne doit pas être estimée comme une fin, mais toujours comme un moyen. Caractériser, c'est apporter un outil archéologique concourant au défrichement des problèmes que pose le Campaniforme. Dans cette optique, il est proposé ici un essai de sériation de l'industrie lithique.

Ainsi, des tendances sont proposées pour enrichir, mais également éprouver la périodisation élaborée par Jean Guilaine. Cette dernière a été soumise à de vives critiques ces dernières années (SALANOVA 2000), mais reste assez communément admise quand elle est abordée avec toutes les réserves nécessaires (GUILAINE 1976 et GUILAINE et al. 2002).

Des limites apparaissent clairement et interdisent une sériation typo-technologiques des industries lithique selon les quatre phases stylistiques de Jean Guilaine. Dans leurs spécificités, ces phases ont d'ailleurs déjà été remises en cause (LEMERCIER 2002 et dans ce volume). Concrètement, il n'est pour l'instant pas possible de différencier les phases 1 (international) et 2 (pointillé géométrique). Si la très faible représentation de l'industrie lithique en contexte campaniforme de la phase 1 est une raison importante liée à cette impossibilité, d'autres arguments apportés par la céramique révèlent la possibilité d'une synchronie entre ces deux phases (*ibidem*). Les phases 3 (rhodano-provencal) et 4 (épicampaniforme/Bronze ancien) ont également été regroupées, non pas du fait de leur synchronie (qui reste néanmoins envisageable en partie), mais à cause de la rareté des contextes épicampaniformes fiables ayant livré une industrie lithique conséquente. L'étude du site du Camp de Laure au Rove montre des spécificités qui laissent entrevoir des perpectives de différenciation avec la phase régionale rhodano-provençale.

A l'instar de la céramique dans son ensemble (décorée et commune), tous les éléments de l'industrie lithique campaniforme ne peuvent pas être sériés. Les phases 1 et 2, et 3 et 4 ont été différenciées, mais un fond commun campaniforme caractéristique reste présent.

Le fond commun: Les modes d'approvisionnements ne semblent pas changer sur toute la période campaniforme. Les matières premières locales sont privilégiées et importées sous forme de fragments de blocs, de gros éclats débités sur les gîtes mêmes, et -plus rarement- de galets alluviaux. Le débitage exclusif de petits éclats (*cf.* infra) est présent pour toutes les phases. Quelques éléments lamellaires sont également constatés. Les grattoirs sur éclat, et les grattoirs unguiformes semblent une grande constante. Les pièces esquillées sur tout type de support sont toujours bien représentées. Une bonne diversité d'armatures foliacées bifaces marque toutes les phases, avec toutefois une préférence pour les armatures ovalaires, cordiformes, lancéolées, à pédoncule, à pédoncule et ailerons, et plus rarement sublosangiques.

Les phases 1 et 2: Les armatures sont les éléments les plus marquants de la différenciation établie. Les types cordiformes et à tendance lancéolée sont privilégiées. Mais si ces dernières peuvent être présentes en contexte régional ou épicampaniforme, il n'en est pas de même pour les armatures à pédoncule et ailerons équarris qui semblent exclusives à la phase 1 / 2. La présence d'éclats axiaux (*cf.* infra) semble également plus marquée, mais cette tendance reste à confirmer.

Les phases 3 et 4: Les armatures ne semblent plus constituer un élément discriminant. Les types du fond commun sont bien présents, mais aucun ne se détache de l'ensemble. Le cas particulier des segments de cercle semble plus pertinent. En effet, ces pièces n'ont été remarquées que pour la phase 3 (rhodano-provençal). Les grandes lames à bords retouchés en silex rubané oligocène (*cf.* infra) semblent apparaître essentiellement durant cette phase, en perdurant néanmoins jusqu'au bronze ancien. On remarquera aussi la tendance à la réalisation de grattoirs plus grands pour la phase 4 (épicampaniforme / Bronze ancien).

Les tendances proposées ici s'appuient sur un constat qui fait apparaître une plus grande facilité de caractérisation pour l'industrie lithique des sites des phases 1 et 2. Le contexte et l'homogénéité de ces séries expliquent en partie cette facilité à caractériser. Les influences des groupes du Néolithique final sont moins prégnantes, et l'absence (ou la présence peu marquée) du phénomène d'acculturation (FURESTIER à paraître a) entre ces groupes et les campaniformes limite les transferts techniques et matériels, et donc les risques de confusion. Les campaniformes de la phase 1 / 2 seraient donc «plus campaniformes» que ceux de la phase 3 / 4. Cependant, que les groupes campaniformes de la phase régionale aient été «néolithisé», ou qu'il aient eux-mêmes «campaniformisé» les groupes locaux, il reste un mélange culturel qui trouble la lecture des caractéristiques de l'industrie lithique pour cette phase. Reconnaître cet état de fait rappelle les difficultés d'identifications de l'industrie lithique campaniforme (COURTIN 1974 et GUILAINE et al. 2002) et incite à la prudence. C'est pour cette raison qu'a été choisi le terme de tendance.

Caractériser, sérier... et après?

Caractériser l'industrie lithique campaniforme et proposer un complément à sa périodisation nous ramène immanquablement aux grandes questions qui motivent les études du Phénomène, et à l'apport que constitue l'industrie lithique.

Le changement de statut social de l'industrie lithique campaniforme est marqué, mais ce changement, qui entraîne, certes, une production moins développée qu'auparavant, ne doit plus être considéré comme une dégénérescence de cet élément mobilier.

Le faible développement des études concernant les industries lithiques campaniformes de l'Europe[6], sont une limite dans l'apport de celles-ci aux problématiques liées aux origines du phénomène. En revanche, avoir caractérisé les industries lithiques nous permet de les intégrer dans les discussions concernant la diffusion et l'évolution chronologique et géographique du Campaniforme. Cette intégration doit se faire en liaison étroite avec les données céramiques (et autres) disponibles. Parmi les questions actuelles, une des plus intéressantes reste celle des relations avec les groupes culturels locaux du Néolithique final. Ces groupes qui ont été décrits récemment (D'ANNA 1995) font l'objet d'un nouveau regard (LEMERCIER et al. à paraître a). D'un point de vue chronologique, le Phénomène campaniforme semble contemporain des groupes de la fin du Couronnien, des groupes Fontbouisse/Rhône-Ouvèze, et des groupes du Bronze Ancien. Le rôle du groupe de Fontbouisse (Languedoc oriental) doit notamment être redéfini, de pair avec le groupe Rhône-Ouvèze, son homologue provençal. En effet, l'influence fontbouisse semble considérable, et on a constaté une présence très fréquente (voire quasi systématique) de tessons à décor fontbuxien (cannelures le plus souvent) en contexte campaniforme Pointillé-géométrique (phase 2). Quant aux phases stylistiques 3 et 4, on rappellera la découverte du vase à décor mixte campaniforme rhodano-provençal / fontbouisse du Mas de Vignolles IV, et une découverte similaire dans la grotte de la Chauve-souris (Donzère, Drôme, fouilles J. Vital). Pour ces deux dernières phases les échanges et le taux d'acculturation sont très développés. En revanche, la présence de tessons

---

[6] Il est en effet illusoire et prématuré d'essayer d'élaborer un catalogue des industries lithiques campaniformes des pays européens concernés. Dans le meilleur de cas, les dernières synthèses reconnaissent les lacunes et la nécessité d'investissements dans ce domaine (LEMERCIER 2002). Dans le pire, elles ignorent totalement cet élément mobilier (GARRIDO-PENA 2000).

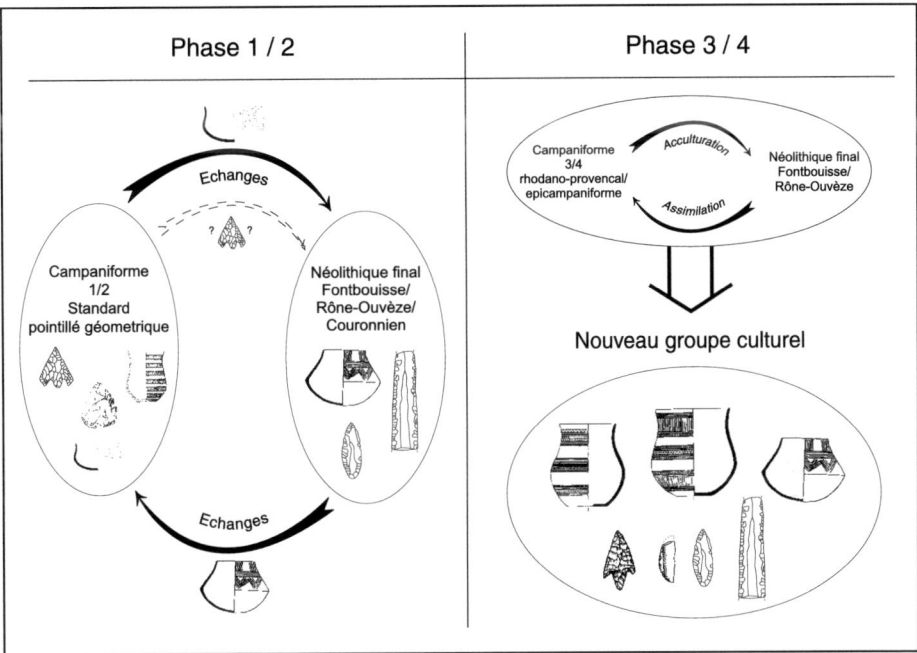

Fig. 3. Schéma synthétique des relations entre Campaniformes et groupes culturels du Néolithique final.

fontbouisses est plus difficile à analyser en contexte campaniforme 1 / 2. Cet élément témoigne en effet d'un contact déjà établi entre Fontbouisses et Campaniformes, alors que les observations réalisées pour l'industrie lithique ne montrent pas de contacts similaires. Cette opposition permet peut-être de proposer un schéma d'acculturation progressive de ces deux groupes culturels forts. Ce schéma est bâti dans l'idée de la diffusion du campaniforme par le biais de contacts, de déplacements humains. Si la diffusion d'une idéologie (STHRAM 1995) peut convenir à l'explication du Campaniforme «standard» (SALANOVA 2000), elle ne colle plus à la phase 2 qui montre une vraie culture matérielle complexe.

Ainsi, on peut proposer l'hypothèse (Fig. 3) d'une installation des campaniformes à partir de la phase 2 (Les Calades, La Balance, Le Fortin du Saut...), établissants alors des rapports avec les cultures du Néolithique final. Les échanges visibles d'un point de vue archéologique, sont limités à quelques éléments de céramique décorée (standard et pointillé géométrique d'un côté, et à cannelures de l'autre). Ces éléments sont peu, ou pas, suivis d'échanges d'objets lithiques. Le statut social de la céramique en tant que marqueur culturel prééminent montre ici sa différence. Chacun des groupes garde alors la majeure partie de leurs spécificités.

Par la suite, les échanges s'accentuent et se traduisent par une acculturation bilatérale. Pour la céramique, c'est l'apparition d'un style nouveau (rhodano-provençal), et pour l'industrie lithique, ce sont des transferts techniques et typologiques. Les pièces spécifiques s'intègrent de part et d'autre: les grandes lames en silex rubané sont «acceptées», les armatures à pédoncule et ailerons se retrouvent également des deux côtés, en perdant le caractère équarris des ailerons. Les grattoirs et les pièces esquillées s'imposent comme l'outillage dominant. Les chaînes opératoires se simplifient (approvisionnement, modes et techniques de débitage...), pour tendre majoritairement vers la production de petits éclats. Enfin, comme pour la céramique, un nouveau type d'outil semble apparaître: le segment de cercle.

Selon le schéma proposé, ce n'est plus une troisième phase constituante du phénomène campaniforme qui est présentée, mais une nouvelle culture du Néolithique final qui n'est ni campaniforme, ni Fontbouisse/Rhône-Ouvèze/Couronnienne, mais un mixage de l'ensemble.

La tentation de provoquer amènerait à dire que le Campaniforme n'existe plus après la phase 2.

Il reste alors un chantier considérable à investir: la compréhension de ce changement culturel. Quels sont les nouveaux statuts des productions observées? Quelles sont leurs nouvelles fonctions? Quels nouveaux besoins les justifient? Développer les études concernant, entre autre, les industries lithiques du troisième millénaire, dans le Sud-est de la France et ailleurs, est un corollaire nécessaire qui doit nous aider à répondre à ces questions[7].

Bien évidemment, de nombreux problèmes restent en suspens. Comme l'ensemble des éléments mobiliers qui constituent la culture matérielle campaniforme, l'industrie lithique ne saurait être considérée comme un marqueur culturel unique... et n'est donc pas un paradis archéologique. Cependant, sa caractérisation a montré qu'elle n'était pas une industrie dégénérescente ou en déclin, et qu'elle est à même d'apporter des éléments nouveaux de réflexion qu'il faut maintenant réinsérer dans une recherche archéologique globale, seule apte à répondre aux attentes que génère un phénomène aussi complexe que le Campaniforme.

Remerciements

J'aimerais ici remercier mes collègues Annabelle Gallin, Christophe Gilabert et Olivier Lemercier pour leur aide.

---

[7] Une grande Provence occidentale bénéficie d'un PCR en cours (LEMERCIER *et al.* à paraître b) et représente en cela un terrain favorable aux réponses à ces questions. En revanche, le Languedoc pâtit d'un manque cruel d'investigation dans ce domaine, et devra être l'objet (dans un avenir qu'il faut espérer proche) d'une attention particulière.

Références

Benz M. / Van Willigen S. (eds) 1998. *Some New Approaches to the Bell Beaker «Phenomenon». Lost Paradise...? Proceedings of the 2nd Meeting of the „Association Archéologie et Gobelets", Feldberg (Germany), 18th - 20th April 1997.* Oxford.

Bailly M. à paraître a. Les industries lithiques taillées campaniformes: contribution à la définition du Campaniforme domestique in: *Temps et Espaces culturels, Rencontres Méridionales de Préhistoire Récente, IVe session, Nîmes, 28-29 octobre 2000.*

— à paraître b. Du Néolithique final à l'âge du Bronze en bassin rhodanien: une première approche du statut des productions lithiques. in: Bailly M. / Furestier R. / Perrin T. (dir.), *Les industries lithiques taillées holocènes du bassin rhodanien: Problèmes et actualités, Actes de la table ronde de Lyon, 8 et 9 décembre 2000.*

Binder D. 1987. Le Néolithique ancien provençal: typologie et technologie des outillages lithiques, Paris.

Binder D. / Gassin B. / Senepart I. à paraître. *Un système technique peut en cacher un autre XXVème Congrès de la Société Préhistorique Française, novembre 2000,* Paris.

Biro T.K. 1991. Bell beaker culture lithic implements from Hungary. *Acta Archaeologica Carpathica* 30, 87-96, Kraków.

Courtin J., 1974. Le Néolithique de la Provence. Paris, *Société préhistorique française*, 360 p. (Mémoire, 11).

D'Anna A. 1995. Le Néolithique final en Provence, in: Voruz J.-L. (dir.), *Chronologies néolithiques. De 6000 à 2000 avant notre ère dans le bassin rhodanien.* Genève, 265-286.

Detrey J. 1997. Approches technologiques et typologiques de l'industrie lithique, in: Othenin-Girard B. (dir.), Le Campaniforme d'Alle, Noir Bois (Jura, Suisse), Porrentruy, Société jurassienne d'Emulation, p. 95-116 (Cahiers d'Archéologie jurassienne, 7).

Dewez M. 1985. La pièce esquillée dans le Paléolithique supérieur de Belgique. *Bulletin de la Société préhistorique française* 82-5, 131-133.

Escalon de Fonton M. 1969. La pièce esquillée: essai d'interprétation. *Bulletin de la Société préhistorique française* 66-3, 76.

Fillion J.P. / Feblot-Augustins J. / Santallier D. 2000. Etude du matériel Néolithique dans la région de Bellegarde (Ain) Materiaux et techniques de débitage du silex sur un site d'approvisionnement du Néolithique final à Villes et Ochiaz (Commune de Chatillon en Michaille-Ain). *Revue d'Archéométrie* 24, 129-147.

Furestier R. 1999. L'industrie lithique campaniforme du sud-est de la France. Premières approches, Mémoire de DEA sous la direction de R. Chenorkian. Aix-en-Provence.

— à paraître a. L'industrie lithique campaniforme du Sud-est de la France dans son contexte Néolithique final/Bronze ancien. Problème d'acculturation? in: *Temps et Espaces culturels, Rencontres Méridionales de Préhistoire Récente, IVe session, Nîmes, 28-29 octobre 2000.*

— à paraître b. Y-a-t-il une production spécifique de support d'outil chez les Campaniformes du Sud-est de la France? Premières caractérisations pour la Provence, in: Bailly M. / Furestier R. / Perrin T. (dir.), *Les industries lithiques taillées holocènes du bassin rhodanien: Problèmes et actualités, Actes de la table ronde de Lyon, 8 et 9 décembre 2000.*

Garrido-Pena R. 2000. *El Campaniforme en La Meseta Central de la Peninsula Ibérica (c. 2500-2000 AC.).* Oxford.

Guilaine J. 1967. *La civilisation du vase campaniforme dans les Pyrénées françaises.* Carcassonne.

GUILAINE J. / CLAUSTRE F. / LEMERCIER O. / SABATIER P. 2002. Campaniformes et environnement culturel en France méditerranéenne, in: *Bell Beakers today. Pottery, people, culture, symbols in prehistoric Europe. International Colloquium, Riva del Garda (Trento, Italy), 11-16 may 1998.* Trento.

JOUSSAUME R. 1981. *Le Néolithique de l'Aunis et du Poitou occidental dans son cadre atlantique.* Rennes.

LE BRUN-RICALENS F. 1989. Correspondance scientifique - Contribution à l'étude des pièces esquillées: la présence de percuteurs à «cupules». *Bulletin de la Société préhistorique française.* 86-7, 196-200.

LEMERCIER O. 2002. *Le Campaniforme dans le sud-est de la France. De l'archéologie à l'Histoire du IIIème millénaire avant notre ère.* Thèse de doctorat, Aix-en-Provence: Université de Provence UMR 6636, 2002, 4 volumes, 1451 p., et 11 cartes hors-texte.

LEMERCIER O. / CONVERTINI F. / D'ANNA A. / DURRENMATH G. / GILABERT C. / LAZARD N. / MARGARIT X. / PROVENZANO N. / PELLISSIER M. / RENAULT S. (à paraître a) - Le Couronnien en Basse-Provence occidentale. Etat des connaissances et nouvelles perspectives de recherches. Objectifs et premiers résultats d'un Projet Collectif de Recherche, 1998-2000, in: *Temps et Espaces culturels, Rencontres Méridionales de Préhistoire Récente, IVe session, Nîmes, 28-29 octobre 2000,* à paraître.

LEMERCIER O. / FURESTIER R. / DUPORT K. / D'ANNA A. (à paraître b) - *Du Néolithique final au Bronze ancien dans le sud-est de la France,* à paraître (communication présentée à la journée SPF de Saintes - février 2000).

LEMONNIER P. 1991. De la culture matérielle à la culture? Ethnologie des techniques et préhistoire, in: PERLÈS C. (dir.), *25 ans d'études technologiques en Préhistoire. XIème Rencontres Internationales d'Archéologie et d'Histoire d'Antibes, 1990.* Juans-les-Pins, 15-20.

PELEGRIN J. 2000. Les techniques de débitage laminaire au Tardiglacière: critères de diagnose et quelques réflexions, in: VALENTIN B. / BODU P. / CHRISTENSEN M. (dir.), *L'Europe centrale et septentrionale au Tardiglaciaire Table-ronde internationale de Nemours, 14-16 mai 1997.* Nemours, 73-86.

PERLES C. 1991. Economie des matières premières et économie du débitage, deux conceptions opposées?, in: PERLÈS C. (dir.), *25 ans d'études technologiques en préhistoire. Bilan et perspectives: Actes des 11e rencontres internationales d'archéologie et d'histoire d'Antibes, 18-20 Octobre 1990.* Juan-les-Pins, 35-45.

RENAULT S. 1998. Economie de la matière première. L'exemple de la production au Néolithique final des grandes lames en silex oligocène du bassin de Forcalquier (04). in: D'ANNA / BINDER (dir.) *Production et identité culturelle, actualités de la recherche. Rencontres méridionales de Préhistoire récente, Actes de la deuxième session, Arles, novembre 1996.* 141-161.

ROUDIL J.-L. / BAZILE F. / SOULIER M. 1974. L'habitat campaniforme de Saint-Côme et Maruejols (Gard), *Gallia Préhistoire.* 17, 181-213.

SALANOVA L. 2000. *La question du Campaniforme en France et dans les îles anglo-normandes. Productions, chronologie et rôles d'un standard céramique.* Paris.

SAUZADE G. 1983. *Les sépultures du Vaucluse du Néolithique à l'Age du Bronze.* Paris.

STRAHM C. (Hrsg.) 1995. *Das Glockenbecher-Phänomen: ein Seminar.* Freiburg.

BELL BEAKERS
COMMON WARE

Similar but different. Bell Beakers in Europe
Czebreszuk J. (ed.)
Poznań 2004

DAS GLOCKENBECHER-PHÄNOMEN
AUS DER SICHT DER KOMPLEMENTÄR-KERAMIK

Christian Strahm (Freiburg, Germany)

1. Einleitung: Eine Standortbestimmung

Momente der Reflexion und der zurückblickenden Besinnung sind zwingend für eine Standortbestimmung in der Wissenschaft. Sie sind vor allem unverzichtbar nach entscheidenden Impulsen, die der Forschung neue Wege und eine neue Richtung gegeben haben. Und genau dies ist die Situation der heutigen Forschung: Vor wenigen Jahren wurden auf der Tagung der Association Archéologie et Gobelets: *„The Bell Beaker 'Phenomenon' - Lost Paradise...?"* auf dem Feldberg im Schwarzwald und auf dem Internationalen Kolloquium: *„Bell Beakers today"* in Riva am Gardasee bestimmte Fragestellungen für die Glockenbecher-Forschung formuliert und ungenügend bearbeitete, oder zu wenig hinterfragte Themenbereiche umschrieben. Dies führte zur Darstellung neuer Theorien, origineller Modelle oder auch nur zu nochmaliger Überarbeitung bekannter Fundkomplexe. Das Kolloquium in Riva hat mit Sicherheit die Forschung neu orientiert und neue Impulse gegeben.

Es ist richtig, wenn wir schon vier Jahre später nach dem Erfolg der neuen Ansätze fragen und abermals eine Standortbestimmung durchführen. Es sind zwar in der Zwischenzeit weder grundlegend neuen Erkenntnisse gewonnen, noch zum Umdenken veranlassende Neufunde geborgen worden - aber es sind zweifelhafte Fakten neu untersucht, unklare Fundgruppen präziser definiert und gewagte Theorien vorsichtiger gefasst worden. Der entscheidende Fortschritt aber ist, dass die Fragestellungen neu und fundiert formuliert worden sind, so dass sich dabei neue Theorien herauskristallisiert haben.

Diese Neuorientierung der Forschung trifft vor allem für zwei Themenbereiche zu, die beide essentiell sind für das Verständnis des gesamten Glockenbecher-Komplexes und ihre Ausdeutung bedingt sich gegenseitig: Zum einen handelt es sich um den ideellen Hintergrund des archäologischen Erscheinungsbildes des Glockenbecher-Komplexes zum anderen um die sogenannte Begleitkeramik, die wir treffender als *Komplementär-Keramik* bezeichnen sollten.

Dass der Glockenbecher und das mit ihm vergesellschaftete, charakteristische Set nicht als herkömmliche archäologische Kultur zu betrachten ist, hat die Forschung mittlerweile deutlich herausgearbeitet. In der kulturellen Evolution waren es bis zu dieser Phase wirtschaftliche Faktoren, die den Kulturwandel bedingten. Mit dem Beginn des 3. vorchr. Jahrtausends ist es offensichtlich ein neues Wissen, das neue Formen und neue soziale Strukturen prägt. Es mag politisch, sozial, ökonomisch oder religiös begründet sein - wir wissen es nicht - aber es sind neue Wertvorstellungen, die das Leben und - wie die streng genormten Grabsitten zeigen - auch das Sterben - bestimmten. Provozierend haben wir formuliert, dass sich an der Wende vom 4. zum 3. Jahrtausend eine neue Ideologie bildet, die einerseits im Glockenbecher-Phänomen, andererseits in der schnurkeramischen Wesensart ihren Ausdruck findet (STRAHM 2002, 178-185).

Die Glockenbecher-Ideologie soll hier nur am Rande (vgl. Kp.4.1.) behandelt werden, sie war schon Gegenstand von Diskussionen, wurde auch in Riva vorgestellt, und es sind seither auch keine neuen Erkenntnisse darüber gewonnen worden. Wir wollen uns vielmehr im folgenden mit der Komplementärkeramik, bzw. der Begleitkeramik befassen, die in der Publikation von Riva neu definiert und bewertet worden ist, und deren massgebende Bedeutung in letzter Zeit durch verschiedene Arbeiten und Diskussionen immer klarer geworden ist. Durch einen Paradigmenwechsel haben wir eine neue Sicht gewonnen, und können dadurch mittlerweile den kulturellen Hintergrund der Begleitkeramik klarer erkennen.

2. These

Mit den folgenden Ausführungen will ich die These aufstellen und begründen, dass es keine allgemeine Begleitkeramik, die allen Glockenbecher-Regionen gemein ist, gibt; eine dem Glockenbecher genuin zuzuordnende, generelle Begleitkeramik mit einem einheitlichen Formenspektrum ist nicht zu erkennen. Es waren vielmehr verschiedene regional differenzierte, den Glockenbecher begleitende Keramikformen vorhanden, die ihre einheimischen Wurzeln hatten. Es handelt sich dabei um eine jeweils regionale Komponente, die auf die einheimische endneolithische Keramik zurückgeführt werden kann. Wir sprechen deshalb in der Folge nicht mehr von einer allgemeinen Begleitkeramik, die durch die Forschungsgeschichte eine irreführende Bedeutung gewonnen hat, sondern von einer *regionalen Komplementär-Keramik*, oder von einer „céramique de tradition régional", bzw. von einer „ware of regional tradition" (BESSE / STRAHM 2001).

In einer ersten Analyse dieser Problematik und dem daraus resultierenden Versuch einen neuen Weg zu gehen, haben wir schon einmal gezeigt, dass der Begriff „Begleitkeramik" methodisch irreführend ist, dass man allenfalls von Begleitkeramiken - besser regionalen Begleitkeramiken - sprechen kann (BESSE / STRAHM 2001,107). Wir haben dann vorgeschlagen, diesen Begriff durch „céramique commune" bzw. „common ware" zu ersetzen. Da dies aber sowohl gemeine, d.h. gewöhnliche, als auch gemeinsame, d.h. einheitliche Keramik bedeutet, schien mir auch diese Kennzeichnung irreführend. Eine Zusammenstellung der Begriffe verdeutlicht ihre unterschiedliche Verwendung:

- Komplementär-Keramik: Ein Keramikspektrum einer Gebrauchsware, die mit dem verzierten Glockenbecher vergesellschaftet ist und in einer regionalen Tradition steht.

- Begleitkeramik: Keramikspektrum einer den verzierten Glockenbecher begleitenden Gebrauchsware, die ursprünglich auf die im östlichen Mitteleuropa aus der karpathenländischen Frühbronzezeit abgeleiteten Keramikformen bezogen wurde. Dieser Begriff wird jedoch oft irreführend auch in anderen Regionen für die den verzierten Glockenbecher begleitende Keramik verwendet. Er soll jedoch auch weiterhin nur auf die in der Ostgruppe des Glockenbecher-Komplexes vorkommende Gebrauchskeramik angewandt werden.
- „Céramique d'accompagnement": Keramikspektrum einer Gebrauchsware mit Formen, die in der Westgruppe den verzierten Glockenbecher begleiten und dort in regionaler Tradition stehen. Dieser Begriff wird irreführend auch für die Begleitkeramik verwendet, so dass auf diese Weise verschiedene Entitäten mit dem gleichen Terminus besetzt sind.
- „Céramique commune", „common ware": Ein erst kürzlich eingeführter Begriff, um die irreführende Verwendung des Begriffs: Begleitkeramik zu umgehen. „Commune" bzw. „commun" ist jedoch ambivalent, so dass auch dieser Terminus nicht weiterführt.

Die Formulierung der These erweckt den Anschein, dass es sich hier lediglich um ein taxonomisches Problem handelt. Doch ging der Klassifizierung und Abgrenzung der Komponenten des gesamten Glockenbecher-Komplexes eine detaillierte Analyse des Fundmaterials voraus. Erst sie erlaubt es, diese weiträumig verbreitete Entität genauer zu beschreiben, die generellen glockenbecherischen Typen zu definieren, und die regionalen, mit dem Glockenbecher verbundenen Elemente zu erkennen. Eine strenge und konsequente Aufgliederung führte dann zwangsläufig zu einer neuen taxonomischen Beschreibung der Komponenten und ohne zusätzliche Argumente wird der Glockenbecher-Komplex erklärbarer: Es gibt offenbar einige wenige allgemein verbreitete, genuin glockenbecherische Objekte (das sog. Glockenbecher-Set) und eine Komponente, die in sich verschieden und in regiona-

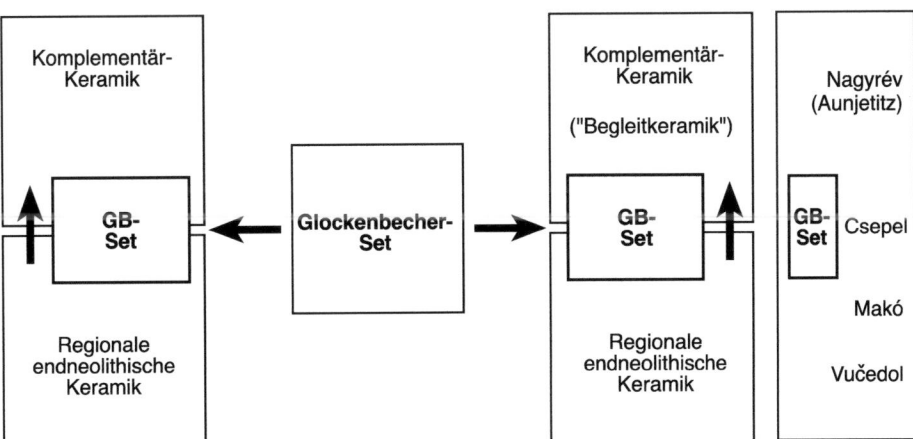

Abb. 1. Die Vernetzung der beiden Glockenbecher-Komponenten: Das Glockenbecher-Set wird von den regionalen endneolithischen Gruppen akkulturiert, ihre Keramik wird die Komplementär-Keramik. Im Feld rechts ist dies am Beispiel der Entwicklung in Ungarn dargestellt.

ler Tradition verwurzelt ist (die regionale Komplementär-Keramik, Abb. 1). Das methodische Vorgehen für die Herausarbeitung der Komponenten, die zu einer Kategorisierung der Funde führten, wurde an anderer Stelle schon ausführlich beschrieben und wird unten nochmals kurz dargestellt (Kp.3.2.6; STRAHM 1995, 8)

3. Die Situation der Forschung

3.1. Die Herausarbeitung der Begleitkeramik

Um die Notwendigkeit einer Neudefinition der Begleitkeramik zu verstehen, ist ein Blick in die Geschichte ihrer Herausarbeitung und eine Analyse der bisherigen Diskussion erforderlich. Ebenso ist die Darstellung der Situation der Forschung der letzten Jahre unverzichtbar, will man zu einem stimmigen Ziel gelangen.

Die Herkunft des Begriffes erstaunt und legt einmal mehr dar, wie eine unklar definierte Benennung, die im Laufe der Forschung unreflektiert mit verschiedenen Inhalten gefüllt und entsprechend gedeutet wird, neue Theorien entstehen lässt. Ein konsequentes Hinterfragen hätte lange Diskussionen erübrigt.

Nachdem schon sehr früh die gesamteuropäische Verbreitung des verzierten Glockenbechers erkannt und anhand bildhafter Vergleiche gedeutet wurde, hat man in den ostmitteleuropäischen Regionen auch seine regelhafte Vergesellschaftung mit einer unverzierten, weniger sorgfältig gearbeiteten Keramik festgestellt. Als erster hat meines Wissens A. Stocký diese Komponente benannt und in Bezug auf den Glockenbecher in der französischen Übersetzung seines berühmten Werkes „La Bohème préhistorique" von einer „Céramique concomitante" geschrieben (STOCKÝ 1926). Auch J. SCHRANIL verwendet schon 1928 den Begriff „Begleitkeramik". Beide Autoren meinen damit eine zusätzliche Keramik, die der Glockenbechererscheinung zu einer umfassend belegten archäologischen Kultur verhalfen. Ähnlich argumentiert etwas später G. Kraft, der in den am Oberrhein gefundenen „Begleitgefässen, die Hinweise auf starkes einheimisches Bevölkerungselement geben," auch die intensiven Beziehungen in die östlichen Glockenbechergruppen erkennt (KRAFT 1941-47,137).

Auch L. Hajek sieht in der damals schon allgemein als Begleitkeramik bezeichneten Formengruppe eine deutliche einheimische Komponente der Glockenbecherkultur. Sie bildet seine dritte Stufe, die mit der Voraunjetitzer und Frühaunjetitzer Kultur parallel geht (HAJEK 1966, 210).

Bis in die 60er Jahre war es das Hauptanliegen der Forschung, den Glockenbecherkomplex überhaupt zu fassen, zu beschreiben und zu gliedern. Dabei spielte auch die Herkunftfrage eine herausragende Rolle. So konzentrierten sich die bekannten Arbeiten von E. Sangmeister zunächst auf die Begründung der bekannten Rückstromtheorie, die nicht zu belegen war, da damals eine weiträumig gültige Chronologie fehlte, die aber der Forschung dennoch wesentliche Impulse gab. Später versuchte er, den Glockenbecherkomplex gesamthaft als archäologische Kultur zu begreifen und stellte die entsprechenden Befunde zusammen (SANGMEISTER 1972). Auch U. Fischer verfolgte ziemlich gleichzeitig das gleiche Ziel (FISCHER 1975), und es ist bezeichnend, dass in beiden Aufsätzen die allgemeine Begleitkeramik kaum eine Rolle spielte. Man betrachtete sie als regionale Erscheinung, als integrierender Bestandteil der Ostgruppe.

Der Paradigmenwechsel, der von den 70er Jahren an die Forschung prägte, wurde im Grunde genommen durch den Aufsatz von E. Neustupný über das jüngere Äneolithikum in Mitteleuropa vorbereitet. Er beruhte auf einem Vortrag, den er 1971 auf dem 1. Internationalen Symposium über Äneolithikum und frühe Bronzezeit auf der Hohen Tatra hielt. Darin stellte er drei mögliche Modelle des Kulturwandels dor, wobei er besonders die kontinuierliche Entwicklung in der Region betonte. Insbesondere weist er auf die einheimischen Wurzeln der Begleitkeramik hin, die eine starke Verbindung zum Vučedol-Komplex aufweist, und ihre Fortsetzung in der Post-Vučedol-Entwicklung im Karpatenbecken findet. Den verzierten Glockenbecher leitet er aus der jüngeren Kultur mit Schnurkeramik Nordwesteuropas ab. Als erster macht er auf die „Zweigleisigkeit......, die für die Glockenbecherkultur so bezeichnend ist: verzierte Becher erscheinen in Begleitung unverzierter 'Begleitkeramik'", aufmerksam (NEUSTUPNÝ 1972, 115).

3.2. Die Deutungen der Begleitkeramik und der Céramique d'accompagnement

3.2.1. Der Ansatz von St. Shennan

St. Shennan hat dann in einem Referat auf dem 3. Internationalen Symposium über die Anfänge der Bronzezeit in Mittel- und Osteuropa, das 1973 in Kraków stattfand und 1975 publiziert wurde, den Paradigmenwechsel konsequent vollzogen und der ganzen Erscheinung eine völlig neue Interpretation gegeben. Er hat die bekannten und stets in den Vordergrund gerückten Elemente beschrieben und festgestellt, dass sie in einem bestimmten, weit verbreiteten Set vorkommen, während die übrigen Beifunde lokaler Herkunft sind. Dies konnte man aber erst erkennen, seit es in den meisten Regionen auch Siedlungsfunde gab. Die regionale Tradition der Gebrauchskeramik wird damit deutlich und man kann das fremde Element, die charakterischen internationalen Glockenbecherformen, die Prestigegüter seien, als eine additive Komponente darstellen. St. Shennan hat diese Theorie, die von dem „Interaction Sphere Model" der nordamerikanischen Archäologie ausging, zusammen mit D. Clarke im bekannten Symposion von Oberried 1974 (LANTING / VAN DER WAALS 1976) nochmals vorgestellt, und 1976 mit C. Burgess auf die angelsächsischen Befunde übertragen (BURGESS / SHENNAN 1976). Die Forschung nahm von diesem Modell vielfach Kenntnis aber eigenartigerweise wurde es weder von der französischen noch von der deutschen Forschung weiterentwickelt, oder gar konkret und eingehend in einer Region überprüft.

3.2.2. Der Ansatz von A. Gallay

Allein A. Gallay hat die neue Theorie aufgenommen und versucht, sie am Material zu prüfen. Er stützte sich dabei besonders auf die Gebrauchskeramik in Glockenbecher-Befunden, die auf einer lokalen Tradition beruht, und definierte dabei verschiedene Verbreitungs- oder Kommunikationsnetze, darunter auch das der östlichen Begleitkeramik (Réseau 3; GALLAY 1979, 233). Er hat damit die Trennung vom Glockenbecher-Package (Glockenbecher-Set), das aus Prestigegütern besteht, und der Komponente einer lokalen Tradition auch in andere Regionen übertragen und im Grunde genommen den Glockenbecher-Komplex in gleicher Weise aufgegliedert, wie wir dies heute auch vorschlagen. Er beschreibt den Glockenbecher-Komplex in den Niederlanden und in England als eine selbständige archäologische Kultur „au plein sens du terme" während z.B. die Begleitkeramik in Mitteleuropa einer anderen Kultur, die ihren Ursprung im Karpatenbecken habe, zuzuordnen sei. Die Glockenbecher-Elemente sind dort eingeführt (GALLAY 1979, 250f.). Gallay hat damit einen entscheideneden Schritt zu einem klaren Verständnis dieser Erscheinung getan, konnte ihn aber nicht konsequent für jede Region vollziehen, da die Kenntnis der lokalen Gruppen und ihrer chronologischen Abfolgen noch zu wenig erarbeitet war. Dieser wegweisende, doch mühsam zu lesende Beitrag blieb bedauerlicherweise grösstenteils unbeachtet.

Den Gedanken, verschiedene Netzwerke des Glockenbecher-Komplexes zu unterscheiden, verfolgte A. Gallay auch in seinem Aufsatz von 1986. Er geht davon aus, dass die Gebrauchskeramik, die lokal hergestellt und kaum weit verbreitet ist, besser als der verzierte Glockenbecher geeignet ist, um „populations" zu bestimmen (1986, 431). Er erkennt die Besonderheit der mit dem verzierten Glockenbecher vergesellschafteten Gebrauchskeramik im Rhônetal und definiert damit den „complexe rodano-rhénan". Man mag gegen die Zusammenfassung der rheinischen und südfranzösischen Komponenten, die wenig typologische Gemeinsamkeiten aufweisen, Einwände haben, richtig ist aber, dass hier eine westliche den Glockenbecher begleitende Gebrauchskeramik erstmals erfasst wird. A. Gallay versäumt es aber, in diesem entscheidenden Beitrag diese Entität klar von der mitteleuropäischen Begleitkeramik abzusetzen, verwendet hier sogar auch den Terminus Begleitkeramik. Er gibt damit der Forschung zu wenig Klarheit, so dass dieser geistreiche, aber schwer zugängliche Aufsatz zwar die Problematik richtig erfasst hat, aber letztendlich auch eine gewisse Unsicherheit geschaffen hat.

In seinem Aufsatz von 1988 hat A. Gallay die Bedeutung der Kommunikationsnetze nochmals unterstrichen und ihre chronologischen und regionalen Unterschiede hervorgehoben (GALLAY 1988). Gleichzeitig lehnt er im Gegensatz zu seinen früheren Ansichten die angelsächsische Theorie eines Glockenbecher-Package ab und erklärt den Glockenbecher-Komplex als besondere Entwicklungsstufe die sich ökonomisch und sozial wenig von der des vorhergehenden Endneolithikum unterscheidet. Auch die anschaulich dokumentierte und instruktive Übersicht von 1998 wiederholt diese Thesen (GALLAY 1998; 2001)

Es ist nicht einfach, die wichtigen und methodisch sehr durchdachten Arbeiten von A. Gallay anzuwenden, denn einerseits hat er die Differenzierung des Glockenbecher-Komplexes seit 1979 richtig dargestellt mit seinen Kommunikationsnetzen (Réseaux 1-6), andererseits hat er mit den komplexen Synthesen eine Einheitlichkeit der gesamten Erscheinung angedeutet, die durch die Befunde nicht gegeben war. Sein Réseaux 2 entspricht im Grunde genommen dem Becher des „Package" und würde mit den typischen nicht-keramischen Funden zusammen das Glockenbecher-Set ergeben. Das Réseau 1 mit den Gobelets AOC, das aus der Kultur mit Schnurkeramik abgeleitet wird, soll den Ausgangspunkt der Entwicklung darstellen. Diese Theorie, die als holländisches Modell in die Forschung eingangen ist, kann aber nicht aufrecht erhalten werden (vgl. dazu STRAHM 1979). Der Herausarbeitung der Réseaux 3, 4, 5 und 6, die als spätere Phasen erkannt werden, wird man zustimmen können. Sie entsprechenden den hier als Keramikgruppen mit regionaler Tradition bezeichneten Komponenten, bzw. der Komplementär-Keramik. Vor dem Hintergrund einer regionalen Differenzierung und der Darstellung der einheimischen Wurzeln der Gebrauchskeramik der verschiedenen Netzwerke hat das Bild von A. Gallay durchaus seine Richtigkeit, aber man gewinnt teilweise auch den Eindruck, dass der Glockenbecher-Komplex als ganzes eine einheitliche archäologische Kultur mit regionalen Unterschieden sei, die mit den Réseaux 3-6 umschrieben werde.

In Bezug auf die Befunde in Frankreich war dies ein wichtiger und weiterführender Schritt, wurde doch damit der gesamte Glockenbecher-Komplex erstmals erfasst. Die Gleichstellung einer westlichen mit der östlichen Begleitkeramik beinhaltete aber auch die Ursache für eine Fehlinterpretation, die, wie so oft in der Urgeschichtsforschung, von einer irreführenden Taxonomie ausging. Einige Autoren übernahmen die Kommunikationsnetze und interpretierten die Gebrauchsware des Glockenbecher-Komplexes als die lokale Ausprägung der weiträumig verbreiteten Glockenbecher-Kultur. Dies bedeutet, dass die „Céramique d'accompagnement" mit der im östlichen Mitteleuropa schon seit langem definierten Begleitkeramik gleichgesetzt wurde. Ein typologischer Vergleich wurde nicht durchgeführt. Dass sie ein unterschiedliches Formenspektrum besitzen, wurde nicht beachtet (Abb.1). Man glaubte, in ihrer Geschlossenheit ein weiteres Argument für die Herausarbeitung einer Glockenbecher-Kultur als umfassend belegte archäologische Kultur („civilisation à part entière") gefunden zu haben.

3.2.3. Der Ansatz von M. Besse

In seinen Ausgrabungen von Les Rances (VD) im westschweizerischen Mittelland hat A. Gallay eine mit dem verzierten Glockenbecher vergesellschaftete Gebrauchskeramik gefunden, die er seinem „Complexe rodano-rhénan" zuordnete, und die er als Bestätigung seines Réseau 6 betrachtete. Eine Aufarbeitung dieser Entität drängte sich auf, und er betraute seine Schülerin M. Besse mit der Aufgabe. Sie legte ihre Studie in der Diplomarbeit von 1992 vor (BESSE 1996). Sie analysierte die mit verzierten Glockenbechern vergesellschaftete Gebrauchskeramik in ganz Frankreich, stellte eine umfangreiche Typologie zusammen und interpretierte sie als Komponente des Glockenbecherkomplexes, der damit zu einer umfassend belegten archäologischen Kultur wurde: „Le Campaniforme doit alors être considéré comme une civilisation à part entière" (BESSE 1996, 34). Sie meinte damit belegen zu können, dass die Gebrauchskeramik in Frankreich ein in sich einheitliches Gepräge hat, und dass sie nicht aus dem Néolithique récent oder Néolithique final abgeleitet werden könne.

Im Grunde genommen wäre mit der Darstellung der Selbständigkeit der „Céramique d'accompagnement" der richtige Weg für ihre Zuordnung innerhalb

107

Similar but different. Bell Beakers in Europe

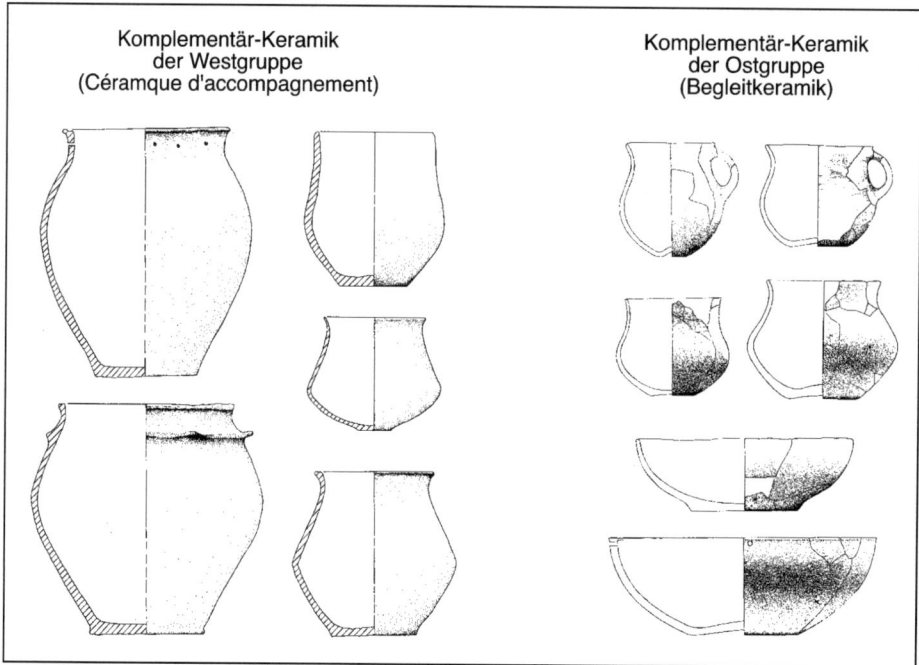

Abb. 2.   Das unterschiedliche Formenspektrum der bisher „Begleitkeramik", bzw. in Frankreich „Céramique d'accompagnement" bezeichneten Entitäten. Es handelt sich um regionale Ausprägungen einer Komplementär-Keramik. (nach Billard 1991 und Engelhardt 1991).

der Westgruppe vorgezeichnet gewesen, und die einheimischen Wurzeln der Glockenbecherkultur in Südfrankreich hätten sich von selbst ergeben. Aber M. Besse übertrug ihre für Frankreich ausgearbeitete Typologie auf die Begleitkeramik im östlichen Mitteleuropa und ging somit zwangsläufig von einer formalen Gemeinsamkeit dieser Keramikgruppen aus. Sie postulierte damit implizit auch eine allgemeine, einheitliche, in ganz Europa verbreitete Begleitkeramik, die den verzierten Glockenbecher ergänzte und man hätte infolgedessen die gesamte Erscheinung als geschlossene Kultur begreifen müssen (Abb. 2).

Diesen gleichen Ansatz verfolgte sie in ihrer Thèse weiter (Besse 2003). Die Gefässtypen sind in den diversen Regionen sehr unterschiedlich vertreten, und es ergeben sich deutliche Verbreitungsschwerpunkte und Abgrenzungen, die den bisher unterschiedenen Gruppierungen gut entsprechen (z.B. Besse 2003, Verbreitungskarten Fig.100 oder Fig.116). Es werden auf diese Weise verschiedene „Domaines" definiert. Die Präsenz einiger dieser Typen in den vorglockenbecherzeitlichen, endneolithischen Kulturen erlaubt es, die lokalen Traditionen aufzuzeigen. Diese wirken sich unterschiedlich in den drei „Domaines" aus, wie dies H. Fokkens für die z.B. für die nordwestliche Region schon festgestellt hat, indem er schreibt, das „in general domestic ware differs sharply from region to region" (Fokkens 1998, 105). Dies bedeutet, dass wir es mit sehr verschiedenen, aber jeweils durch die einheimischen Wurzeln bestimmten, Komponenten zu tun haben, womit aber auch die initiale These einer gemeinsamen, überregionalen Begleitkeramik falsifiziert wird. Doch die Arbeit zeigt die Bedeutung dieser Fundgruppe und fordert weitere regionale Untersuchungen.

3.2.4. Der Ansatz von O. Lemercier

Aus der bisherigen kritischen Analyse der Forschungssituation geht hervor, dass die Komplementär-Keramik aus Frankreich schwer zu verstehen war und fundarme Befunde zu Fehldeutungen geführt haben. Das grosse Interesse der Forschung an dieser Glockenbecher-Region zeigt aber, dass dort ein Schlüssel zum besseren Verständnis der gesamten Erscheinung liegen könnte. Es ist deshalb interessant, abschliessend hier noch eine neueste Arbeit zu betrachten, die als breite Regionalstudie konzipiert war, und die die heutige Problematik der Komplementärkeramik am deutlichsten aufzeigen kann. Es handelt sich um die Thèse von O. Lemercier, die er 2002 in Aix-en-Provence vorgelegt hat (LEMERCIER 2002). Er hat aus der Erkenntnis heraus, dass das Glockenbecher-Problem nicht von seiner Totalität her gelöst werden kann, gefordert, dass zunächst regionale Studien anzustreben seien, um später zu einem ganzheitlichen Verstehen zu gelangen. Er führt diesen Ansatz dann auch modellhaft durch: Er definiert als Grundlage für seine Gliederung den frühen verzierten Glockenbecher, oder seinen „style 1", bzw. den „standard", der nie mit anderer Keramik vorkommt. Dann unterscheidet er in Südostfrankreich (neben den verschiedenen bekannten Glockenbecher-Zierstilen) drei Arten von unverzierten Gefässen, die mit verzierten Glockenbechern vergesellschaftet sind:

a. eine unverzierte Keramik in einem glockenbecherischen Formenspektrum. Dies ist der unverzierte Glockenbecher; er ist Bestandteil des interregional verbreiteten Glockenbecher-Sets,

b. weiter eine „Céramique commune", die mit „style 2" (pointillé géometrique) zusammen vorkommt. Sie scheint sich gänzlich an die lokale groupe Rhône-Ouvèze anbinden zu lassen (LEMERCIER 2002, 205),

c. schliesslich eine weitere „Céramique commune", die jeweils zu seinem „style 3" (rhodano-provençal) oder „style 4" (barbelé) gehört, und die von den einheimischen endneolithischen Gruppen übernommen ist, u.a. von der groupe Rhône-Ouvèze. Sie stellen jeweils mit den Glockenbechern dieser Stile eine „culture archéologique complète" dar.

Wenn man alle Aussagen in Betracht zieht, heisst dies, dass der Ursprung der unverzierten Keramik der letzten beiden Gruppen im einheimischen Néolithique récent oder final zu suchen ist. Dies bedeutet aber auch, dass es eine allgemeine, einheitliche „Céramique commune" nicht gibt, sondern jeweils regionale Ausprägungen, die von der Glockenbecherpopulation übernommen worden sind. Diese Konsequenz würde sehr gut mit den Ergebnissen der Ostgruppe übereinstimmen und scheint von entscheidender Relevanz zu sein. Sie wäre eine Interpretation der Akkulturation der Glockenbecherleute.

3.2.5. Fazit

Die Analyse der Forschungssituation hat dazu geführt, dass durch die vergleichende gesamteuropäische Darstellung des Glockenbecher-Komplexes die besondere Stellung der den Glockenbecher begleitenden Keramik, d.h. der Komplementär-Keramik erkannt, und dass daraus neue Ansätze entwickelt werden konnten. Während man vor einem Jahrhundert noch beeindruckt war von der weiten Verbreitung gleicher Typen und darin die archäologische Manifestation einer besonderen Bevölkerungsgruppe sah, bemühte man sich in der Folge zu den Glockenbechern ergänzende Artefakte hinzuzufügen, um dann eine konventionelle, archäologische Kultur zu beschreiben. Später erkannte man, dass es lediglich ein bestimmtes Set oder „package" von besonderen Objekten gab, die eine weiträumige Verbreitung haben. Dass diese Erscheinung für die New Archaeology, oder später für die konzeptuelle Archäologie, exemplarische Bedeutung gewann, erstaunt nicht. Man entwarf vielfach beachtete Modelle, die sich stets auf die Interpretation der auffälligen Prestigegüter konzentrierte. Die Gebrauchskeramik, d.h. die Komplementär-Keramik hatte daneben untergeordnete Bedeutung, wurde methodisch und begrifflich unzureichend erfasst und vor allem regional nicht differenziert, so dass Irrwege vorprogrammiert waren. Die Diskussion war festgefahren, die Deutungen durch antizipierende Benennungen geprägt, so dass sich daraus zwingend die Konsequenz ergibt, die gesamte Glockenbecher-Problematik, insbesondere die Frage der Herausarbeitung der Komplementär-Keramik mit einem neuen Ansatz anzugehen. Dieser beinhaltet in erster Linie die Aufstellung einer schlüssigen Terminologie und deren äquivalente Anwendung auf die regionalen Gruppierungen. Er soll im folgenden dargestellt werden, um sich auf neuen Wegen der Deutung des gesamten Glockenbecher-Komplexes anzunähern.

3.2.6. Der Ansatz des Seminars von Freiburg

Nach der ausführlichen Darstellung der Problematik der Herausarbeitung der Komplementär-Keramik innerhalb des Glockenbecher-Komplexes ist es offenkundig, dass nur ein neuer Anfang eine überall gültige Lösung bringen konnte. Wir haben deshalb in einem Seminar in Freiburg, das anfänglich als methodische Aufarbeitung des gesamten Glockenbecher-Komplexes angelegt war, diesen neuen Weg gesucht. Es war uns allen klar, dass nur ein konsequentes und kohärentes methodisches Vorgehen bei seiner Bestimmung und vor allem bei seiner Benennung zum Ziele führen kann und unabdingbare Voraussetzung ist.

Wir haben uns entschlossen, die Funde des gesamten Glockenbecher-Komplexes neu zu gliedern und in eindeutige, überregional gültige Kategorien zu fassen, wobei stets darauf geachtet wurde, dass jeder Schritt nachvollziehbar ist. Wir wollten unvoreingenommen und möglichst unbelastet vom heutigen Forschungsstand, bzw. bisheriges Wissen ausser acht lassend, das Material neu ordnen.

Es sind sehr unterschiedliche Fundkomplexe, die mit dem Etikett Glockenbecher versehen worden sind; sie sind stets in irgendeiner Weise, oft auch nur indirekt, mit einem sogenannten Glockenbecher kombiniert. Sie enthalten auch recht unterschiedliche Objekte, die zu ordnen waren.

In einem ersten Schritt haben wir alle Artefakte, die mit dem Glockenbecher in Verbindung gebracht worden sind, zusammengestellt, um überhaupt die Gesamtheit zu erfassen und eine möglichst breite Grundlage zur Klassifizierung zu erzielen. Diese berücksichtigt auch die Befundzusammenhänge, die entscheidendes Kriterium für die Differenzierung waren. Wir definierten den charakteristischen Glockenbecher und prüften alle damit zusammen vorkommenden Komponenten. Diese wurden wiederum auf ihre weitere Vergesellschaftung hin untersucht. Auf diesem induktiven Wege liess sich der Glockenbecher-Komplex ohne jede Prämisse beschreiben und damit auch neue Grundlagen für seine Deutung schaffen.

Ausgangspunkt bildete also eine eindeutige Definition des Glockenbechers selbst. Wir sind dabei impressionistisch - im Sinne vom M. Malmer (MALMER 1962, XXXII und 881) - vorgegangen und haben ihn als Kategorie I benannt. Dann haben wir diejenigen Funde, die mit dem definierten Glockenbecher und nur mit diesem vergesellschaftet sind zur Kategorie II zusammengefasst; schliesslich wurden die Funde, die auch mit anderem endneolithischen oder frühbronzezeitlichen Material vorkommen, zusammengestellt, und als Kategorie III bezeichnet. Dieses an sich einfache Vorgehen beruht zwar zunächst auf sujektiven, typologischen Kriterien für die Bestimmung der Typen und verzichtet auf mathematisch genaue Masse oder Verhältniszahlen für deren Definition. Es soll aber dazu dienen, den gesamten Glockenbecher-Komplex einheitlich zu fassen. Die Kategorien stellen - das muss immer wieder betont werden - eine Beschreibung, eine Erleichterung des Vorgehens dar, eine Interpretation wird damit nicht vorweggenommen. Die Unterscheidung von Kategorie II und III könnte allerdings kulturell bewertet werden, doch stellt auch diese Aussage schon eine Interpretation dar und muss für jede Region einzeln erbracht werden.

3.2.7. Die Kategorien

Kategorie I

Die Kategorie I umfasst allein den als „Standard" charakterisierten Glockenbecher, den L. Salanova jüngst (SALANOVA 2000, 193) klar beschrieben hat: Er ist definiert durch eine bewusste Auswahl und Anwendung bestimmter Merkmale in seinem gesamten Herstellungsprozess; er besteht aus einem sehr feinen Ton, der im Brand eine orange-rote Tönung ergibt, und er hat ein charakteristisches, regelmässiges S-Profil; er ist verziert mit horizontalen, mehrfachen und alternierend schräg schraffierten Bändern oder sich wiederholenden Linien ausgeführt in Stempeltechnik mit Hilfe von Muscheln, Kämmen oder Schnüren. Diese klare Definition erlaubt es meines Erachtens, den weiträumig verbreiteten Typ des Glockenbechers von seinen regionalen Ausprägungen, wie z.B. dem Zonen -, Metopen -, Veluwe -, oder Ciempozuelo - Becher etc., die eine regionalspezifische Verzierung aufweisen, abzugrenzen.

Innerhalb dieser Kategorie gibt es den maritimen, bzw. internationalen oder paneuropäischen Becher, sowie den AOC- und den AOO-Becher.

Kategorie I beschreibt damit keine „Fazies" und auch keinen „Stil", denn mit diesem Verständnis könnte sie auch um weitere Formen, z.B. glockenbecherisch verzierte Schalen, erweitert werden.

Kategorie II

Kategorie II wird durch Objekte definiert, die ausschliesslich mit dem definierten Standard-Glockenbecher (Kategorie I) oder nur unter sich vergesellschaftet sind. Sie werden also nie in einem nicht-glockenbecherischen Kontext anzutreffen sein - es sei denn, es handelt sich um eindeutige, vereinzelt auftretende Importfunde.

Sie wird vor allem gebildet von den charakteristischen Kleinfunden der Glockenbecher-Ausstattung, wie z.B. der gestielten Pfeilspitze, dem bogenförmigen Knochenknebel, dem Kupferdolch oder der Palmela-Spitze. An keramischen Funden gehören in diese Kategorie die wenigen allen Glockenbecher-Regionen gemeinsamen Typen, wie z. B. die Schalen. Ebenso sind die Formen der regionalen Stile, wie der rhodano-provençalische oder der pyrenäische Stil, dazuzurechnen, sofern sie nur mit Glockenbechern vergesellschaftet sind.

Die allgemein verbreiteten Typen der Kategorie I und II bilden das sog. Glockenbecher-Set oder „package", das in der Forschung schon seit einiger Zeit diskutiert wird (Abb. 3, vgl. Kp. 4.1).

Kategorie III

Kategorie III wird definiert durch die Objekte, die mit Glockenbechern, die aber auch in zeitlich und räumlich benachbarten Gruppen vorkommen. Bei der Keramik handelt es sich um Gefässformen mit regionaler Tradition, d.h. um eine allgemein endneolithische Keramik. Dazu gehört im östlichen Mitteleuropa in erster Linie die sog. Begleitkeramik. Über ihre forschungsgeschichtliche Bedeutung und über die irreführende Übertragung des Begriffes auf westeuropäische Glockenbecher-Gruppen wurde oben schon diskutiert (Kp. 3.2.3), und wir haben vorgeschlagen, ihn durch den Begriff „Komplementär-Keramik" zu ersetzen. In diese Kategorie sind auch weitere mit dem Glockenbecher vergesellschaftete Formenspektren einzuordnen, die überall in regionaler Tradition stehen oder zumindest ganz allgemein dem Endneolithikum zugerechnet werden.

Die Subsumierung verschiedener, den Glockenbecher begleitenden Entitäten unter eine Kategorie trägt wesentlich zur Klärung des gesamten Glockenbecher-Komplexes bei. Dieser lässt sich dadurch klar gliedern und die unterschiedlichen Komponenten können eindeutig auseinandergehalten werden. Die Beschreibung wird dadurch zwangsläufig vom folgenden Schritt, nämlich der Interpretation, getrennt.

Das beschriebene Vorgehen, d.h. die Einordung aller Artefakte in die drei Kategorien wurde auch für jede Region angewendet. Es hat sich gezeigt, dass dies mühelos durchführbar ist; es gab keine grundsätzlichen Probleme, Zuordnungen waren selten umstritten. Der Gesichtspunkt einer umfassenden und einheitlichen Darstellung des gesamten Glockenbecher-Komplexes war vorrangig.

4. Die Komponenten des Glockenbecherkomplexes.

Anhand der beschriebenen Kategorien lässt sich der gesamte Glockenbecher-Komplex zwanglos darstellen. Dieser lediglich beschreibende erste Schritt ist Grundlage für die folgende Interpretation, die sich aus der Vergesellschaftung und der Ver-

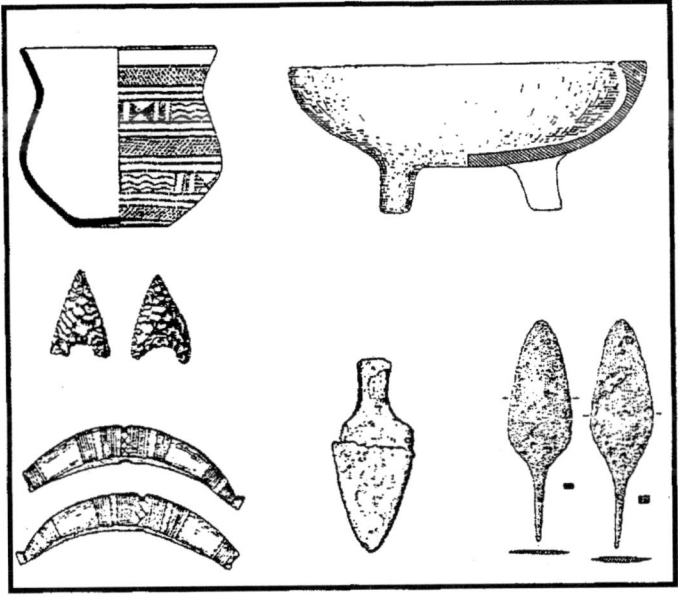

Abb. 3.   Das Glockenbecher-Set.

breitung der Kategorien ergibt. Sie führt zur Theorie, den Glockenbecher-Komplex als ein Zusammenwirken von zwei entgegengesetzt verankerten Komponenten zu verstehen: Die erste Komponente besteht aus dem semiotischen Ausdruck einer Philosophie oder Ideologie, die zweite ist die archäologische Manifestation einer regionalen ansässigen Bevölkerung.

4.1. Das Glockenbecher-Set

Die erste Komponente wird gebildet aus Kategorie I, dem definierten Glockenbecher, und von der Kategorie II, den ausschliesslich mit dem Standard-Glockenbecher vergesellschafteten Artefakten. Beide Kategorien zusammen ergeben das Glockenbecher-Set (Abb. 3). Dieses enthält neben dem verzierten Glockenbecher auch die Füsschenschale, die charakteristischen Pfeilspitzen, den bogenförmigen Knochenknebel, den Kupferdolch mit rechteckiger Griffplatte und die Palmelaspitze, die zwar nur der Westgruppe bekannt ist. Es ist anzunehmen, dass auch andere Objekte zu dieser besonderen Ausstattung zu zählen sind, die aber dann auch in späteren Gemeinschaften verwendet werden, so dass die Definition nicht mehr greifen würde. Konsequenterweise werden sie nicht zum Set gerechnet. In diesem Sinne hat z.B. St. Shennan, der als erster dieses „package" beschrieb (SHENNAN 1975, 175) auch Armschutzplatten, V-förmig durchbohrte Knöpfe, Ahlen und Ohrringe hier subsumiert. Es handelt sich offensichtlich um eine persönliche Ausstattung, die dem Träger eine bestimmte Funktion gab. Sie ist oft auch nur partiell belegt, da es möglicherweise verschiedene Abstufungen gab, oder weil die Norm nicht streng eingehalten werden musste. Man muss sich auch vorstellen, dass dieses Set nur die überlieferten Objekte umfasst, sie sind mit Sicherheit zu ergänzen mit weiteren vergänglichen Zeichen und Symbolen mit denen sich der Träger zu erkennen geben wollte. Einen Eindruck dieser Ausstattung könnten vielleicht die bekannten Stelen von Sion und Aosta geben (DORNHEIM 2004).

4.2. Die Komplementärkeramik

Die zweite Komponente des Glockenbecher-Komplexes wird durch die Kategorie III beschrieben, die die Komplementär-Keramik und die übrigen nicht keramischen Funde umfasst.

Gemäss der oben angeführten Definition sind es die Artefakte, die regionalen Bezug haben, und die der ansässigen Bevölkerung zuzuordnen sind. Sie beinhalten keine Semiotik, sind keine Zeichen, sondern sind alltägliche Objekte und die Keramik ist die Gebrauchsware. Ihre Formen sind vornehmlich durch die unmittelbare Funktion bestimmt und es sind somit Mittel der Subsistenzsicherung, und sie sind Zeugnis einer agrarischen Gemeinschaft.

Daraus ergibt sich auch zwangsläufig die unterschiedliche regionale Ausprägung dieser Artefakte, insbesondere der Komplementär-Keramik und in der Regel haben die Formen auch ihre regionalen Wurzeln (vg. Abb. 2). Erst die gesamte Entität bildet dann die archäologische Manifestation der wirtschaftenden, subsistenzsichernden Bevölkerung und entspricht einer archäologischen Kultur im herkömmlichen Verständnis.

4.3. Die Komponenten des Glockenbecher-Komplexes in einzelnen Regionen.

Die entworfene Gliederung des Materials in Kategorien kann nicht Selbstzweck sein und darf nicht bloss als akademisches Gedankenspiel gesehen werden. Sie hat zum Ziel den gesamten Problemkreis besser zu verstehen. Sie ist folglich nur relevant, wenn sie am Befund getestet wird. Dieser Überprüfung sollen die folgenden Kapitel gewidmet sein, und wir wollen die dargestellte Dichotomie des Glockenbecher-Komplexes in einigen ausgewählten Regionen aufzeigen. Es wird dies in unterschiedlichem Masse gelingen, doch werden wir sehen, dass die beiden Komponenten in fast allen Gebieten vorhanden sind, auch wenn die jeweilige Forschungssituation das Bild vereinzelt verschleiert.

Allerdings beinhaltet die Definition einer Komplementär-Keramik und der Nachweis ihres regionalen Bezugs auch ein taxonomisches Problem: Wenn sie in der jeweiligen regionalen, endneolithischen Kultur wurzelt, bzw. diese regionale, endneolithische Kultur darstellt, später als Bestandteil des Glockenbecher-Komplexes existiert, und in der Folge auch ohne Glockenbecher-Bezug vorkommt, handelt es sich stets um die gleiche archäologische Entität, die in einigen Regionen in Phasen, in anderen als Einheit gesehen wird. Es bestünde eigentlich kein Anlass, sie in Bezug auf den Glockenbecher speziell zu benennen, und genau genommen ist das Glockenbecher-Set dann komplementär zu dieser Entität. Trotzdem wollen wir an der vorgelegten Definition festhalten: Denn die Komplementär-Keramik bezeich-

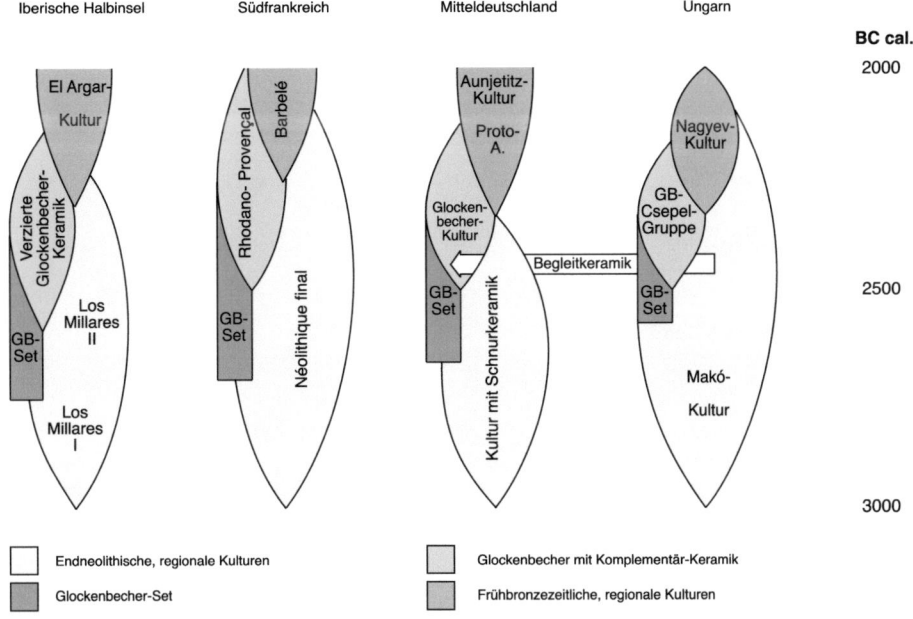

Abb. 4. Ein Spindelmodell der endneolithischen Kulturen in einigen ausgewählten Glockenbecher-Provinzen und die Akkulturation des Glockenbecher-Sets: Dieses hat sich verbreitet und - zunächst abgegrenzt von den einheimischen Kulturen - bestimmte Siedlungslagen besetzt. Es folgt eine Phase der Akkulturation in der die Glockenbecherelemente (oder -Weltanschauung) von der einheimischen Gesellschaft aufgenommen wurde (oder umgekehrt). Dokumentiert ist dies durch den verzierten Glockenbecher und die regionale endneolithische Keramik, die in diesem Zusammenhang taxonomisch zur Komplementärkeramik wird. In einer weiteren Phase werden die beiden Komponenten assimiliert und es entstehen neue archäologische Kulturen, die in der Tradition der Glockenbecher-Kultur stehen.

net nicht eine kulturelle Einheit sondern lediglich ihre Funktion in Bezug auf den Glockenbecher-Impact. Sie ist zudem auch Bestandteil einer regionalen, endneolithischen, bzw. frühbronzezeitlichen Kultur. Diese dialektische Betrachtung soll mit der Grafik (Abb. 4) zum Ausdruck gebracht werden. Sie erweitert das Schema über die Vernetzung der beiden Glockenbecher-Komponenten (Abb. 1) mit dem Hintergrund der Darstellung von archäologischen Kulturen als Spindelmodell.

4.3.1. Östliches Mitteleuropa

Die Theorie der Dichotomie des Glockenbecherkomplexes lässt sich am deutlichsten am Beispiel der Ostgruppe darstellen, weil sich hier die kulturellen Differenzierungen an dem reich belegten und gut publizierten Material paradigmatisch aufzeigen lassen. Zudem liegen mit den zahlreichen Grabfunden auch auswertbare geschlossene Fundkomplexe vor.

Dabei müssen wir die Betrachtungen in der Peripherie der Ostgruppe, in Ungarn, ansetzen, da hier die beschriebene Situation besonders deutlich zu Tage tritt: Dank der Arbeiten von N. Kalicz und R. Kalicz-Schreiber kennen wir die kulturelle

Similar but different. Bell Beakers in Europe

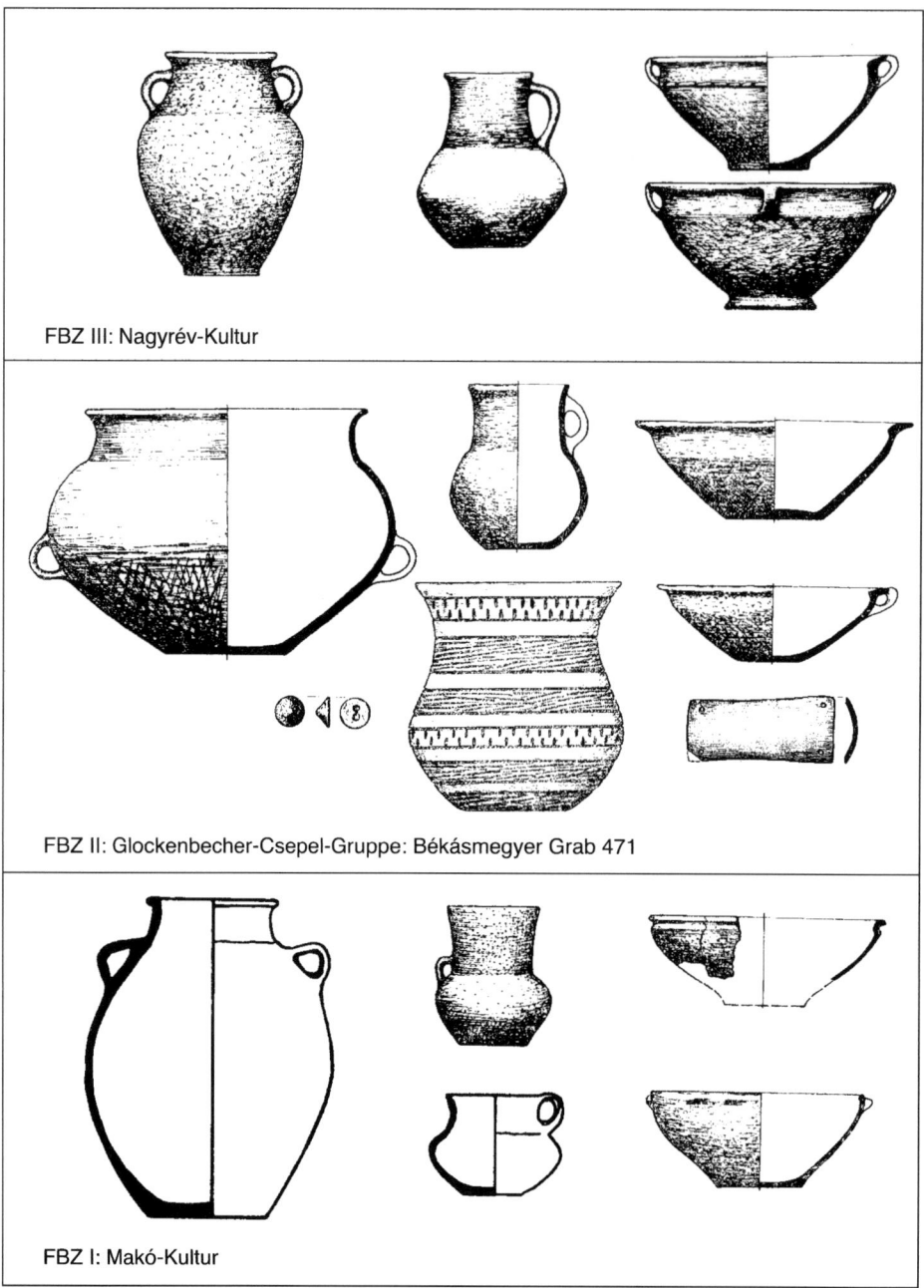

Abb. 5: Die frühbronzezeitliche Entwicklung in Ungarn: Das einheimische Formeninventar der Makó (Zók - Vučedol) - Kultur entspricht in der Frühphase demjenigen der „Begleitkeramik". Ein Teil der Makó-Kultur übernimmt den verzierten Glockenbecher, ihr Formenspektrum wird eine Komplementär-Keramik. Beide Komponenten bilden die Csepel-Gruppe (Funde nach KALICZ 1984).

Abfolge der Kulturen des 3. Jahrtausends im Karpatenbecken gut (KALICZ 1984). Zwar sind die chronologischen Argumente nicht immer erkennbar dargelegt und es scheint, dass es vor allem typologische Kriterien waren, die für die Autoren wegleitend waren. Nach der Kupferzeit, in der das Karpathenbecken Teil einer ägäischen Koine war, entfaltete sich ein grosser karpatenländischer Kulturenkomplex der mit der Vučedol- und Makó-Kultur einsetzt. Diese nach ungarischer Terminologie schon als Frühbronzezeit I bezeichnete Entwicklung setzt sich typologisch kontinuierlich fort in der Frühphase der Nagyrév-Kultur und leitet über in die mittelbronzezeitliche Madarovce- und Vatya-Kultur. Die verschiedenen Kulturen sind charakterisiert durch die formalen Veränderungen einiger Grundformen wie der Schale, der Schüssel, dem Topf und vor allem dem Krug (Abb. 5). In diese klare und typologisch nachvollziehbare Abfolge dringt das Glockenbecher-Phänomen ein und wird von den einheimischen Kulturen akkulturiert. Ein beispielhafter Beleg dafür ist das Grab Nr. 471 von Békásmegyer. Als Beigaben enthält es neben Armschutzplatte, V-Knopf und zwei typischen Glockenbechern, drei Schalen, eine Schüssel und ein Krug, die alle für die frühe Nagyrév-Kultur, bzw. ganz allgemein für die frühe Bronzezeit im östlichen Mitteleuropa definierend sind (KALICZ-SCHREIBER 1984, Tf. 31).

Die Formen der Begleitkeramik, bzw. der Komplementärkeramik, sind also schon vor dem Erscheinen der Glockenbecher als einheimisches Element vorhanden und werden von diesen übernommen, wobei allerdings nicht zu entscheiden ist, wer hier die gebende, wer die aufnehmende Gemeinschaft ist – war das Glockenbecherphänomen so stark und dominierend, dass es andere Gesellschaften geprägt hat, oder so attraktiv, dass es von anderen Gemeinschaften übernommen werden wollte? Jedenfalls wird damit das typische Formenspektrum Schale, Schüssel, Krug als sog. Begleitkeramik der Ostgruppe intergrierter Bestandteil des Glockenbecher-Komplexes und gemäss den oben beschriebenen terminologischen Festlegungen vervollständigt sie das Glockenbecher-Phänomen zur Glockenbecher-Kultur (ENGELHARDT 1991)

Dieses im Karpathenbecken herausgearbeitete Modell kann in allen Regionen der Ostgruppe angewandt werden. Allein ausserhalb von Ungarn kennen wir keine vor-glockenbecherzeitliche Keramik der gleichen Ausprägung, so dass wir annehmen müssen, dass sich die Begleitkeramik vom Karpathenbecken ausgehend nach Westen und Nordwesten im Zuge einer frühbronzezeitlichen Expansionswelle ausgebreitet hat und in Mitteldeutschland und Bayern das Glockenbecher-Phänomen akkulturiert hat (STRAHM 2001, 181). Die Glockenbecher-Kultur in Niederösterreich und die Csepel-Gruppe in Transdanubien würden dann als eine Art östlicher „Rückstrom" zu bezeichnen sein.

4.3.2. Nordwesteuropa

Die Aufgliederung des Glockenbecherkomplexes in heterogene Komponenten ist in seiner Nordwestgruppe bei erster Betrachtung nicht erkennbar, die Theorie der Dichotomie scheint nicht anwendbar. Es gibt zwar Glockenbecher, die der Definition entsprechen, auch das Glockenbecher-Set liegt als geschlossener Komplex vor (DRENTH / HOGESTIJN 2001, 326), aber Mischformen und -kombinationen sind in überwiegender Zahl vorhanden. Insbesondere sind es v.a. die Verbindungen mit der

Kultur mit Schnurkeramik, die das kulturelle Bild prägen. Sie haben auch das sog. „holländische Modell" generiert: Da man aufgrund, der damaligen 14C-Daten eine vermeintlich allmähliche Ablösung der Schnurkeramik durch die Glockenbecher-Einflüsse zu erkennen glaubte, leitete man auch den Glockenbecher aus der Schnurkeramik ab (VAN DER BEEK / FOKKENS 2001, 301). Die Forschung, die sehr bald diese neue Theorie verallgemeinerte, suchte den Ursprung der gesamten Glockenbecher-Erscheinung in dieser Region und übersah, dass diese Abfolge - wenn sie denn richtig war - allein für die Niederlande Gültigkeit haben konnte. In anderen Gegenden setzt die Glockenbecher-Entwicklung früher ein, so dass in den Niederlanden lediglich eine Verbindung, bzw. Aufnahme einheimischer Elemente durch die Glockenbecher-Gemeinschaft in Erwägung gezogen werden kann (zur Kritik am holländischen Modell vgl. STRAHM 1979). Die Aufgliederung in Komponenten ist nicht offenkundig aber eine Kombination von Elementen verschiedener kultureller Herkunft ist auch hier erkennbar.

Klarer ist die Situation auf den britischen Inseln: Beispielhaft sind die Befunde von Monknewtown oder Swarkeston 4 Barrow, Derbyshire (GREENFIELD / APSIMON 1960), wo typische Becher mit einer einheimischen Grobkeramik vergesellschaftet sind. C. Burgess hat darin schon 1976 eine regionale Komponente erkannt, die sich mit dem Glockenbecher-Package verbindet: „Here, as with many 'Beaker domestic ware' assemblages there is a combination of good Beaker vessels with Beaker traits of varying importance, and a quantity of sherds possessing nothing in their form or decoration not already present in later Neolithic ceramics. Instead of scrutinising these assemblages assiduously for signs of Beaker influence, stamping them automatically with a Beaker label, the products of separate Beaker communities, the time has come to re-examine them with an alternative hypothesis in mind: that these are indigenous domestic assemblages in which Beaker is only one element, often not the largest, although it may be the most attractive and at present is certainly the most easily recognisable." (BURGESS / SHENNAN 1976, 320s.).

4.3.3. Frankreich

In Frankreich ist die Situation der Forschung auch nicht unbedingt geschaffen, die Komponenten des Glockenbecher-Komplexes direkt herauszuarbeiten. Doch führt gerade hier die unsere Theorie der Dichotomie des Glockenbecher-Komplexes zu einem besseren Verständnis des Übergangs vom Neolithikum zur Bronzezeit. Es sind mehrere Gründe, die einer differenzierten Analyse entgegenstehen. Zunächst gibt es in Frankreich in der gesamten Urgeschichte kaum je einheitliche Entwicklungen. Erst mit der Latène-Zeit bildet sich eine kulturelle Geschlossenheit heraus. Doch gerade das Endneolithikum und die Frühbronzezeit zeichnen sich durch eine starke regionale Diversität aus und teilweise sind die Kulturen sogar nur periphere Manifestationen von ausserhalb. Andererseits stehen hier die Komponenten des Glockenbecher-Komplexes in starker gegenseitiger Vernetzung und in intensiver Wechselwirkung mit den einheimischen Gruppierungen, so dass eine Entflechtung ohne theoretische Vorgaben kaum möglich ist. Dies ist nicht zuletzt auch bedingt durch die spröde Quellenlage: In Frankreich gibt es nur wenig geschlossene Fundkomplexe dieser Zeit, Einzelgräber fehlen grösstenteils, fast alle Befunde enthalten beide Glockenbecher-Komponenten, eine regionale Entflechtung ist somit nur auf indirektem Wege möglich, indem man zunächst die eindeutig einheimische Komponente bestimmt. Diese ist gut aufgearbeitet, hat aber bisher trotz der zahlreichen modernen Ausgrabungen recht wenig Material erbracht, so dass einzelne Gruppen nur schwer zu definieren sind. Mit Hilfe dieses methodischen Vorgehens erzielte O. Lemercier in seiner Dissertation: „Le campaniforme dans le sud-est de la France" beachtliche Erkenntnisse über die Zusammensetzung des gesamten Glockenbecher-Komplexes. Er konnte die schon bisher in der Forschung skizzierten Stile klar beschreiben und unterschied (LEMERCIER 2002, 76), den internationalen und den AOC-Becher neben einem vom internationalen abgeleiteten „style pointillé géometrique" für die älteren Phasen, und später seien unter dem Einfluss von aussen die regionalen Glockenbecher-Facies „Rhodano-provençal" und „Barbelé" entstanden, die als selbständige archäologische Kulturen zu betrachtet werden müssen. Für unsere Fragestellung sind die typologischen Vergleiche der den frühen Glockenbecher begleitenden Keramik entscheidend (vgl. Kp. 3.2.4.). Sie gliedert sich in eine sehr feine Keramik mit glochenbecherischen Formen (d.h. es handelt sich um unverzierte Glockenbecher), und in eine Fein- und Grobkeramik, die ein lokales Formenspektrum aufweist. Dieses findet sich in der Rhône-Ouvèze Gruppe wieder (CAULIEZ 2001). Die Analyse von O. Lemercier konnte also eine lokale Komponente aufzeigen, die den internationalen, bzw. den davon abgeleiteten Becher begleitet. dies bedeutet, dass wir auch in Südfrankreich eine Unterscheidung zwischen der Komponente Glockenbecher-Set (hier vertreten durch den Standard) und der Komponente Glockenbecher mit lokaler Keramik, der Komplementär-Keramik, erkennen können. Die Differenzierung wird auch in dem Schema von O. Lemercier, das hier vereinfacht wiedergegeben wird, deutlich (Abb. 6). In Südfrankreich drängen die schwierigen Befunde die Theorie der Dichotomie des Glockenbecher-Komplexes zwar nicht gerade auf, aber sie führt zu einem schlüssigen Bild der Entwicklung.

4.3.4. Iberische Halbinsel

Die Iberische Halbinsel hat in der Glockenbecher-Forschung schon immer eine besondere Stellung eingenommen, da dort nicht nur äusserst bedeutungsvolle und vielfältige Funde entdeckt worden sind, sondern weil man dort auch beharrlich den Ursprung des Glockenbechers suchte. Die Keramik ist reich verziert und die typischen horizontalen Stempelmuster finden sich nicht nur auf den Bechern, sondern auch auf Schalen und Schüsseln, so dass man den Eindruck einer stilistisch geschlossenen Entität gewann. Das Formenspektrum, das durch die Mannigfaltigkeit der Typen breiter als in anderen Regionen ist, schien denn auch eine umfassend belegte archäologische Kultur zu repräsentieren. Eine Diskussion über verschiedene Komponenten des Glockenbecher-Komplexes drängte sich hier nicht auf, und kürzlich formulierte M. Kunst dies folgendermassen: „Während im übrigen Europa die 'Begleitkeramik' der Glockenbecher eine grosse Rolle spielt, ist ein solcher oder ähnlicher Begriff auf der Iberischen Halbinsel nicht vorhanden, aber auch nicht angemessen." (KUNST 2001a, 94). Die genuin glockenbecherische Komponente ist hier vielgestaltiger als anderswo, und sie beschränkt sich nicht auf ein Set oder „package" von wenigen Formen. Dennoch handelt es sich dabei hauptsächlich um

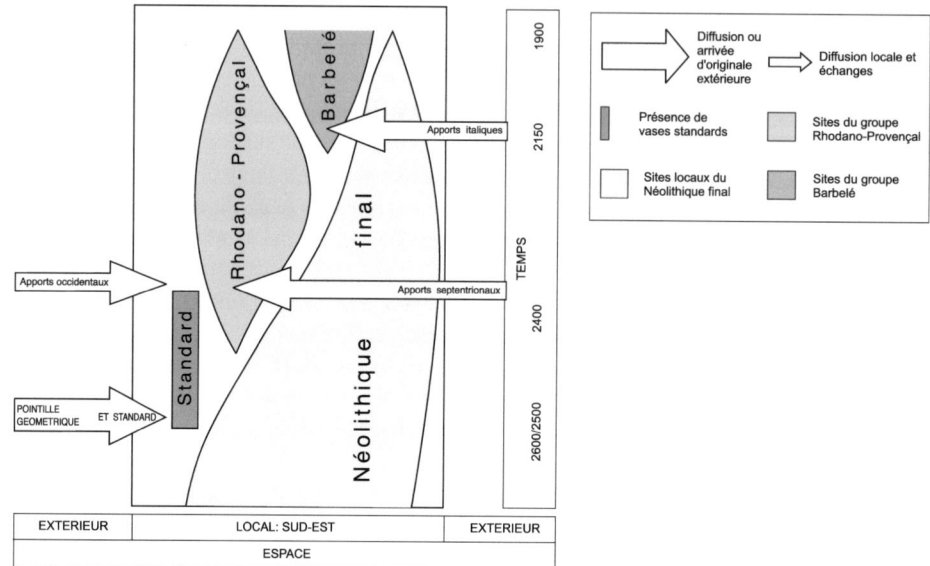

Abb. 6. Die Entwicklung der Kulturen des jüngeren Endneolithikum in Südfrankreich: Im Néolithique final breitet sich der „Standard-Glockenbecher" von Westen her aus und bildet den „style pointillé-géometrique" dessen Komplementär-Keramik aus der lokalen Gruppe Rhône-Ouvèze abgeleitet ist. Später sind daraus die regionalen Glockenbecher-Kulturen mit dem „style Rhodano-Provençal" und dem schon frühbronzezeitlichen „style barbelé" entstanden, während das Néolithique final daneben weiterexistierte.

Funde mit besonderer Symbolik, denen man grossen Prestigewert zuordnen möchte, und sie werfen die Frage ihrer besonderen Bedeutung auf.

Auf der anderen Seite wird gerade in neuester Zeit immer wieder die Kontinuität der spätneolithischen Kulturen, die bis in die Frühbronzezeit andauert, hervorgehoben, und sie kann gut belegt werden. So hat etwa M. Carrilero Millan in einer stratigraphischen Grabung in Ciavieja (Almeria) vorglockenbecherzeitliche Schichten mit einem Los Millares I-Formeninventar untersucht. Die gleichen Formen finden sich dann in den glockenbecherischen Schichten, teilweise mit Glockenbecher-Verzierung, zusammen mit echten Glockenbechern. Dieses Formenspektrum setzt sich dann fort in der El Argar-Kultur, so dass man folgende Entwicklung nachzeichnen könnte (Abb. 7).

Ein gleiche Abfolge postuliert auch M. Kunst für Portugal, indem er schreibt: „There are typological similarities between Portuguese earlier Chalcolithic pottery and Bell Beaker ware, especially, on the one hand, between 'beakers' and the cylindrical 'copos', and, on the other hand, between 'Palmela bowls' and the typical Chalcolithic 'plates' with thick rims..." (KUNST 2001b, 84).

Die angeführten Befunde und Feststellungen belegen, dass auf der Iberischen Halbinsel die gleiche Situation vorliegt wie in anderen Regionen. Der Glockenbecher-Komplex besteht auch hier aus zwei Komponenten, aus einem glockenbecherspezifischen Ensemble, das formenreicher als anderswo ist, und aus einer Kom-

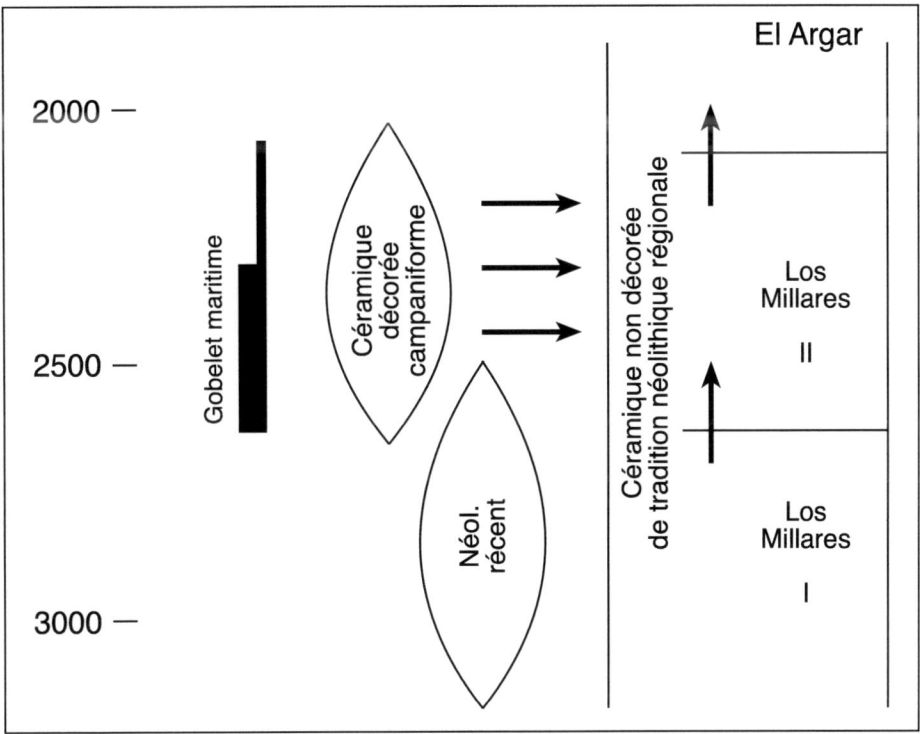

Abb. 7. Entwurf der Darstellung der Kulturentwicklung in Südostspanien: Neben dem älteren Endneolithikum, dessen „Céramique non décorée de tradition régionale" bis in die El Argar-Kultur weitergeführt wird, erscheint mit Los Millares II der maritime Glockenbecher mit einer „Céramique à technologie fine". Gleichzeitig entsteht eine regionale „Céramique décoré campaniforme" (vgl. auch Abb. 4; nach M. CARRILERO MILLAN 1989–90).

plementär-Keramik, die die einheimische, spätneolithische und frühchalkolithische Tradition fortsetzt, die teilweise auch mit Glockenbecher-Mustern verziert wird und in die Argar-Kultur überleitet. Die Theorie der Dichotomie des Glockenbecher-Komplexes ist somit auch hier anwendbar.

4.3.5. Italien

Allein in Italien sind die Verhältnisse bezüglich der Komplementär-Keramik noch unklar. Dies mag zum einen daran liegen, dass die Glockenbecher-Elemente an sich hier äusserst komplex und vielgestaltig sind, zum andern daran, dass die Befunde auch schwer zu interpretieren sind. Es gibt zwar in Norditalien ein keramisches Spektrum, das der Begleitkeramik der Ostgruppe entspricht (NICOLIS 2001, 212), das jedoch infolge der fehlenden eindeutigen Vergesellschaftung ebenso als frühbronzezeitlich angesehen werden kann. Auch die sog. „Ceramica alla squame" die teilweise mit Glockenbechern vergesellschaftet erscheint, könnte die Funktion einer Komplementär-Keramik innehaben, doch gibt es auch hier zu wenig klare

Similar but different. Bell Beakers in Europe

Befunde. Wichtig sind v. a. die Belege der neuen Ausgrabungen von Neto – Via Verga in Sesto Fiorentino, wo maritime und AOC-Becher mit einer lokalen Einstichverzierten Keramik vergesellschaftet sind (SARTI 1997, 367). Sie bezeugen eine Verbindung von Glockenbechern mit einheimischer Komplementär-Keramik. Der in diesem Band vorliegende Beitrag von L. Sarti und V. Leonini wird hier weiterführen und eine neue Grundlage für unsere Fragestellung schaffen.

5. Ein Ansatz für die Deutung

Es war Zielsetzung der vorangegangen Ausführungen, die Artefakte, die eine interkulturelle Entität von Prestigeobjekten, d.h. das Glockenbecher-Set, begleiten, zu bestimmen und ihre originären Wurzeln zu untersuchen. Damit soll ein besseres Verständnis des gesamten Glockenbecher-Komplexes gewonnen werden. Es konnte dabei gezeigt werden, dass es in jeder Region eine einheimische Komponente gibt, die sich in erster Linie an der Keramik, die wir als Komplementär-Keramik bezeichnet haben, festmachen lässt. Damit ist auch offenkundig, dass es keine allgemeine und überregional einheitliche Begleitkeramik gibt.

Mit dieser Aufgliederung in Komponenten, d.h. der Theorie der Dichotomie des Glockenbecher-Komplexes kann die gesamte Erscheinung m.E. eindeutig und anschaulich beschrieben und ein neuer Ansatz für eine Interpretation gewonnen werden. Dies soll in einem kurzen Ausblick noch angedeutet werden.

Nachdem die beiden Komponenten des Glockenbecher-Komplexes unterschiedlich definiert worden sind, beruht auch ihre Interpretation auf unterschiedlichen Voraussetzungen. Die erste Komponente, das Glockenbecher-Set ist seit seiner ersten Beschreibung durch S.J. Shennan schon oft behandelt worden und hat unterschiedliche Deutungen erfahren (SHENNAN 1975; BURGESS / SHENNAN 1976; CLARKE 1976; SHERRAT 1987; STRAHM (ed.) 1995; BENZ / VAN WILLIGEN (eds) 1998; GALLAY 2001; STRAHM 2002). Man war sich stets darin einig, dass es sich um ein Ensemble von Objekten mit bestimmtem Symbolgehalt handelt, das ausserhalb der Tradition einer herkömmlichen archäologischen Kultur steht. Man hat es mit dem Peyote-Kult in Mexiko verglichen (Burgess), mit dem Interaction Sphere Model zu erklären versucht (Shennan) oder als Exchange-Network gedeutet. Es sei Indiz von kultischen Trinksitten mit euphorisierenden Getränken (Sherratt) oder eine Vernetzung von sozioökonomischen Réseaux archäologisch-linguistischer Entitäten (Gallay). Wir haben versucht einige Wertvorstellungen, die mit dem Set zum Ausdruck gebracht werden sollen, zu benennnen und dieses Phänomen als Crémade-Modell bezeichnet (Abb. 8; BENZ et al. 1998, 181 ff.; STRAHM 2002, 183ff. dort auch die Hintergründe der Entstehung des Modells). Wir betrachten das Set als archäologischen Niederschlag eines neuen Wissens, einer Ideologie. Den eigentlichen Inhalt dieser Ideologie, die sowohl einen politischen, ökonomischen wie auch religiösen Hintergrund haben kann, werden wir wohl nie erfahren können, wir können nur festhalten, dass sie offenbar sehr erfolgreich war. Ihre materielle Manifestation ist massgebend, ihre Wirkung ein Phänomen, weshalb wir auch von einem Glockenbecher-Phänomen sprechen.

Dieses neue Wissen hat sich sehr schnell ausgebreitet, war sehr dynamisch und überzeugend oder attraktiv und wurde bereitwillig aufgenommen. Belegt wird dies

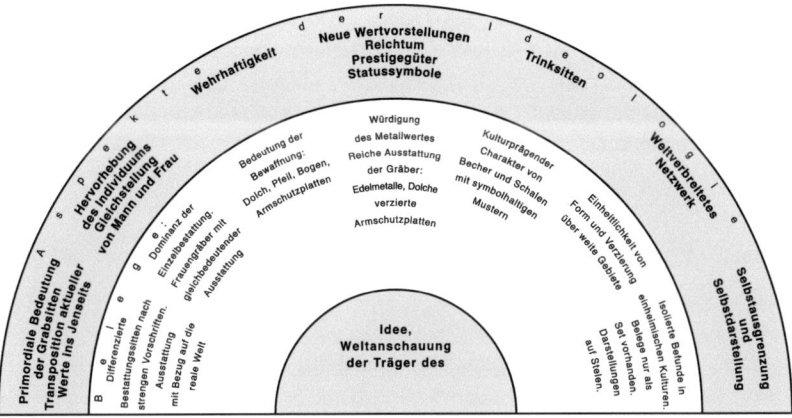

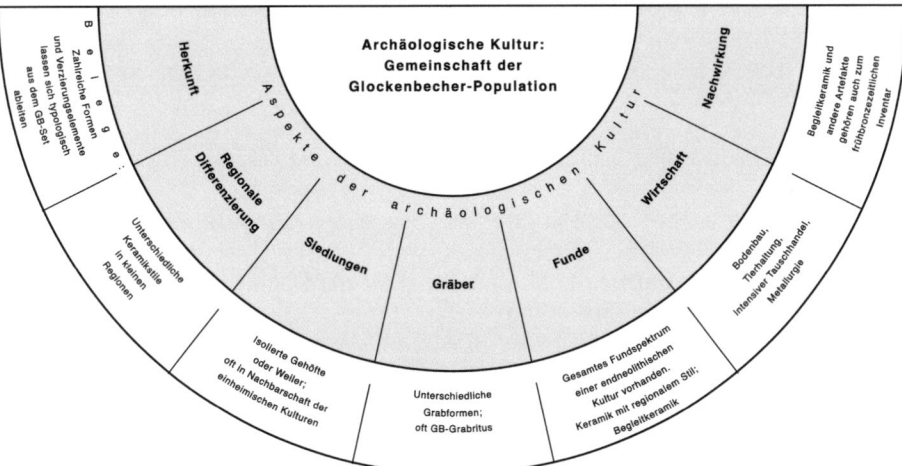

Abb. 8. Das Crémade-Modell: Graphische Darstellung der Werte, die die glockenbecherische Weltanschauung mitprägen und der darus hervorgegangenen Glockenbecher-Kultur, die aus der Akkulturation mit den regionalen endneolithischen Kulturen entstanden ist.

durch die zweite Komponente des Glockenbecher-Komplexes, durch die Komplementär-Keramik. Sie ist regional differenziert, steht jeweils in der Tradition der einheimischen archäologischen Kultur, die allerdings in einigen Gebieten noch ungenügend herausgearbeitet ist. Die Komplementär-Keramik, die in der Ostgruppe schon lange als Begleitkeramik beschrieben worden ist, belegt die intensive Akkulturation des Glockenbecher-Phänomens, indem sie glockenbecherische Elemente aufnimmt, d.h. die einheimische Keramik mit glockenbecherischen Mustern verziert oder Typen des Glockenbecher-Sets in das gesamte Formeninventar integriert. Die beiden Komponenten, Glockenbecher-Set und Komplementär-Keramik, bilden eine neue Entität, und in unserer Wahrnehmung wandelt sich dadurch das Glockenbecher-Phänomen zur Glockenbecher-Kultur, die damit eine umfassend belegte archäologische Kultur wird, die die archäologische Manifestation einer agrarisch wirtschaftenden Gemeinschaft repräsentiert.

Literaturverzeichnis

BENZ M. / GRAMSCH A. / WIERMANN R. / VAN WILLIGEN S. 1998. Rethinking Bell Beakers. In: BENZ M. / VAN WILLIGEN S. (eds), *Some New Approaches to the Bell Beaker 'Phenomenon'. Lost Paradise...?* BAR International Series 690. Oxford, 181-192.

BENZ M. / VAN WILLIGEN S. (eds) 1998. *Some New Approaches to the Bell Beaker 'Phenomenon'. Lost Paradise...?* BAR International Series 690. Oxford.

BESSE M. / STRAHM CH. 2001. The Components of the Bell Beaker Complex, In: NICOLIS F. (ed.), *Bell Beakres Today. Pottery, people, culture, symbols in prehistoric Europe.* Trento, 103-110.

BESSE M. 1996. *Le Campaniforme en France:* analyse de la céramique d'accompagnement. BAR International Series 635. Oxford.

2003. L'Europe du 3e millénaire avant notre ère: les céramiques communes au Campaniforme. *Cahiers d'archéologie romande* 94. Lausanne.

BURGESS C. / MIKET R. (eds) 1976. *Settlement and Economy in the third and second millenia B.C.* BAR 33. Oxford.

BURGESS C. / SHENNAN, S.J. 1976. The beaker phenomenon: Some suggestions. In: BURGESS C. / MIKET R. (eds) *Settlement and Economy in the third and second millenia B.C.* BAR 33. Oxford. 309-326.

CARRILERO MILLAN M. 1989-90. *Ciavieja (El Ejido).* Cuadernos de Preistoria de la Universidad de Granada 14-15, 109-136.

CAULIEZ J. 2001. *La céramique du Néolithique final du Sud-Est de la France.* Maîtrise d'Archéologie, Université de Provence.

CLARKE, D.L. 1976 *The Beaker network -social and economic models.* In: LANTING, J.N. / J.D. VAN DER WAALS (eds), Glockenbechersymposion. Oberried 1974, 459-488.

D'ANNA A. 1995 Le Néolithique final en Provence. In: Voruz J.-L. (ed), *Chronologies néolithiques.* Ambérieu-en-Bugey., 265-286.

DEMOULE J.-P. / GUILAINE J. (eds) 1986. *Le Néolithique de la France. Hommage à Gérard Bailloud.* Paris.

DORNHEIM S. 2004. *Voreisenzeitliche anthropomorphe Stellen Südfrankreichs, Norditaliens und des Wallis: Ein einheitliches Phänomen?* Magisterarbeit Freiburg SS 2003.

DRENTH E. / HOGESTIJN, W.J.H. 2001 *The Bell Beaker Culture in the Netherlands: the state of research in 1998.* In: NICOLIS F. (ed.) Bell Beakers Today. Pottery, people, culture, symbols, in prehistorical Europe. Trento, 309-332.

ENGELHARDT B. 1991. *Beiträge zur Kenntnis der Glockenbecherkultur in Niederbayern.* Vorträge 9. Archäologentag Deggendorf, 65-84.

FISCHER U. 1975. Zur Deutung der Glockenbecherkultur. *Nassauische Annalen* 86, 1-13.

GALLAY A. 1979. Le Phénomène Campaniforme: une nouvelle hypothèse historique. *Archives Suisses d'Anthrop. gén.* 43,2, 231-258.

1986. Autonomie du Campaniforme rhodano-rhénan. In: DEMOULE J.-P. / GUILAINE J. *Le Néolithique de la France,* 431-446.

1988. Le Phénomène Campaniforme: l'heure des remises en question. *Arenera* 5, 6-13.

2001. *L'énigme campaniforme*. In: Nicolis F. (ed.), *Bell Beakers today. Pottery, people, culture, symbols in prehistoric Europe*. Trento, 41-57.

Greenfield E. / Apsimon A.M., 1960. The excavation of Barrow 4 at Swarkeston, Derbyshire. *Derbyshire Archeological Journal* 80.

Hájek L. 1966. Die älteste Phase der Glockenbecherkultur in Böhmen und Mähren. *Památky archeologické* 57, 210-241.

Kalicz N. 1984. *Die Makó-Kultur*. In: Tasic N. (ed.), *Kulturen der Frühbronzezeit des Karpatenbeckens und Nordbalkans*. Beograd, 93-107.

Kalicz-Schreiber R. 1984. *Komplex der Nagyrév-Kultur*. In: Tasic N. (ed.), *Kulturen der Frühbronzezeit des Karpatenbeckens und Nordbalkans*. Beograd, 133-190.

Kraft G. 1947. Neue Glockenbecherfunde am Oberrhein. *Badische Fundberichte* 17,1941-47, 127-137.

Kunst M. 2001a. Die Kupferzeit der Iberischen Halbinsel. In: *Hispania Antiqua*. Denkmäler der Frühzeit, 67-99.

2001b. *Invasion? Fashion? Social Rank?* In: Nicolis F. (ed.), *Bell Beakers Today. Potterey, people, culture symbols in prehistoric Europe*. Trento, 81-90.

Lanting, J. / Van Der Waals D. 1976. Beaker culture relations in the Lower Rhine Bassin. In: Lanting, J.N. / van der Waals, J.D. (eds), *Glockenbechersymposion*. Oberried 1974, 1-80.

Lemercier O. 2002. *Le Campaniforme dans le sud-est de la France*. Thèse, Université de Provence, Aix-Marseille I.

Malmer M. 1962 *Jungneolithische Studien*. Lund.

Müller J. (ed.) 2002. *Vom Endneolithikum zur Frühbronzezeit: Muster des sozialen Wandels*. UPA Bd. 90. Bonn.

Neustupný E. 1972. Das jüngere Äneolithikum in Mitteleuropa. *Musaica* 23, 91-120.

Nicolis F. (ed.) 2001 *Bell Beakers today. Pottery, people, culture, symbols in prehistoric Europe*. Proceedings of the International Colloquium. Riva del Gaarda 1998. Trento.

Nicolis F. 2001. Some observations on the cultural setting of the Bell beakers of Northern Italy. In: Nicolis F. (ed.), *Bell Beakers today. Pottery, people, culture, symbols in prehistoric Europe*. Trento, 207-227.

Salanova L. 2000. *La question du Campaniforme en France et dans les îles anglo-normandes*. Paris.

Sangmeister E. 1972. Sozial-ökonomische Aspekte der Glockenbecherkultur. *Homo* 72, 188-203.

Sarti L. 1997. Il Campaniforme di Neto-Via Verga a Sesto Fiorentino. *Rivista di Scienze Preistoriche* 48, 367-398.

Schránil J. 1928. *Die Vorgeschichte Böhmens und Mährens*. Berlin.

Shennan S. J. 1975. Die soziale Bedeutung der Glockenbecherkultur in Mitteleuropa. *Acta Archaeologica Carpatica 15, 173-179*.

1976. Bell Beakers and their Context in Central Europe. In: Lanting, J.N. / van der Waals, J.D. (eds), *Glockenbechersymposion*. Oberried 1974, 231-240.

Sherratt A. 1987. Cups that cheered. In: Waldren R.C. / Kennard R.C. (eds) *Bell Beakres of the West Mediterranean*. BAR, International Series 331. Oxford, 81-114.

Stocký A. 1926. *La Bohème préhistorique*. Praha.

Strahm Ch. 1979. Die Kalibration und die Herkunft der Glockenbecher. *Archives Suissses d'Anthropologie générale 43, 2, 285-293*.

1995. (ed.) *Das Glockenbecher-Phänomen*. FAS 2. Freiburg.

2001. Das Kulturenkonzept und das Periodisierungskonzept. In: *Hemmenhofener Skripte* 2, 177-184.

2002. Tradition und Wandel der sozialen Strukturen vom 3. zum 2. vorchr. Jahrtausend. In: MÜLLER J. (ed.), *Vom Endneolithikum zur Frühbronzezeit: Muster sozialen Wandels.* UPA 90. Bonn, 175-194.

TASIC N. (ed.), 1984. *Kulturen der Frühbronzezeit des Karpatenbeckens und Nordbalkans.* Beograd.

VAN DER BEEK Z. / FOKKENS H. 2001. 24years after Oberried: the 'Dutch Model' reconsidered. In: NICOLIS F. (ed.), *Bell Beakers Today. Potterey, people, culture symbols in prehistoric Europe.* Trento, 301-308.

VORUZ J.-L. (ed.) 1995. *Chronologies néolithiques.* Ambérieu-en-Bugey.

Similar but Different. Bell Beakers in Europe
Czebreszuk J. (ed.)
Poznań 2004

BELL BEAKER COMMON WARE DURING THE THIRD MILLENNIUM BC IN EUROPE

Marie Besse (Geneva and Neuchâtel, Switzerland)

Summary

The Bell Beaker Culture embodies the transition between the Neolithic and the Bronze Age during the third millennium BC. It is generally defined by different types of decorated pottery, by the undecorated Bell Beakers and by a set of artefacts such as archer's arm-guards, Palmela points, tongued daggers and arciform pendants. Another pottery style is associated with this culture: the Begleitkeramik, or common ware.

Although several studies have been carried out on this time period, it is still badly defined as a whole. Does it represent an ideology? Populations? Migrations of one or several human groups? In one or several peopling waves? Coming from and going where?

This study attempts to answer these questions based on Bell Beaker common ware, despite the heterogeneous nature of archaeological documentation, whereas preceding research has focalised on decorated pottery.

Our research is based on the study of Bell Beaker sites with common ware in continental Europe. Eight hundred sites have been studied, located in the eleven following countries: Germany, Austria, Belgium, France, Hungary, Italy, the Netherlands, Poland, the Czech Republic, Slovakia and Switzerland. The pottery was grouped in eighty-three types. Preferential associations of these pottery types with a particular type of site (settlement, grave, deposit) as well as their geographical distribution, have made it possible to interpret synchronically the cultural components acting during the third millennium BC in Europe. Furthermore, to determine the geographic zones from which originate some components, the origin of the main pottery types was sought for in the Late Neolithic substratum. Three cultural domains were discovered: the eastern Domain, centred on the Czech Republic, the northern Domain, centred on the Netherlands, and the southern domain, including France and northern Italy. Thus, the transition mechanisms between the Late Neolithic and the Bell Beaker Culture are very different from one domain to another. The cultural changes are so important in the southern Domain that one can invoke an important (population?) renewal, whereas the eastern and northern Domains are characterised by transition without a major discontinuity.

This study has made it possible to propose a synthesis of the pottery components in Europe during the third millennium BC, and also to differentiate the geographical areas responsible for their formation.

Introduction

The Bell Beaker Culture embodies the transition between the Neolithic and the Bronze Age during the third millennium BC. It is generally defined by different types of decorated pottery, by undecorated Bell Beakers, and by a set of artefacts such as archer's arm-guards, Palmela points, tongued daggers and arciform pendants. Another pottery style is associated with this culture: the Begleitkeramik, or common ware.

Although several studies have been carried out on this time period, it is still badly defined as a whole. Does it represent an ideology? Populations? Migrations of one or several human groups? In one or several peopling waves? Coming from and going where?

This study attempts to answer these questions based on Bell Beaker common ware, despite the heterogeneous nature of archaeological documentation, whereas preceding research has focalised on decorated pottery.

The relation with the substrate where the Bell Beaker Culture emerged and developed needs to be studied systematically. In all of Bell Beaker Europe – with the relative exception of Corded Ware pottery distribution – there is a discontinuity between pottery from the regional substrate and Bell Beaker decorated pottery. In effect, not a single pottery belonging to the cultures of the regional Late Neolithic or Chalcolithic carries the same decorations as those belonging to the Bell Beaker Culture. This gives reason to wonder whether there exists Bell Beaker common ware of a type already present within the regional substrate (Late Neolithic or Chalcolithic), that is, if there may be a relationship between Late Neolithic and Bell Beaker Cultures based on the common ware.

Archaeologists generally discern three categories of Bell Beaker objects according to the context of their discovery (BESSE / STRAHM 2001). Bell Beaker pottery consists, on one hand, of *decorated Bell Beaker Culture*; this is the standard defined by Laure Salanova (SALANOVA 2000) (category 1), and on the other, of *decorated Bell Beaker pottery of the regional facies* (category 2).

We also admit that common ware consists on one hand of *Bell Beaker common ware* (category 2) and on the other, of *Bell Beaker common ware of regional tradition* (category 3).

Methods

We have built a dataset of 800 sites located in Germany (n=283), Austria (n=18), Belgium (n=6), France (n=140), Hungary (n=13), Northern Italy (n=34), the Netherlands (n=7), Poland (n=18), the Czech Republic (n=274), Slovakia (n=1) and Switzerland (n=6) (BESSE 2001) (Fig. 1).

We have described the common ware from each site according to pottery types. We defined 83 types (BESSE 2001, Fig. 47), which we compared, at each site, to pottery from the regional Late Neolithic substrate, which made it possible to differentiate Bell Beaker common ware from pottery of regional traditions.

According to the frequency of each pottery type in a known context, we determined main and secondary types. For the graves, the main types are those present at 25 sites at least. However, this limit was fixed at 10 sites for the settlements. In this way, we selected 26 main pottery types (Fig. 2). The 57 remaining types are considered as being secondary.

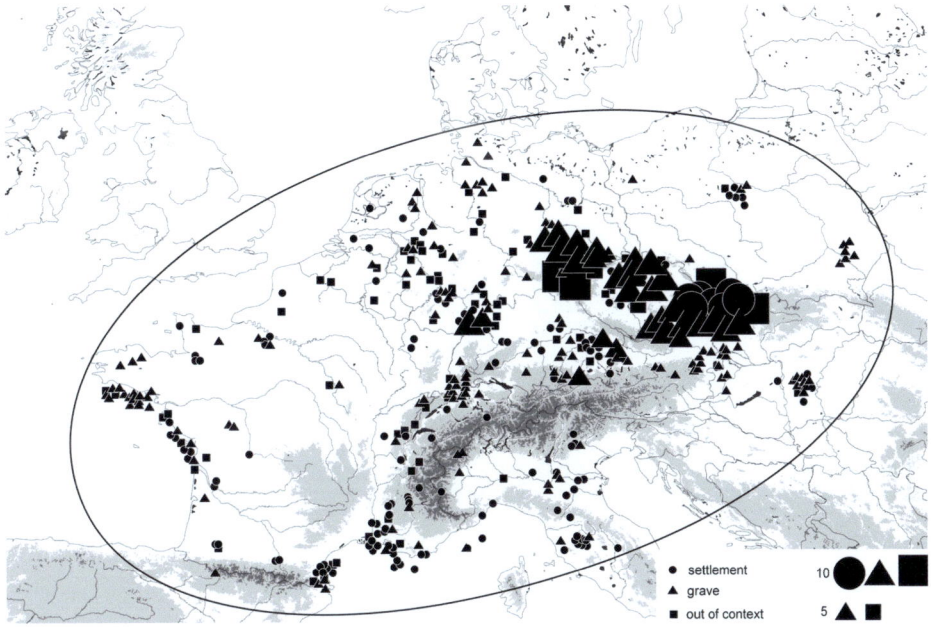

Fig. 1. Map of the geographic distribution of the sites with Bell Beaker common ware in continental Europe.

Main pottery types (n=26): geographical distribution

Type 1: undecorated Bell Beaker, tall type. S-shaped profile. Generally flat-based. The ratio of the height over the body diameter is greater than one

Type 1 has been identified at 66 sites, including 43 graves, 19 settlements and 4 discoveries out of context. This pottery type is not present in Austria, Belgium, Hungary and Slovakia. It is most frequently encountered in Germany and in Western France, and most often associated with a funerary context, with the exception of southern and central France, where it is found in settlements.

Type 2: undecorated Bell Beaker, low type. S-shaped profile. Generally flat-based. The ratio of the height over the body diameter is equal to or less than one

Type 2 has been identified at 173 sites, including 116 graves, 36 settlements, and 21 sites out of context. It is one of the most frequent pottery types, particularly in the region of Elbe-Saale in Germany where it is found inside graves. It is also present in the South of Germany and in the Czech Republic. In Moravia, it is equally represented in settlements and graves.

Type 4: edge underlined by a cordon which is most often triangular in section

129

Similar but Different. Bell Beakers in Europe

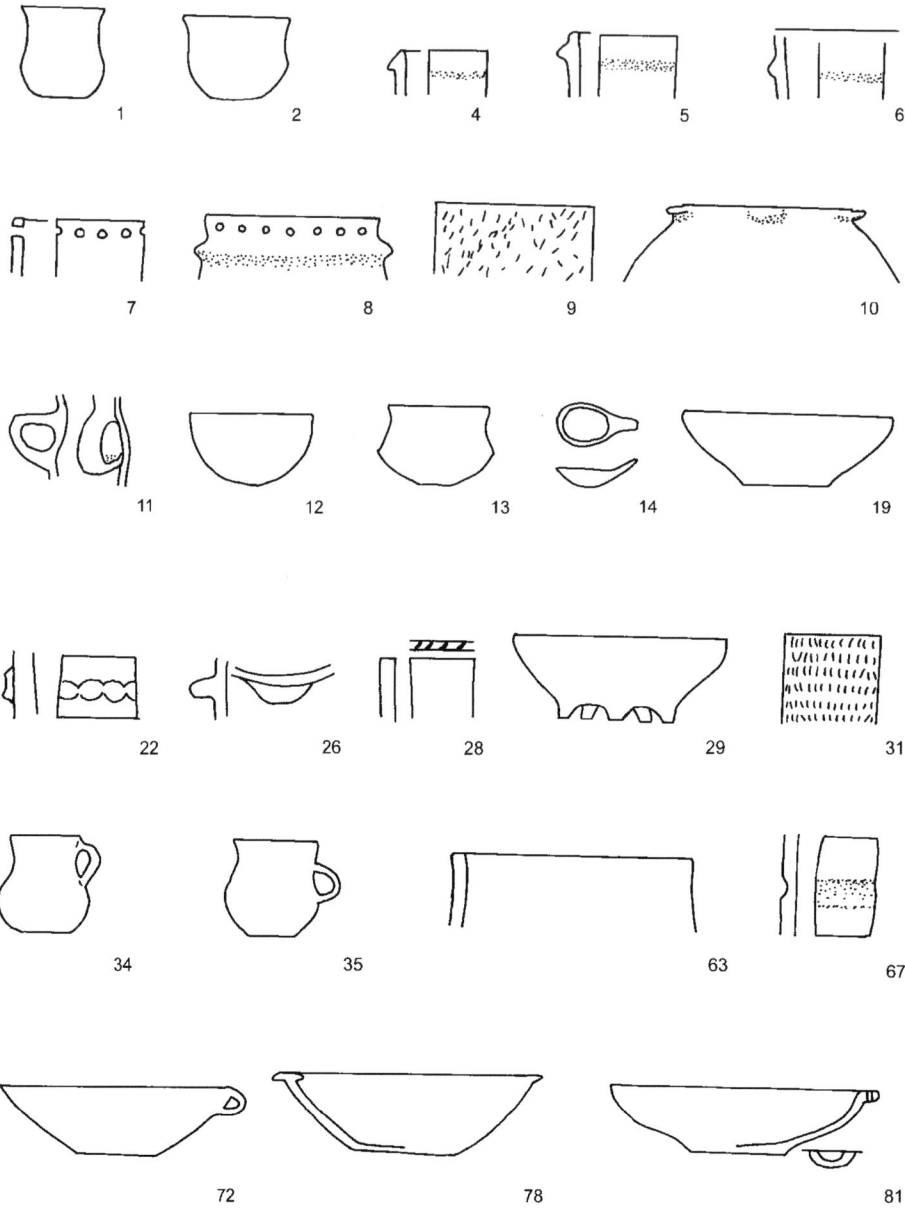

Fig. 2. The twenty-six main types of Bell Beaker common ware in continental Europe.

Type 4 was present at 24 sites, including 2 graves, 19 settlements, and 3 sites out of context. It is most frequently found in the South of France, as well as in eastern and central eastern France. Several regions do not possess this pottery: Germany (with the exception of Bavaria), Austria, Belgium, northern and western France, Hungary, the Netherlands, Poland, the Czech Republic and Slovakia. It is clearly associated with settlements.

Type 5: *horizontal cordon which is, most often triangular in section, and obviously placed under the rim*

Type 5 has been identified at 95 sites, including 13 graves, 64 settlements, and 17 sites out of context. It is found in several regions, but it is absent from northern Germany (western Mecklemburg-Pomerania and North-West), in Austria, Poland and Slovakia. It is mainly associated with settlements, in particular in southern, central-western, northern and eastern France, as well as in northern Italy.

Type 6: *horizontal cordon, position on the vase unknown*

Type 6 was present at 37 sites, including 3 graves, 29 settlements, 1 deposit and 4 sites out of context. As the type is represented by a horizontal cordon whose position on the vase is unknown, it might be covered by type 5 (cordon under the rim). Type 6 is mainly encountered in the southeastern half of continental Europe, France and northern Italy. It is almost exclusively associated with settlements.

Type 7: *rim underlined by a row of traversing and equidistant perforations*

Type 7 was present at 26 sites. It is mainly encountered in settlements (n=23), but was also found in 3 graves. It is predominant in the South of France and is absent from the eastern regions. It has mostly been discovered in settlements in the South of France.

Type 8: *rim underlined by a row of traversing and equidistant perforations above a horizontal cordon, which is most often triangular in section*

Type 8 was identified at 40 sites. It was mostly found in settlements (n=34) and was identified in 2 graves and 4 out of context discoveries. It is predominant in southern France and northern Italy, and is clearly associated with settlements. It is not found in the northern part of continental Europe.

Type 9: *fingernail (or small spatula) decorations; disordered fingernail marks*

We identified type 9 at 21 sites, including 4 graves, 13 settlements, and 4 sites out of context. It is mainly known in settlements in northern Italy and France.

Type 10: *hand-grip under the rim*

Type 10 has been recognised at 66 sites including 48 settlements, 14 graves and 4 sites out of context. It is mainly present in Moravia; more precisely in settlements.

Type 11: *handle which cannot be located on the pottery*

Type 11 has been identified at 65 sites including 53 settlements, 8 graves and 4 sites out of context. It is similar to type 34 (handle attached to the pottery's rim, possibly a pitcher) and to type 35 (handle clearly attached under the pottery's rim, possibly a pitcher). Type 11 is mainly found in settlements in Moravia and northern Italy.

Type 12: small hemispherical round-based bowl

>Type 12 was present at 19 sites, including 13 settlements, 3 graves and 3 discoveries out of context, mostly in settlements in the South of France.

Type 13: carination

>We identified type 13 at 23 sites, including 15 settlements, 6 graves and 2 sites out of context. This type was discovered in several regions, with the exception of the most northern part of continental Europe. It is mainly linked to settlements.

Type 14: spoon

>Spoons were identified at 18 sites, including 15 settlements, 2 graves and 1 site out of context. It is located in several regions and, naturally, in settlements.

Type 19: flat-based bowl

>Type 19 was found at 106 sites. It is one of the most often represented types. It is preponderant in graves (n=76) and quite frequent in settlements (n=23). Some discoveries were made out of context (n=7). It is mainly located in the eastern half of continental Europe in a funerary context.

Type 22: fingered cordon

>The fingered cordon is present at 72 sites, including 55 settlements, 9 graves and 7 sites out of context. It is spread sporadically over several regions, with the exception of settlements in Moravia and northern Italy, where it is well represented.

Type 26: hand-grip, position on the vase unknown

>We identified type 26 at 17 sites, including 14 settlements and 3 sites out of context. It is thus exclusively associated with settlements, and can be found in France, Bavaria and Moravia.

Type 28: rim notched with fingernail or spatula impressions

>We recognised Type 28 at 31 sites, including 39 settlements, 7 graves and 4 sites out of context. It was mainly identified in settlements in Moravia and northern Italy.

Type 29: polypod cup

>Type 29 was discovered at 78 sites, including 14 settlements, 56 graves and 8 sites out of context. It is one of the most frequent types of the Bell Beaker Culture in continental Europe. It is mainly represented in a funerary context in the Czech Republic and in the Elbe-Saale region in Germany. Some settlements scattered over several countries also contained this pottery type.

Type 31: fingernail (or small spatula) decoration: aligned fingernail marks

>Type 31 was identified at 63 sites, including 24 settlements, 15 graves and 24 sites out of context. This pottery type is found in all of continental Europe with the exception of its most eastern regions, that is, the Czech Republic, Slovakia, Hungary and Poland. It is found in settlements as well

as in funerary contexts according to the region under consideration. In northern Italy, it is only found in settlements, whereas in South-West Germany, it is found in settlements as well as in graves.

Type 34: handle attached to the rim of the pottery: possibly a pitcher

Type 34 is frequent, with 269 cases, including 47 in settlements, 202 in graves, 1 in a deposit and 19 discoveries out of context. It is the most frequent pottery type in continental Europe. It is mainly located in graves, in the Czech Republic, in Bavaria, in Austria and in the Elbe-Saale region (Germany). It is also present in a few settlements, in Moravia, northern Italy, and Bavaria.

Type 35: handle clearly attached under the rim of the pottery: possibly a pitcher

We identified type 35 at 128 sites, including 17 settlements, 100 graves, 1 deposit and 10 discoveries out of context. This pottery type is clearly associated with graves in the eastern part of the Bell Beaker Culture. It is mainly found in the Czech Republic and the southern part of Germany (South-West, Bavaria, Elbe-Saale region). In some rare instances, it was also identified in settlements in France, Italy, and Hungary.

Type 63: straight rim and flattened lip

We recognised type 63 at 48 sites, including 37 settlements, 4 graves, 1 deposit and 6 sites out of context. It is mainly found in settlements in almost all of continental Europe, in particular in settlements in France, Moravia and Italy.

Type 67: horizontal corrugation

Twenty sites contained type 67 potteries, including 10 settlements, 5 graves and 5 sites out of context. It is mainly, and sporadically, found in north-western Germany, the Netherlands, northern France and in the Elbe-Saale region (Germany). It is associated with settlements and graves.

Type 72: low bowl with a ribbon-like handle

Type 72 concerns 48 sites: 15 settlements, 31 graves and 2 discoveries out of context. It is mostly found in the eastern part of the Bell Beaker Culture's distribution, that is, in the Czech Republic, in the Elbe-Saale region (Germany), in Bavaria, Austria and Hungary. It seems to be mostly associated with graves, although in Moravia the settlements with this pottery type were almost as numerous as the graves.

Type 78: bowl with a flattened rim, T-shaped lip

Type 78 was identified at 157 sites, including 60 settlements, 83 graves and 14 sites out of context. This pottery type is one of the most frequent in continental Europe, being found primarily in the Czech Republic. In Moravia, it is most often found in settlements rather than in graves, whereas in Bohemia, it is very frequent in graves. Southern Germany (South-West and Bavaria) as well as Austria, Hungary and Poland rarely contain samples of this pottery type in graves.

Type 81: bowl with a horizontal handle or a perforated hand-grip

Type 81 was found in 39 sites, of which 6 settlements, 31 graves and 2 discoveries out of context. It is mainly found in the eastern part of the Bell Beaker Culture. This pottery type was most often found in graves in the Czech Republic and Bavaria. In northern Italy, three settlements contained this pottery type.

Association of the main pottery types with settlements and graves

The types mainly present in settlements are types 4, 5, 6, 7, 8, 9, 10, 11, 12, 13, 14, 22, 26, 28, 31, 63 and 67, type 26 being found only in settlements (Fig. 3). Types found mainly in a funerary context are types 1, 2, 19, 29, 34, 35, 72, 78 and 81 (Fig. 4).

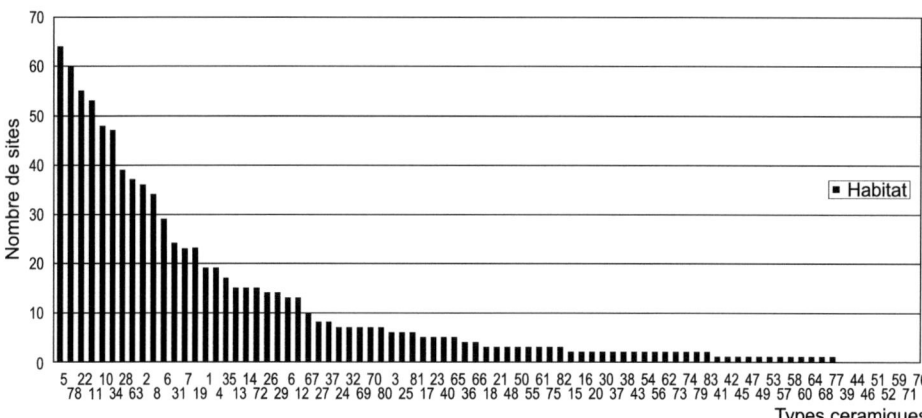

Fig. 3. Common ware during the Bell Beaker Culture in continental Europe: histogram indicating in descending order the number of settlements possessing the pottery types.

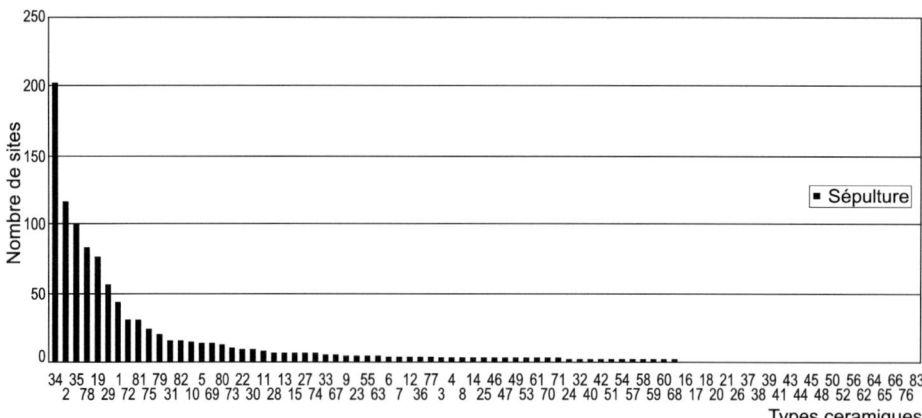

Fig. 4. Common ware during the Bell Beaker Culture in continental Europe: histogram indicating in descending order the number of graves possessing the pottery types.

Analyses

In order to measure the degree of inter-association of these pottery types, we carried out multidimensional scaling and cluster analyses. These two types of analyses were based on Euclidean distances calculated from the frequencies of the pottery types in each region. Multidimensional scaling concerned pottery types (Fig. 5) and regions (Fig. 6). First of all, and very interestingly, the central European regions (Bohemia, Moravia, Austria, Hungary, Bavaria and Poland) cluster together very clearly (Fig. 6, 7), and are distinct from the rest of continental Europe. Secondly, as for countries which aren't associated with central Europe, France, with the exception

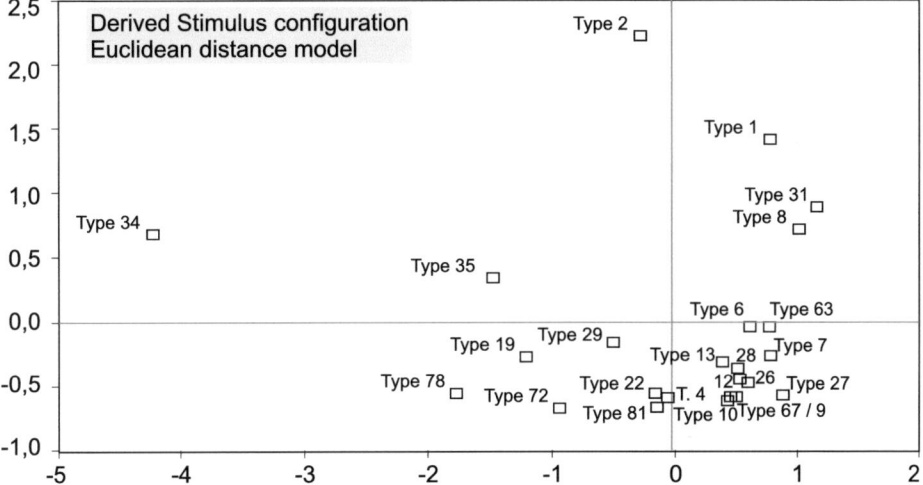

Fig. 5. Illustration of the multidimensional scaling analysis based on the pottery types.

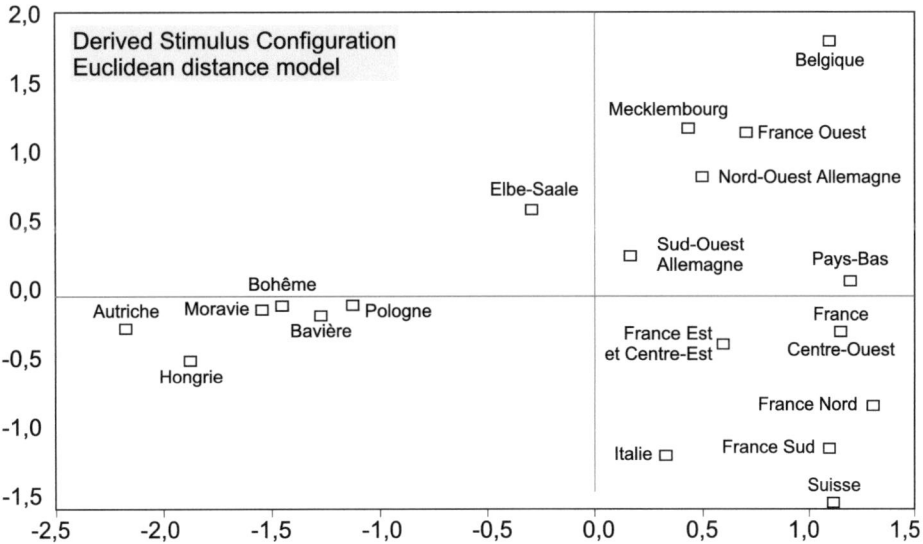

Fig. 6. Illustration of the multidimensional scaling analysis based on the twenty regions.

Similar but Different. Bell Beakers in Europe

of its western part, clusters with Switzerland and Italy. Finally, a third group associates western France, Belgium, the Netherlands, north-western Germany, Mecklemburg-Pomerania and south-western Germany (Fig. 7). According to the distribution of the pottery types, we can identify three geographically distinct cultural groups: an eastern domain, a northern domain and a southern domain (Fig. 8). The eastern

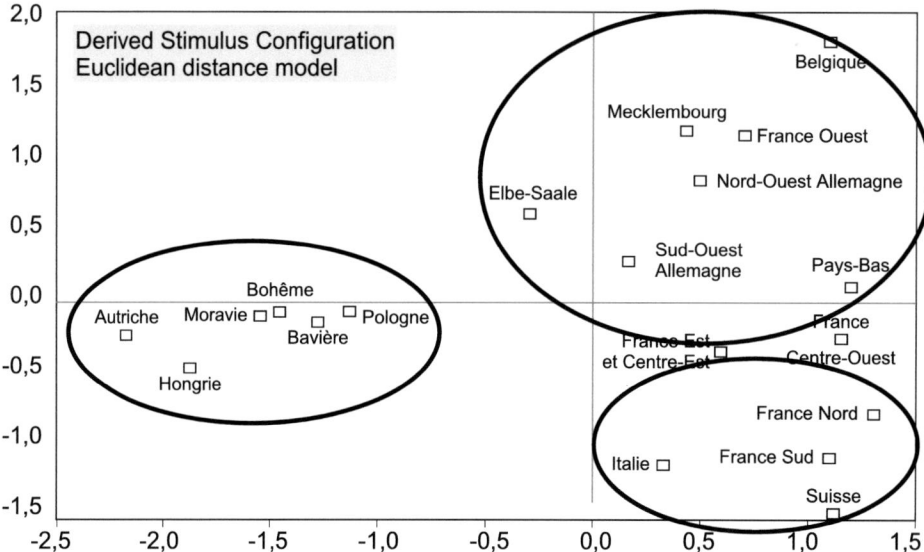

Fig. 7. Illustration of the multidimensional scaling analysis based on the twenty regions: the ellipses were added later.

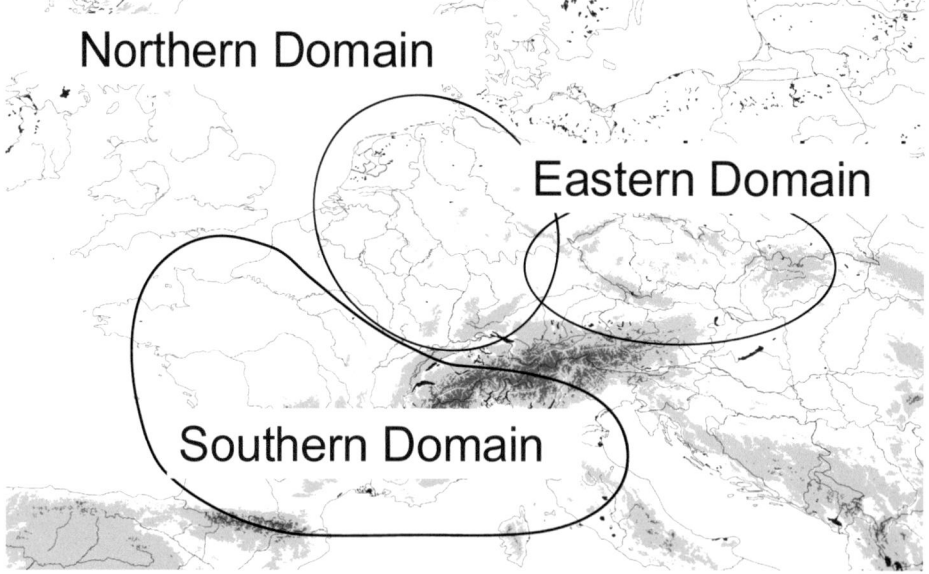

Fig. 8. Bell Beaker common ware in continental Europe: presentation of the three cultural domains.

domain includes the Czech Republic, Bavaria, Elbe-Saale in Germany, Austria, Poland and Hungary. The southern domain includes Switzerland, northern Italy and France with the exception of the most western and eastern reaches of this country. The northern domain includes Belgium, the Netherlands, north-western and south-western Germany and the eastern part of France near the German border.

The eastern domain

Twelve pottery types were observed in the eastern domain: types 2, 10, 19, 22, 28, 29, 31, 34, 35, 72, 78 and 81 (Fig. 9).

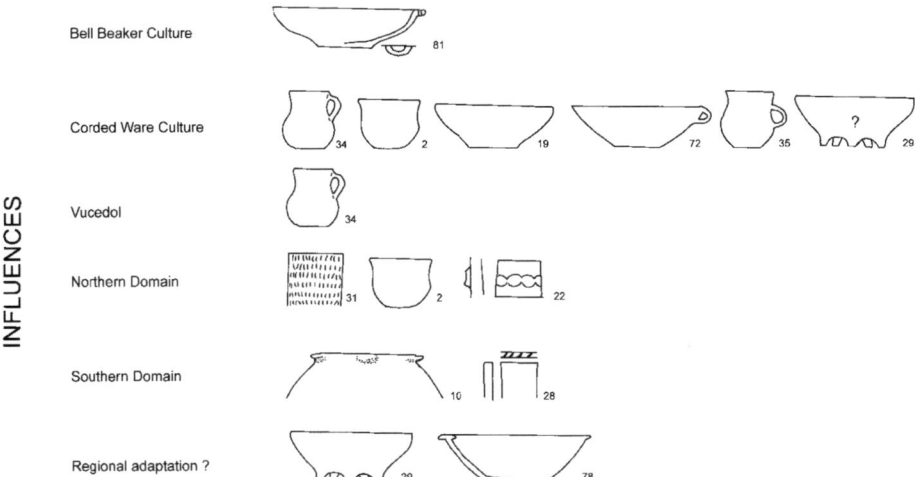

Fig. 9.   Bell Beaker common ware from the eastern domain: components and possible influences.

When studying Bell Beaker Culture common ware, one realises that it is a reflection of the complex relationships existing between different cultural groups, and that the regional substrate represented by the Corded Ware Culture plays an important role. Some forms of common ware are already present during the Corded Ware Culture of this region. These are types 2, 19, 34, 35 and 72

Bavaria: ENGELHARDT (1978, Fig. 3; 1986, Fig. 15; 1991, Fig. 1, 2; 1989, Fig. 28), HOPPE / WEISS (1983, Fig. 18), KREINER (1983, Fig. 20), NADLER / SÖRGEL (1997, Fig. 24), MATUSCHIK (1998, Fig. 1, 3, 7, 8, 9), KRAUTWURST (1999, Fig. 2) , PFAUTH (1987, Fig. 22), BIRKNER (1933, Fig. 1) and RIEDER (2000, Fig. 7).

Bohemia: PLESLOVÁ-ŠTIKOVÁ (1972), KYTLICOVÁ (1960, Fig. 15-17), HAVEL (1978, Pl VI), HAVEL / KOVARIK (1992, Pl. 2-3), BUCHVALDEK (1978, Pl. 4-5, Fig. 5-8; 1981, Pl. 1-3; 1986, Pl. 44, 46, 48-49; 1992, Fig. 1-3), NEUSTUPNÝ E. / SMRZ (1989), BUCHVALDEK / KOUTECKÝ (1970, Fig. 1-127), BŘEZINOVÁ / TUREK (1999, Fig. 6, 9), BUCHVALDEK / NOVOTNÝ / PLESLOVÁ-ŠTIKOVÁ (1988, Fig. 4).

Moravia: ŠEBELA (1981, Fig. 2, 1993, Fig. 126, 128-132), MIKULKOVÁ (1999, Fig. 1, 2), PEŠKA (1989), PEŠKA / RAKOVSKY (1990, Fig. 6, 7), BUCHVALDEK (1966, Pl. I –XXIII; 1986, Pl. 60-61; 1961; 1981, Fig. 4; 1992, Fig. 1-3), LUDIKOVSKY / ONDRÁČEK (1970-1971, Fig. 2), BUCHVALDEK / NOVOTNÝ / PLESLOVÁ-ŠTIKOVÁ (1988, Fig. 5).

These pottery types are predominant in the Czech Republic, in particular Bohemia.

Two pottery types originate from the local substrate and are also found in the substrates of other regions. These are types 2 and 34. The pitcher with a handle (type 34) is present during the Corded Ware Culture of this eastern group, but also in other cultural groups, for instance Vučedol in Croatia (SCHMIDT 1945, NEUSTUPNÝ 1984), in the groups of Makó-Kosihý-Čaka in Hungary (MOUCHA 1981) and of Somogyvár, in the Carpathian Basin (BUCHVALDEK 1981). Some authors believe that the Begleitkeramik originates from the Carpathian Basin (BERTEMES / HEYD 1996, TUREK 1998). The undecorated low Bell Beaker (type 2) is present during the Bohemian Corded Ware Culture (Czech Republic), in the German region of Elbe-Saale, but also during the Corded Ware Culture of the northern region, in particular in the Netherlands and in north Germany (LOUWE KOOIJMANS 1974, Fig. 6, 46, 48-52; LANTING 1973).

Bowls with flat bases and T-shaped lips (type 78) are occasionally decorated. This pottery type seems to be a local adaptation of a type of decorated pottery.

The same is true for polypod cups, which are also occasionally decorated. However, it seems that the situation here is more complex, as some rare cases have been discovered in the Corded Ware Culture of western Mecklemburg-Pomerania (NILIUS 1981); the Bell Beaker Culture of this region does not possess any such cups. Admittedly, the latter is not very well known, and it is often assimilated with the „Individual Burials Civilisation". Some polypod cups have also been found within the context of the regional Corded Ware Culture, in particular in the Elbe-Saale region (MATTHIAS 1974, Pl. 94, 5, Pl. 113) and in Denmark, during the „Individual Burials Civilisation" (LICHARDUS / LICHARDUS-ITTEN 1985, Fig. 43, 33). Some of the corded polypod cups from the Elbe-Saale region are decorated; others are made of wood (BEHRENS 1973, Pl. 54; BUCHVALDEK 1978, Pl. 5, 1). While we wish to remain cautious given the small amount of remains of this type, we can tentatively propose that these Bell Beaker polypod cups originated locally, from the Corded Ware Culture. They seem to represent an adaptation of this pottery type, which can be detected either by the transition from corded decorations to Bell Beaker decorations, or by the complete disappearance of decorations. Influences from the north or from the south may also have played a role. In the Mediterranean Basin, polypod cups are numerous and are often decorated (ATZENI 1987, Fig. 9;1995, Fig. 31, 3;1998, Fig. 5, 15). Other examples are not decorated (TUSA 1997, Fig. 17; ATZENI 1998, Fig. 5-7). Thus, we can also imagine influences stemming from the Mediterranean Basin; initially, these may have induced the presence of polypod decorated cups in central Europe, which then lost their decorations. This corresponds to the chronology which is generally proposed for these regions, with decorated pottery being present during early phases and undecorated pottery appearing during more recent phases.

Flat-based bowls (type 19) occasionally bearing a small vertical handle (type 72) are present within the regional substrate (MARSCHALL 1983, Pl. 2, b; MATTHIAS 1974, Pl. 96, 1), whereas bowls with a horizontal hand-grip (type 81) – a perforated hand-grip or a handle – originate from somewhere else.

Decorations with impressed fingernail or spatula lines (type 31) are present during the Corded Ware Culture of the northern domain, in particular in the Netherlands and north-western Germany (LANTING / VAN DER WAALS 1976; VAN DER BEEK / FOKKENS 1998).

Small hand-grips under the pottery rim (type 10) are found in different pre-Bell Beaker cultural groups in Western Europe, such as the Vérazien and the group of Gord-Deûle-Escaut, but they are uncommon during the Bell Beaker Culture of these regions. It is therefore difficult to imagine an influence from the south-west towards the north-east, as these hand-grips are more numerous in the eastern domain. As for vases with notched lips (type 28), they are sparsely distributed over the whole of continental Europe and seem to come from a pre-Bell Beaker Culture in northern Italy (the White-Ware group) (BARFIELD et al. 1975-1976, Fig. 23) and from the Tuscan Eneolithic (MARTINI / MORANDI 1986-1987).

Thus, many external influences may have acted in this region. Nevertheless, the stock from the regional Corded Ware Culture substrate seems to dominate, as the types which are most frequently encountered originate from the substrate of the regional Corded Ware Culture.

The regional Neolithic basis – the substrate – is therefore central to the emergence of the eastern domain Bell Beaker Culture.

The northern domain

Fourteen pottery types belong to the northern domain: types 1, 2, 5, 7, 8, 9, 22, 27, 28, 31, 29, 34, 35 and 67 (Fig. 10).

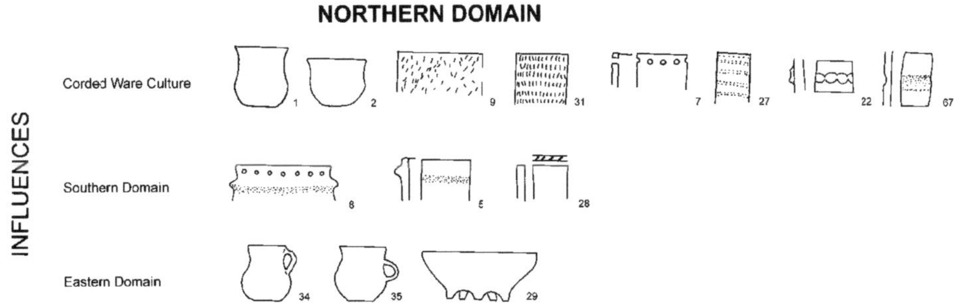

Fig. 10. Bell Beaker common ware from the northern domain: components and possible influences.

The Corded Ware Culture plays an important role in the evolution towards the Bell Beaker Culture. Types 1, 2, 7, 9, 22, 27, 31 and 67 are present during both Cultures. Apart from the undecorated bell beakers (types 1 and 2), these are mainly types of decoration (corrugations, circular impressions, fingernail or spatula decorations, impressed cordons).

Similar but Different. Bell Beakers in Europe

Corrugations also exist within the regional Corded Ware Culture substrate, as well as in the Elbe-Saale region (MATTHIAS 1987, Pl.1, 7).

Impressed cordons are present in the Corded Ware Culture of the Middle Rhine region (BANTELMANN 1989, Pl.1, j).

Influences from the eastern domain can be inferred from the presence of single-handled pitchers (types 34 and 35) and polypod cups (type 29).

Influences from southern Europe are also perceptible. These may have followed the Rhine-Rhône axis, as edges underlined by a cordon are abundant in pre-Bell Beaker Culture contexts in the southern domain.

Influences from the south are also apparent in type 8 potteries (rim underlined by a cordon with a row of traversing perforations between the rim and the cordon), but the situation is slightly different from type 5, as type 8 has not been discovered within the substrate. It is probably associated with decorated Bell Beaker pottery. Its southern origin can be inferred from its density, which is more important than in northern continental Europe. As for vases with notched lips (type 28), they are sparsely distributed over the whole of continental Europe and seem to come from a pre-Bell Beaker Culture in northern Italy (the White-Ware group) (BARFIELD *et al.* 1975-1976, Fig. 23) and from the Tuscan Eneolithic (MARTINI / MORANDI 1986-1987).

In this region, the regional Neolithic substrate plays an important role in the emergence of the Bell Beaker Culture, as the most frequent types originate from the Corded Ware substrate.

The southern domain

Nineteen types associated with the common ware were identified (Fig. 11): types 1, 2, 4, 5, 7, 8, 9, 10, 12, 13, 19, 22, 27, 28, 29, 31, 34, 35 and 63.

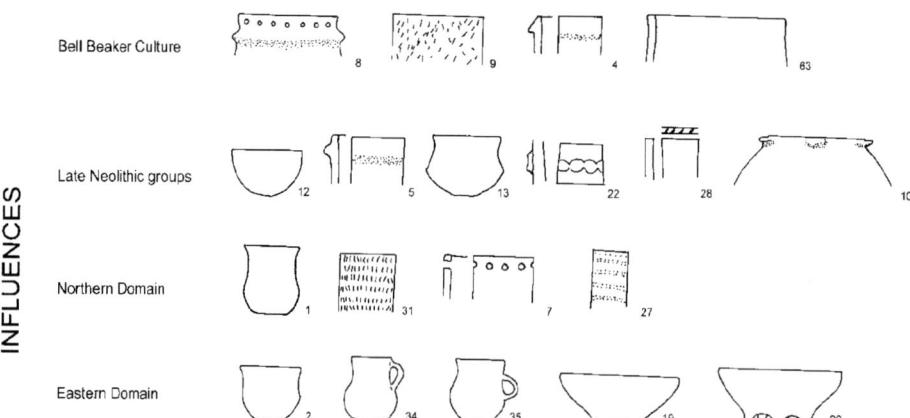

Fig. 11. Bell Beaker common ware from the southern domain: components and possible influences.

The types which originate from various Late Neolithic groups are:
- pottery represented by edges underlined by a triangular cordon (type 5)

  Vérazien: ABELANET (1980, Fig. 1, 2), BARBAZA (1980, Fig. 1), DUDAY / GUILAINE (1980, Fig. 1, 2, 4), GRIMAL (1980, Fig. 1), GUILAINE (1980, Fig. 1, 2, 3, 5), GUILAINE / JACOBIESKI (1980, Fig. 1), GUILAINE / VAQUER / BOUISSET (1980, Fig. 1, 2, 3, 4, 5), MARTIN COLLIGA (1980, Fig. 1, 2), TAFFANEL / TAFFANEL (1980, Fig. 1, 2), TARRUS (1980) / VAQUER (1980, Fig. 1; 1998, Pl. 9, p. 491);

  Tuscan Eneolithic: CREMONESI et al. (1998, Pl. 8), MARTINI / MORANDI (1986-1987, Fig. 3-8), SARTI / CARLINI / MARTINI (1999-2000, Fig. 3-10), COCCHI GENIK (1998), COCCHI GENIK / CREMONESI (1989);

- the small round-based hemispheric bowl (type 12)

  Vérazien: ABELANET (1980, Fig. 1, 2), BARBAZA (1980, Fig. 1), DUDAY / GUILAINE (1980, Fig. 1, 2, 4), GRIMAL (1980, Fig. 1), GUILAINE (1980, Fig. 1, 2, 3, 5), GUILAINE / JACOBIESKI (1980, Fig. 1), GUILAINE / VAQUER / BOUISSET (1980, Fig. 1, 2, 3, 4, 5), MARTIN COLLIGA (1980, Fig. 1, 2), TAFFANEL / TAFFANEL (1980, Fig. 1, 2), TARRUS (1980) and VAQUER (1980, Fig. 1 , 1998, Pl. 9, p. 491);

  Late Neolithic of Provence: D'ANNA (1995a, Fig. 2, 4, 1995b, Fig. 1, 2, 4, 1999, Fig. 2, 3), GUTHERZ / JALLOT (1995), VAQUER (1998, Pl. 13, p. 495), COURTIN (1974, Fig. 68, 69, 70, 76, 77, 83, 103, 111, 113, 114);

- vases with hand-grips under the rim (type 10) JEUNESSE / PÉTREQUIN / PININGRE (1998, Pl. 27 and 28),

- carenated containers (type 13)

  Fontbouisse: VAQUER (1998, Pl. 12, p. 494), GUTHERZ (1975) and GASCO (1976); Gord-Deûle-Escaut: BLANCHET (1984, Fig. 18, 19, 21, 22, 24), CONSTANTIN / BLANCHET (1998, Pl. 11) and PRAUD / MARTIAL (2000, Fig. 2);

- fingered cordons (type 22)

  Fontbouisse: VAQUER (1998, Pl. 12, p. 494), GUTHERZ (1975) and GASCO (1976);

  Tuscan Eneolithic: CREMONESI et al. (1998, Pl. 8), MARTINI / MORANDI (1986-1987, Fig. 3-8), SARTI / CARLINI / MARTINI (1999-2000, Fig. 3-10), COCCHI GENIK (1998), COCCHI GENIK / CREMONESI (1989);

- and notched edges (type 28)

  Remedello Group: BAGOLINI et al. (1998, Pl. 14), GAMBARI / VENTURINO GAMBARI (1985, Pl. 1, 1990, Fig. 1-3), BIAGI (1995, p. 215), GIUGGIOLA et al. (1966), CORNAGGIA CASTIGLIONI (1971, pl. 13-19), COLINI 1898-1902;

  Spilamberto Group: BAGOLINI et al. (1998, Pl. 13), BAGOLINI (1981), BAGOLINI et al. (1988), BAGOLINI et al. (1998).

Three pottery types appear at the same time as the decorated beakers and do not originate from a pre-Bell Beaker horizon in continental Europe. These are potteries with straight rims and flattened lips (type 63), potteries rimmed by a triangular cordon (type 4) and potteries whose rim is underlined by a row of traversing perforations, which are themselves situated above a triangular cordon (type 8). The type consisting of a small bowl with an umbilicated base can be added to this list (type 36), as it has been found at seven sites in southern France and does not originate from Late Neolithic cultures of this region. Misaligned fingernail or spatula impressions (type 9) are present in scarce pre-Bell Beaker levels in northern Italy and northern Europe. It is therefore difficult to settle where this type of decoration comes from.

Influences from the eastern domain can be detected in several instances: single-handled pitchers (types 34 and 35), low undecorated Bell Beakers (type 2), and flat-based bowls (type 19). Polypod cups may also reflect eastern influences, unless they are adaptations of Mediterranean decorated types.

High undecorated Bell Beakers (type 1), circular impressed decorations (type 27) or rows of spatula impressions (type 31) and potteries with rows of perforations under the rim (type 7) all reveal influences from the northern domain.

In this region, only six of the 19 pottery types present (types 5, 10, 12, 13, 22 and 28) originate from cultural groups of the regional substrate. There are therefore 13 types specific to the Bell Beaker Culture, and some bear traces of external influences. We can assert that the typological assortment is largely renewed when these series are studied at the level of a domain.

Conclusions

It is essential to grasp the importance of the regional Neolithic basis in the emergence of the Bell Beaker Culture, as well as the influences that the regions occasionally exert over each other. During the Bell Beaker Culture, several networks of influences acting between the different domains can be perceived. They vary in their importance.

The regional substrates of the eastern and of the northern domains, that is, the Corded Ware Culture, seem to play a major role in the emergence of the Bell Beaker Culture. Some Corded Ware Culture pottery types persist during the Bell Beaker Culture, and make up the best part of the latter's pottery types. Furthermore, decorated pottery in this region is proportionally less frequent than undecorated pottery.

This is not the case within the southern domain, where the transition between the Late Neolithic and the Bell Beaker Culture is more radical. Bell Beaker pottery types are new; few of them originate from cultures of the regional substrate during the end of the Neolithic. Furthermore, sites with decorated pottery are much more numerous than sites with common ware only, which emphasizes the renewal of cultural components during the Bell Beaker Culture.

In the southern domain, the substrate does not seem to herald the Bell Beaker Culture, whereas in the northern and eastern domains, the Corded Ware substrate seems to have played an important role in the founding of the Bell Beaker Culture.

What is more, the Bell Beaker sites of the southern domain do not occupy the same locations as Late Neolithic sites. This is not the case during the Corded Ware Culture: Bell Beaker sites seem to have been founded as a function of the latter. Also, the Bell Beaker Culture is often contemporaneous with the Corded Ware Culture, or at least with a recent phase of the Corded Ware Culture.

At the end of the Neolithic, the southern domain is characterised, by multitudinous regional groups whose geographic extension is limited, whereas at the same time, the Corded Ware Culture occupies most of central and eastern Europe. The importance of the Corded Ware Culture is also perceptible in the continuity of funerary rituals. Where the Corded Ware Culture is accompanied by single graves, the same is true for the Bell Beaker Culture. A different situation prevails in the southern domain, as collective graves exist from the Late Neolithic onwards, whereas during the Bell Beaker Culture, these are reused, or else individual graves are built (Fig. 12).

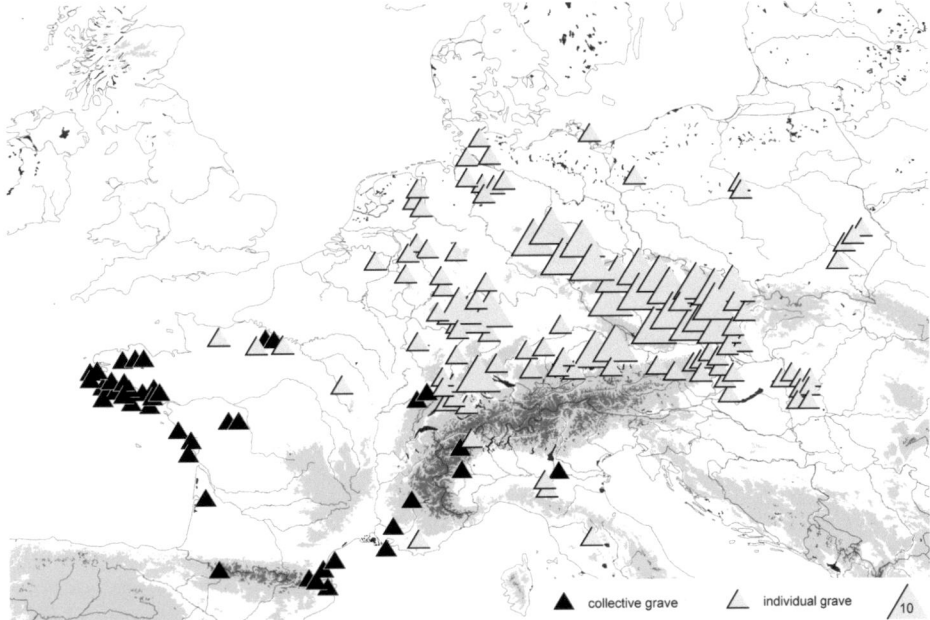

Fig. 12. Distribution map of the individual and collective graves with common ware during the Bell Beaker Culture in continental Europe.

Thus, the transition mechanisms leading to the Bell Beaker Culture are very different. These changes are very important in the southern domain, whereas in the eastern and northern domains, the transition is much smoother.

(Translation: Suzanne Eades)

Bibliography

ABELANET J. 1980. Stations du Néolithique final du type de Veraza en Rousillon. In: GUILAINE J. (ed.), *Le groupe de Véraza et la fin des temps néolithiques dans le Sud de la France et la Catalogne. Colloque (Narbonne, 3-4 juin 1977)*. Paris, 55-60.

ATZENI E. 1987. *La preistoria del Sulcis Iglesiente*. Cagliari.

ATZENI E. 1995. La „cultura del vaso campaniforme" nella necropoli di Locci-Santus (S. Giovanni Suergiu). In: Santoni V. (ed.), *Carbonia e il Sulcis Archeologia e territorio*. Editrice S'Alvure, 119-143.

ATZENI E. 1998. La Cultura del bicchiere campaniforme in Sardegna. In: NICOLIS F. / MOTTES E. (eds), *Simbolo ed enigma: il bicchiere campaniforme e l'Italia nella preistoria europea del III millennio a.C. Catalogo di mostra (1998, Riva del Garda)*, 243-253.

BAGOLINI B. 1981. *Il Neolitico e l'età del Rame: ricerca a Spilamberto - S. Cesario, 1977-1980.* Bologna.

BAGOLINI B. / FERRARI A. / STEFFE G. 1988. La necropoli di Spilamberto (Modena). In: L'età del Rame in Europa. Congresso int. (Viareggio, 15-18 ott. 1987). *Rassegna di archeologia* (Firenze), 7, 614-615.

BAGOLINI B. / FERRARI A. / STEFFE G. 1998. Il recente Neolitico di Spilamberto (Modena). *Bullettino di paletnologia italiana*, 89, 92-200.

BAGOLINI B. / Pedrotti A. / Barfield L. / NICOLIS F. 1998. L'Italie septentrionale. In: GUILAINE J. (ed.), *Atlas du Néolithique européen, 2A: l'Europe occidentale*. Liège: Service de préhist. de l'Univ. (Etudes et rech. archéol. de l'Univ. de Liège, ERAUL; 46), 233-341.

BANTELMANN N. 1989. Frühschnurkeramische Siedlungware am nordlichen Oberrhein. In: BUCHVALDEK M. / PLESLOVÁ-ŠTIKOVÁ E. (eds), *Das Äneolithikum und die früheste Bronzezeit (C14 3000-2000 b.c.) in Mitteleuropa: kulturelle und chronologische Beziehungen. Int. Symposium, 14 (Prag-Liblice, 20-24.10.1986)*. Praha, 301-304.

BARBAZA M.. 1980. Le mobilier lithique (pierre taillée) de la station de plein air de Saint-Antoine à Caux-et-Sauzens (Aude). In: GUILAINE J. (ed.), *Le groupe de Véraza et la fin des temps néolithiques dans le Sud de la France et la Catalogne. Colloque (Narbonne, 3-4 juin 1977)*. Paris, 50-54.

BARFIELD L.H. / BIAGI P. / BORELLO M.-A. 1975-1976. *Scavi nella stazione di Monte Covolo (1972-73). Part. I.* Annali del Museo di Gavardo 12, 7-149.

BEHRENS H. 1973. *Die Jungsteinzeit im Mittelelbe-Saale-Gebiet.* Berlin.

BERTEMES F. / HEYD V. 1996. Définition et origine de l'âge du Bronze ancien en Europe centrale. In: MORDANT C. / GAIFFE O. (eds), *Cultures et sociétés du Bronze ancien en Europe. Colloque sur les Fondements culturels, techniques, économiques et sociaux des débuts de l'âge du Bronze. Congrès nat. des Soc. savantes, 117, section de pré- et protohistoire (Clermont-Ferrand, 27-29 oct. 1992)*. Paris, 13-36.

BESSE M. 2001. L'Europe continentale, la région Rhin-Rhône et l'habitat de « Derrière-le-Château » (Ain, France) ou la céramique commune du Campaniforme. Genève: département d'anthropologie et d'écologie de l'Université (Thèse de doctorat, non publ.).

BESSE M. / STRAHM C. 2001. The components of the Bell Beaker Complex. In: NICOLIS F. (ed.), *Bell Beakers today: pottery, people, culture, symbols in prehistoric Europe: volume 1. Int. Colloquium (11-16 May 1998 ; Riva del Garda, Trento)*. Trento, 103-110.

BIAGI R. 1995. Val Pennavaira (Savona). In: MAGGI R. / MARTINI F. / SARTI L. (eds), *Guide archeologiche: Preistoria e Protostoria in Italia, 6: Toscana e Liguria. Int. congress of prehistoric and protohistoric sciences, 13 (Forlì, 8-14 sept. 1996)*. Forlì, 206-217.

BIRKNER F. 1933. Die schnurkeramische Kultur in Südbayern. *Bayerische Vorgeschichtsblätter* 11, 1-18.

BLANCHET J.-C. 1984. *Les premiers métallurgistes en Picardie et dans le Nord de la France: Chalcolithique, âge du Bronze et début du Premier âge du Fer.* Paris.

BŘEZINOVÁ H. / TUREK J. 1999. Šňůrové a raně středověké pohřebiště v severním předpolí Pražského hradu - archeologický výzkum v Lumbeho zahradě. The Corded Ware and Early Medieval cemetery in northern vicinity of Prague Castle. *Archeologické rozhledy* 51, 653-687.

BUCHVALDEK M. 1966. *Die Schnurkeramik in Böhmen.* Praha.

1978. *Otázka kontinuity v Českomoravském mladším eneolitu — Zur Frage der Kontinuität im jüngeren Äneolithikum in Böhmen und Mähren.* Praha, 35-64.

1981. Das Karpatenbecken und die Schnurkeramik in Böhmen und Mähren. In: *Die Frühbronzezeit im Karpatenbecken und in Nachbargebieten. Int. Symposium (Budapest-Velem, 1977)*. Budapest, 41-48.

1986. Zum gemeineuropäischen Horizont der Schnurkeramik. *Praehistorische Z.* 61, 129-150.

1992. Grundlegende und Teilveränderungen in der Schnurkeramik. In: BUCHVALDEK M. / STRAHM C. (eds), *Die kontinentaleuropäischen Gruppen der Kultur mit Schnurkeramik. Schnurkeramik Symposium (Prag, 1990)*. Praha, 61-66.

BUCHVALDEK M. / KOUTECKÝ D. 1970. *Vikletice: ein schnurkeramisches Gräberfeld*. Praha.

BUCHVALDEK M. / NOVOTNÝ B. / PLESLOVÁ-ŠTIKOVÁ E. 1988. The Copper Age in Czechoslovakia. In: L'età del Rame in Europa. Congresso int. (Viareggio, 15-18 ott. 1987). *Rassegna di archeologia* 7, 105-142.

COCCHI GENICK D. 1998. *L'antica età del Bronzo nell'Italia centrale: profilo di un'epoca e di un'appropriata strategia metodologica*. Firenze, 410 p..

COCCHI GENICK D. / Grifoni Cremonesi R. 1989. *L'età del Rame in Toscana*. Viareggio.

CONSTANTIN C. / BLANCHET J.-C. 1998. Le Nord de la France (Bassin Parisien). In: GUILAINE J. (ed.), *Atlas du Néolithique européen, 2B: l'Europe occidentale*. Liège, 585-651.

CORNAGGIA CASTIGLIONI O. 1971. La cultura di Remedello: problematica ed ergologia di un facies dell'Eneolitico padano. *Memorie della Soc. Italiana di Sci. Naturali e del Museo Civico di Storia Naturale di Milano*, 20, 1.

COURTIN J. 1974. *Le Néolithique de la Provence*. Paris.

CREMONESI G. / GRIFONI CREMONESI R. / RADI G. / TOZZI C. / NICOLIS F. 1998. L'Italie septentrionale. In: GUILAINE J. (ed.) *Atlas du Néolithique européen, 2A: l'Europe occidentale*. Liège, 165-231.

D'ANNA A. 1995a. La fin du Néolithique dans le Sud-Est de la France. In: CHENORKIAN R. (ed.) *L'homme méditerranéen: mélanges offerts à Gabriel Camps, professeur émérite de l'Université de Provence*. Aix-en-Provence, 299-333.

1995b. Le Néolithique final en Provence. In: VORUZ J.-L. (ed.) *Chronologies néolithiques: de 6000 à 2000 ans avant notre ère dans le Bassin rhodanien. Colloque, Rencontre sur le Néolithique de la région Rhône-Alpes, 11 (Ambérieu-en-Bugey, 19- 20 sept. 1992)*. Ambérieu-en-Bugey, 265-286.

1999. Le Néolithique final en Provence. In: Vaquer J. (ed.), *Le Néolithique du Nord-Ouest méditerranéen. Congrès préhist. de France, 24 (Carcassonne, 26-30 sept. 1994)*. Paris, 147-159.

DUDAY H. / GUILAINE J. 1980. Le niveau vérazien de la grotte des Chambres d'Alaric à Moux (Aude). In: GUILAINE J. (ed.), *Le groupe de Véraza et la fin des temps néolithiques dans le Sud de la France et la Catalogne. Colloque (Narbonne, 3-4 juin 1977)*. Paris, 42-46.

ENGELHARDT B. 1978. Neue Grabfunde der Schnurkeramik aus Niederbayern. *Archäologisches Korrespondenzblatt* 8, 4, 285-291.

1986. Weitere schnurkeramische Grabfunde aus Niederbayern. *Das archäologische Jahr in Bayern*, 45-47.

1989. Die schnurkeramische Doppelbestattung von Künzing. *Das archäologische Jahr in Bayern*, 55-57.

1991. Beiträge zur Kenntnis der Glockenbecherkultur in Niederbayern: kurze Einführung in die Glockenbecherkultur. In: SCHMOTZ K. (ed.), *Vorträge des 9. Niederbayerischen Archäologentâges (Deggendorf, 1991)*. Buch am Erlbach, 85-96.

GAMBARI F. M. / VENTURINO GAMBARI M. 1985. La ceramica a fori passanti nel quadro dell'Eneolitico dell'Italia nord-occidentale. *Sibrium* 18, 61-79.

GASCO J. 1976. *La communauté paysanne de Fontbouisse*. Carcassonne.
GIUGGIOLA O. / IMPERIALE G. / LAMBERTI G. / PIACENTINO G. / VICINO G. 1966. Un rifugio del Neolitico medio nel Finalese: l'Arma delle Anime. *Rev. d'études ligures* 32, 1/2, 106-250.
GRIMAL J. 1980. L'occupation vérazienne de la vallée de l'Hérault. In: GUILAINE J. (ed.), *Le groupe de Véraza et la fin des temps néolithiques dans le Sud de la France et la Catalogne. Colloque (Narbonne, 3-4 juin 1977)*. Paris, 72-75.
GUILAINE J. 1980. Le groupe de Véraza et la fin des temps néolithiques en Languedoc et Catalogne. In: GUILAINE J. (ed.), *Le groupe de Véraza et la fin des temps néolithiques dans le Sud de la France et la Catalogne. Colloque (Narbonne, 3-4 juin 1977)*. Paris, 1-10.
GUILAINE J. / JACOBIESKI G. 1980. La Cauna de Vergues (Villeneuve-Minervois, Aude). In: GUILAINE J. (ed.), *Le groupe de Véraza et la fin des temps néolithiques dans le Sud de la France et la Catalogne. Colloque (Narbonne, 3-4 juin 1977)*. Paris, 47-48.
GUILAINE J. / VAQUER J. / BOUISSET P. 1980. Stations véraziennes d'Ouveillan (Aude). In: GUILAINE J. (ed.), *Le groupe de Véraza et la fin des temps néolithiques dans le Sud de la France et la Catalogne. Colloque (Narbonne, 3-4 juin 1977)*. Paris, 55-60.
GUTHERZ X. 1975. *La culture de Fontbouisse: recherches sur le Chalcolithique en Languedoc oriental*. Garons.
GUTHERZ X. / JALLOT L. 1995. Le Néolithique final du Languedoc méditerranéen. In: VORUZ J.-L. (ed.) *Chronologies néolithiques: de 6000 à 2000 ans avant notre ère dans le Bassin rhodanien. Colloque, Rencontre sur le Néolithique de la région Rhône-Alpes, 11 (Ambérieu-en-Bugey, 19- 20 sept. 1992)*. Ambérieu-en-Bugey, 231-263.
HAVEL J. / KOVARIK J. 1992. Die Schnurkeramischen Gräberfelder in Praha - Jinonice. In: BUCHVALDEK M. / STRAHM C. (eds), *Die kontinentaleuropäischen Gruppen der Kultur mit Schnurkeramik. Schnurkeramik Symposium (Prag, 1990)*. 95-98.
HAVEL J. 1978. Pohřebni ritus kultury zvoncovitých pohárů v Čechách a na Moravě. *Praehistorica* VII (Varia Archaeologica). Praha, 91-117.
HOPPE F. / WEISS B. 1983. Ein Begräbnisplatz der Schnurkeramik bei Bergrheinfeld, Landkreis Schweinfurt, Unterfranken. *Das archäologische Jahr in Bayern*, 37-38.
JEUNESSE C. / PETREQUIN P. / PININGRE J.-F. 1998. L'est de la France. In: GUILAINE J. (ed.), *Atlas du Néolithique européen, 2A: l'Europe occidentale*. Liège, 501-584.
KRAUTWURST R. 1999. Einige „bronzezeitliche" und „urnefelderzeitliche" Funde im Nürberger Land: schnurkeramische Wellenleistentöpfe. *Archäologisches Korrespondenzblatt* 29, 3, 3, 325-334.
KREINER L. 1983. Die erste schnurkeramische Mehrfachbestattung in Südostbayern aus Straubing-Wallmühle, Niederbayern. *Das archäologische Jahr in Bayern*, 39-40.
KYTLICOVÁ O. 1960. Eneolitické pohřebiště v Brandýsku — Das äneolithische Gräberfeld in der Gemeinde Brandýsek. *Památky archeologické* 51, 2, 442-474.
LANTING J.N. 1973. Laat-neolithicum en Vroege Bronstijd in Netherland en N.W.-Duitsland: continue ontwikkelingen. *Palaeohistoria* 15, 216-317.
LANTING J.N. / VAN DER WAALS J.D. 1976. Beaker Culture Relations in the Lower Rhine Basin. In: LANTING J.N. / VAN DER WAALS J.D. (eds), *Glockenbecher Symposion (Oberried, 1974)*. 1-80.
LICHARDUS J. / LICHARDUS-ITTEN M. / BAILLOUD G. / CAUVIN J. collab. 1985. *La protohistoire de l'Europe: le Néolithique et le Chalcolithique*. Paris.
LOUWE KOOIJMANS L. 1974. *The Rhine/Meuse Delta: four studies on its prehistoric occupation and Holocen geology*. Leiden.
LUDIKOVSKÝ K. / ONDRÁČEK J. 1970-1971. Hrob se snurovou keramikou z Morkůvek. *Sborník Československé Spolecnosti Antropologické pri CSAV* 4, 35-39.
MARSCHALL O. 1983. Ein schnurkeramischer Grabfund und die ur- und frühgeschichtliche Besiedlung der Gemarkung Hedersleben, Kr. Eisleben. *Ausgrabungen und Funde* 28, 4, 165-176.

MARTIN-COLLIGA A. 1980. Le Vérazien en Catalogne. In: Guilaine J. (ed.), *Le groupe de Véraza et la fin des temps néolithiques dans le Sud de la France et la Catalogne. Colloque (Narbonne, 3-4 juin 1977).* Paris, 76-82.

MARTINI F. / MORANDI R. 1986-87. L'Eneolitico di Sesto Fiorentino - Via Leopardi (Firenze). *Rassegna di archeologia* 6, 217-249.

MATTHIAS W. 1974. *Kataloge zur mitteldeutschen Schnurkeramik, Teil IV: Südharz-Unstrut-Gebiet.* Berlin

1987. *Kataloge zur mitteldeutschen Schnurkeramik, Teil VI: Restgebiete und Nachträge.* Berlin.

MATUSCHIK I. 1998. Der „Kettenhocker" von Sengkofen: ein Beitrag zur Kenntnis der Schnurkeramischen Kultur in Südbayern. In: FRITSCH B. / MAUTE M. / MATUSCHIK I. / MÜLLER J. / WOLF C. (eds), *Tradition und Innovation: prähistorische Archäologie als historische Wissenschaft: Festschrift für Christian Strahm.* Rahden, 223-255.

MIKULKOVÁ B. 1999. Výskov-Nosalovice (okr. Výskov). *Prehled výzkumu* (Brno) 39, 308-309.

MOUCHA V. 1981. Südostliche Elemente in der mährischen und böhmischen Gruppe der Glockenbecherkultur. In: *Die Frühbronzezeit im Karpatenbecken und in Nachbargebieten. Int. Symposium (Budapest-Velem, 1977).* Budapest, 115-123.

NADLER M. / SORGEL W. 1997. Der Hochberg bei Mittelburg: eine schnurkeramische Höhensiedlung. *Das archäologische Jahr in Bayern*, 49-51.

NEUSTUPNÝ E. 1984. The Bell Beaker Culture in East Central Europe. In: GUILAINE J. (ed.), *L'Âge du Cuivre européen: civilisations à vases campaniformes.* Paris, 107-119.

NEUSTUPNÝ E. / SMRŽ Z. 1989. Čachovice: pohřebiště kultury se šňůrovou keramikou a zvoncovitých pohárů — Čachovice: a Corded Ware and Bell Beaker Cemetary. *Památky archeologické* 80, 2, 282-383.

NILIUS I. 1981. Beitrag zur Stellung der Einzelgrabkultur in Mecklenburg. *Jahresschrift für mitteldeutsche Vorgeschichte* 64, 63-87.

PEŠKA J. 1989. Die Anfänge der Bronzezeit in Ostmähren. In: BUCHVALDEK M. / PLESLOVÁ-ŠTIKOVÁ E. (eds), *Das Äneolithikum und die früheste Bronzezeit (C14 3000-2000 b.c.) in Mitteleuropa: kulturelle und chronologische Beziehungen. Int. Symposium, 14 (Prag — Liblice, 20-24.10.1986).* Prague, 193-199.

PEŠKA J. / RAKOVSKÝ I. 1990. *Břeclavsko v pozdní době kamenné.* Mikulov.

PFAUTH U. 1987. Funde der Schnurkeramik von Landersdorf. *Das archäologische Jahr in Bayern*, 50-51.

PLESLOVÁ-ŠTIKOVÁ E. 1972. Eneolitické osídlení v Lysolajích u Prahy — Die äneolitische Besiedlung in Lysolaje bei Prag. *Památky archeologické* 63, 1, 3-141.

PRAUD I./ MARTIAL E. 2000. *Une nouvelle occupation du Néolithique final dans la vallée de la Deûle, à Annoeullin (nord). Journée d'information de l'Assoc. pour les études interrég. sur le Néolithique (Paris, 2 déc. 2000).* Saint-Germain-en-Laye, (Internéo; 3), 131-141.

RIEDER K.H. 2000. Ein Gräberfeld der Schnurkeramik aus Ingolstadt. *Das archäologische Jahr in Bayern*, 17-18.

SALANOVA L. 2000. *La question du campaniforme en France et dans les îles anglo-normandes: productions, chronologie et rôles d'un standard céramique.* Paris.

SARTI L. / CARLINI C. / MARTINI F. 1999-2000. L'Eneolitico di Volpaia a Sesto Fiorentino: primi dati sulle produzioni fittili e litiche. *Rivista di Scienze Preistoriche* 50, 189-227.

SCHMIDT R. R. 1945. *Die Burg Vucedol.* Zagreb.

ŠEBELA L. 1981. Die Mährische Schnurkeramik und die Frübronzezeit. *Slovenská Archeólogia* 19, 1, 181-189.

ŠEBELA L. 1993. Lid s šňůrovou keramikou. In: PODBORSKÝ V. (ed.), *Praveki dejiny Moravy.* Brno, 204-218.

TAFFANEL O. / TAFFANEL J. 1980. Le Vérazien de Mailhac (Aude). In: Guilaine J. (ed.), *Le groupe de Véraza et la fin des temps néolithiques dans le Sud de la France et la Catalogne. Colloque (Narbonne, 3-4 juin 1977).* Paris, 33-37.

TARRUS J. 1980. Le Néolithique final (Vérazien) à Serinya (Gérone). In: GUILAINE J. (ed.), *Le groupe de Véraza et la fin des temps néolithiques dans le Sud de la France et la Catalogne. Colloque (Narbonne, 3-4 juin 1977).* Paris, 72-75.

TUREK J. 1998. The Bell Beaker Period in North-West Bohemia. In: BENZ M. / VAN WILLIGEN S. (eds), *Some New Approaches to the Bell Beaker „Phenomenon": Lost Paradise...?. Meeting of the Assoc. Archéologie et Gobelet, 2 (Feldbreg, Germ., April 18-20, 1997).* Oxford, 107-119.

TUSA S. 1997. *L'insediamento dell'età del bronzo con Bicchiere Campaniforme di Marcita, Castelvetrano (Trapani).* Trapani.

VAN DER BEEK Z. / FOKKENS H. 1998. 24 Years After Oberried: the „Dutch Model" Reconsidered. In: NICOLIS F. (ed.), *Bell Beakers Today: pottery, people, culture, symbols in prehistoric Europe. Int. Colloquium (Riva del Garda, Trento, 11-16 May 1998): abstracts.* Trento, 45-47.

VAQUER J. 1980. Le groupe de Véraza: essai sur l'évolution de la culture matérielle. In: GUILAINE J. (ed.), *Le groupe de Véraza et la fin des temps néolithiques dans le Sud de la France et la Catalogne. Colloque (Narbonne, 3-4 juin 1977).* Paris, 84-93.

    1998. Le Midi méditerranéen de la France. In: GUILAINE J. (ed.), *Atlas du Néolithique européen, 2A: l'Europe occidentale.* Liège, 413-500.

Similar but Different. Bell Beakers in Europe
Czebreszuk J. (ed.)
Poznań 2004

LA CERAMIQUE DOMESTIQUE DU CAMPANIFORME DE L'ITALIE CENTRALE ET SEPTENTRIONALE

Valentina Leonini (Siena, Italy)

Summary

The knowledge of the Bell Beaker Culture in Italy improved after the discover of new sites and the re-examination of old collections. In order to point out the state of we attempt to carry out a preliminary synthesis.

The analysis focused on the study of the common ware assemblages associated with the Bell Beaker pottery. The starting point of the research is represented by the study of the archeological sites discovered in the Florentine area, which, so far, correspond to the most significant Italian core of Bell the Beakers Culture; as a second step we considered the sites of Northern Italy discovered in a recognized context.

Afterward the assemblages of the Italian sites are compared with the ones of Southern-East France, since traditionally the decorated ware of this regions is matched up. It is possible to distinguish in the Italian assemblages two major components depending on the different sites: one is typically Bell Beaker characterized by pottery with sinuous profile decorated often by finger printed ribbons and impressions placed on the rim, frequently with the presence of handles; the other is related to different local Calcolithic traditions.

The paper attempts to illustrate the state of the on going research.

Résumé

La découverte de nouveaux gisements et l'étude de vieilles collections a récemment amélioré la connaissance du Campaniforme en Italie; on a pourtant aperçu la nécessité d'essayer une première synthèse sur l'état des connaissances.

On a choisi de considérer les céramiques domestiques, qui sont en général peu connues et rarement publiées par rapport aux ensembles décorés.

Les ensembles considérés sont d'abord les gisements de la région de Firenze, en Italie centrale, qui constituent à ce moment le noyau le plus significatif de la présence campaniforme en Italie continentale; on considère ensuite les habitats d'Italie septentrionale dont le contexte stratigraphique soit fiable. Le dernier niveau de l'étude est la comparaison des céramiques italiennes avec des séries du Midi français, desquelles les céramiques campaniformes décorées italiennes sont traditionnellement approchées.

Dans le cadre de ce colloque on se propose de exposer l'état de la recherche, encore en cours. Cet article présente l'état de la recherche et certains résultats préliminaires d'une thèse de Doctorat en Archéologie, qui devrait être terminée à la fin de l'année 2002.

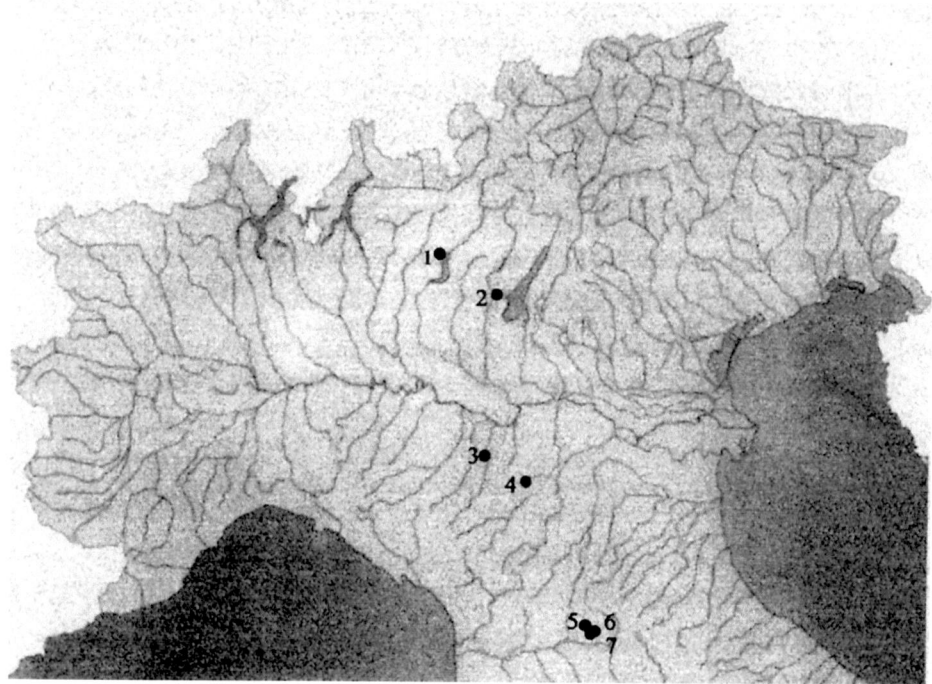

Fig. 1. Habitats campaniformes en Italie centrale et septentrionale: 1. Lovere; 2. Monte Covolo; 4. Sant'Ilario d'Enza; 5. Rubiera; 6. Querciola; 7. Lastruccia; 8. Semitella.

Le sujet de la recherche est l'analyse directe de la céramique commune associée à la céramique campaniforme décorée sur des sites d'habitat d'Italie centrale et septentrionale; seuls les ensembles dont le contexte stratigraphique est fiable ont été considérés.

Ces dernières années, la connaissance du troisième millénaire en Italie septentrionale a progressé grâce à la découverte de nouveaux sites aux pieds des Alpes lombardes et dans la plaine de Sesto Fiorentino en Toscana. Il s'agit de sites comme Lovere et Monte Covolo en Lombardia et Lastruccia en Toscana qui présentent d'importantes séquences stratigraphiques; ils permettent d'observer le développement du Campaniforme et de l'Epicampaniforme et, parfois, de saisir certains rapports avec les cultures énéolithiques locales.

Les sites

Italie centrale: Toscana

La recherche a commencé par l'analyse de plusieurs sites campaniformes de la plaine de Sesto Fiorentino, dans la région de Firenze (Fig. 1 nn. 5-7). Certains d'entre eux sont déjà connus: Querciola (Sarti 1997), Lastruccia (Sarti 1995-96), d'autres sont partiellement publiés: Semitella, Bulimacco-Cilea, Campo del Sorgo (Martini *et al.* 1999; Martini *et al.* 1996; Sarti / Martini 1993), Sassaiola (Volante 2001).

Les sites de Querciola, Semitella et Lastruccia sont les plus importants en raison de leur étendue et de la grande quantité de mobilier.

À Querciola (SARTI 1997) la céramique commune est très abondante et très variée au point de vue typologique. Les formes sont pour la plupart profondes et moyennes, les formes basses sont plus rares. Les bords éversés sur des parois convexes sont caractéristiques de l'ensemble (Fig. 2). Des formes basses et moyennes de la céramique décorée sont aussi présentes parmi les morphologies de la céramique commune: écuelles à bord épaissi, souvent à anse horizontale (*cuencos*), tasses (Fig. 3, 4). Parmi les éléments de décoration, les cordons, surtout digités, sont prédominants (Fig. 5). Les éléments de préhension, souvent appliqués sur les cordons, sont nombreux. Il y a également des perforations en lignes sous le bord (Fig. 6). Enfin, des fragments qui ont été interprétés comme pieds de différentes morphologies ne sont jamais associés à des formes reconstituables, il n'est donc pas possible d'établir s'il s'agissait de vases décorés ou communs (Fig. 7).

La production céramique de Querciola montre l'introduction dans la région florentine d'un ensemble étranger à la tradition énéolithique toscane. Pourtant, la présence d'une composante qui peut être attribuée au faciès précampaniforme – dont les rapports avec l'Italie péninsulaire, et spécialement avec la Tyrrhénienne moyenne et l'Adriatique moyenne, sont caractéristiques – est également importante: on peut reconnaître parmi ces caractères précampaniformes des traitements spécifiques des surfaces, comme l'application d'écailles d'argile imbriquées (*squame*) ou disposées pour former un motif décoratif qu'on appelle *a rosetta*, les parois striées par brossage (*Besenstricht*); certaines des formes simples aux parois rectilignes, qui sont cependant très génériques, pourraient également être attribuées à la composante de tradition locale (Fig. 8, 9).

Le site de Semitella (SARTI / MARTINI 1993, BALDUCCI 1997-98), qui se trouve à quelques dizaines de mètres de Querciola, semble représenter un moment légèrement postérieur; cette phase est caractérisée, au point de vue typologique, par une augmentation des formes basses, qui sont souvent carénées (Fig. 10). Les éléments de la tradition précampaniforme sont moins nombreux, alors que d'autres éléments sont présents qui se développent avec les phases finales du Campaniforme et au Bronze ancien local: tasses et écuelles carénées, fréquence des anses verticales, souvent coudées (SARTI, ce volume).

L'habitat de Lastruccia (SARTI 1995-96 et ce volume) présente une importante séquence stratigraphique du Campaniforme évolué jusqu'au début de l'âge du Bronze moyen. La première phase est la moins importante du fait de son extension et de la quantité de mobilier découvert. Les caractères généraux ne diffèrent pas de ceux de Querciola, mais sont représentés par une moindre variété de types.

Les sites de cette première phase du Campaniforme en Toscana témoignent de la présence d'un faciès campaniforme local dont la production céramique est très homogène. Si on considère aussi d'autres éléments, non céramiques, on remarque encore une fois l'existence de ces deux composantes, dont une constitue une rupture avec la tradition énéolithique, l'autre, au contraire, en conservant certains aspects.

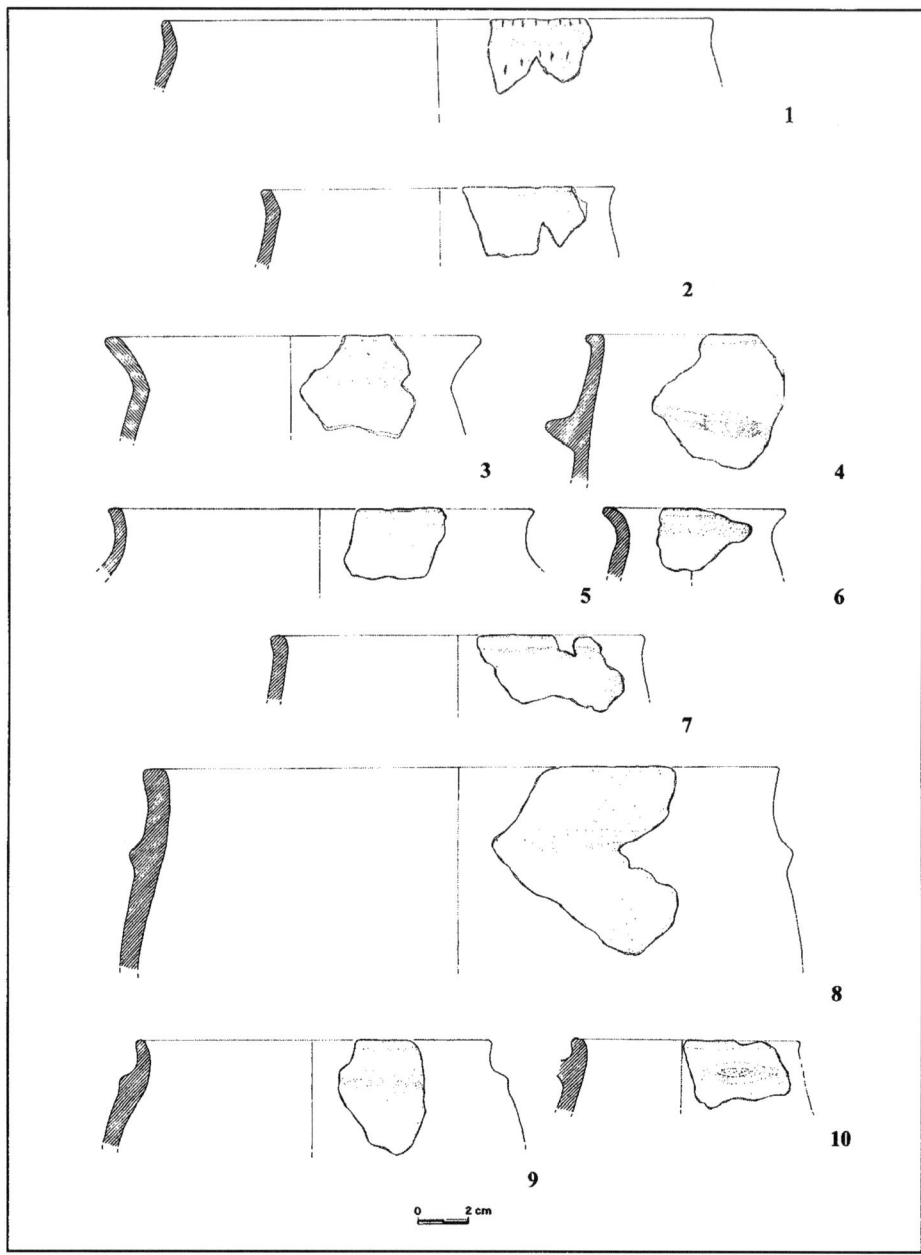

Fig. 2.   Querciola (SARTI 1997).

On peut citer parmi les éléments originaux les suivantes:
- le répertoire de la céramique décorée et d'une partie de la céramique commune;
- les modes de l'implantation dans des paléolits (MARTINI *et al.* 1999; SARTI / MARTINI 2001a);

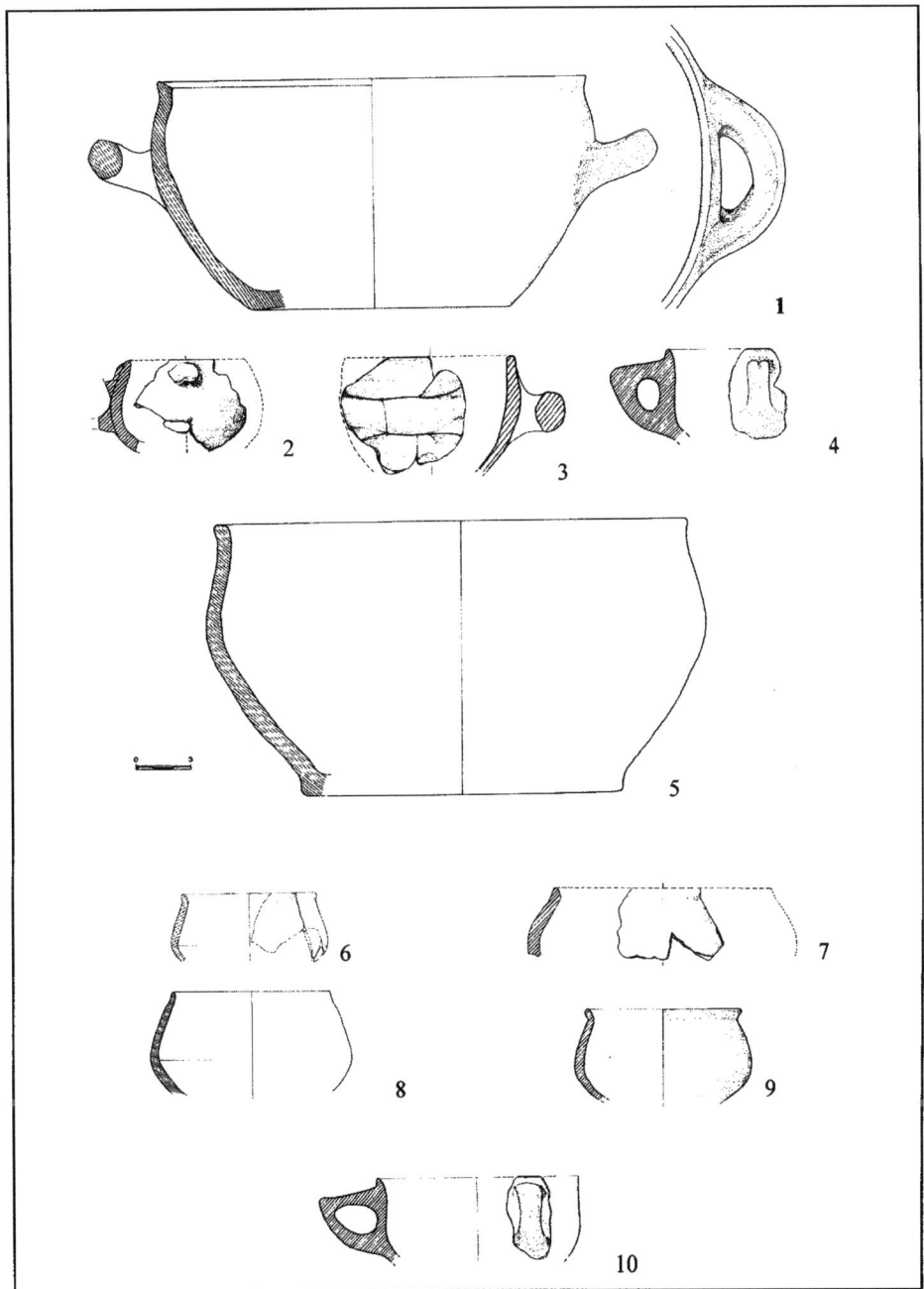

Fig. 3. Querciola (SARTI 1997).

Similar but Different. Bell Beakers in Europe

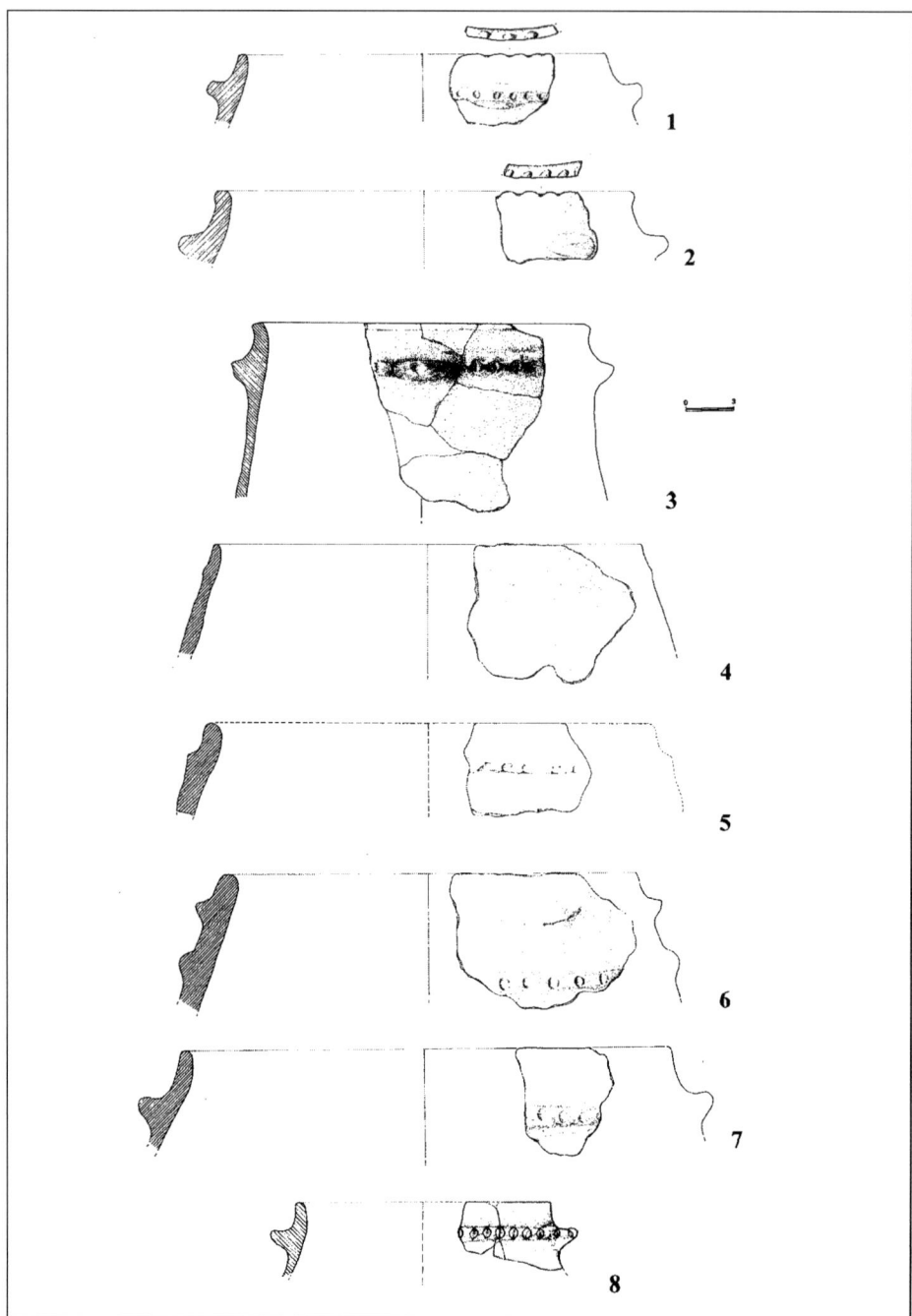

Fig. 4. Querciola (SARTI 1997).

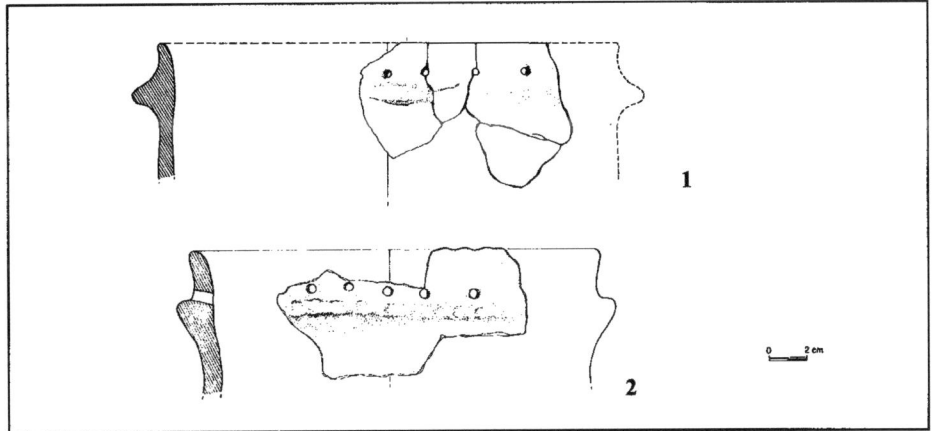

Fig. 5. Querciola (Sarti 1997).

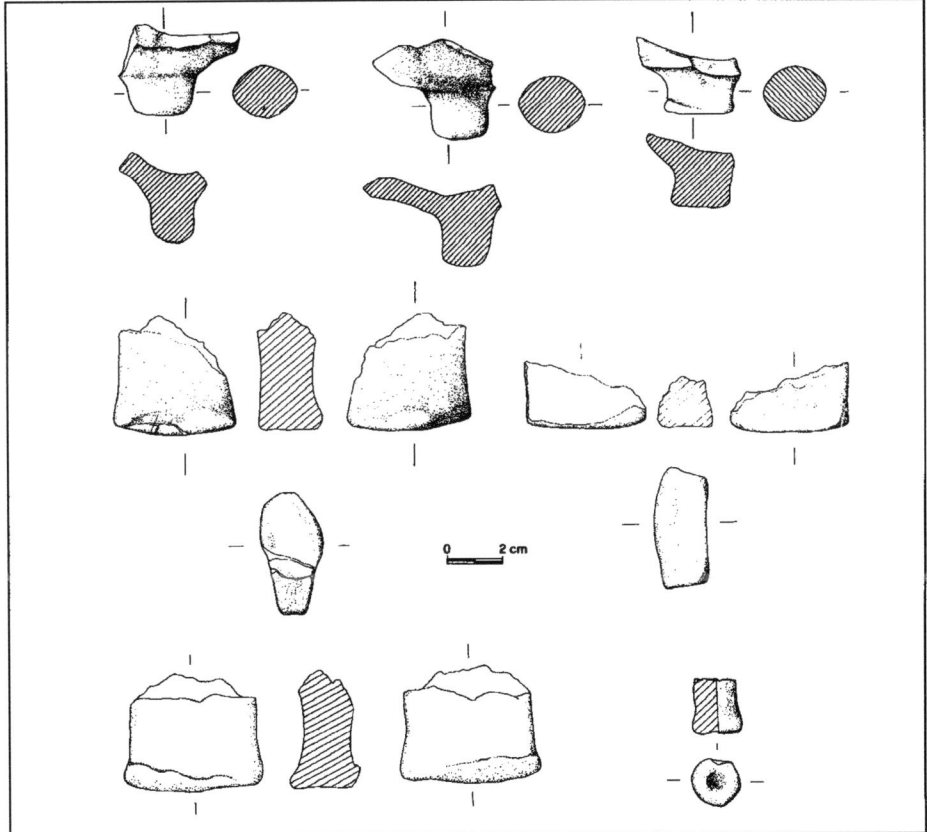

Fig. 6. Querciola (Sarti 1997).

Similar but Different. Bell Beakers in Europe

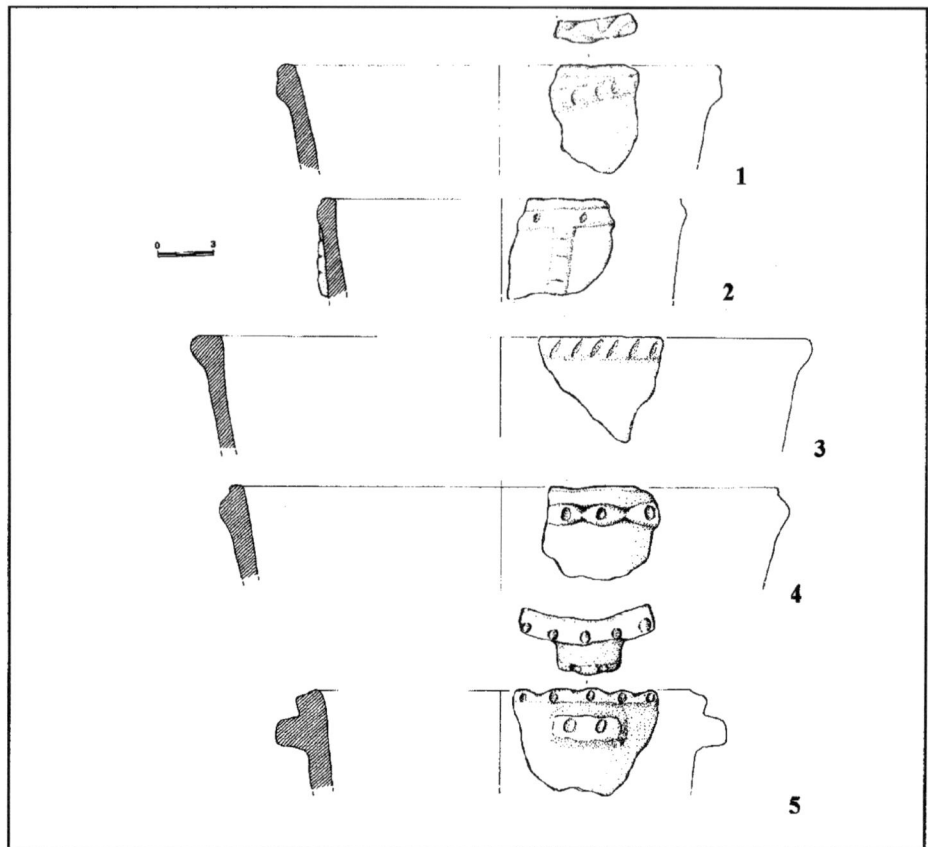

Fig. 7. Querciola (SARTI 1997).

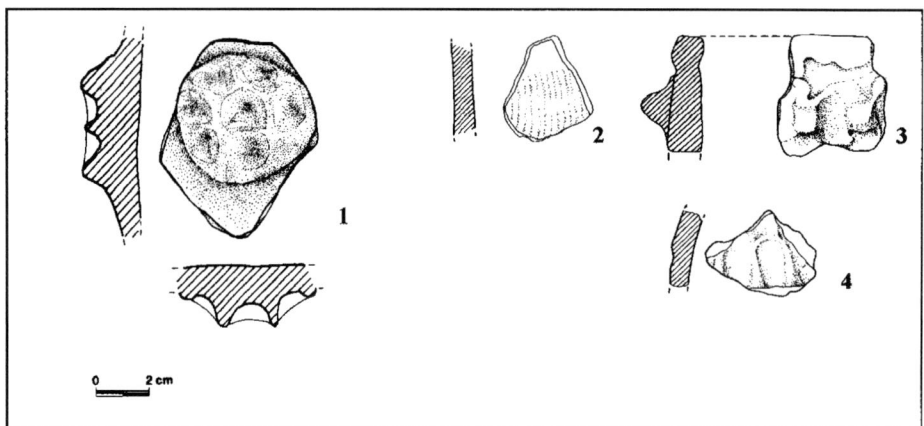

Fig. 8. Querciola (SARTI 1997).

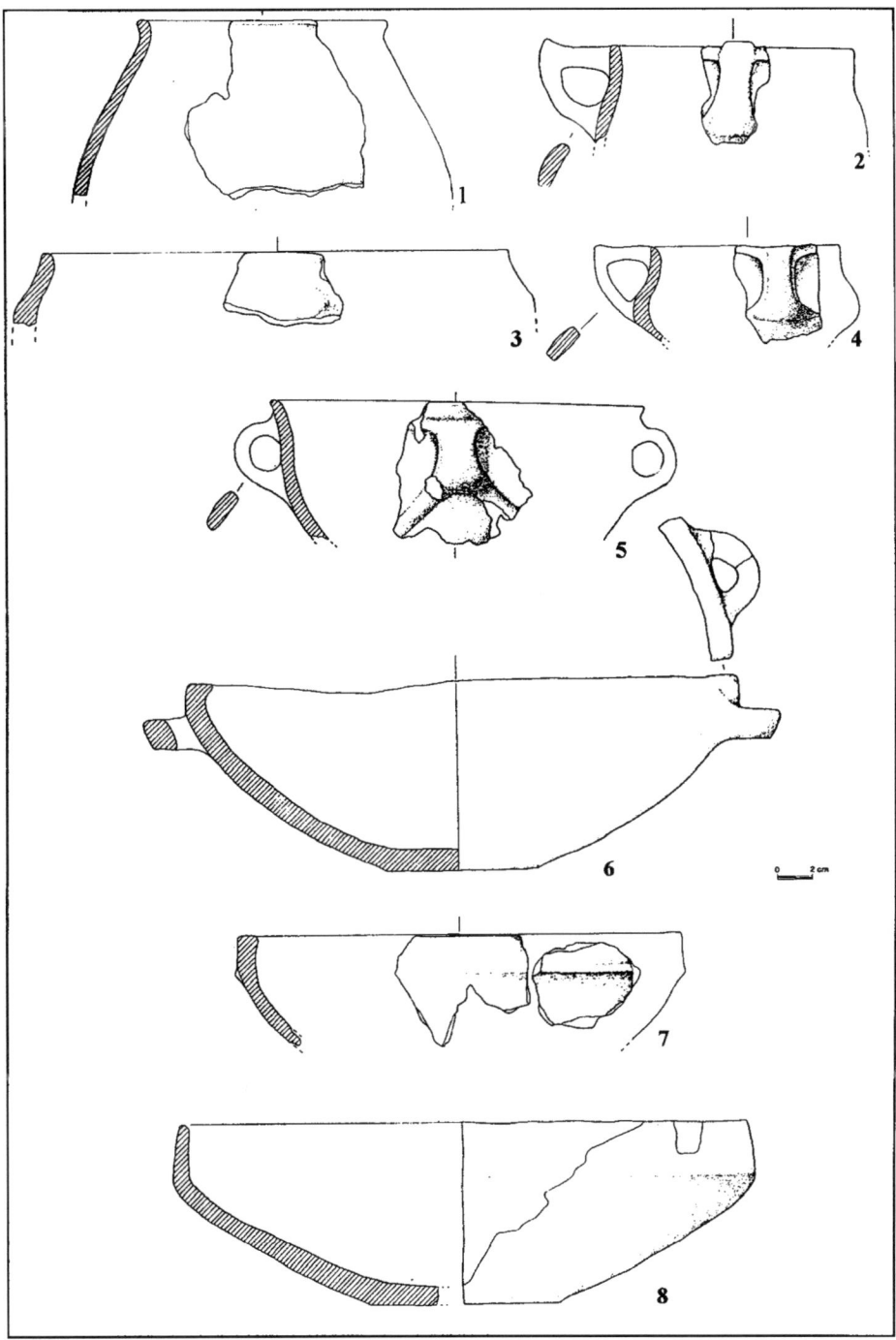

Fig. 9. Semitella (Balducci 1997-1998).

Similar but Different. Bell Beakers in Europe

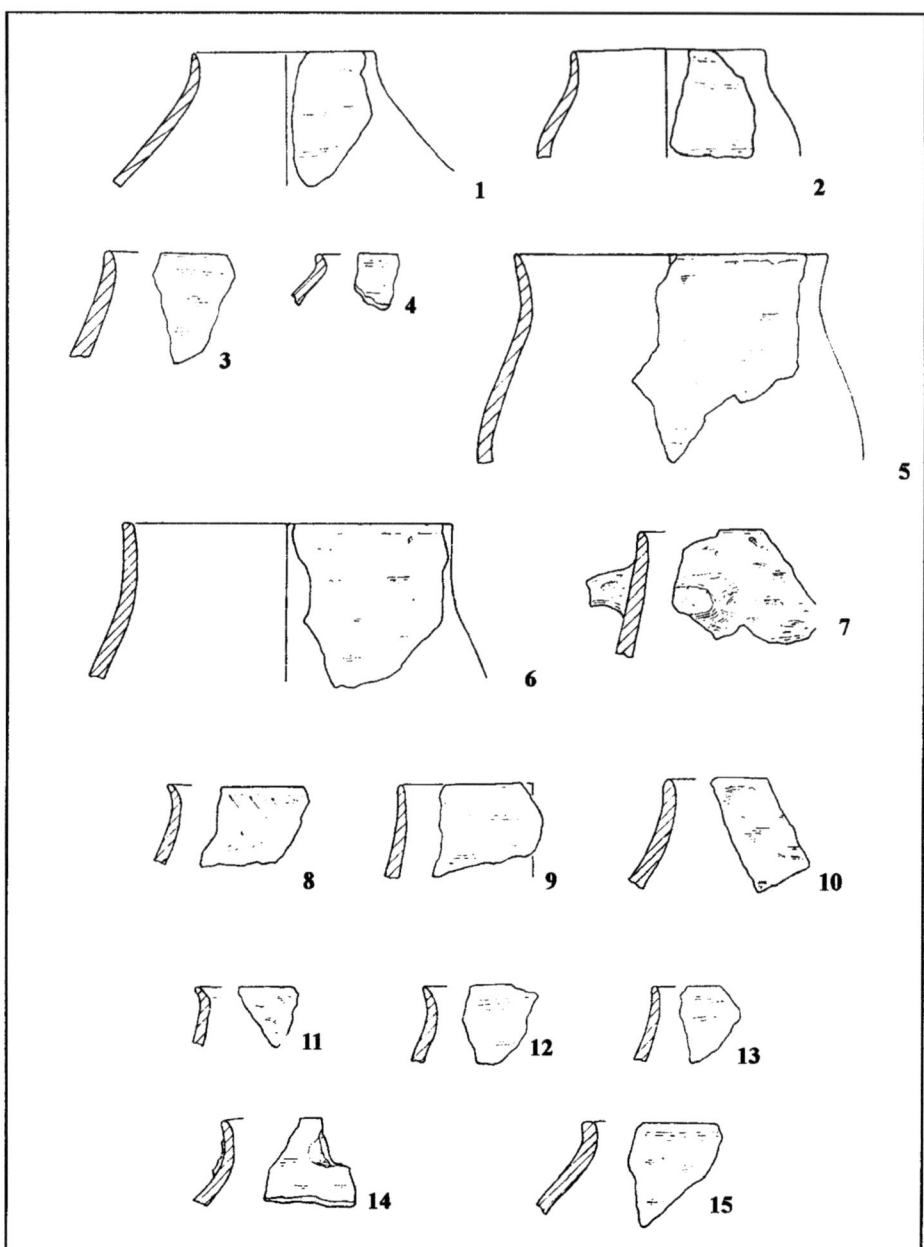

Fig. 10. Sant'Ilario d'Enza (Barfield 1975).

- l'augmentation de l'importance de l'élevage des bovidés, processus qui avait déjà été remarqué pour les premières phases de l'âge du cuivre en Toscana (Corridi 1997);
- l'introduction de certaines innovations dans la sphère cultuelle, comme la sépulture de bovidés de Semitella (Sarti / Martini 1993; Sarti / Anastasio 2001) et la structure complexe de Via Bruschi (Sarti et al. 1987-88);

et parmi les éléments de tradition énéolithique:
- le territoire d'approvisionnement des matières premières, spécialement argileuses et lithiques (Martini et al. 1996; Cipriani et al. 2000-01);
- le choix des sites pour les implantations: ils sont concentrés dans une aire limitée, qui était déjà connue avant;
- une partie du répertoire céramique et les techniques de fabrication.

Pour ce qui concerne les industries lithiques, il est très difficile de saisir les rapports avec les cultures précédentes, à cause de la faible quantité de matériel trouvé.

En conclusion, il est possible de remarquer que la composante du substrat énéolithique en Toscana est plus importante pour la formation de l'ensemble campaniforme local que ce qu'on ne le pensait jusqu'à aujourd'hui, aussi bien pour l'artisanat comme pour d'autres choix culturels.

L'Italie septentrionale: Emilia Romagna

J'ai réexaminé les séries de Sant'Ilario d'Enza (Barfield et al. 1975) et Rubiera (Bermond Montanari et al. 1982). Les deux sites ont connu une fréquentation de brève durée; ils n'ont pas été fouillés intégralement et ils demeurent presque les seuls témoignages archéologiques du troisième millénaire dans cette région.

À Sant'Ilario d'Enza le complexe de la céramique commune est caractérisé par un pourcentage très haut de formes profondes et moyennes à profil sinueux, à cols de morphologies et dimensions variées (Fig. 11). Parmi les éléments les plus caractéristiques de l'ensemble, il faut citer la fréquence des anses verticales (Fig. 12), les impressions digitées sur les bords et les impressions éparpillées sur les parois des pots; ces impressions sont obtenues par l'utilisation de divers outils, mais celles réalisées à l'ongle sont les plus nombreuses (Fig. 13). Les cordons et les éléments de décoration plastiques en général sont absents.

Un seul fragment qui pourrait être en relation avec la tradition énéolithique locale a été analysé: il s'agit d'un tesson décoré à bandes d'argile imbriquées.

L'ensemble est très homogène, caractérisé par un nombre limité de types céramiques.

La céramique commune de Rubiera définit un ensemble plus complexe et riche de types céramiques; comme à Sant'Ilario, les formes profondes et moyennes sont prédominantes, mais des formes basses sont aussi présentes. Les profils sinueux, avec une certaine variété de morphologie, sont les plus fréquents (Fig. 14).

Les nombreuses impressions sur le bord des pots caractérisent fortement la céramique de Rubiera (Fig. 15, 16); une variante originale, qui n'est pas connue ailleurs jusqu'à présent, est le type à bord retourné ou épaissi à décor quadrillé incisé (Fig. 14 nn. 4-8). De rares décorations à l'ongle sur le parois, proches du type de Sant'Ilario, sont présentes.

A l'inverse de ce qui est observé à Sant'Ilario, les éléments de préhension sont très rares, alors que les décorations plastiques et spécialement les cordons digités sont bien présents (Fig. 16).

On ne connaît pas la préhistoire de la région où se trouvent ces deux sites pour les phases précédentes le campaniforme; les seules données proviennent de quelques ramassages de surface, en cours d'étude (Tirabassi comm. pers.), et semblent montrer la présence sur le territoire d'un faciès céramique à parois "non lisses", peut être du type de Spilamberto (Bagolini 1981). Il ne semble donc pas exister de liaison entre le Campaniforme et le substrat local; au contraire, le campaniforme semble être tout à fait étranger dans la région et il ne semble pas non plus avoir eu des relations d'échanges avec les groupes indigènes, excepté pour la présence du seul tesson à bandes d'argile imbriquées à Sant'Ilario. Mais, il faut rappeler encore une fois que cette hypothèse se fonde sur des données encore insuffisantes.

Pour ce qui concerne les rapports entre les deux sites, on observe à la fois des affinités et des différences, aussi bien pour la céramique commune que pour les vases ornés. Ce double constat demeure difficile à comprendre: la chronologie absolue (Nicolis 1998) ne permet pas de proposer une périodisation et il n'est pas possible non plus d'évoquer des fonctions différentes pour ces deux sites, envisagés comme des habitats à brève durée d'occupation.

Très récemment, des affinités liées à la technologie céramique ont été mises en évidence (Bermond Montanari 2001), parmi lesquelles l'utilisation de chamotte dans les pâtes et le type de cuisson à basse température, qui s'ajoutent aux éléments communs aux deux sites émiliens.

Lombardia

Le site le plus important de ceux examinés en Lombardia est Lovere (Poggiani Keller 1999-2000); il s'agit d'un site multistratifié, dont la fréquentation, qui débute au néolithique ancien, se poursuit jusqu'à la fin de l'âge du Bronze. Au sein de cette séquence, on peut observer deux couches énéolithiques, deux couches campaniformes et une couche épicampaniforme.

Les deux niveaux campaniformes diffèrent par l'apparition, dans la couche supérieure, de quelques formes carénées. On peut, comme ailleurs, distinguer deux composantes pour la céramique commune. L'une est caractérisée par la prédominance de formes profondes et moyennes à profil sinueux, souvent à bords digités, par la présence de anses et de préhensions, par les cordons digités (Fig. 17). L'autre composante montre un très fort caractère énéolithique local, comme le confirme l'examen des niveaux d'occupation antérieurs (Fig. 18); le faciès précampaniforme présent peut être identifié au type White ware défini pour le site de Monte Covolo (Barfield *et al.* 1975-76): formes profondes simples aux parois rectilignes, pâtes très grossières présentant des inclusions non calibrées, fréquence du brossage, fausses (et plus rarement vraies) perforations en ligne sous le bord. La séquence stratigraphique même confirme celle de Monte Covolo, qui se trouve aussi aux

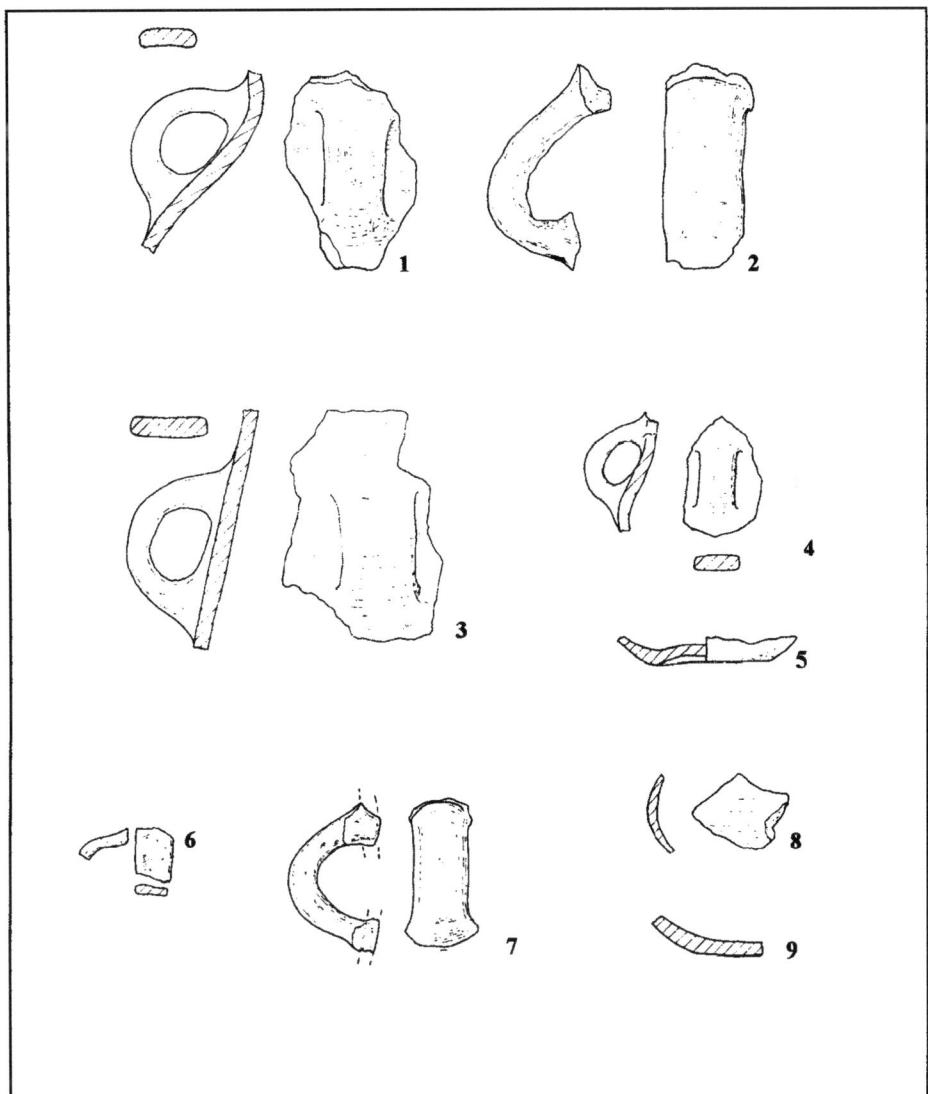

Fig. 11. Sant'Ilario d'Enza (BARFIELD 1975).

pieds des Alpes, mais dans ce dernier site l'association des éléments originaux avec la composante précampaniforme n'est pas certaine, à cause de la disposition stratigraphique. Les fouilles de Monte Covolo ont été récemment reprises, mais les données ne sont pas encore disponibles.

On peut observer, en Lombardia, l'existence d'une importante rupture culturelle au passage entre le Néolithique final et l'Enéolithique, représentée par les productions céramiques, les matières premières, les techniques de fabrication, la technologie lithique (BARFIELD 2001; POGGIANI KELLER 1999-2000; POGGIANI KELLER et al. à paraître), alors que le campaniforme ne semble introduire que quelques éléments nou-

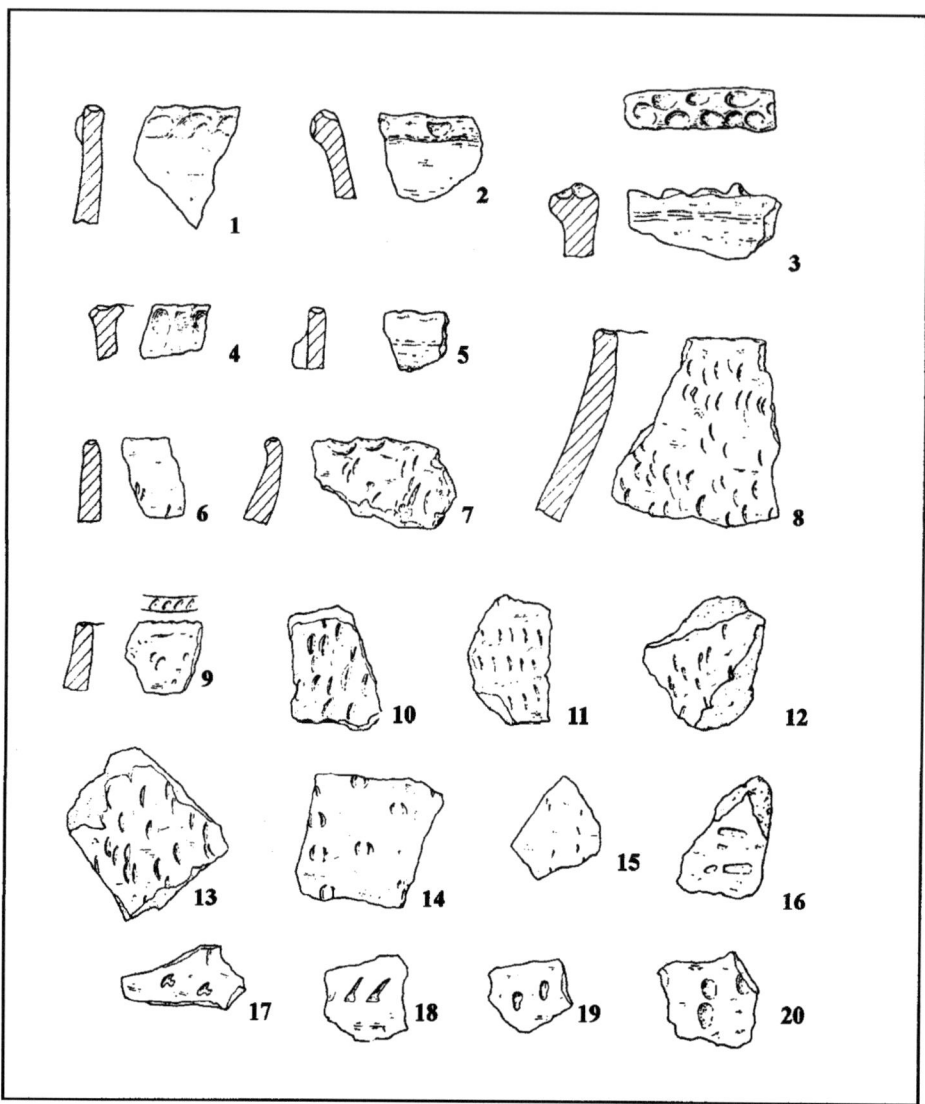

Fig. 12. Sant'Ilario d'Enza (BARFIELD 1975).

veaux dans un substrat très fort. Les autres aspects de la vie de ces sites sont encore en cours d'étude et ne peuvent pas encore nous aider à comprendre les processus culturels qui se sont déroulés au cours du troisième millénaire.

Considérations générales

Les sites considérés ici pour l'Italie centrale et septentrionale, et quelques autres en cours d'étude, montrent une situation complexe pour la céramique commune. Tous les ensembles décrits partagent certains caractères typologiques et structurels, parmi lesquels:

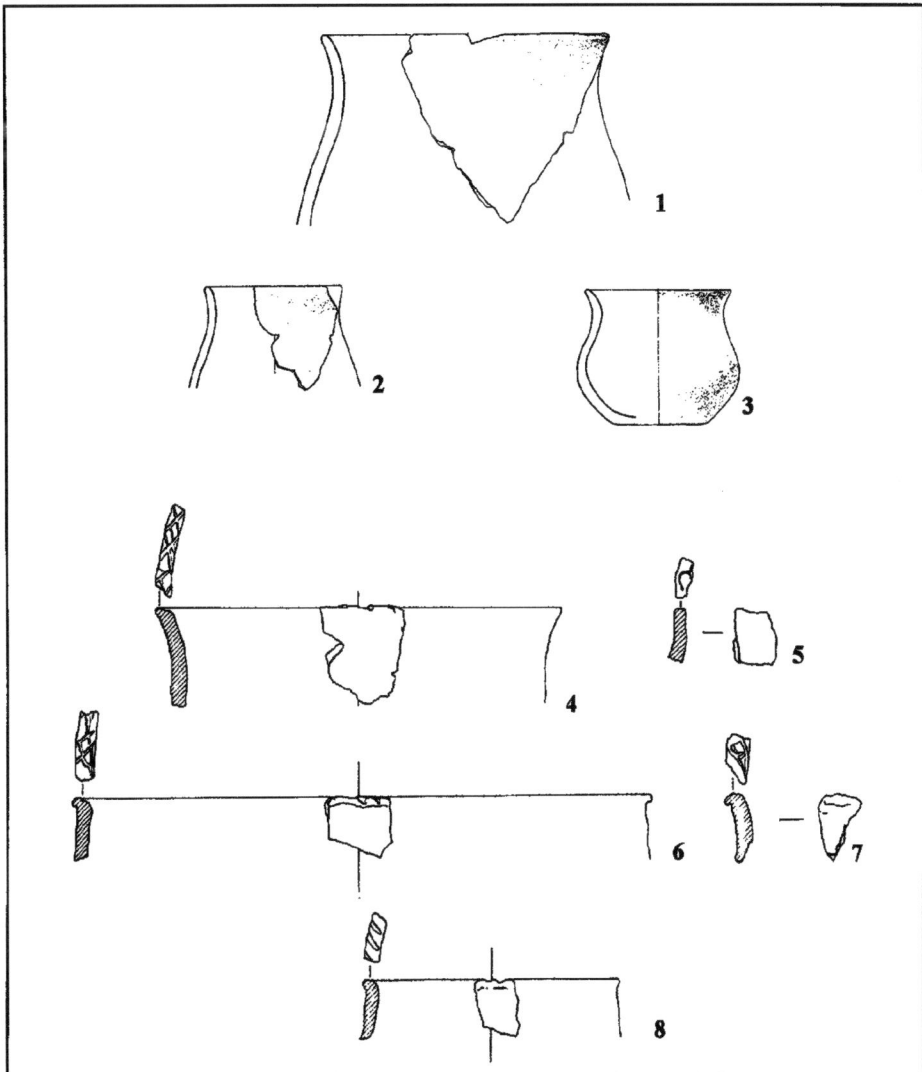

Fig. 13. Rubiera (BERMOND MONTANARI 1982).

- la forte prédominance de formes profondes et moyennes à profil sinueux;
- la fréquence de anses verticales et des éléments de préhension;
- la fréquence des cordons, pour la plupart digités, même en association avec les anses/préhensions;
- la fréquence des bords décorés: digités ou, plus rarement, incisés.

L'importance de l'un ou de l'autre de ces éléments est variable selon les sites considérés: par exemple, à Sant'Ilario les anses sont très nombreuses et les cordons absents, à Rubiera on remarque une importance particulière des bords décorés, parmi lesquels il y a un type exclusif de ce site; dans les ensembles toscans les

Similar but Different. Bell Beakers in Europe

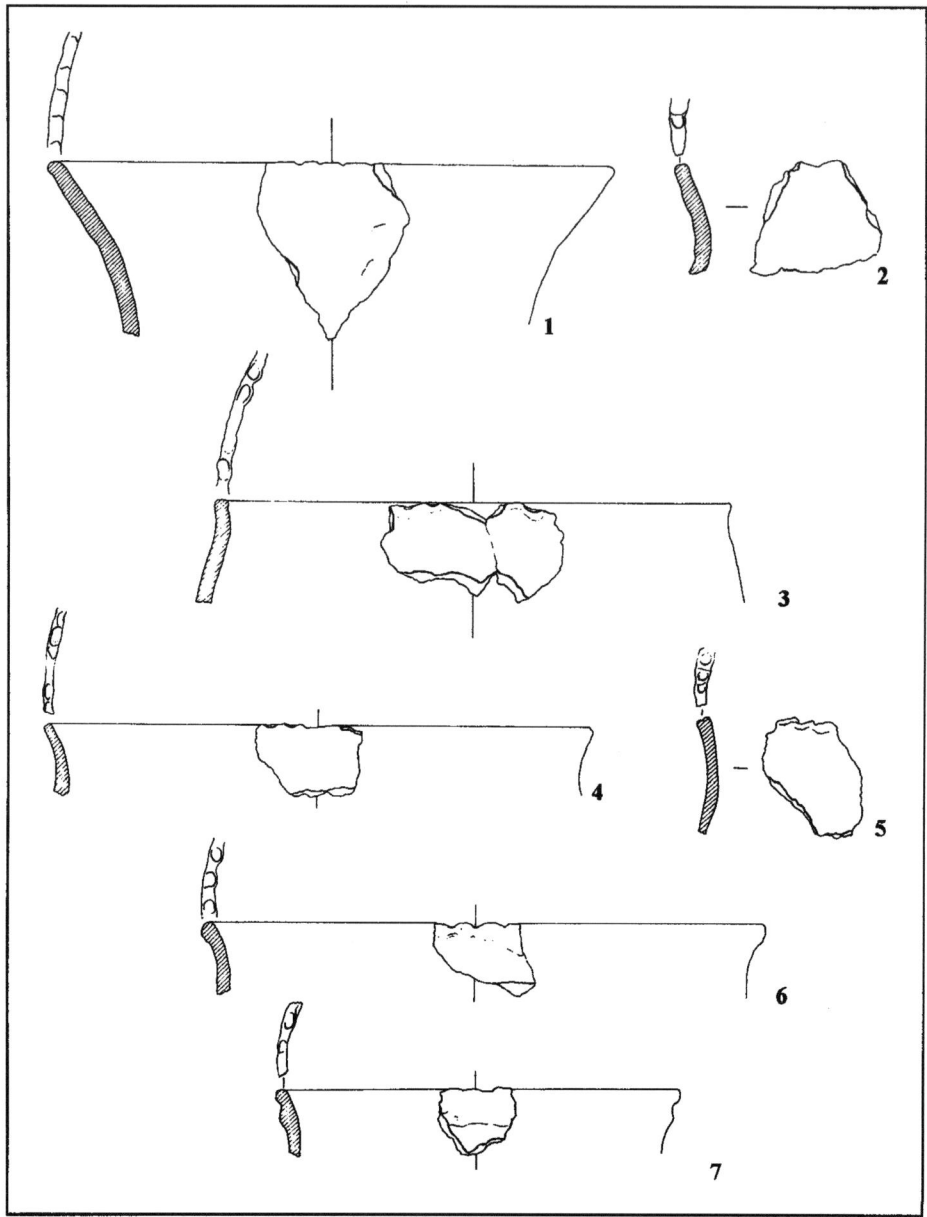

Fig. 14.   Rubiera (BERMOND MONTANARI 1982).

anses sont nombreuses et les impressions sur le bords plus rares; en Lombardia on trouve enfin des cordons verticaux, comme à Il Cristo di Gazzo Veronese, un site de la région du Veneto, du coté oriental du lac de Garda, qui est partiellement publié (SALZANI 1998).

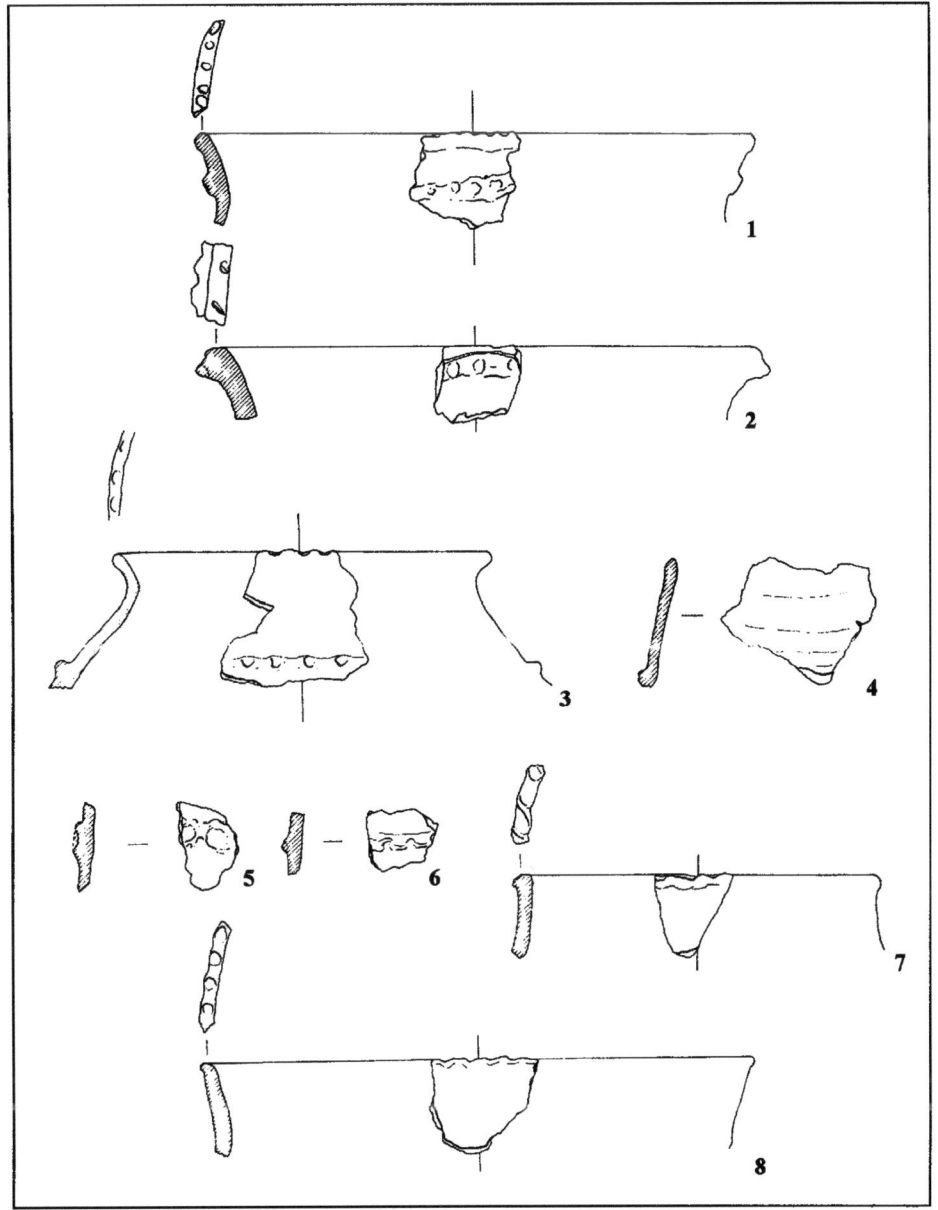

Fig. 15. Rubiera (BERMOND MONTANARI 1982).

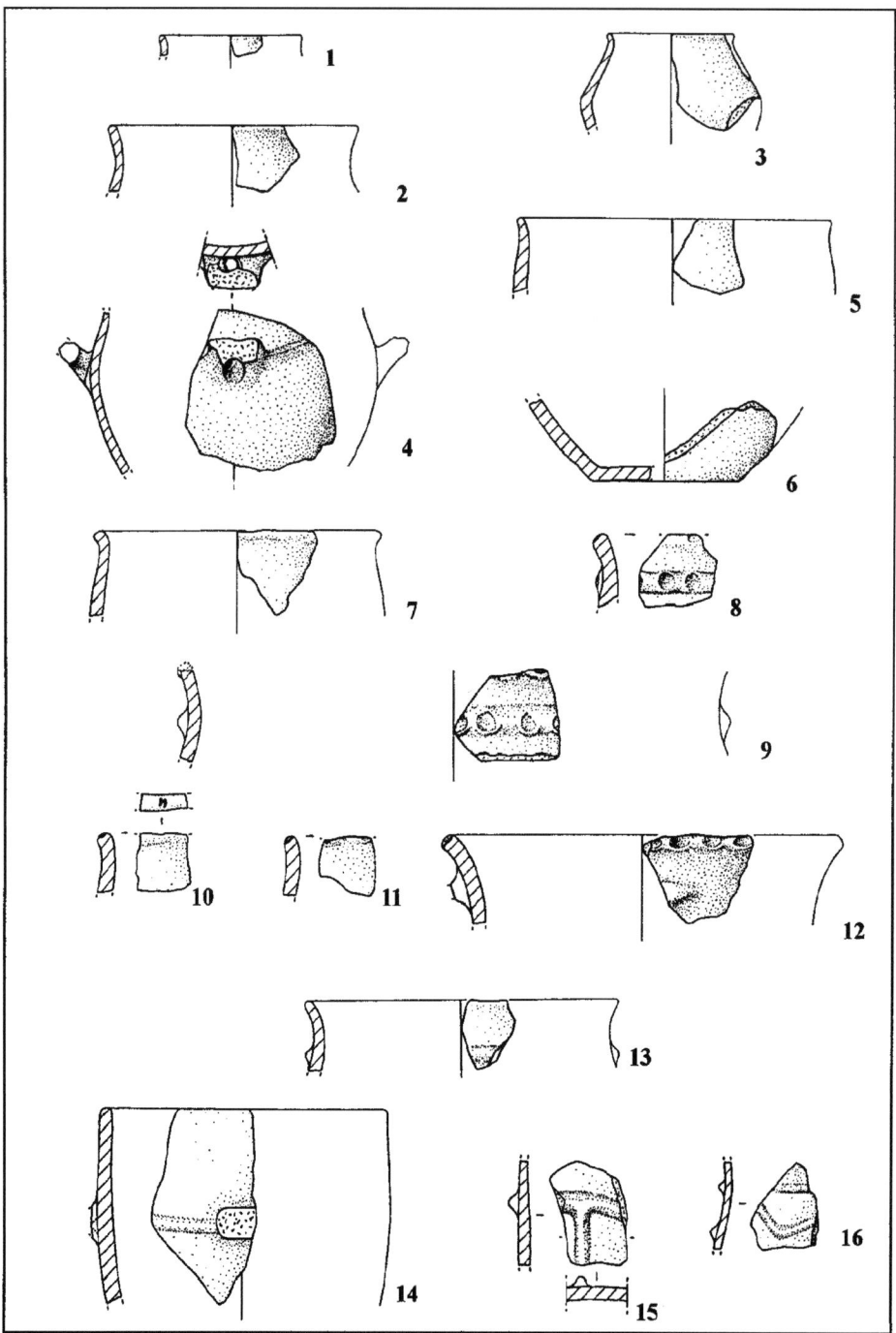

Fig. 16. Lovere (POGGIANI KELLER 1999–2000).

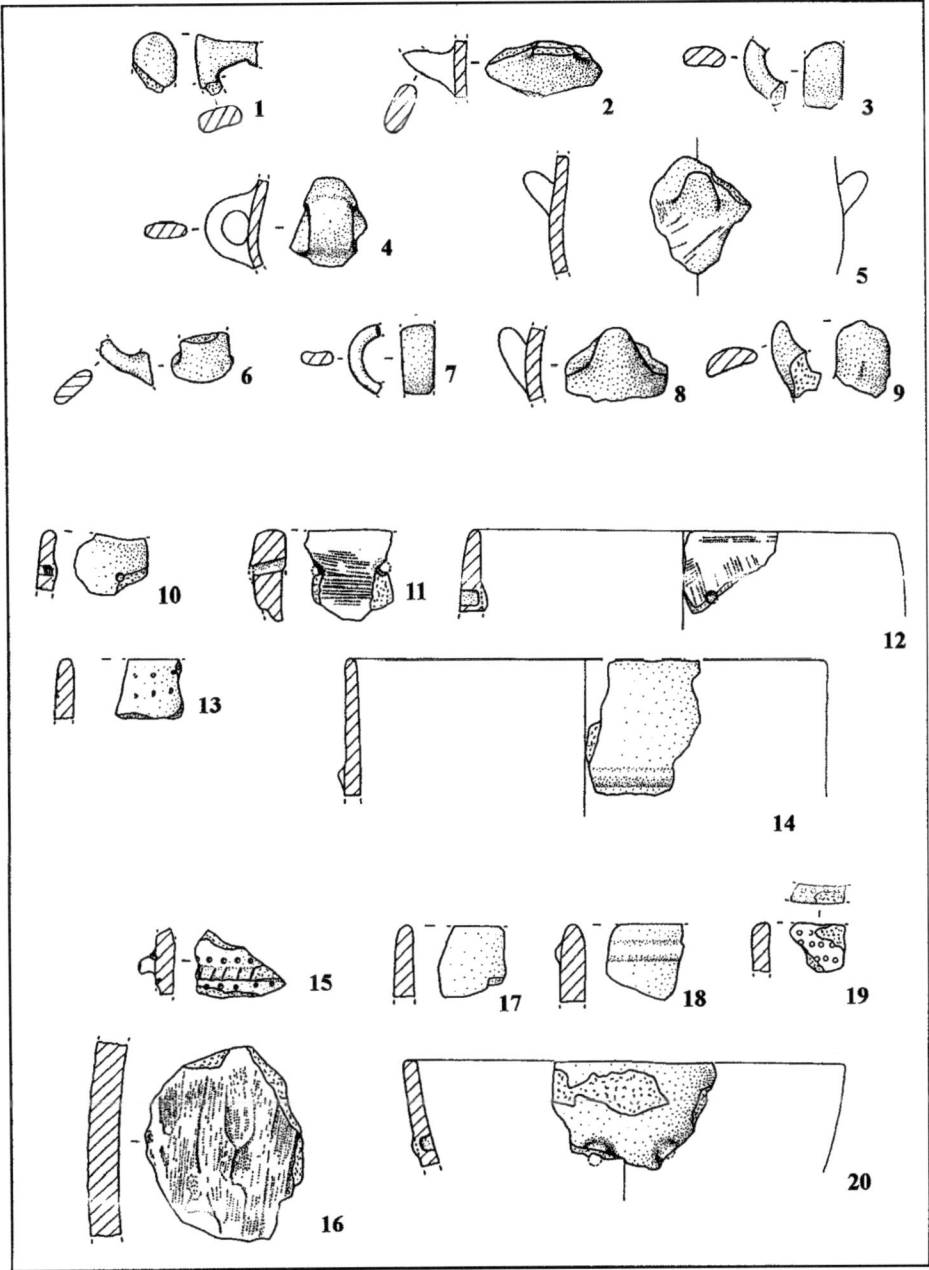

Fig. 16. Lovere (POGGIANI KELLER 1999–2000).

Les sites présentés se différencient entre eux par l'existence de certains aspects spécifiques:
- à Querciola il y a des éléments à perforations en ligne sous le bord et de pieds de deux morphologie principales, cylindriques et trapézoïdaux;
- dans tous les sites toscans on trouve des écuelles à bord plat épaissi parfois à anse horizontale;
- à Sant'Ilario les impressions à l'ongle éparpillées sur les parois, qu'on trouve aussi, mais bien plus rarement, à Rubiera;
- certains éléments technologiques (dont je propose ici quelques données, quoique les analyses ne soient pas toutes effectuées): la présence de chamotte à Sant'Ilario, Rubiera et Lovere, absente en Toscana; tout ce qui concerne les techniques de production semble constituer des groupes régionaux;
- un ensemble de formes et de traitements des surfaces qui pourraient être expliqué comme une composante de tradition locale et donc être strictement régionale. Il est plus difficile de saisir ce rapport pour les sites émiliens, où on ne connaît presque pas les cultures précampaniformes, il pourrait cependant ne pas exister; une faible importance est aussi remarquée pour le substrat à Monte Covolo, mais la stratigraphie n'est pas aussi fiable. Dans le cadre d'un rapport avec le substrat local on pourrait interpréter aussi d'autres éléments culturels: par exemple, la continuité de certaines productions lithiques en Lombardia et, peur être, en Veneto (BARFIELD 2001, POGGIANI KELLER et al. à paraître); en Toscana, la faible quantité de mobilier lithique pour l'énéolithique ne permet pas de proposer une interprétation, mais les données connues ne semblent pas invalider cette hypothèse. Les choix économiques, en Lombardia comme en Toscana, semblent eux aussi montrer une certaine continuité, comme les implantations, au moins pour ce qui concerne le choix des sites: en Toscana il y a cependant une stratégie d'implantation nouvelle qui apparaît au Campaniforme (SARTI / MARTINI 2001b).

Conclusions

À ce stade de la recherche il me semble donc possible de proposer l'existence de deux composantes distinctes pour la céramique commune du Campaniforme.

Il s'agit tout d'abord d'une céramique campaniforme spécifique, que j'ai considéré, pour le moment, comme un ensemble homogène, mais des détails montrant une certaine diversité régionale apparaissent déjà. Le caractère de ce Campaniforme d'Italie centrale et septentrionale, comme le montre la céramique commune, est local, néanmoins de très importantes relations avec d'autres régions d'Europe peuvent avoir eu un rôle déterminant pour la formation de ce faciès: les plus significatives semblent avoir été l'aire centro-orientale, particulièrement la Bohème, la Moravie, la basse Saale, et le couloir Rhône-Rhin (BESSE 2001). Une comparaison avec le mobilier de quelques habitats de la France méridionale est en cours dans le cadre de la thèse, et l'étude doit prochainement s'étendre à l'Europe centrale.

L'autre composante est due aux substrats locaux et diffère d'une région à l'autre; c'est à partir de l'intégration de ces deux composantes qu'on peut suivre le développement des faciès du premier âge du Bronze en continuité stylistique et stratigraphique avec les phases précédentes, comme le montrent trois sites stratifiés - Lovere, Monte Covolo et Lastruccia - (ASPES / FASANI 1972; POGGIANI KELLER 1999-2000; NICOLIS 2001). A partir de ce moment on remarque aussi l'apparition d'un nouveau réseau de relations entre l'Italie du nord et d'autres régions européennes.

Bibliographie

ASPES A. / FASANI L. 1972. Aspetti e problemi dell'antica età del Bronzo in Italia settentrionale, *Rassegna di Archeologia* 7, 418-422.

BAGOLINI B. (ed.) 1981, *Il neolitico e l'età del rame. Ricerca a Spilamberto e a S. Cesario 1977-1980*. Vignola.

BALDUCCI C. 1997-98. *Il Campaniforme di Semitella a Sesto Fiorentino: la produzione fittile*, Università degli Studi della Tuscia di Viterbo, Facoltà di Conservazione dei Beni Culturali, Anno Accademico 1997/98, tesi di laurea, inedita.

BARFIELD L.H. 2001. Beaker lithics in northern Italy, in: NICOLIS F. (ed.), *Bell Beakers today. Pottery, people, culture, symbols in prehistoric Europe. Proceedings of the International Colloquium, Riva del Garda (Trento, Italy) 11-16 may 1998*. Trento, 507-518.

BARFIELD L.H. / BIAGI P. / BORRELLO M.A. 1975-76. Scavi nella stazione di Monte Covolo (1972-73). Parte I. *Annali dl Museo di Gavardo* 12, 7-160.

BARFIELD L.H. / CREMASCHI M. / CASTELLETTI L. 1975. Stanziamento Del vaso campaniforme a Sant'Ilario d'Enza (Reggio Emilia), *Preistoria Alpina* 11, 155-199.

BERMOND MONTANARI G. 2001. Forme insediative e aspetti sepolcrali del Campaniforme dell'Italia settentrionale, in: NICOLIS F. (ed.) 2001, *Bell Beakers today. Pottery, people, culture, symbols in prehistoric Europe. Proceedings of the International Colloquium, Riva del Garda (Trento, Italy) 11-16 may 1998*. Trento, 199-206.

BERMOND MONTANARI G. / CREMASCHI M. / SALA B. 1982, Rubiera: insediamento del vaso campaniforme, *Preistoria Alpina* 18, 79-109.

BESSE M. 2001. Bell Beaker Common Ware: a discussion of its problems illustrated by the Rhone-Rhine corridor, in: NICOLIS F. (ed.) 2001, *Bell Beakers today. Pottery, people, culture, symbols in prehistoric Europe. Proceedings of the International Colloquium, Riva del Garda (Trento, Itlay) 11-16 may 1998*. Trento, 277-287.

CIPRIANI N. / DINI M. / GHINASSI M. / MARTINI F. / TOZZI C. 2000-01. L'approvvigionamento della materia prima in alcuni tecnocomplessi della Toscana appenninica, *Rivista di Scienze Preistoriche* LI, 337-388.

CORRIDI C. 1997. Archeozoologia, in: SARTI (ed.) 1997, *Querciola. Insediamento campaniforme a Sesto Fiorentino*. Firenze.

MARTINI F. / PALLECCHI P. / SARTI L. 1996. *La ceramica preistorica in Toscana. Artigianati e materie prime dal Neolitico all'età del Bronzo*. Firenze.

MARTINI F. / Poggesi G. / Sarti L. (eds.) 1999. *Lunga memoria della piana. L'area fiorentina dalla preistoria alla romanizzazione*. Firenze (guida della mostra).

NICOLIS F. 1998. Alla periferia dell'impero: il bicchiere campaniforme nell'Italia settentrionale, in: NICOLIS F. / MOTTES E. (eds.), *Simbolo ed enigma. Il bicchiere campaniforme e l'Italia nella preistoria europea del III millennio a. C., Catalogo della mostra (Riva del Garda, 12 maggio-30 settembre 1998)*. Trento, 47-68.

NICOLIS F. 2001. Some observations on the cultural setting of the Bell Beakers of Northern Italy, in: NICOLIS F. (ed.) 2001. *Bell Beakers today. Pottery, people, culture, symbols in prehistoric Europe. Proceedings of the International Colloquium, Riva del Garda (Trento, Itlay) 11-16 may 1998*. Trento, 207-227.

POGGIANI KELLER R. 1999-2000. Lovere (Bergamo): una sequenza stratigrafica esemplare dal Neolitico antico al Bronzo finale in area prealpina, *Rivista di Scienze Preistoriche* L, 297-374.

POGGIANI KELLER R. / MARTINI F. / BAIONI M. / LO VETRO D. à paraître, Monte Covolo tra tardo neolitico ed età del rame. Strutture e materiali degli scavi 1998-1999. *Atti del Congresso Il declino del mondo neolitico. Ricerche in Italia centro-settentrionale fra aspetti peninsulari, occidentali e nordalpini, Pordenone 5-7 aprile 2001*.

SALZANI L. 1998. Capanna dell'età del Rame a Gazzo Veronese, in: NICOLIS F. / MOTTES E. (eds.), *Simbolo ed enigma. Il bicchiere campaniforme e l'Italia nella preistoria europea del III millennio a. C., Catalogo della mostra (Riva del Garda, 12 maggio-30 settembre 1998)*. Trento, 77-79.

SARTI L. 1995-96. Cronostratigrafia del Campaniforme in area fiorentina: dati preliminari dall'insediamento di Lastruccia, *Rivista di Scienze Preistoriche* XLVII (1995-96), 239-260.

SARTI L. (ed.) 1997. *Querciola. Insediamento campaniforme a Sesto Fiorentino*. Firenze.

1998a. Aspetti insediativi del Campaniforme nell'Italia centrale, in: NICOLIS F. / MOTTES E. (eds.), *Simbolo ed enigma. Il bicchiere campaniforme e l'Italia nella preistoria europea del III millennio a. C., Catalogo della mostra (Riva del Garda, 12 maggio-30 settembre 1998)*. Trento, 137-201.

SARTI L. / ANASTASIO S. 2001, The ox grave from Semitella (Sesto Fiorentino, Firenze), in: NICOLIS F. (ed.), *Bell Beakers today. Pottery, people, culture, symbols in prehistoric Europe. Proceedings of the International Colloquium, Riva del Garda (Trento, Itlay) 11-16 may 1998*, 649-651.

SARTI L. / BIRTOLO R. / FOGGI B. / MAGI M. / MARTINI F. 1987-88. Il tumulo eneolitico di via Bruschi a Sesto Fiorentino, *Rivista di Scienze Preistoriche* XLI. Trento, 139-198.

SARTI L. / MARTINI F. 1993. *Costruire la memoria. Archeologia preistorica a Sesto Fiorentino (1982-1992)*. Firenze.

SARTI L. / MARTINI F. (eds.) 2000, *Insediamenti e artigianati dell'età del Bronzo in area fiorentina. Le ricerche archeologiche nei cantieri CONSIAG (1994-1996)*. Firenze.

2001a. *L'Eneolitico in area fiorentina: appunti e riflessioni*, Atti incontro di studio *Recenti acquisizioni, problemi e prospettive della ricerca sull'Eneolitico dell'Italia centrale*. Arcevia 1999.

2001b. Strategie insediative del Campaniforme in Italia centrale, in: NICOLIS F. (ed.), *Bell Beakers today. Pottery, people, culture, symbols in prehistoric Europe. Proceedings of the International Colloquium, Riva del Garda (Trento, Itlay) 11-16 may 1998*. Trento, 187-198.

VOLANTE N. 2001. Il Campaniforme di via della Sassaiola (Sesto Fiorentino, Firenze), *Rassegna di Archeologia* 16, 157-169.

Regional point of view

Similar but Different. Bell Beakers in Europe
Czebreszuk J. (ed.)
Poznań 2004

BURIALS AND BEAKERS: SEEING BENEATH THE VENEER IN LATE NEOLITHIC BRITAIN

Alex Gibson (Bradford, Great Britain)

During the majority of the C20th the perceived wisdom regarding the Beaker 'invasions' of Britain was that round-headed warriors dominated and subjugated the local populations. Fundamental to this theory was the appearance in the archaeological record of single, crouched inhumations beneath round barrows (Fig. 1). These burials were often accompanied by the pots themselves as well as various 'toolkits' of both a martial (arrowheads, wristguards, daggers and battle-axes) and a more mundane (copper awls, flint strike-a-lights and leatherworking tools) nature. Rich burials, associated with rare grave goods such as goldwork and jet and amber items, further illustrated the importance of these new people. Previous 'native' or insular burial traditions had involved the deposition of multiple inhumations or cremations beneath long barrows or within chambered tombs. Therefore, not only did the Beaker round barrow stand in marked contrast to what had gone before, but also the Beaker celebration of the individual must surely reflect fundamental changes in belief systems and/or the manifestation of new social identities.

The Beaker introduction of this burial tradition remained unchallenged in the archaeological literature despite the circularity of argument that it involved. For example, „Beaker people" introduced single crouched inhumations beneath round barrows therefore any crouched inhumation beneath a round barrow must, by necessity, be Beaker or post-Beaker in date. This was to an extent supported by the association of early Bronze Age (post-Beaker) vessels such as Food Vessels with a similar burial rite as well as early Bronze Age Urn forms accompanying cremation burials below similarly shaped mounds. Unaccompanied inhumations, without datable grave goods, were also seen to be early Bronze Age in date for the burial rite that they involved was held to be a Beaker introduction.

The lasting appeal of this thesis was largely due to its simplicity. This was despite some very obvious and well-known contradictions. Firstly, for example, not all Neolithic long barrows covered burials. There were, for instance, only the fragmentary remains of three individuals below Giants Hills II in Lincolnshire (EVANS / SIMPSON 1991) and there were no burials at all beneath the South Street long barrow in Wiltshire (ASHBEE *et al.* 1979). Secondly, the absence of burials in some passage graves was always attributed to later robbing; an explanation that was as difficult to prove as it was to argue against. Thirdly, there were also Neolithic and therefore

Similar but Different. Bell Beakers in Europe

Fig. 1. How it probably wasn't. The reconstruction of the burial of a man with Beaker and dagger from BATEMAN 1848.

pre-Beaker round barrows that had been excavated at the beginning of the 20th C. The round barrow of Duggleby Howe in Yorkshire, for example was not only associated with earlier Neolithic pottery, but also covered individual inhumations and cremations (KINNES *et al.* 1983) (Fig. 2). These were admittedly in large numbers but they comprised discrete burials and not the jumbles of disarticulated bones that were more common in long barrow contexts.

The long barrow and chambered tomb burials also demonstrated that the Neolithic populations practised excarnation. The burials were generally composed of disarticulated bones and there was evidence for the sorting of bones and probably also the removal of others. The finding of partly articulated human remains in the ditch of the causewayed enclosure at Hambledon Hill in Dorset seemed to provide at least one location for this excarnation process. Sub-rectangular 'mortuary enclosures' were also interpreted as enclosures where bodies were allowed to decompose prior to their incorporation in long barrows or chambered tombs. The singular lack of human remains from excavated examples of these sites however, was either attributed to the local soil conditions or to the fact that the remains had been removed to the long barrows; another circular argument that still persists in some of the literature. However, contracted inhumations within the Fussell's Lodge and Nutbane long barrows (ASHBEE 1966; MORGAN 1959) and an extended but complete burial in the passage of the chambered tomb at Hazleton (SAVILLE 1990) also seemed to suggest that some of the excarnation process may also have taken place within the tombs.

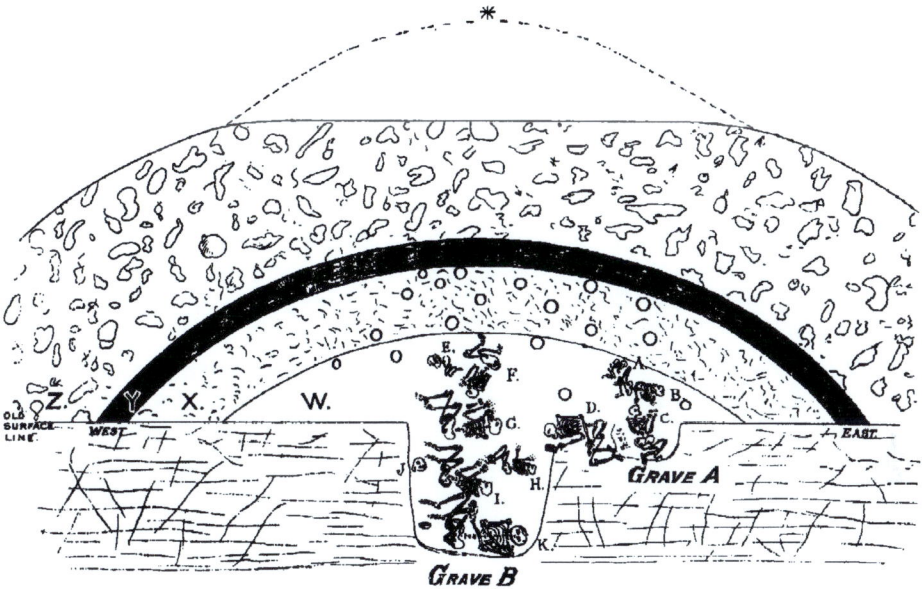

Fig. 2. Section through the Neolithic round barrow of Duggleby Howe. From MORTIMER 1905.

It has been recognised for some time that this simple dichotomy between the multiple of the Neolithic and the individual of the Bronze Age can no longer be seen to be valid. Firstly the wide application of radiocarbon dates, even discounting those with uncertain integrity, has served to demonstrate that the Neolithic in Britain now occupies some one and a half to two thousand years: a much longer timespan that had been previously envisaged. Secondly, there would appear to be a gap of as much as five hundred years between the end of the construction of long barrows and the introduction of Beakers. Thirdly, the Beaker presence at some chambered tombs and passage graves as well as their presence in the ditches of some long barrows suggest continued interest in the „old ways". Fourthly, radiocarbon dating of unaccompanied inhumations is disproving their early Bronze Age date and we are now aware that there is a complexity of burial practices throughout the Neolithic and Bronze Age that is far more intricate or multifarious than had previously been envisaged.

Discussion of the complexity of Neolithic and Bronze Age burial practices has been undertaken notably by PETERSEN (1972), but also by, *inter alia*, KINNES (1979), THOMAS (1999) and WOODWARD (2000). Other authors such as BRODIE (1994) and VAN DER LINDEN (undated) have demonstrated how so-called «Beaker» burial practices were already established in the indigenous later Neolithic. However, the post-Beaker early Bronze Age has been given less attention and there is evidence to suggest that both multiple and individual burials continued to be made and that the process of excarnation continued to be practiced. This paper is not intended to be a definitive review, but rather to give some instances of the complexity of burial types during this period, to illustrate that collective burial, individual burial, token burial, and excarnation all continued to be practiced throughout the Beaker period in Britain and finally to highlight a major avenue for future research. Furthermore, it is my opinion that the „Beaker burial", with its all-too-familiar pottery, might therefore be regarded as a veneer which catches the eye and draws attention away from the chipboard beneath. The chipboard in this instance is the practice of a variety of modes of burial throughout the third and earlier second millennia BC.

There are various strands of interrelated evidence and burial practices that we might consider. The first is individual burial, the second is multiple burial, the third examines cremation and inhumation and the fourth considers exposure and articulation/disarticulation. Finally, the question of the absence or presence of grave goods is relevant to all these other issues. Before embarking on this review, however, it is first necessary to define some terms of reference. By individual burial, I mean the deposition of a single discrete corpse. By multiple burial I mean the deposition in the same context of the remains of more than one individual.

Individual Inhumations

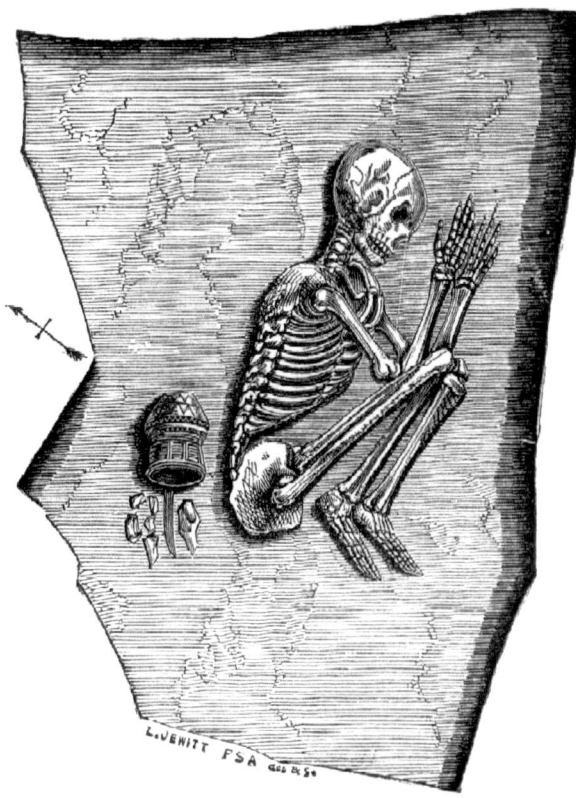

Fig. 3. Contracted Beaker burial from Smerrill Moor. From BATEMAN 1861.

Individual crouched (Fig. 3) or flexed inhumations in graves or cists and associated with a Beaker or Food Vessel have come to almost typify the burial record of the final Neolithic and earlier Bronze Age. Such graves are abundant in the reports of both the early barrow diggers and recent excavators alike. However, and as mentioned above, circular arguments are often at play and because an inhumation is flexed, it is therefore assumed to be Bronze Age. This need not be the case.

Mention has already been made of the individual burials in the chambered tomb of Hazelton (SAVILLE 1990) and Nutbane (MORGAN 1959) above. At the former site, an extended inhumation was placed in the passage to the northern chamber. At the latter site, the crouched inhumations of three adult males and an adolescent were placed within the mortuary structure (Fig. 4). The interpretation of the mortuary structures beneath earthen long barrows is a continuing debate however, the sorting of bones within some of these structures suggests that they were accessible for at least part of their existence. Once more these individuals may have been left to decay prior to the intended sorting of the defleshed bones. Both these examples suggest periodic or episodic individual burials but that the importance of the integral individual was diminished once in a skeletal state.

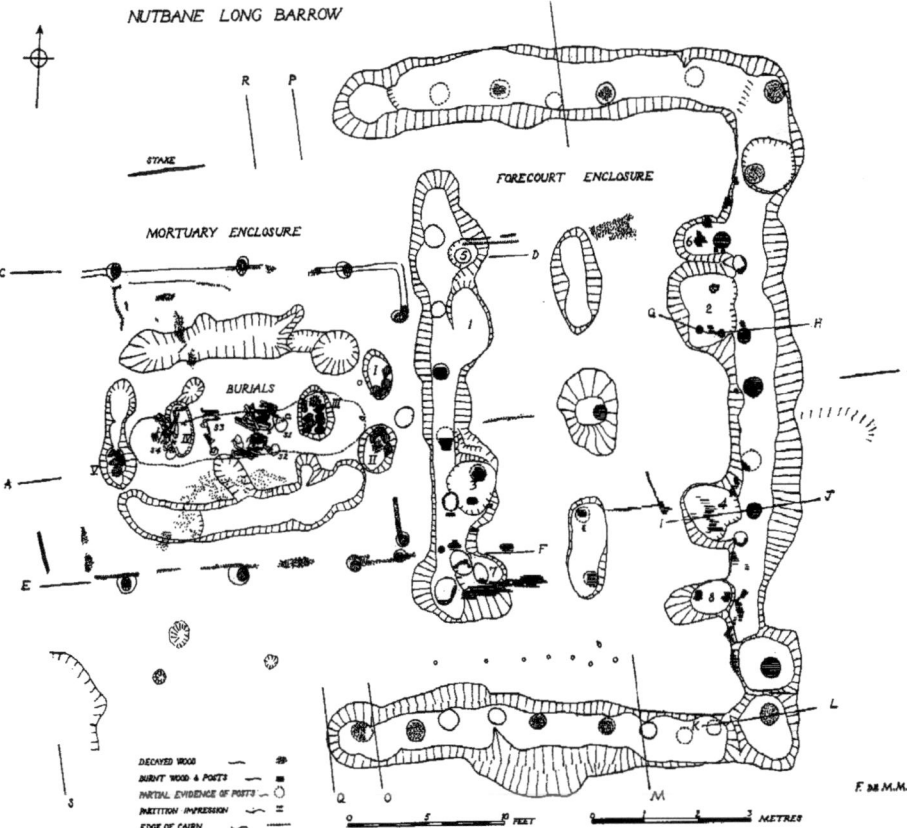

Fig. 4. Neolithic contracted inhumations in the mortuary house of the long barrow at Nutbane, Hants. From MORGAN 1959. Copyright and by courtesy of the Prehistoric Society.

In the ditches of the middle Neolithic causewayed enclosure at Windmill Hill, burials were placed within the silts (SMITH 1965). The graves of two children here as well as from the main causewayed enclosure ditch at Hambledon Hill (information by Frances Healy) has led some to consider that a more cavalier attitude towards infant mortality was held in the Neolithic. However this may be simplistic and the fact that these burials are being placed in contexts where other ritually charged structured depositions are being made suggests that they are not casual disposals.

Similar but Different. Bell Beakers in Europe

Fig. 5. The grave group from Liffs Low, Derbyshire. From BATEMAN 1861.

Below the giant round barrow of Duggleby Howe in Yorkshire a pit c. 2.7 m deep contained at is base the articulated body of an adult male associated with fragments of round-based bowl of early to middle Neolithic date. Two further adult males and a child were buried in an articulated state in the fill of this pit. The lower of the two males was associated with a lozenge arrowhead, also of early to middle Neolithic date and an antler macehead which has produced a radiocarbon date of c. 3500 Cal BC though it may have been a curated item – an heirloom deposited with the burial. At Liffs Low in Derbyshire (BATEMAN 1861) (Fig. 5) a contracted inhumation lay below a round barrow and was associated with a package of artefacts including edge-polished Seamer-type axes and boars tusks as well as a small, round-based flask so far unique in Britain but with similarities to the Corded Ware ceramics of northern Europe.

At Alfriston in Sussex (Fig. 6), a contracted burial of a young female was found below an oval mound (DREWETT 1975) associated with Carinated Bowl pottery (from the primary ditch silts). Below a similar monument in the Thames Valley at Radley the crouched inhumations of an adult male and female were associated with a flint arrowhead, knife and jet „belt slider" of middle Neolithic date around 3000 BC (Fig. 6) (BARCLAY / HALPIN undated). At Linch Hill Corner at Stanton Harcourt in Oxfordshire a contracted inhumation of a female was associated with an edge-polished knife and jet belt slider of middle Neolithic affinity (Fig. 6) (BARCLAY et al. 1995). And at Dorchester I, also in Oxfordshire, a crouched inhumation was central to a segmented ring-ditch (ATKINSON et al. 1951).

There was also a flat grave cemetery at Barrow Hills, Radley, in which was found the contracted burials of a child, adult female and adult male all in individual graves. The male and the child both had associated grave goods in the form of flint flakes of undiagnostic type (1 with the child, 3 with the male). These burials might have been attributed to the Beaker or Bronze Age periods according to conventional wisdom but a radiocarbon date from each burial placed the group in the mid to late fourth millennium BC. These inhumations clearly illustrate the benefit of dating unaccompanied burials or burials with undiagnostic artefacts and illustrate that contracted inhumations in discrete graves predate Beakers by over 500 years.

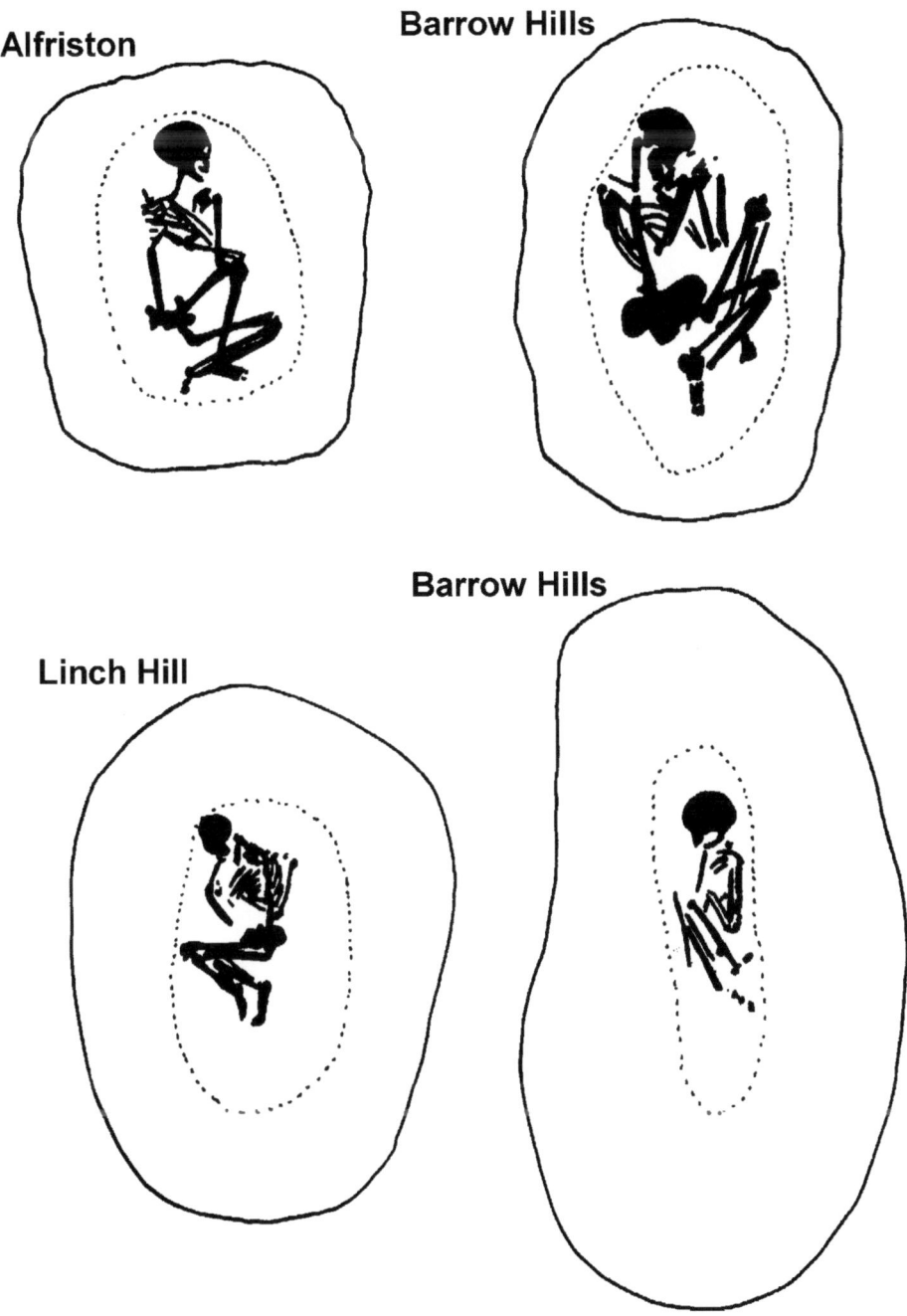

Fig. 6. Neolithic contracted inhumations from graves. 1 - Alfriston, Sussex (after Drewett 1975); 2 - Radley, Oxfordshire (after Barclay / Halpin undated), 3 - Linch Hill, Oxford (after Barclay et al. 1995).

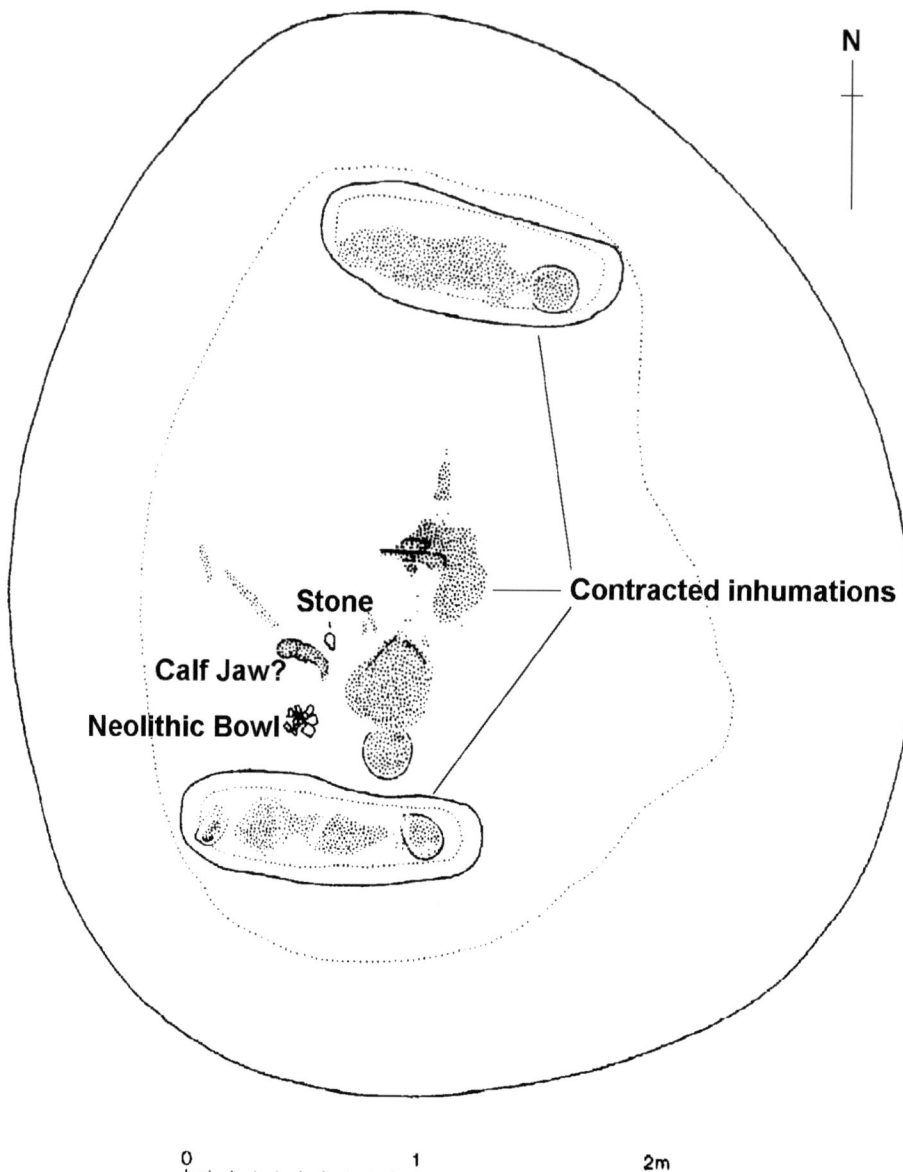

Fig. 7. Multiple central burial from a ring-ditch at Four Crosses, Powys. Copyright and by courtesy of the Clwyd-Powys Archaeological Trust.

Multiple inhumations

Multiple burials, the perceived burial right of the Neolithic, occur in both an articulated and disarticulated state. The long barrows and chambered tombs have already been mentioned above however such burials also occur in other contexts. For example, in the Severn Valley, at Four Crosses in northern Powys, a large pit lay beneath the centre of a round barrow and covered the contracted inhumations of three individuals (Fig. 7); one in the centre and one each at the head and foot of the central burial (WARRILOW *et al.* 1986). They were radiocarbon dated to c. 3300-2900 Cal BC and associated with a small undecorated round-based bowl with a sinuous „S" profile.

Burials directly associated with Peterborough Ware pottery for the middle Neolithic are rare but a cist burial containing multiple disarticulated burials was found in a rock shelter at Church Dale in Derbyshire (BURGESS 1980) and was associated with a decorated Mortlake style bowl. This has sometimes been taken to represent a transitional phase between the multiple burials of the Neolithic and the cist burials of the early Bronze Age.

A pit burial containing the remains of seven individuals and associated with Beaker pottery was found at South Dumpton Down in Kent (PERKINS undated). The sequence of burial was difficult to determine given the overlapping and intricate nature of the skeletons (Fig. 8) but radiocarbon dates from the top and bottom of

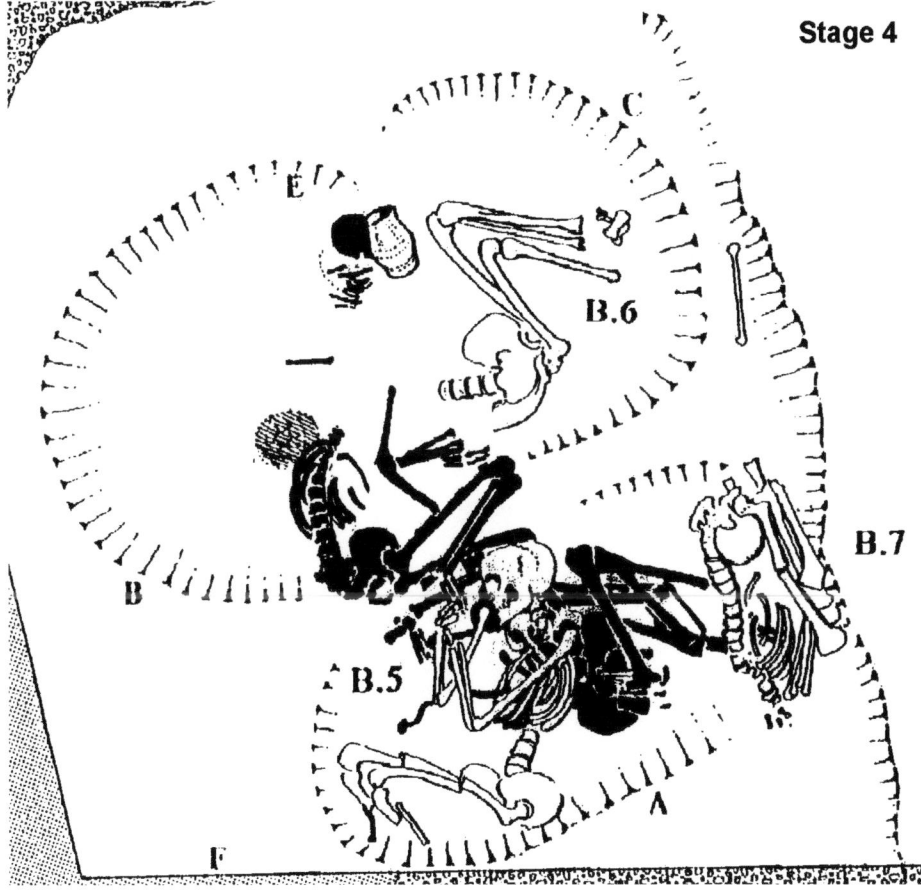

Fig. 8. Multiple Beaker inhumations from South Dumpton Down, Kent. Copyright and by courtesy of the Trust for Thanet Archaeology.

the deposit are statistically indistinguishable at c. 2000-1750 Cal BC. At Bee Low, in Derbyshire, associated with an All Over Cord decorated Beaker were the disarticulated remains of seven individuals (Fig. 9) (MARSDEN 1970). In the top of a natural mound at Hendre, in North Wales, a pit contained the fragmentary and disarticulated remains of a 25 year old male and three children of approximately 8, 6 and 4 years old (BRASSIL / GIBSON 1999). This deposit was radiocarbon dated to c. 1890-1680 Cal BC. Another example of this practice is a cist discovered at Linlithgow in west Lothian (COOK 2000) where the skeletal remains of at least 1 adult and 5 children were radiocarbon dated to just before c. 2000 Cal BC. The adult was represented by the skull and a fragment of femur and, given that the immature bones survived moderately well, it seems either that the entire adult skeleton was not deposited or else substantial parts were removed.

Numerous other instances of multiple inhumations exist in the Beaker and early Bronze Age periods (PETERSEN 1972) and a comprehensive review is beyond the scope of this paper. However it is also worth noting Petersen's observation that there are, in addition and particularly in Yorkshire, instances of burials apparently accompanied by cremations, a practice that can also be dated to the late fourth millennium BC at, for example, Trelystan, Powys (BRITNELL 1982). The mixture of cremation and inhumation at Duggleby Howe has already been mentioned above and instances of cremations within the fills of graves will be outlined below.

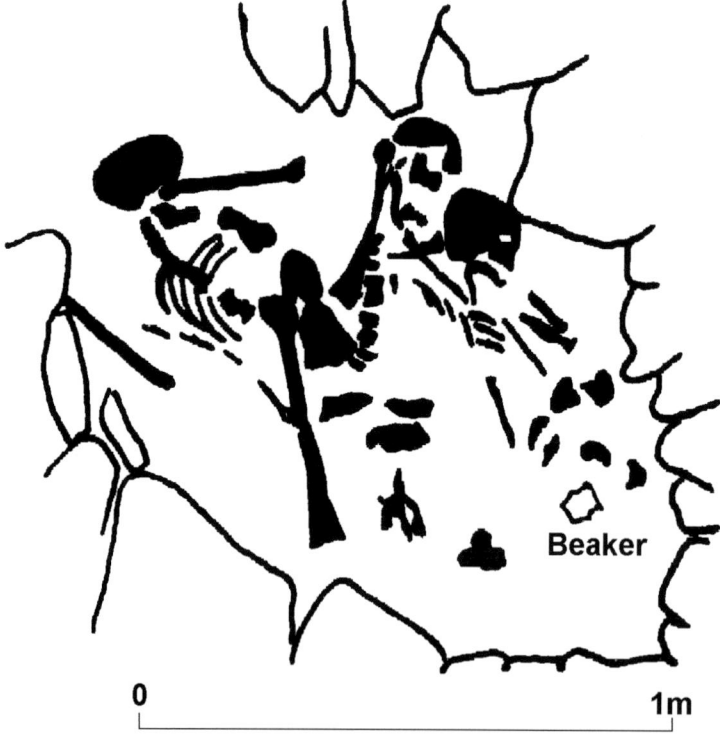

Fig. 9. Multiple Beaker inhumations from Bee Low, Derbyshire (after MARSDEN 1970).

Cremations

Cremation deposits in the earlier Neolithic are rare though crematoria have been identified below some long and round barrows. Certainly by the middle Neolithic, however, the practice is becoming more common. The cremations within the mound of Duggleby Howe, for example, are well-known though their precise dating remains uncertain. The cremation deposits in the Aubrey Holes at Stonehenge are likely to date to this period as are the cremations from the ring-ditches in the cursus complex at Dorchester on Thames (ATKINSON et al. 1951). Secondary cremation deposits in a penannular ring-ditch at Sarn-y-bryn-caled in Powys (Fig. 10) were from a phase of the monument associated with Peterborough Ware and dated to c. 3000 Cal BC (GIBSON 1994) which is in close agreement for the mixed inhumation and cremation burial at nearby Trelystan mentioned above. This date also acts as a *terminus ante quem* for the cremation of a female in the basal silts of the same monument at Sarn-y-bryn-caled.

Fig. 10. Middle Neolithic cremations *in situ* at Sarn-y-bryn-caled Site 2. Cremation 1 is primary and cremation 2 is from the upper silts, dated to c. 3000 Cal BC. Copyright and by courtesy of the Clwyd-Powys Archaeological Trust.

Later Neolithic cremations are more difficult to identify largely due to a lack of associated datable artefacts but there are occasional associations of Grooved ware with cremations at, for example, Winhill and Eddisbury (KINNES 1979). The association of Beakers with cremations, particularly in northern Britain, suggest that it was a predominant burial rite before the arrival of Beakers and, of course, cremation continued to be widely practised in the earlier Bronze Age accompanied by a variety of Food Vessel and Urn forms suggesting an unbroken practice continuing behind the Beaker veneer. As with unaccompanied inhumations above, now that cremated bone can be radiocarbon dated, such unaccompanied cremations may hold some surprises.

The identification of cremated remains can be difficult depending heavily on the fragment size. The identification of sex, age and whether more than one individual is represented relies on the size, shape and duplication of diagnostic skeletal elements. This raises some interesting questions regarding perceived wisdoms, questions which may not actually be answerable. For example, if no body parts are duplicated in a cremation deposit, are we necessarily correct in assuming that only one individual is present? Possibly, indeed probably, but as discussed below, if bones were being selected for inhumation burial, why not for cremation too?

Certainly there are multiple cremations in the Bronze Age. At the Sarn-y-bryn-caled timber circle in Powys, fragments of two individuals comprised the primary burial (GIBSON 1994) as evidenced by a duplicated left petrous temporal. The easy and obvious explanation for this is the re-use of a pyre site and the accidental recovery of a fragment from an earlier cremation. However, how many of the other bone fragments were from this second individual but cannot be identified because they are not duplicated? In other instances, the evidence is not so contentious. At Trelystan, only a few miles from Sarn-y-bryn-caled, the cremated remains of a mature male and female were contained in the same Food Vessel Urn (BRITNELL 1982). A pit cut into the subsoil beneath a cairn at Carneddau, also in Powys contained the cremated remains of two children. On the other side of the country at Weasenham Lyngs, Norfolk, a central grave associated with a Collared urn contained the cremated remains of three or four adults, likely to have been 3 male and one possible female (PETERSEN / HEALY 1986).

At Tandderwen in Denbighshire (Fig. 11), the central burial in the ring ditch had originally been an inhumation in a wooden coffin and associated with a Beaker. This burial had been partially disturbed by the insertion of a second coffin burial, this time containing the cremated remains of five individuals (two adult males, an adult female and two children) (BRASSIL et al. 1991). Cremation 2 at the same site, associated with a Food Vessel Urn comprised the remains of an adult male, an adolescent and a young child. Cremation 8 from the unenclosed part of the Tandderwen cemetery comprised the remains of two adults and though the burial was unaccompanied, it produced a radiocarbon date of c. 1600 Cal BC.

Articulation / disarticulation

Disarticulated remains are abundant in the Neolithic period and the process of excarnation is widely accepted amongst archaeologists. However, there would also appear to be a growing amount of evidence to suggest that excarnation was just as commonplace in the Bronze Age and a regionalised re-assessment of Bronze Age burials is overdue. The best evidence will come from inhumation burials where the ground conditions are favourable towards the preservation of bone.

At Hemp Knoll, near Avebury, for example, a child inhumation lacked hand and foot bones. A Beaker burial from Manston in Kent (Fig. 12), though arranged to resemble a crouched inhumation, lacked vertebrae, pelvis, both upper arms and both mandibles (PERKINS / GIBSON 1990). At Aldwincle in Northamptonshire, the beaker burial in barrow 2 was disarticulated and the bones had been lightly burnt but not cremated (JACKSON 1976). At Grendon, in the same county, an area of Bronze Age pits produced an adult and child inhumation in Pit 9 with the pelvis and lower limbs missing from the adult. From Pit 6 at the same site, the complete burial record comprised only a fragment of rib and a tibia and fibula with some attached foot bones: a lower leg burial (GIBSON / MCCORMICK 1985). In Northumberland, A dagger grave at Newborough contained what appeared to have been a contracted inhumation but analysis of the bones proved that only the lower part of the body was represented. The «head» was in fact the pelvis and the «arms» and «legs» com-

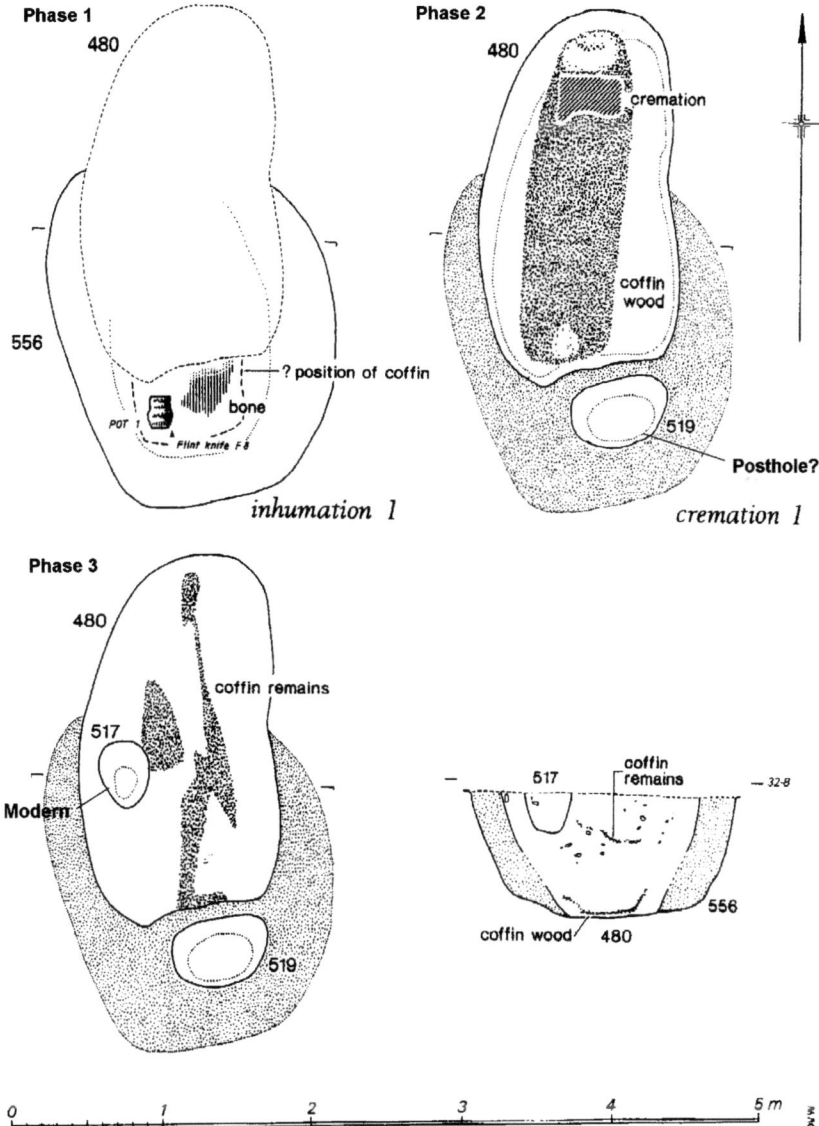

Fig. 11. Burial sequence in the central pit within a ring-ditch at Tandderwen, Denbigh. Copyright and by courtesy of the Clwyd-Powys Archaeological Trust.

prised one leg each (NEWMAN / MIKET 1973). A similar scenario was encountered at Chealamy, Strathnaver, in northern Scotland where the beaker was associated with only the lower half of a body (GOURLAY 1984). At Dalgetty, in Fife, it seems, from the size of the pits and from the dental evidence (the only skeletal evidence to survive), that severed heads may have been the only body parts to have been buried (WATKINS 1982).

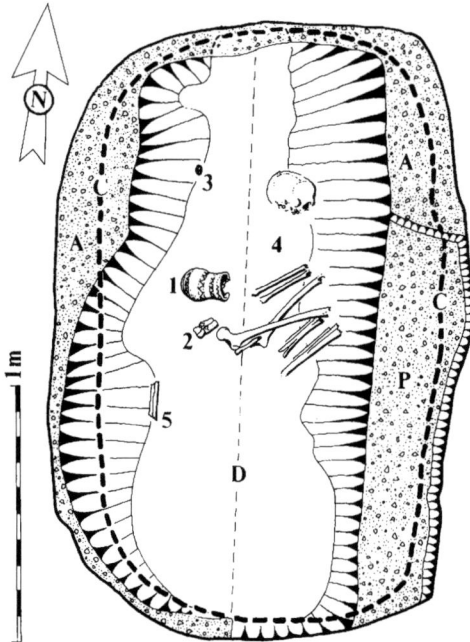

Fig. 12. Disarticulated and incomplete burial from Manston, Kent. Copyright and by courtesy of The Trust for Thanet Archaeology.

Even ostensibly complete burials may occasionally provide evidence for exposure or excarnation. At Bredon Hill in Worcestershire, for example, a central pit beneath a barrow contained the remains of two individuals, a male first and a female added later, both associated with Beakers. The later, female, skeleton was the more complete but within the skull were found shells of the carnivorous snail *Oxychilus* as well as the pellet from a bird of prey such as a kite or buzzard (THOMAS 1965). Even one of the woman's toe bones was also found in the skull! These remains were found during the cleaning of the skull in the laboratory and could not have found their way into the skull after burial or during excavation. That the corpse was exposed prior to burial is the only explanation. Thomas and his specialists not only conclude that the completeness of the skeleton does not suggest a lengthy period of exposure but they also observe that the only way the pellet could have entered the skull was through the *foramen magnum* at the base. They therefore suggest that it is very likely that the corpse had been decapitated and that the brain had been removed prior to burial. It seems therefore that the process of excarnation may have been mechanically accelerated by human agency.

The completeness of cremations is often difficult to judge and complete combustion and/or a cavalier approach to the collection of cremated remains may be invoked to account for examples with less than expected bulk. A modern cremation of an adult might produce in the region of 3 kg of bone (MCKINLEY 1989). Allowing for collection difficulties in prehistory, we might expect at least 2 kg from a complete cremation. However, a cremation from Hemp Knoll in Wiltshire, for example associated with a Food Vessel of the early Bronze Age weighed only 72 g. The individual was adult and therefore the cremation cannot represent the whole body (ROBERTSON-MACKAY 1980). At Meldon Bridge, in Peebles the Neolithic and Bronze Age cremations produced a maximum of 1325 g of bones and the smallest deposits comprised just a few fragments (SPEAK / BURGESS 1999). Of the 14 documented adult or youth cremations, only 3 are recorded as producing more than 1 kg of bone and 9 are recorded as weighing under 150 g. It is clear that far from entire bodies are being deposited. There are also instances of cremations where substantial body parts have been found to be missing. At Welsh St Donats 3, in South Glamorgan, for example, burial E had been poorly cremated but lacked a tibia and humerus while cremation 6 at the same site lacked an arm (EHRENBERG *et al.* 1982).

Overwhelming evidence for the selection of human bone in the Bronze Age comes from three Bronze Age cremation deposits at Treiorwerth and Bedd Branwen on Anglesey (Fig. 13) (LYNCH 1991) where the only bone present comprised the ear bones of children. While these small bones may be resilient to cremation, it seems unlikely that no other skeletal elements would have survived.

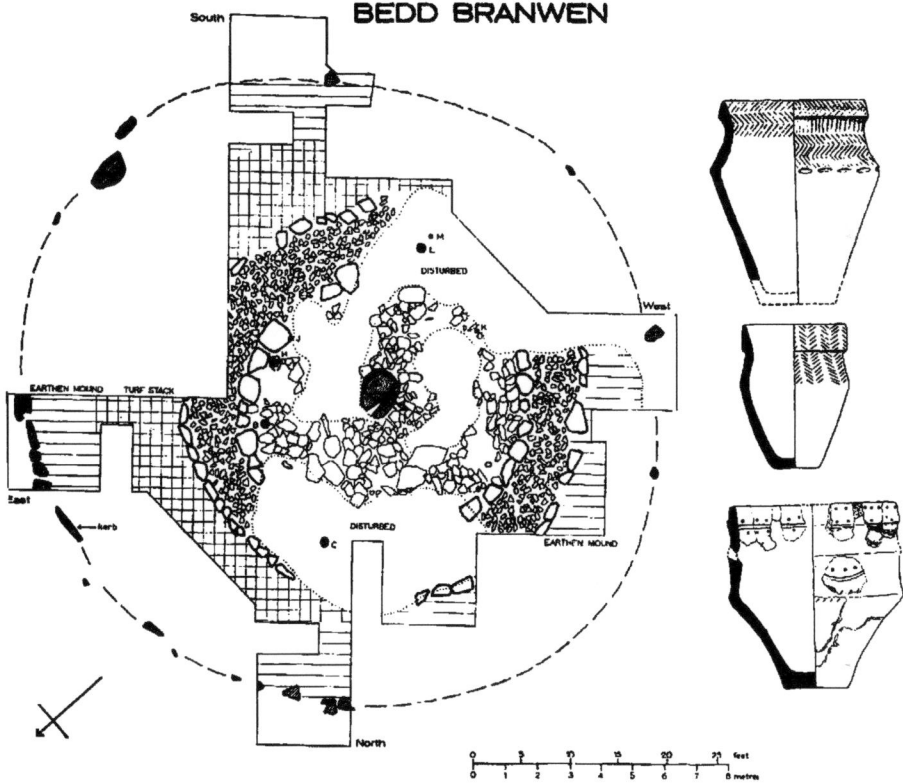

Fig. 13. Bedd Branwen, Anglesey, and pots J, M and E which contained infant ear-bones. From LYNCH 1991. Copyright and by courtesy of Frances Lynch.

The incompleteness and/or disarticulation of some Bronze Age inhumations and cremations clearly suggests exposure or mechanical excarnation prior to final deposition. This may also be detected in some cremations. Occasionally (and again reassessment is badly needed) the pits in which cremations have been found have been reddened by the action of fire. This has sometimes been interpreted as proving that the cremations were still hot when deposited but this is clearly erroneous. Cremations cool quickly and only fire as opposed to hot items will be sufficient to burn the sides of the pit. It seems that some pits may actually have been the site of the cremation. This is especially so at Carneddau in Powys, where a pit beneath a small addition to Cairn I was heavily burnt and was filled with a mixture of charcoal and the cremated remains of an adult male. At a maximum of 0.8 m across, a complete body could not have been cremated in this pit and it is likely that defleshed bones had been dropped into a raging fire set within the pit. The fact that the bone and charcoal was thoroughly mixed suggests that the fire was being stoked throughout the process (GIBSON 1993). This was also the case at pit 29 beneath cairn II at the same site, where the calcined bones of two children were thoroughly mixed with charcoal in a fire-reddened pit.

Therefore, in the Beaker and post-Beaker Bronze Age, there is a growing amount of data for the burial of incomplete corpses either by cremation or inhumation. The process of excarnation, well accepted in Neolithic contexts clearly continues through into the second millennium. Once more the Beaker veneer can be pulled away.

Sequential burial

As has been mentioned above, it would appear that at both megalithic tombs as well as within the mortuary houses of earthen long barrows, there was a time or times when access was allowed to the burials. Thus some bones were sorted into piles while others were doubtless removed. Burial does not seem to have been a final act, therefore, but rather part of a process, perhaps involving one or more rights of passage, concerning, death, laying out, excarnation, sorting of the skeletal remains and final deposition. With each stage, the deceased may have been endowed with different meanings or significances, perhaps increasing or even decreasing in importance with each stage. Once again this might also be seen to be happening in the Beaker period and earlier Bronze Age and this aspect has recently been discussed by WOODWARD (2000).

A case has already been made for the extension of 'Neolithic' burial practices of multiple burial, excarnation and skeletal selection into the Bronze Age. We need now to look at the practice of burial replacement or disturbance. Mention has already been made of the Bredon Hill Beaker burial where the burial of an adult male was replaced with the burial of an adult female causing disturbance to the original burial. Clearly the grave pit was still visible when the second burial was made. This is also the case at Amesbury G71 (CHRISTIE 1967) where the burial of an adult in a pit had been deposited. This was then dug out and the body of an adult male was deposited in the same pit. Below a round barrow at West Cotton, Northants, a pit containing a disarticulated burial was dig into and a Beaker contracted inhumation placed within this larger grave (WINDELL 1989). At Bowthorpe, Norfolk, there was a complex sequence of recutting graves and pits (LAWSON 1986). Grave 39, for example, cut grave 28. Both had held contracted inhumations though the bone preservation was very poor. Beaker sherds were found in the fill of the lower grave. At Shrewton 5k in Wiltshire, an adult male was buried with a Beaker and copper alloy dagger in a pit 2.25 m deep (GREEN / ROLLO-SMITH 1984). Into the upper fill of this pit was inserted the contracted inhumation of a second adult male, also associated with a Beaker. These burials, like the other examples quoted are clearly sequential. At Monkton-Minster, in Kent (Fig. 14), a Beaker inhumation had been placed in a grave with a pile of disarticulated bones representing another adult.

Was this a simultaneous deposit or were the bones from an earlier burial pushed aside to make room for the later one? Depending on soil conditions, it might take a burial between five and fifteen years to deflesh which suggests that, if sequential, the grave may have been marked for a considerable time. However, the possibility that the first corpse was defleshed before burial and as discussed above must also be considered.

At Gravelly Guy ring-ditch X, 6-8, in Oxfordshire (BARCLAY *et al.* 1995) there had been five successive burials in the centre of a ring ditch (Fig. 15). The primary burial had been dug out by the later insertions and an original inhumation is inferred. The second inhumation, of a male adult, was accompanied by a bronze dagger, Beaker, wristguard, scraper, copper alloy awl, whetstone and antler rod and two flint flakes.

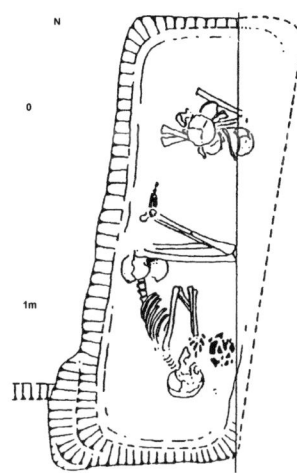

Fig. 14. The Beaker contracted inhumation and disarticulate burial from Monkton-Minster, Kent. Copyright and by courtesy of the Trust for Thanet Archaeology.

He had probably been buried in a coffin. The third burial was cut into the second at a higher level and contained the crouched inhumation of a young adult female. She was associated with a beaker, copper alloy awl and a flint scraper. Comparatively little time seems to have elapsed between these burials. Two cremation pits were then dug into the backfill of the third grave. The first contained the remains of an infant with a few unburnt and disarticulated adult bones. The second comprised the remains of an adult female. Clearly there is a sequence of use and reuse at this site. The grave is being revisited much as chambered tombs and long barrows were although the manner in which the graves were revisited is clearly different in detail given the obvious physical differences between pits and chambers.

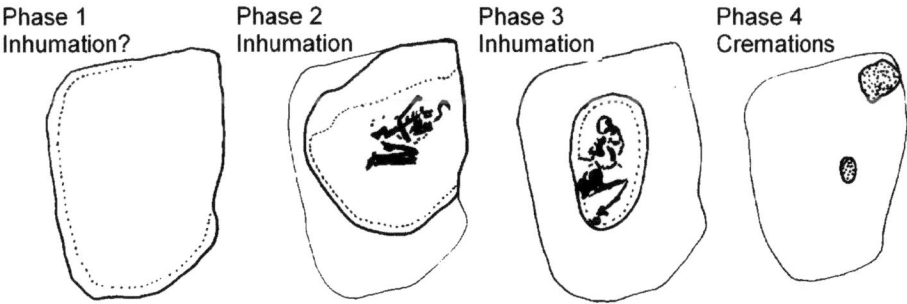

Fig. 15. The recut grave sequence at Gravelly Guy, Oxford (after BARCLAY *et al.* 1995).

A similarly complex sequence was recorded at Tandderwen in Denbighshire (BRASSIL *et al.* 1991). Here, within the central grave complex of a ring-ditch, an inhumation had been interred in a coffin with a Beaker and a flint knife (the bone was too decayed for analysis). A second grave was dug into the first and into this was inserted a dug-out coffin containing the multiple cremation already discussed above. This grave may have been marked by a standing post. The coffin stain measured 2.2 m long yet the cremation deposit occupied a discrete rectangular area to the northern end of the coffin. The excavators therefore considered it likely that this grave had also held an inhumation burial but that this had not survived in the acid soil. The multiple cremation deposit is also interesting because it appeared to be layered and that the remains of each individual (2 adult males, adult female, adolescent, child) were broadly restricted to these individual layers. It is possible therefore that this too was a sequential deposit, perhaps in a box or other organic container.

Conclusion

This brief review of the complexity of burial practices during the third and early second millennia BC in Britain indicates that the perceived split between the multiple inhumations of the Neolithic and the individual burials of the early Bronze Age is no longer tenable. Instead practices involving the deposition of complete, incomplete, articulated, disarticulated, inhumations and cremations are practised throughout the period. The process of excarnation, so commonly observed in the Neolithic, seems to be equally common in the early Bronze Age. This is evidenced by both incomplete and complete inhumations as well as by small and token cremation deposits: cremation pits could not have coped with complete corpses. This important aspect of early Bronze Age burial ritual has not really received the attention it deserves and regional syntheses are needed. Contracted inhumations appear in the archaeological record well before the advent of Beakers and the only distinguishing feature about the «Beaker burial» would be the presence of the pot itself. Grave goods start to appear from the middle of the third millennium and increase in complexity into the early Bronze Age (see KINNES 1979 and THOMAS 1999 for discussions of this). The presence of a Beaker and its associated package of artefacts may simply be a logical extension of this grave good development. After all, the Beaker artefact package must initially have been regarded as exotic with links to Europe and foreign histories. Furthermore, the «Beaker inhumation» is itself, at least in part, a myth since both complete and incomplete skeletons are found as well as articulated and disarticulated remains. The burial practices of this period, therefore, may be like cheap furniture... it's not the veneer that is important but rather what is happening underneath.

What seems certain from the above review is that the sentiment of „Rest in Peace", generally wished upon the deceased of modern times, does not seem to have been a sentiment widely understood by our Neolithic and Bronze Age forebears. It appears that the dead did not rest easy.

Acknowledgements

I would like to thank John McIlwaine for providing information on natural defleshing processes and I am also grateful to Dave Perkins of the Trust for Thanet Archaeology, Bill Britnell of the Clwyd-Powys Archaeological Trust, Julie Gardiner of the Prehistoric Society and Frances Lynch for permission to use illustrative material.

Bibliography

ASHBEE P. 1966. The Fussell's Lodge long barrow excavations, 1957. *Archaeologia* 100, 1-80.

ASHBEE P./ SMITH I.F. / EVANS J.G. 1979. Excavation of three long barrows near Avebury. *Proceedings of the Prehistoric Society*, 45, 207-300.

ATKINSON R. / PIGGOTT C.M. / SANDARS, N. 1951. *Excavations at Dorchester, Oxon*. Oxford.

BARCLAY A. / HALPIN C. undated. *Excavations at Barrow Hills, Radley, Oxfordshire. Volume I: The Neolithic and Bronze Age Monument complex*. Oxford.

BARCLAY A. / GRAY M. / LAMBRICK G. 1995. *Excavations at the Devil's Quoits, Stanton Harcourt, Oxfordshire, 1972-3 and 1988*. Oxford.

BATEMAN T. 1848. *Vestiges of the Antiquities of Derbyshire*. London.

1861. *Ten Years' Diggings in Celtic and Saxon Grave Hills in the Counties of Derbyshire, Stafford and York*. London.

BRASSIL K. / GIBSON, A.M. 1999. A Grooved Ware pit group and Bronze Age multiple inhumation at Hendre, Rhydymwyn, Flintshire. In: R. CLEAL / A. MACSWEEN (eds) *Grooved Ware in Britain and Ireland*, 89-97. Oxford.

BRASSIL K. / OWEN G. / BRITNELL W.J. 1991. Prehistoric and early medieval cemeteries at Tandderwen, near Denbigh, Clwyd. *Archaeological Journal* 148, 46-97.

BRODIE N. 1994. *The Neolithic-Bronze Age Transition in Britain*. BAR 238. Oxford.

BURGESS, C. 1980. *The Age of Stonehenge*. London.

CHRISTIE P.M. 1967. A barrow cemetery of the second millennium BC in Wiltshire. *Proceedings of the Prehistoric Society* 33, 336-366.

COOK M. 2000. An early Bronze Age multiple burial cist from Mill Road Industrial Estate, Linlithgow, West Lothian. *Proceedings of the Society of Antiquaries of Scotland* 130, 77-91.

DREWETT, P. 1975. The excavation of an oval burial mound of the third millennium BC at Alfriston, East Sussex. *Proceedings of the Prehistoric Society* 41, 119-152.

EHRENBERG M. / PRICE J. / VALE V. 1982. The excavation of two bronze age round barrows at Welsh St Donats, South Glamorgan. *Bulletin of the Board of Celtic Studies* 29 (4), 776-842.

EVANS J.G. / SIMPSON, D.D.A. 1991. Giants Hill 2 long barrow, Skendleby, Lincolnshire. *Archaeologia* 109, 1-45.

GIBSON, A.M. 1993. The excavation of two cairns and associated features at Carneddau, Carno, Powys, 1898-90. *Archaeological Journal* 150, 1-45.

GIBSON A.M. / MCCORMICK A. 1985. Archaeology at Grendon Quarry, Northamptonshire, Part 1: Neolithic and Bronze Age sites excavated in 1974-5. *Northamptonshire Archaeology* 20, 23-44.

GOURLAY R. 1984. A short cist Beaker inhumation from Chealamy, Strathnaver, Sutherland. *Proceedings of the Society of Antiquaries of Scotland* 114, 567-71.

JACKSON D.A. 1976. The excavation of Neolithic and Bronze Age sites at Aldwincle, Northants, 1967-71. *Northamptonshire Archaeology* 11, 12-70.

KINNES I. / SCHADLA-HALL / T. CHADWICK P. / DEAN P. 1983. Duggleby Howe reconsidered. *Archaeological Journal* 140, 83-108

LAWSON A. J. 1986. The excavation of a ring-ditch at Bowthorpe, Norwich, 1979. *Barrow Excavations in Norfolk, 1950-82, East Anglian Archaeology* 29, 20-49.

LYNCH F. 1991. *Prehistoric Anglesey*, 2nd ed.

MARSDEN B.M. 1970. The excavation of the Bee Low round cairn, Youlgreave, Derbyshire. *Antiquaries Journal* 50, 186-215.

MCKINLEY J. 1989. Cremations: expectations, methodologies and realities. In: ROBERTS C.A., LEE F. / BINTLIFF J. (eds) *Burial Archaeology. Current Research, Methods and Developments*, 65-76. BAR 211. Oxford.

MORGAN F. DE M. 1959. The excavation of a long barrow at Nutbane, Hants. *Proceedings of the Prehistoric Society* 25, 15-51.

MORTIMER J.R. 1905. *Forty Years' Researches into British and Saxon Burial Mounds of East Yorkshire*. London: Brown & Sons.

NEWMAN T.G. / MIKET R.F. 1973. A Dagger Grave at Allerwash, Newborough, Northumberland. *Archaeologia Aeliana* I (5th series), 87-95.

PERKINS D. undated. *Two Evaluations: Dumpton Gap and South Dumpton Down, Broadstairs*. Broadstairs.

PETERSEN F. 1972. Traditions of multiple burial in later Neolithic and early Bronze Age Britain. *Archaeological Journal* 129, 22-55.

PETERSEN F. / HEALY F. 1986. The excavation of two round barrows and a ditched enclosure on Weasenham Lyngs, 1972. *Barrow Excavations in Norfolk, 1950-82, East Anglian Archaeology* 29, 70-103.

ROBERTSON-MACKAY M.E. 1980. A «head and hoofs» burial beneath a round barrow with other Neolithic and Bronze Age sites on Hemp Knoll, near Avebury, Wiltshire. *Proceedings of the Prehistoric Society* 46, 123-176.

SAVILLE A. 1990. *Hazelton North. The Excavation of a Neolithic Long cairn of the Cotswold-Severn Group*. BAR 13. London.

SMITH I.F. 1965. *Windmill Hill and Avebury. Excavations by Alexander Keiller 1925-1939*. Oxford.

SPEAK S. / BURGESS C. 1999. Meldon Bridge: a centre of the third millennium BC in Peeblesshire. *Proceedings of the Society of Antiquaries of Scotland* 129, 1-118.

THOMAS J. 1999. *Understanding the Neolithic*. London.

THOMAS N. 1965. A double Beaker burial on Bredon Hill, Worcestershire. *Birmingham Archaeological Society Transactions and Proceedings* 82, 58-76.

VANDER LINDEN M., undated. Perpetuating traditions, changing ideologies: the Bell Beaker culture in the British Isles and its implications for the Indo-European problem. In: HULD M.E. / JONES-BLEY K. / DELLA VOLPE A. / DEXTER M.R. (eds) *Proceedings of the 12th Annual UCLA Indo-European Conference, Journal of Indo-European Studies Maonograph 40,* 269-286. Washington.

WARRILOW W. / OWEN G. / BRITNELL W. 1986. Eight ring-ditches at Four Crosses, Lalndyssilio, Powys, 1981-85. *Proceedings of the Prehistoric Society* 52, 53-88.

WATKINS T. 1982. The excavation of an early Bronze Age cemetery at Barns Farm, Dalgetty, Fife. *Proceedings of the Society of Antiquaries of Scotland* 112, 48-141.

WINDELL D. 1989. A late Neolithic 'ritual focus' at West Cotton, Northamptonshire. In: GIBSON A. (ed), *Midlands Prehistory. Some Recent and Current Researches into the Prehistory of Central England*, 85-94. BAR British Series 204. Oxford.

WOODWARD A. 2000. *British Barrows: A Matter of Life and Death*. Stroud.

Similar but Different. Bell Beakers in Europe
Czebreszuk J. (ed.)
Poznań 2004

HISTORICAL MODEL OF SETTLING AND SPREAD OF BELL BEAKER CULTURE IN THE MEDITERRANEAN FRANCE

Olivier Lemercier (Aix-en-Provence, France)

Summary

Here we present some elements of reflexion which are developped in a PhD thesis taken during March 2002 in Aix-en-Provence (LEMERCIER 2002). This work concerned all the bell-beaker elements present in more than 300 sites in the South East of France wherein almost 1200 pots were discovered.This study permitted to confirm the existence of 4 stylistics assemblages and most of the chronology based upon the decorated ceramics that J. Guilaine proposed. The analysis of these assemblages, both in their context of dicovery and their location, allows to set a new interpretation of the settling and development of the bell-beaker culture in the mediterranean France and to question the nature of the phenomenon itself. The first bell-beaker settling, that match with the geometric dotted style, can be regarded as counters established along the mediterranean shore, the mouths of the main rivers and the rivers themselves.In these sites, the artifacts immediately appear mixed with elements of local cultures, nevertheless these settlements present particular geography and topography which make them unic among the local settlements. Their origin must be located in the south western area (iberic peninsula, maybe atlantic coast). Standardized pots are spread from these sites towards the inland populations. This first diffusion goes beyond the South East of France, following the Rhone river. The development of a regional stylistic group, called „rhodano-provençal" like the „pyrénéen" group, squares with a phase of acculturation of the local population under iberic influence. As this acculturation goes, new elements from the north east area appear, showing that the south east area has become a relay in an important road for communication and exchanges. The apparition of the „barbelé" style may be the result of the arrival of new people from Italy in the country (at work). Both artifacts and sites data show that Bell Beaker culture should be considered, buring this first phase of apparition in the mediterranean and atlantic Europe, not as a simple diffusion of a fashion, a rite or even of objects, but as a cultural spread with its phases of exploration, settling and acculturation of the local populations. From the iberic origin (Portugal?) of this first phenomenon to its spread until the far eastern parts of Europe, great lines of communication appear; they will permit numerous multipolar exchanges of ideas, artifacts and populations.

Résumé

Ce court article a pour but de présenter quelques éléments de réflexion issus d'une thèse de Doctorat soutenue en mars 2002 à Aix-en-Provence (LEMERCIER 2002). Le travail a pris en compte

Similar but Different. Bell Beakers in Europe

tous les éléments campaniformes présents sur plus de 300 sites recensés qui ont livré les fragments de près de 1200 vases décorés, dans le sud-est de la France. Il permet de confirmer l'existence de 4 ensembles stylistiques et, en grande partie, la chronologie proposée par Jean Guilaine à partir de la céramique décorée. L'analyse de ces ensembles, de leur contexte de découverte et de leur répartition permet de proposer une nouvelle interprétation de l'implantation et du développement du Campaniforme en France méditerranéenne, en s'interrogeant, au-delà sur la nature même du phénomène. Les premières implantations campaniformes, qui correspondent au style pointillé géométrique, peuvent être comprises comme des comptoirs implantés le long du littoral méditerranéen, aux embouchures des principaux fleuves et le long de ceux-ci. Ces implantations sont immédiatement marquées par une mixité avec des éléments des cultures locales mais présentent à la fois une géographie et des topographies particulières qui les isolent au sein des implantations indigènes. Leur origine est très probablement sud-occidentale (Ibérique et peut-être atlantique). A partir de ces sites, des vases standardisés sont diffusés vers l'intérieur des terres auprès des populations locales. Cette première diffusion dépasse très largement le sud-est de la France pour s'étendre au-delà en remontant le Rhône. Le développement d'un groupe stylistique régional „Rhodano-Provençal", comme celui du groupe „Pyrénéen", correspond à une phase d'acculturation des populations locales sous l'influence ibérique qui se poursuit mais avec l'apparition de nouveaux éléments d'origine nord-orientale, montrant que le sud-est est devenu une sorte de relais sur une importante voie de communication et d'échanges. L'apparition du style barbelé traduit sans doute l'arrivée dans la région de nouveaux groupes d'origine italique. Les données des mobiliers et des sites montrent que le Campaniforme doit être compris, dans cette phase initiale d'apparition en Europe méditerranéenne et probablement atlantique, non comme la simple diffusion d'une mode, d'un rite ou d'objets mais bien comme une expansion culturelle avec ses phases d'exploration, d'implantation et d'acculturation des populations locales. De l'origine ibérique (Portugal?) de ce premier phénomène à son extension jusqu'aux confins de l'Europe, ce sont de grandes voies de communication qui apparaissent et vont permettre de nombreux échanges multipolaires d'idées, de mobiliers et sans doute de populations.

Zusammenfassung

Im Folgenden werden einige Teilergebnisse aus einer Dissertation vorgestellt, die im März 2002 an der Universität Aix-en-Provence vorgelegt wurde (LEMERCIER 2002). In dieser Arbeit wurden sämtliche Glockenbecher-Elemente (1200 verzierte Gefässe bzw. Gefässfragmente) aus über 300 südostfranzösischen Fundstellen mit annähernd berücksichtigt. Diese Untersuchung bestätigt das Vorhandensein von vier Stilgruppen und die Gültigkeit der von J. Guilaine auf der Basis der verzierten Keramik vorgeschlagenen Chronologie weitgehend. Die Analyse dieser Gruppen, ihrer Fundumstände und ihrer Verbreitung führt uns dazu, das Aufkommen und die Ausbreitung der Glockenbecher im mediterranen Südfrankreich und darüber hinaus die Frage nach dem Wesen des Phänomens neu zu interpretieren. Die ersten Glockenbecher-Niederlassungen (Style pointillé-géométrique) können als Kontore interpretiert werden, die entlang der Mittelmeerküste, nahe der Mündungen oder entlang der Hauptflüsse erbaut werden. Diese Niederlassungen sind durch die Aufnahme von Elementen aus den einheimischen Kulturen charakterisiert, heben sich jedoch durch eine besondere geographische und topographische Lage von den Siedlungen der einheimischen Kulturen ab. Ihre Herkunft ist höchstwahrscheinlich im Südwesten zu suchen (iberische Halbinsel oder atlantische Küstengebiete). Von diesen Siedlungen aus breiten sich stark standardisierte Gefässe ins Landesinnere innerhalb der einheimischen Bevölkerung aus. Diese erste Ausbreitung reicht bis weit über Südostfrankreich hinaus und folgt dem Rhonetal in nördlicher Richtung. Die Entwicklung von regionalen Stilen wie die „Groupe Rhodano-provençal" oder „Groupe pyrénéen" ist das Ergebnis einer Akkulturation lokaler Bevölkerungsgruppen unter iberischem Einfluss. Hinzu kommen neue Elemente nordöstlicher Herkunft, die deutlich machen, dass Südostfrankreich zu einer Etappe innerhalb eines wichtigen Kommunikations- und Austauschweges geworden ist. Das Aufkommen des „Style barbelé" spiegelt wahrscheinlich die Ankunft neuer Bevölkerungsgruppen aus Italien wieder. Die materielle Kultur und die Fundstellen zeigen, dass die Glockenbecher bereits in einer frühen Phase nicht nur als Ausdruck der Ausbreitung einer Mode, eines Rituals oder von besonderen Objekten verstanden werden sollten, sondern als das Ergebnis einer kulturellen Ausbreitung mit einer Pionierphase, einer Konsolidierungsphase und schliesslich einer Phase der Akkulturation lokaler Bevölkerungsgruppen. Zwischen der Entstehung des Phänomens auf der iberischen Halbinsel (Portugal?) und seiner Ausbreitung über ganz Europa kommen die grossen Kommunikationswege zum tragen und ermöglichen die Ausbreitung von Ideen, Gütern und Menschengruppen.

Framework and context of the study

The South of France is one of the richest regions concerning Bell Beakers. We present a brief synthesis of it, under the direction of J. Guilaine, during the Congress of Riva del Garda (GUILAINE et al. 2002). Since this day, the realisation of a PhD thesis concerning a large part of the South of France, the south-east corner, has permitted us to precise several aspects and to make new assumptions (LEMERCIER 2002). We have been able to record more than 300 sites in this area (Fig. 1), where almost 1200 Bell Beaker decorated vases were found.

At the same time, the presence of easily identifiable distinct styles, whose definition is based on decorative patterns, the existence of closed sets, the large part of domestic sites, and an increasing knowledge of the chrono-cultural context shall enable us to propose a spatial and temporal scheme of appearance and development of the Bell Beakers in this area and, furthermore, to draw informations about the origin and the nature of the phenomenon itself, as we expected at the beginning of this work (LEMERCIER 1998).

1. The reports

1.1. The Bell Beaker styles in the south-east of France[1]

The decorated ceramics of Style 1 (corded, linear spotted, international and mixed decorations) are present not as entire dish sets but as few standardised items (beakers) which fit into the criteria defined by L. Salanova (SALANOVA 2000). They are not associated with a specific domestic ceramic and, most of time, they appear in the local contexts of the Final Neolithic, such as settlements and graves. We still do not know where they were produced, as we are waiting for more abundant analysis. The raw material they were made of may be from this area, but the way they were realised squares with specific technical traditions. The „new" items associated with this style are scarce and of metallic ware. Last important fact: the ceramics that belong to style 1 appear also among assemblages where style 2 prevails.

The ceramics of style 2 (geometric spotted decorations „pointillé géométrique") show a variety of decorative patterns, with few atlantic standard, and numerous morphologies, marked by the abundance of low shapes. A fine undecorated but

---

[1] Figures of the ceramics are published in LEMERCIER 1998 and GUILAINE et al. 2002.

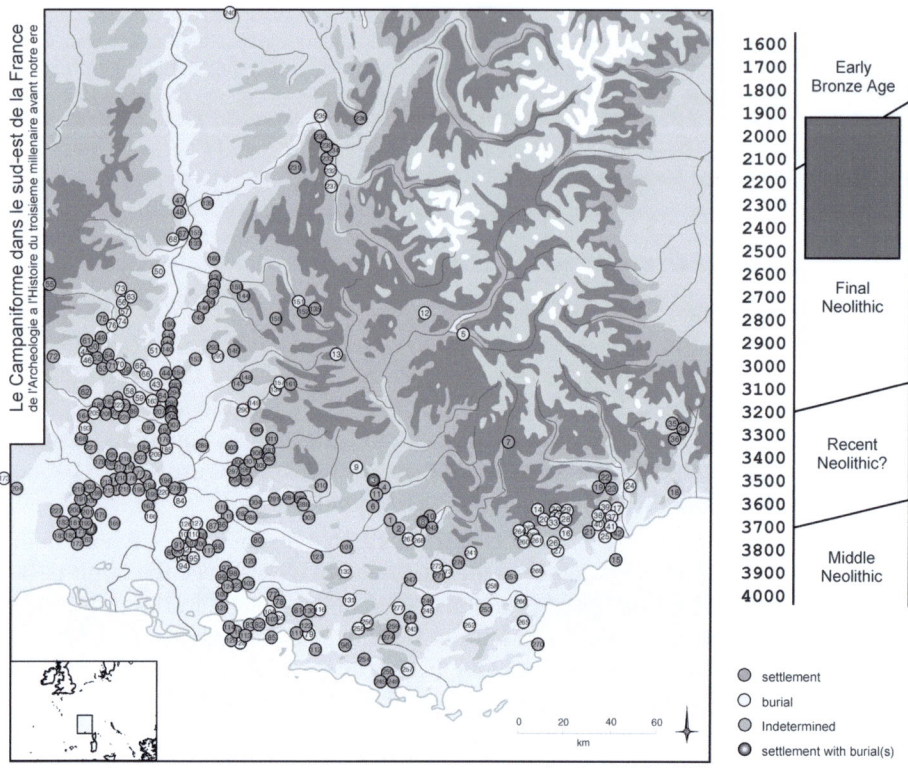

Fig. 1.   Bell Beaker settlements in the South-East of France.

specific ceramic is present. Few sites provide the ceramics of style 2, they are essentially located in the left bank of the low Rhône valley. There, these pots are associated with remains that can be linked to the local Fontbouisse and Rhône-Ouvèze groups. The domestic ceramic belongs to the local tradition, Rhône-Ouvèze or Fontbouisse, but some Bell Beaker characteristics can be distinguished. We can observe some transfers of techniques between the Bell Beaker productions, locally made, and the Rhône-Ouvèze ones, even some cases of stylistic mixity among the decorated ceramics. There are other elements that can be considered as specific, such as metallic items, jewels and, maybe, a lithic tool-kit. The sites often have a particular topography. Some houses were discovered and the whole domestic and agro-pastoral activities were recognised. There are few graves, all collective and most of time located in caves.

The ceramics of style 3 (incised, incised-and-stamped and complex spotted decorations of the „rhodano-provençal" group defined by J. Courtin (COURTIN 1967; 1974) show many morphologies, the low shapes being very important. The decorations are very diverse too. We can observe some decorations imitating the barbed wire pattern. These decorated potteries are associated with many undecorated ceramics, among them a specific domestic ware; together they constitute the entire vessel kit. Many types of jewels and metallic items and the lithic industry are specifics for

Bell Beaker. These assemblages are present in a lot of sites in the entire area of study. In most of this region the sites are homogeneous and no association with elements of local styles can be observed. Nevertheless, in the „département" of the Gard and in some sites along the Rhône there are artifacts of the Fontbouisse tradition associated with Bell Beakers. Concerning the sites of the style 3, the types of settling and architectures vary from a district to another. All the activities are present, some sites may even have been complementary. The graves are abundant and various, but still the dolmens and the caves were more often used.

The decorated ceramics of style 4 (incised decorations and barbed wire pattern) are marked at the same time by the Bell Beaker tradition and specificities concerning the morphologies and the technique of decoration itself. They are associated with a domestic ceramic and specific elements such as scarce bronze items. The contexts are almost homogeneous, but we often discover some vases of style 4 associated with rhodano-provençal assemblages or in rhodano-provençal sites. Among the various kinds of settlings, the sites in the heights are the more abundant. Sometimes they are associated with enclosures that may be regarded as fortifications. There are less sites than for the other styles and we do not find them all around the area of study, as we are used to do with the rhodano-provençal Bell Beakers. The graves are mostly collective deposits in caves, but there are some individual ones.

1.2. A domestic Bell Beaker: a Bell Beaker culture

Another important observation concerning these assemblages is the obvious domestic characteristic of the Bell Beakers in the south-east of France.

Both the number and the quota of the habitations among the recorded sites is very important. Even if all the non-funeral sites cannot be considered as strictly domestic sites, they represent more than two thirds of the recorded sites, contrary to what is known for the other areas.

Thus we can assume that the Bell Beaker culture is not a funeral phenomenon, even if there are Bell Beaker elements in the graves, in almost a hundred graves (LEMERCIER et al. to be published).

Moreover, the domestic sites where Bell Beaker elements are found can be specific or pure, namely free from any element of the local final Neolithic.

In these sites, whose domestic architecture must be regarded as culturally invested as in the local groups of the final Neolithic, all the activities of handcraft (pottery, tool-kit making ...) and subsistence (agriculture or at least grain stocking, rearing and hunting) are present.

Finally, the Bell Beaker is a „normal" material culture.

All these remarks are valid for the sets of styles 2, 3 and 4. The style 1, that includes some elements of the standard, cannot be considered as a material culture in the general sense, but as a „facing" in the assemblages of the local final Neolithic.

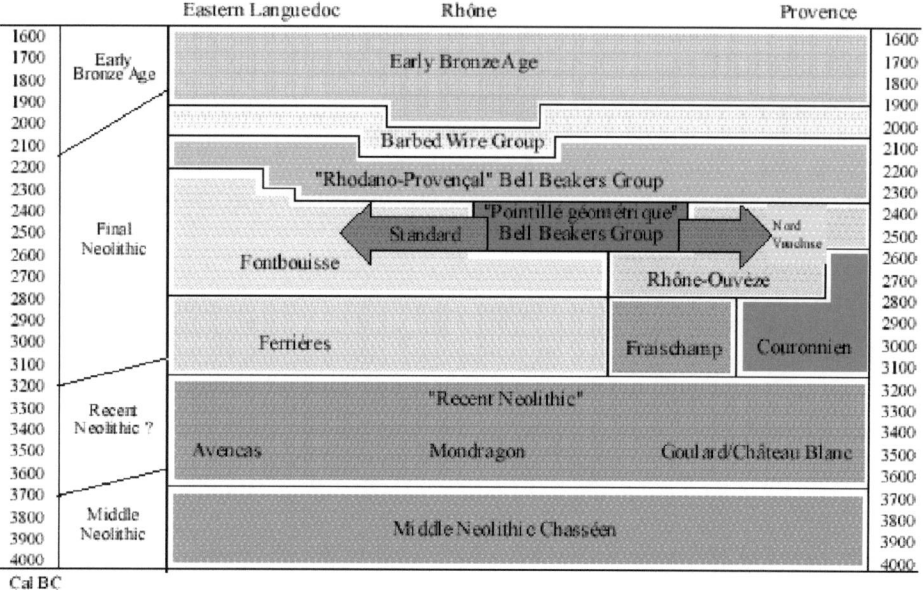

Fig. 2. Chronology of the fourth and third millenium BC archaeological groups in the South-East mediterranean France.

1.3. Bell Beakers and local cultures

The relationships between the Bell Beaker and the local cultures of the final Neolithic are recognised in certain assemblages, at least for the styles 1 and 2 and in few cases for style 3. For all those cases in the south-east of France, the local cultures are the Fontbouisse group and mostly the Rhône-Ouvèze group in Provence, which is the result of the main influence of the Fontbouisse group over the local Couronnien group.

Contrary to what we once thought during this study, no association between Couronnien and Bell Beaker elements could be proved or considered as valid.

As we have described yet, there are two types of associations. Either it is a simple „facing" the presence of standardised Bell Beaker vases (style 1) among complete and specific assemblages of local groups, either a mixed set which even presents technical shifts and cases of stylistic mixity (style 2).

In fact, one could think that the Bell Beaker culture did not appear in a world totally with no population (Fig. 2).

With the Bell Beaker phenomenon, we are lucky we can observe the different phases of a main change in the material culture, what we cannot do for the other transitional phases of the Neolithic.

2. Implications and interpretations

2.1. The chronological articulation of the styles

The general succession of the two main styles is obvious:

A first set is composed by elements linked to the styles widely spread in Europe (styles 1 and 2). They are associated with elements of the local cultures of the final Neolithic. The second set consists of the specific regional elements of the rhodano-provençal group and the barbed wire group, which are generally independent.

Within these sets the succession of the different styles is difficult to establish. The analysis of the contexts of discovery and the associations of remains does not enable us to determinate if, in this area, the style 1, with elements of the standard, is anterior to the style 2, with geometric spotted decorations. Analysing the styles 3 and 4 in the same way, we find out they are, in part at least, contemporary. The barbed wire style is the only one whose dates constitute an actual chronological phase during the Bell Beaker phenomenon.

2.2. The origin of the Bell Beaker elements present in the south-east of France

Here we question ourselves about the origins of the Bell Beaker elements, about the constitution of the different assemblages: is it the result of a local evolution or of some distinct inflows?

If we look for elements of comparison out of the area of study, we find (Fig. 3):

- For the early phase (style 1 and 2): the presence of identical elements in western Languedoc and beyond, the Iberic Peninsula until the atlantic coast. The style 2 (spotted geometric decorations) present a particular repartition that follows the mediterranean coastway and concentrates at the mouths of the rivers and along them, but avoids the inlands, contrary to certain isolated elements of style 1.

- For the rhodano-provençal Bell Beakers: once more we turn west towards the Pyrénéen group and the iberic groups for comparisons. At the same time, the presence of northern elements can be assumed, but it must have been a secondary influence.

- I have not made further researches for the barbed wire group. The subject is studied nowadays in several specific ways (VITAL et al. 1999; LEMERCIER to be published). Still, we can remark that the origin of these elements may be partly Bell Beaker. However, some morphological features remind us the Bell Beakers of central Italy, but the decorative patterns look like elements from north eastern Italy and Slovenia, yet their precise chronological place is to be established.

Whereas the potential geographical origins of the different elements remain imprecise, we can conclude there were several inflows, both successive and from distinct origins. Among these inflows the Iberic Peninsula plays a great role, as the western Languedoc.

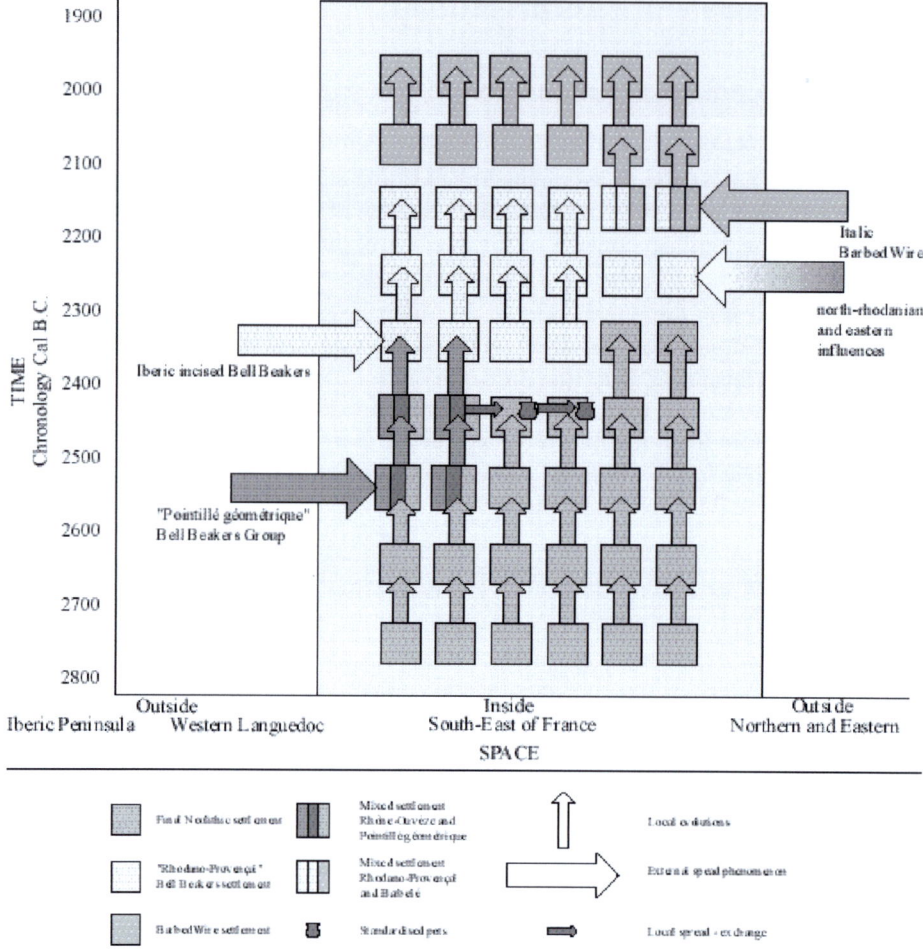

Fig. 3. Historical Model of settling and spread of Bell Beakers culture in the South-East of France.

2.3. A spatial and temporal scheme and its interpretation

We still find it difficult to date the apparition of the Bell Beaker culture in the southeast of France, though there is an hypothetical date: the middle of the third millennium B.C. Its origins is western, we could not discover any actual characteristic from the northern areas. The Rhône axis is important, but only for south-north direction at first.

Two hypothesises can be proposed:

The first hypothesis is the chronological succession of the styles1 and 2. The vases of the standard would fit into a very little important first spread, some contacts preceding the settling of actual sites where we can find items of style 2 (geometric spotted decorations).

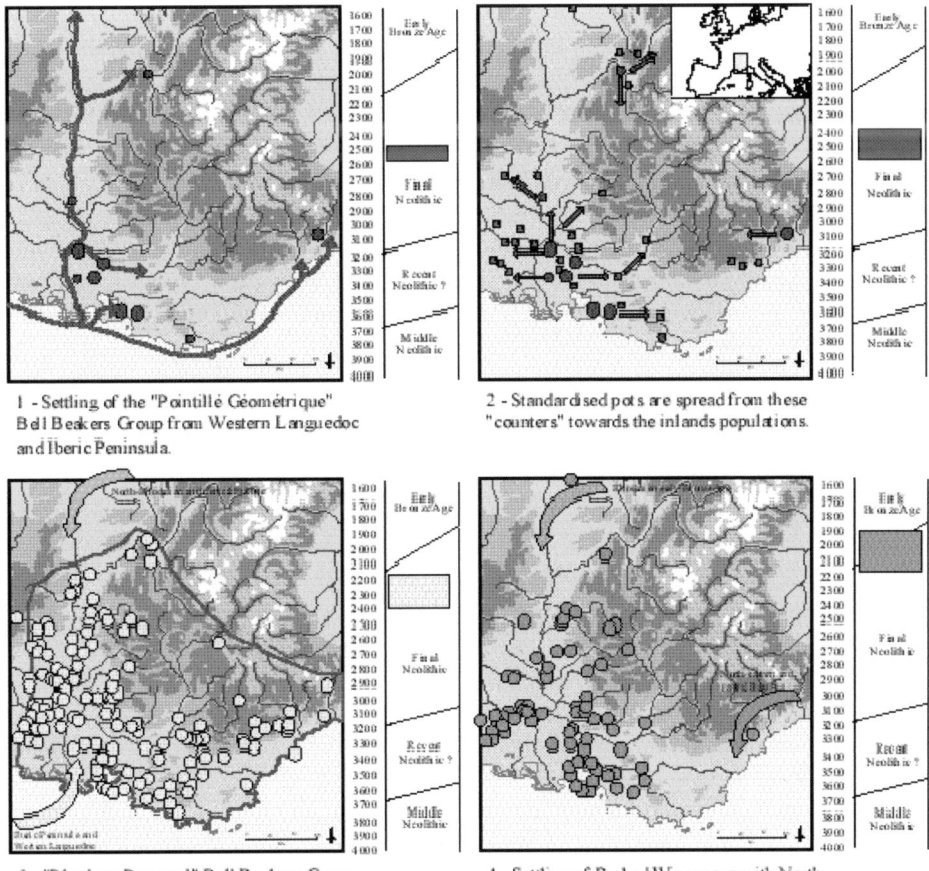

Fig. 4. Historical Model of settling and spread of Bell Beakers culture in the South-East of France.

This would square with the scheme proposed by J. Guilaine (GUILAINE 1967; 1976). Yet another hypothesis, a functional one, would propose a strict synchronism of the styles 1 and 2, which was observed in some sites.

With this point of view, the isolated vases of style 1 would be the result of the diffusion of standardised beakers from the settling of the styles 1 and 2 towards the inlands. This diffusion would have produced „counters", established close to the indigenous people, along the routes of communication. This hypothesis seems to be the most satisfying one to explain the assemblages we can observe.

The diffusion of the geometric spotted style is concentrated in the Mediterranean coast, in the mouths of the rivers and along the main rivers, but it continues beyond the south-east of France, following the Rhône (Fig. 4).

The second hypothesis concerns the development of the rhodano-provençal Bell Beaker: it would be the result of the acculturation of the local cultures. The possible comparisons show that repeated contacts must unite the south-east of France and the Iberic Peninsula during this period. As some elements show the influence of northern and eastern areas, the south-east of France seems to have become a kind of relay on an important route of communication and exchange which spread goes beyond this region towards north. At this time, Bell Beakers reach the borders of the area and may displace all the local cultures.

For the barbed wire group, the frequency of the reoccupation of the rhodano-provençal settlements and the presence of imitation of the barbed wire pattern in assemblages of the style 3 indicate a phase of partial synchrony. However, the dates show that the barbed wire group is to be distinguished of the Bell Beaker culture and continues after the change of millennium.

Synthesis and interrogation

In this area, the Bell Beaker phenomenon is constituted by a succession of historical events, it is neither a fashion or a simple diffusion of objects and their use. The analysis of the remains and the sites has shown that human groups actually moved. The distribution of the sites and their nature itself recall the protohistoric models proposed for the Greek settling in the same area. These models can be summed up like this: explorations, contacts, settlings, diffusions and acculturation/assimilation.

If this model squares perfectly with the archaeological of the South of France, it may be not valid for the areas close to the Iberic Peninsula, the atlantic coast and the lands along the Rhône. Yet, the ways the populations reacted to these contacts and settlings may have been different and may have generated various situations.

Within the South of France there are important differences from a district to another, for example the group of Fontbouisse seems to have strongly resisted in the eastern Languedoc, where the Bell Beakers arrives later than in Provence.

Nevertheless, one of the most important facts is the opening of main routes of communication and exchange through Europe, across the mediterranean South of France and the Rhône valley and beyond the Alps, that created the conditions for the development of the Bronze Age. From this point of view, the development of the barbed wire group in the South of France, with its probable italic origin, remains anecdotal. At the same time, a new movement from the east and the north going through the Rhône valley marks the actual appearance of the early Bronze Age.

Whatever the application of these ideas on the archaeological data, the questions they provoke are abundant and important.

Where is the actual origin of the Bell Beakers we can trace until the Iberic Peninsula (confirmed by radiocarbon dating)? And above all, why did this expansion follow two directions: along the Atlantic coast and the northern Mediterranean coast? The situation in Portugal in the middle of the third millennium, with the exacerbation of the characteristics of the final Neolithic (extreme density of sites, fortifications and building of monuments, social and individual markers) may constitute the only one answer to these two questions.

Finally, these few remarks do not suffice to explain the function and the appeal of the Bell Beakers towards the local populations from the Bell Beaker settlings, sometimes far in the inlands. This diffusion must have a sense that the quality of making and decoration of these vases, or their novelty, does not permit to justify and make us think of an ideological dimension (STRAHM 1997).

Remerciements:

Je remercie Anabel Gallin et Samuel van Willigen pour leur traductions de ce texte et des résumés en langues anglaise et allemande, et Robin Furestier pour avoir présenté en mon absence forcée cette communication au symposium de Poznań 2002.

Bibliography

COURTIN J. 1967. La culture du vase campaniforme en Provence, note préliminaire, *Cahiers Ligures de Préhistoire et d'Archéologie* 16, 27-36.

    1974. *Le Néolithique de la Provence*, Paris.

GUILAINE J. 1967. *La civilisation du vase campaniforme dans les Pyrénées françaises*, Carcassonne.

    1976. La civilisation des gobelets campaniformes dans la France méridionale, in: GUILAINE J. (dir.): *La Civilisation des vases campaniformes, IXe Congrès de l'UISPP, Colloque XXIV*, Nice, 197-213.

GUILAINE J. / CLAUSTRE F. / LEMERCIER O. / SABATIER P. 2002. Campaniforme et environnement culturel en France méditerranéenne. In: NICOLIS F. (ed.). *Bell Beakers today. Pottery, people, culture, symbols in prehistoric Europe. Proceedings of the International Colloquium, Riva del Garda (Trento, Italy), 11-16 May 1998. Volume 1*, Trento, 229-275.

LEMERCIER O. 1998. Phénomène, culture et tradition: statuts et rôles du Campaniforme au IIIe millénaire dans le Sud-Est de la France, *Bulletin de la Société Préhistorique Française* 95-3, 365-382.

    2002. *Le Campaniforme dans le sud-est de la France. De l'Archéologie à l'Histoire du troisième millénaire avant notre ère*. Thèse de Doctorat, Aix-en-Provence: Université de Provence / ESEP, 4 volumes, 1451 p. (dont 487 figures, 35 cartes) et 11 cartes hors-texte.

    to be published. *L'origine du groupe „barbelé" de la transition Campaniforme – Bronze ancien dans le sud-est de la France. L'hypothèse italique*, en préparation.

LEMERCIER O. / PELLISSIER M. / TCHEREMISSINOFF Y. to be published. Campaniforme et sépultures. Au-delà du standard. La place du Campaniforme dans l'évolution des sépultures du sud-est de la France au troisième millénaire avant notre ère. In: CHAMBON P. (dir.): *Les sépultures du Néolithique final et du Bronze ancien (2700-2000 av. J.-C.), Table ronde internationale de Sion, 2001*, à paraître.

SALANOVA L. 2000. *La question du Campaniforme en France et dans les îles anglo-normandes. Productions, chronologie et rôles d'un standard céramique*, Paris.

STRAHM C. 1997. Le Campaniforme: phénomène et culture. In: *L'énigmatique Civilisation Campaniforme*, Dijon.

VITAL J. / CONVERTINI F. / JALLOT L. / LEMERCIER O. / LOISON G. (dir.) 1999. *Projet Collectif de Recherche: Composantes culturelles des premières productions céramiques du bronze ancien dans le sud-est de la France, Rapport 1999: Provence-Alpes-Côte d'Azur*, Valence: CAP, 135 p., 33 fig.

L'Epicampaniforme en Italie Centrale:
stratigraphies, datations radiometriques, productions lithiques et ceramiques

Lucia Sarti (Siena, Italy)

Résumé

Le Campaniforme est un des aspects les plus importants des activités de recherche dans la région de Firenze (Italie centrale); à la fin du troisième millénaire on a dans ce territoire une importante croissance démographique, due au développement du phénomène campaniforme, dont l'importance pour nombre de gisements n'a pas de comparaisons ailleurs en Italie.

Ce développement se déroule entre la fin du troisième millénaire et la première moitié du deuxième, où la tradition campaniforme garde dans la région de Firenze une grande importance pour ce qui concerne soit l'organisation des espaces d'habitat, soit les choix économiques, soit les productions d'artisanat.

La recherche sur le campaniforme de Firenze concerne actuellement l'analyse des contextes les plus récents, au débout du deuxième millénaire, à l'âge du Bronze, en particulier, l'étude de certains grands gisements, Lastruccia, Madonna del Piano, Termine Est, récemment mis au jour. Il est donc possible de proposer une sériation continue en trois phases du Bronze ancien local jusqu'à la moitié du deuxième millénaire, lorsqu'ils commencent les aspects caractéristiques du Bronze moyen.

Summary

The Bell Beakers Culture represents one of the most interesting subjects among the researches in the Florentine plain; at the end of the III millennium B.C the occupation of this area, seems to intensify as confirmed by the demographic increase related to the Bell Beaker Culture phenomenon. This particular development, when compared to other Italian regions, is also denoted by the high density of archaeological evidences.

Such development starts in the last centuries of the III millennium B.C. and continues in the following millennium. During this period, the Bell beakers tradition in the Florentine area maintains a high impact on the organization of the settlements, on the economic strategies, and on the artefact productions.

The researches related to the Bell Beaker Culture are actually focussed on the analyses of the latest contexts which refer to the Bronze Age, in particular at the beginning of the II Millennium B.C.

An extensive study of complexes from the beginning of the Bronze Age was recently carried out on three lately discovered large sites, Lastruccia, Madonna del Piano and Termine est. It is now possible, with this new data , to give a detailed account of the uninterrupted development of the Early Bronze Age until the half of the II millennium B.C., when cultural aspects specific of the Middle Bronze Age appear. Therefore we propose a chrono-stratigrafic sequence of the first Bronze Age subdivided in three phases.

Le Campaniforme marque l'introduction d'une nouvelle phase culturelle en Toscane à la deuxième moitié du troisième millénaire. Plusieurs sites, environ quinze, appartiennent à cette période. Ils se trouvent le long du pied des collines, autour de 45-50 m au dessus du niveau de la mer, probablement aux alentours des rives du bassin lacustre, aujourd'hui disparu. Il s'agit d'habitats, avec des structures couvertes et des zones fonctionnelles situées à l'extérieur des structures memes.

L'économie est mixte: l'environnement humide favorise l'agriculture et l'élevage dispose d'espaces ouverts et des collines pour les pâturages. La sépulture de *Bos* trouvée dans l'habitat de Semitella pourrait trouver une explication en relation avec le développement de l'élevage des bovidés. L'activité de déboisement intensif attesté au Campaniforme pourrait etre liée à l'élargissement des aires destinées à l'agriculture et au pâturage. La peche et la chasse sont des activités secondaires.

Le rituel funéraire n'est documenté que par la structure de Via Bruschi: il s'agit d'une fosse placée dans une structure à tumulus, très élaborée et complexe (SARTI *et al.* 1987-88).

Les productions artisanales – céramiques, lithiques, métalliques – sont bien documentées. L'étude du mobilier a permis de proposer une sériation culturelle, confirmée par des datations radiométriques (SARTI 1997; 1995-96; SARTI / MARTINI 2001).

La dynamique évolutive de l'industrie céramique du Campaniforme de l'aire florentine présente des affinités avec celle du Midi français, selon une physionomie qu'on pourrait définir comme «méditerranéenne»; notre production définit un caractère original qui réélabore de rares apports du substrat énéolithique local avec d'autres, plus importants et nombreux, qui trouvent des comparaisons dans les régions de l'Europe continentale, centrale et orientale, aussi bien que dans la France méridionale ou, plus rarement, dans la péninsule ibérique. L'importance des éléments qui marquent une rupture avec les cultures indigènes est amplifiée par la présence d'une structure funéraire comme Via Bruschi et de la sépulture de bovidé (SARTI / ANASTASIO 2001).

Il est encore difficile d'expliquer les modalités de diffusion et le rôle de la production campaniforme dans l'aire florentine et en Italie centrale en général; l'explication ne doit pas avoir été univoque dans les différents contextes. La documentation permet de proposer l'hypothèse de l'arrivée de nouvelles idéologies ou d'un nouveau goût qui s'insèrent dans la réalité régionale dans les derniers siècles du troisième millénaire. Cela est démontré par les éléments de la tradition céramique toscane présents au sein des ensembles du Campaniforme évolué. Telle intégration est plus évidente aux premiers siècles du millénaire suivant, avec la création d'aspects plus régionaux.

Aux début du deuxième millénaire la tradition campaniforme garde encore une grande importance dans le territoire: pour l'organisation des espaces d'habitat, pour les modes de subsistance, pour les artisanats. L'étude des ensembles du premier âge du Bronze a été récemment développé par l'analyse de plusieurs niveaux d'habitat trouvés sur trois sites: Lastruccia, Madonna del Piano, Termine Est. Il est donc possible de détailler le développement continu du Bronze ancien local, jusqu'au milieu du deuxième millénaire, avec une périodisation chronostratigraphique en trois phases (SARTI / MARTINI 2000).

La typologie des implantations des habitats du début de l'âge du Bronze fait partie d'un canon standardisé, qui trouve ses antécédents dans la stratégie d'implantation du Campaniforme local. Il s'agit d'implantations dans des paléolits, en exploitant les dépôts de graviers du fond des canaux probablement pour leur fonction de drainage. Des apports artificiels de gravier et cailloux mélangés à des déchets céramiques et osseux complétaient le remplissage, qui constituait le pavage où se trouvent les mobiliers et certaines structures domestiques. Une telle intervention, préliminaire aux implantations, est constamment présentes sur tous les sites.

Les données analytiques relatives aux structures de drainage, aux trous de poteau, aux fosses, et la vérification de la distribution spatiale des objets, sont les seules données qui permettent de proposer l'hypothèse de la présence de structures couvertes; il n'y a aucune indication directe des élévations et les fragments d'argile rubéfiée, parfois avec empreintes de clayonnage, dont la distribution ne présente aucune concentration particulière, ne permettent pas d'aller plus loin. La morphologie des concentrations est elliptique très allongée, suivant la direction du paléolit et limitée à celui-ci en largeur. La faible profondeur des trous de poteau laisse penser à des couvertures légères.

Au cours du Bronze ancien et à la transition au Bronze moyen, les drainages deviennent progressivement moins importants et relatifs à des structures moins profondes. Cette tendance devient plus évidente au Bronze moyen, pendant lequel les implantations sont localisées près des paléolits et non à l'intérieur. Il semblerait donc qu'on abandonne définitivement au Bronze moyen cette stratégie d'implantation dans les paléolits, apparue avec le Campaniforme évolué, transmise à l'Epicampaniforme et encore présente – quoique moins importante – dans une deuxième phase du Bronze ancien.

La gestion du terroir montre une exploitation intensive et diversifiée des ressources locales, en continuité avec la stratégie de complémentarité entre la plaine et les reliefs proches qui existait déjà pour les premiers groupes néolithiques. L'approvisionnement des matières premières est quasi exclusivement local. L'industrie lithique est obtenue sur silex et jaspe locaux; l'usage de l'obsidienne est rare, la stéatite et le Dentalium sont les seuls matériaux exogènes.

La périodisation culturelle et chronologique proposée se fonde sur l'étude de trois sites multistratifiés: Lastruccia, Madonna del Piano et Termine Est.

Une première phase du Bronze ancien est appelée Epicampaniforme en raison des strictes liaisons observées avec le Campaniforme évolué. Un caractère fondamental pour sa définition est l'abondance des éléments de décor de style campaniforme, dont la proportion est proche de celle constatée pour le Campaniforme évolué. Quelques exemples de décor incisé, présentant un motif simplifié par rapport au Campaniforme, apparaissent associés aux éléments plus proches du style précédent. La céramique décorée selon le style campaniforme est constituée spécialement par des formes simples globulaires et par formes composées des ensembles campaniformes. Des formes à anses horizontales ou verticales et des écuelles à bord épaissi, parfois décoré, pouvant porter une ou deux anses horizontales sont présentes; ces dernières deviennent cependant moins fréquentes à l'Epicampaniforme.

Au sein du corpus de récipients décorés épicampaniformes, de nouvelles morphologies apparaissent: les tasses de forme composée à carène vive et celles globulaires à bord éversé.

L'organisation du décor conserve la disposition en bandes horizontales; quelques fois le motif n'est pas délimité. On observe un changement de l'organisation du décor, à partir des techniques et des motifs préexistants. Le décor varie entre deux tendances extrêmes: l'une vers la surabondance des signes, qui occupent une bonne partie de la surface, l'autre vers la simplification des ornementations, où le remplissage des bandes horizontales tend à disparaître. Les dispositions verticales et obliques deviennent fréquentes, mais elles n'arrivent que très rarement à former des motifs en métopes.

Les motifs nouveaux qui apparaissent associés à ceux de tradition campaniforme, en sont cependant inspirés de façon plus lointaine. Ils présentent une bande décorée souvent unique; les remplissages sont plus simples que ceux des décors campaniformes: traits verticaux, lignes brisées, chevrons.

La céramique commune montre aussi d'importants changements, même si une forte continuité structurale avec la tradition campaniforme est remarquable.

Les formes prédominantes sont simples et peuvent être profondes, moyennes ou basses. Les anses verticales asymétriques – parmi lesquelles les anses coudées sur des vases ou des tasses sont prédominantes, alors que les anses horizontales deviennent plus rares.

Le goût pour les décors imprimés est confirmé par la présence de plusieurs bords et languettes traités par ce décor, qui étaient plus rares au Campaniforme évolué.

La deuxième phase du Bronze ancien présent une raréfaction des éléments décorés. Les décors de type campaniforme, obtenus au peigne et au poinçon, sont dans la plupart des cas moins nombreuses que ceux liés aux innovations décoratives à incisions peu profondes et bien plus rarement à cannelures élaborées selon des schémas complexes. On peut encore y reconnaître une tradition campaniforme très lointaine. Le goût pour les bandes non délimitées se généralise. La décoration constituée par une seule bande horizontale sur la largeur maximale des pots est aussi présente.

Les formes globulaires et celles à carène douce sont encore présentes, alors que les formes basses à bord plat épaissi disparaissent. Les types décorés originaux sont constitués par des formes carénées et des écuelles hémisphériques. Un des types nouveaux de la céramique commune est le pot globulaire à bord épaissi et cordon lisse horizontal à la base du col. Les vases à cordons souvent multiples, lisses ou plus rarement digités sont bien présentes. Il y a quelques exemplaires de vases bitronconiques. Les tasses composées comprennent soit les types sinueux de la phase précédente, soit des types profonds à gorge plus ou moins évidente; les carènes peuvent être accentuées ou douces. On observe la rareté des anses horizontales et l'abondance des anses coudées à appendice ou en forme de lacet.

Parmi les ensembles attribués à la deuxième phase, on observe certaines différences typologiques qui peuvent indiquer une périodisation fine.

Dans la troisième phase du Bronze ancien on a une réduction des éléments décorés. Il s'agit encore de morphologies carénées, sur lesquelles le décor est disposé en bandes horizontales parfois marginées. Les ornements sont encore traditionnels et on trouve aussi des décors incisés qui suivent des motifs complexes assez lointains du goût campaniforme.

Les formes profondes sont prédominantes dans la céramique commune. On observe des éléments globulaires et ceux à bord dégagé. Les cordons, appliqués surtout sur les formes profondes, sont lisses horizontaux ou festonnés, plus rarement digités. Parmi les tasses on ne trouve plus les éléments à profil sinueux de type campaniforme. On remarque la fréquence des écuelles à bord rentrant, apparues sporadiquement à la phase précédente. Les anses coudées et celles en lacet de développent ultérieurement. On observe la présence sporadique de traitements des surfaces par brossage et imprimées à l'ongle.

Les industries lithiques de la première phase du bronze ancien montrent elles aussi des ressemblances avec les productions campaniformes.

À la deuxième phase on observe des comportements structuraux qui conservent des liaison avec la tradition précédente (progression du Substrat, rareté des foliacés, présence des segments), mais des aspects qui ne se développent qu'à la phase suivante apparaissent déjà: développement des grattoirs frontaux courts, faible pourcentage des pièces écaillées.

La troisième phase du Bronze ancien présente des éléments innovants qui remplacent certaines aspects campaniformes. Les liaisons avec la tradition demeurent ici de nature stylistique.

Il est intéressant de souligner les variations des géométriques, et spécialement des segments, qui sont caractéristiques du Campaniforme évolué. À partir du passage au Bronze ancien, ils ne sont qu'un élément à peine présent et perdurent jusqu'à la deuxième phase; néanmoins, ils témoignent d'une évolution phylétique du Campaniforme. Les foliacés, qui étaient aussi très importants au sein des industries campaniformes de production de pointes pédonculées et pièces bifaciales, deviennent moins nombreuses à l'Epicampaniforme et ne réapparaissent qu'à la fin de la deuxième phase. Les pointes foliacées pédonculées montrent une évolution stylistique vers des types petits et peu élancés. Leur production augmente avec l'introduction d'une plus grande diversité typologique à la fin de la deuxième phase. Les autres types de foliacés qui étaient présents au Campaniforme disparaissent alors à l'Epicampaniforme.

Une catégorie différente d'outils est obtenue sur un calcaire local à texture fine. Ce groupe se différencie de l'industrie en jaspe et en silex par des dimensions – moyennes et grandes – et par la technique de débitage mise en oeuvre; le but à atteindre est la production de tranchets ou de tranchants prononcés. Les classes reconnues du point de vue typologique sont des racloirs, des denticulés, des pièces écaillées, des grattoirs du type *rabots* et des choppers. La retouche est écailleuse large, parfois scalariforme.

L'hypothèse d'une évolution culturelle graduelle et continue des ensembles locaux du premier âge du Bronze, qui se développent à partir d'un substrat

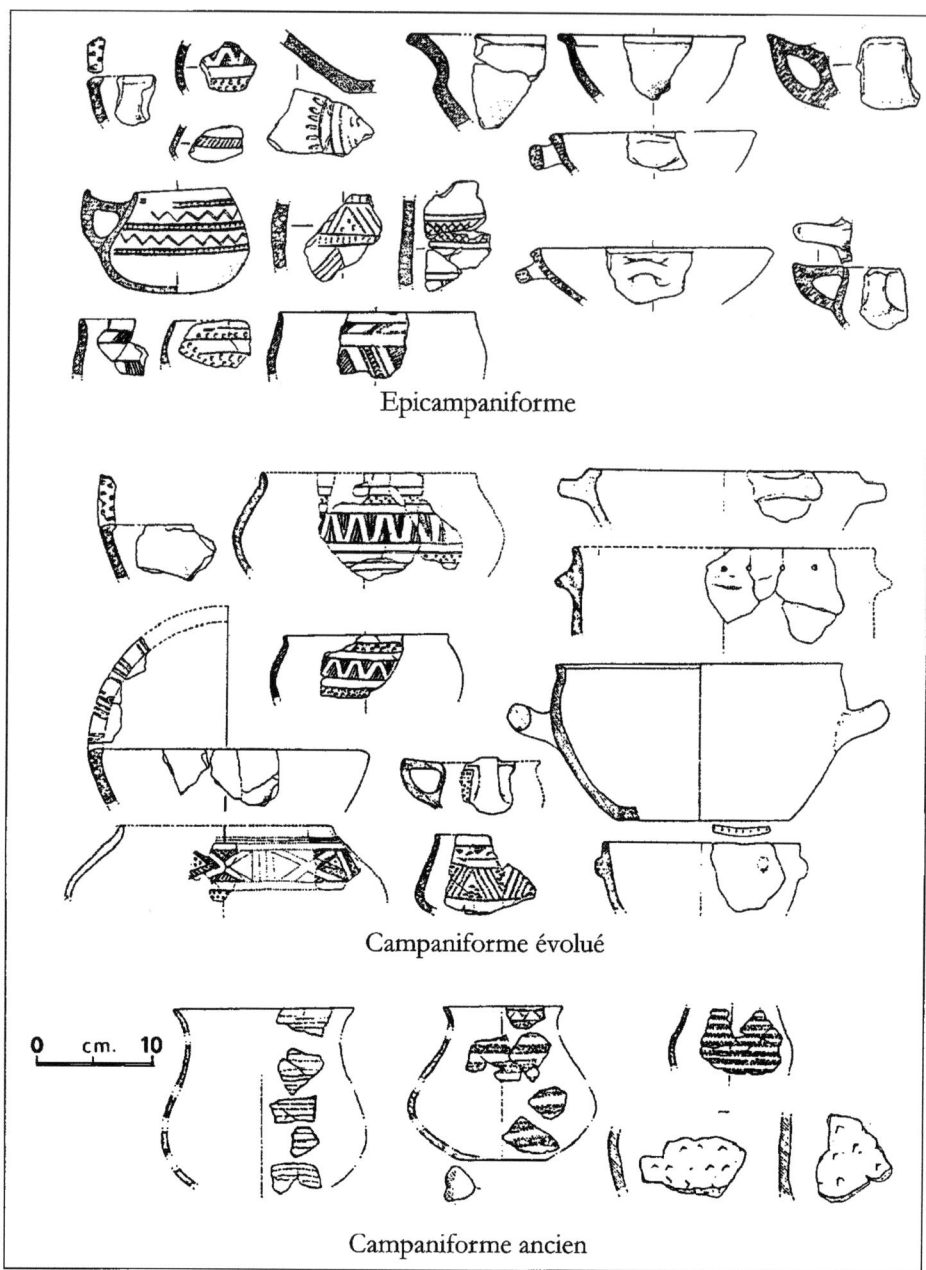

Fig. 1.   Sèquence du Campaniforme dans la région de Firenze.

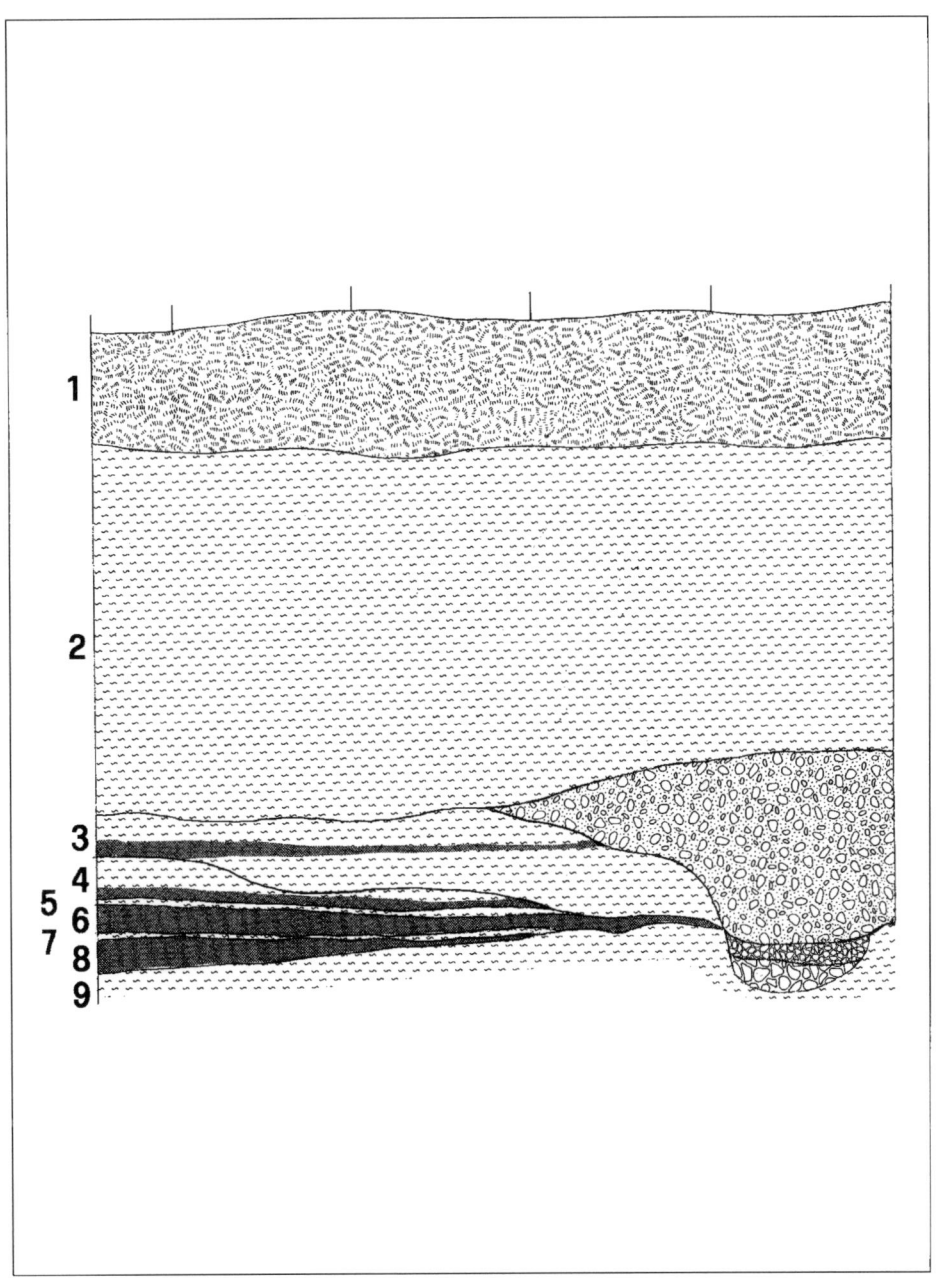

Fig. 2. Schéma stratigraphique de Lastruccia 3.

Similar but Different. Bell Beakers in Europe

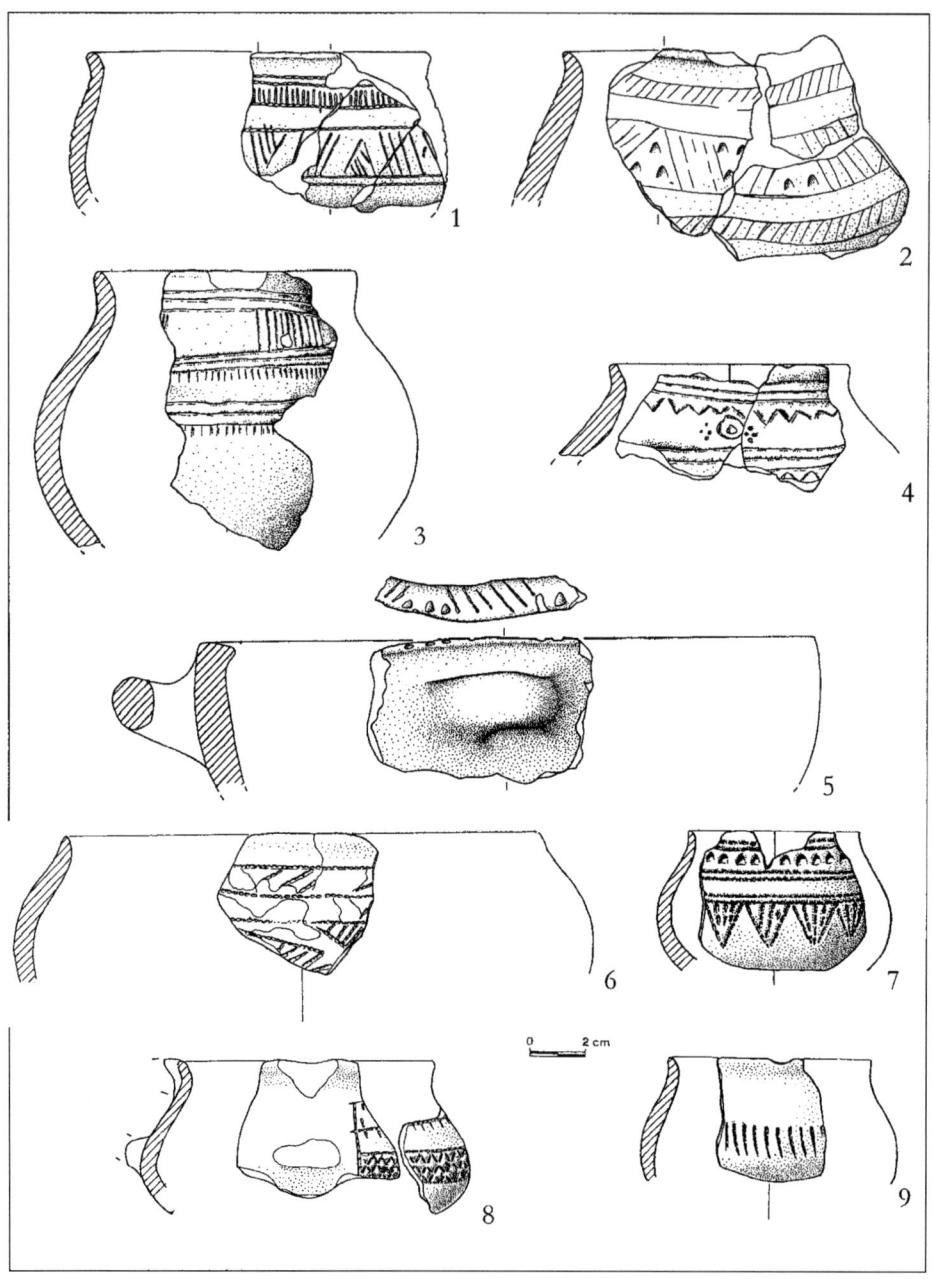

Fig. 3. Céramique de la phase 1: Lastruccia 3 couche 8 (nn. 1–5); Lastruccia 2A couche C2–3 (nn. 6–9).

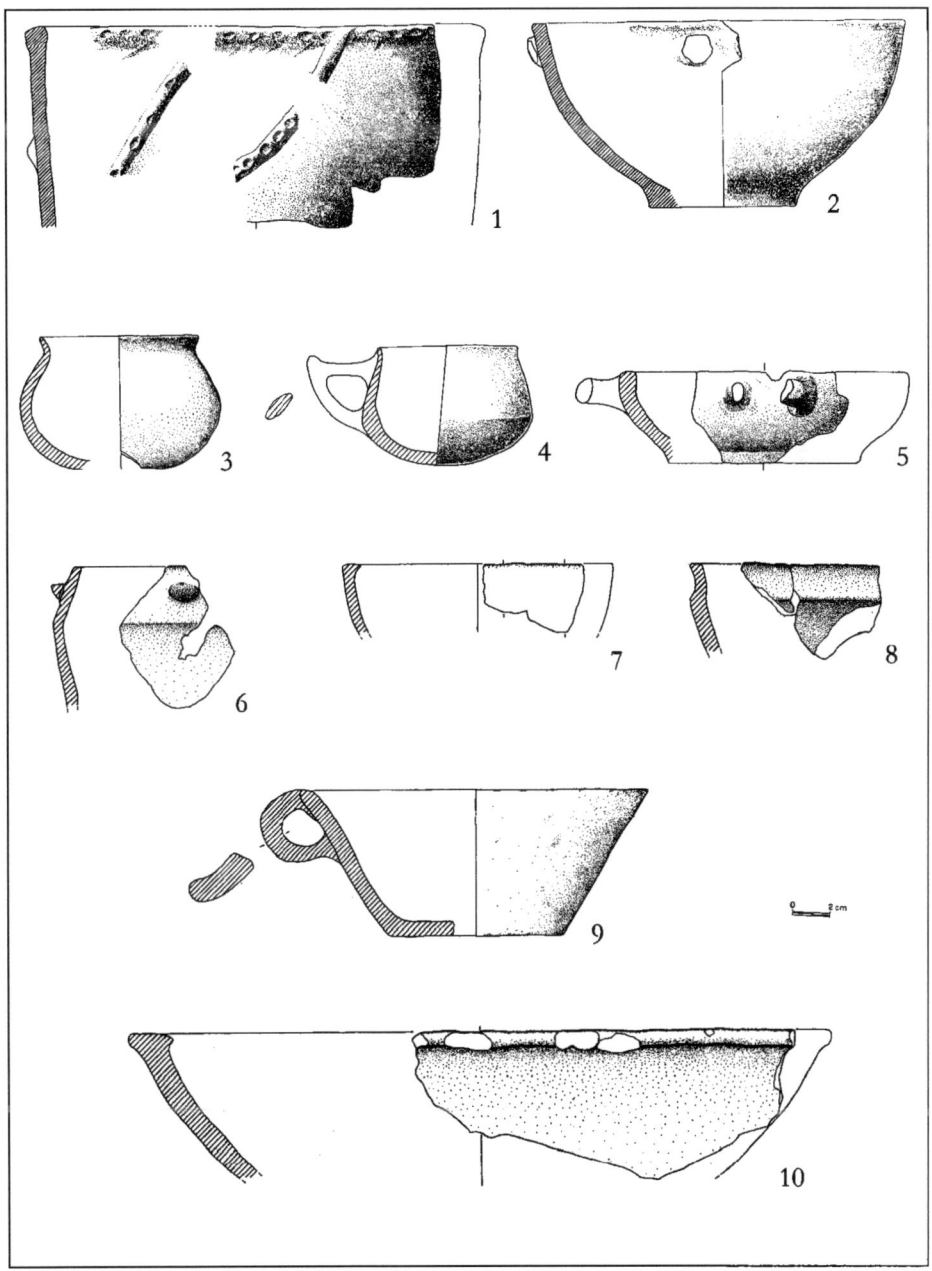

Fig. 4. Céramique de la phase 1: Lastruccia 2A couche C 2–3 (nn. 1–5); Lastruccia 3 couche 8 (nn. 6–10).

Similar but Different. Bell Beakers in Europe

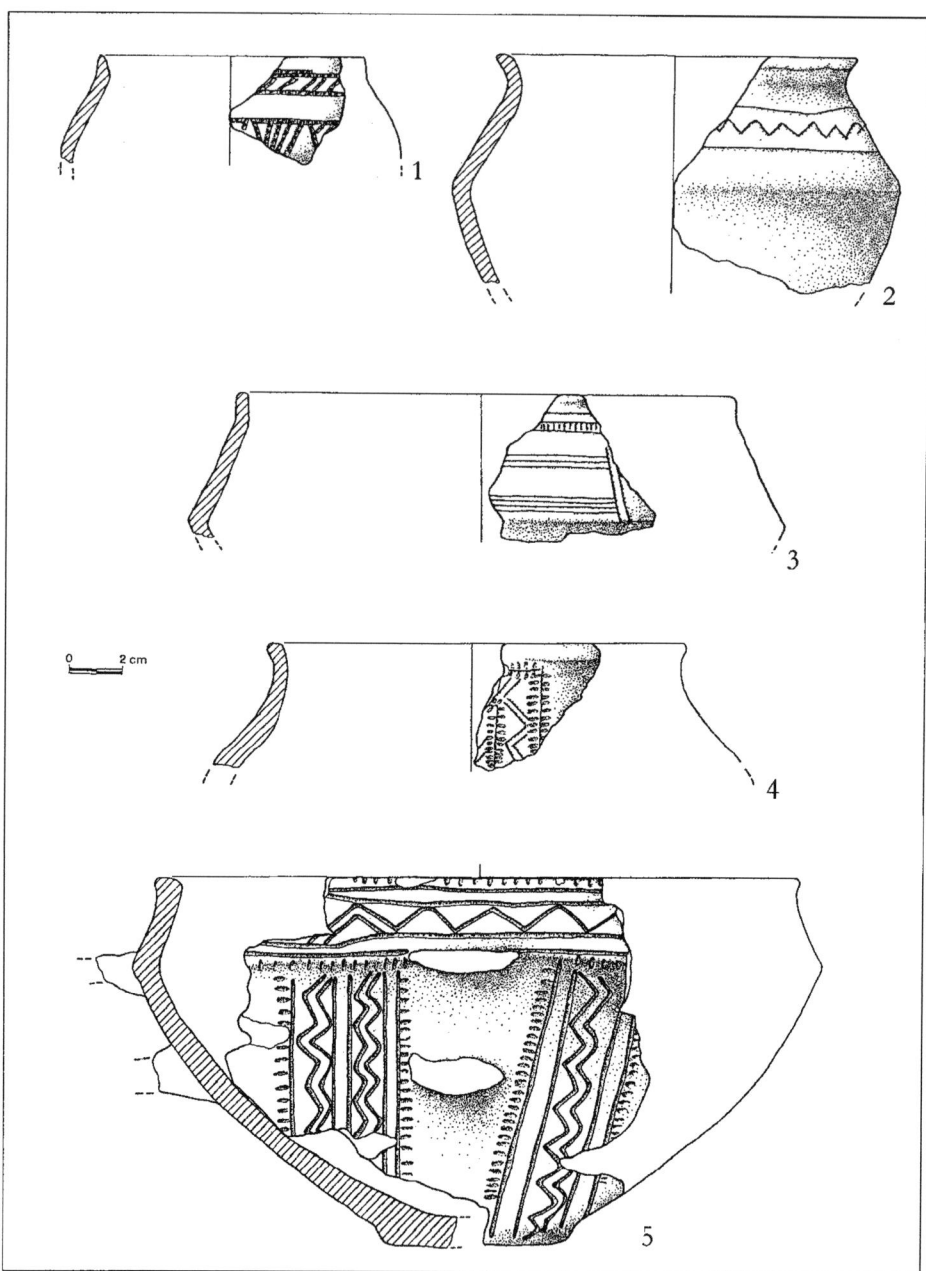

Fig. 5. Céramique de la phase 2: Lastruccia 3, couche 6.

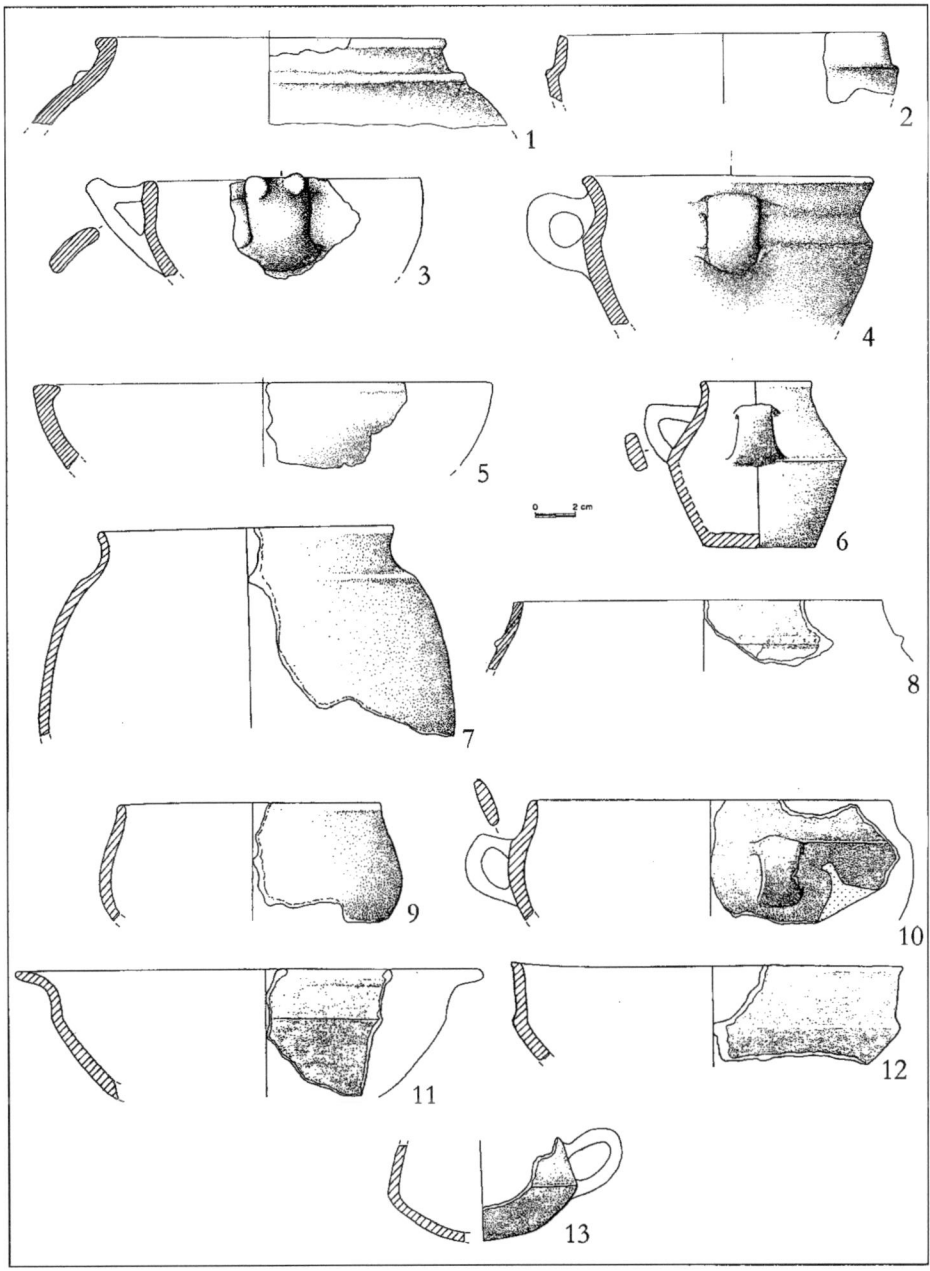

Fig. 6. Céramique de la phase 2: Lastruccia 3, couche 6 (nn. 1–5); Termine Est 2, couche 3E (nn. 6–13).

Similar but Different. Bell Beakers in Europe

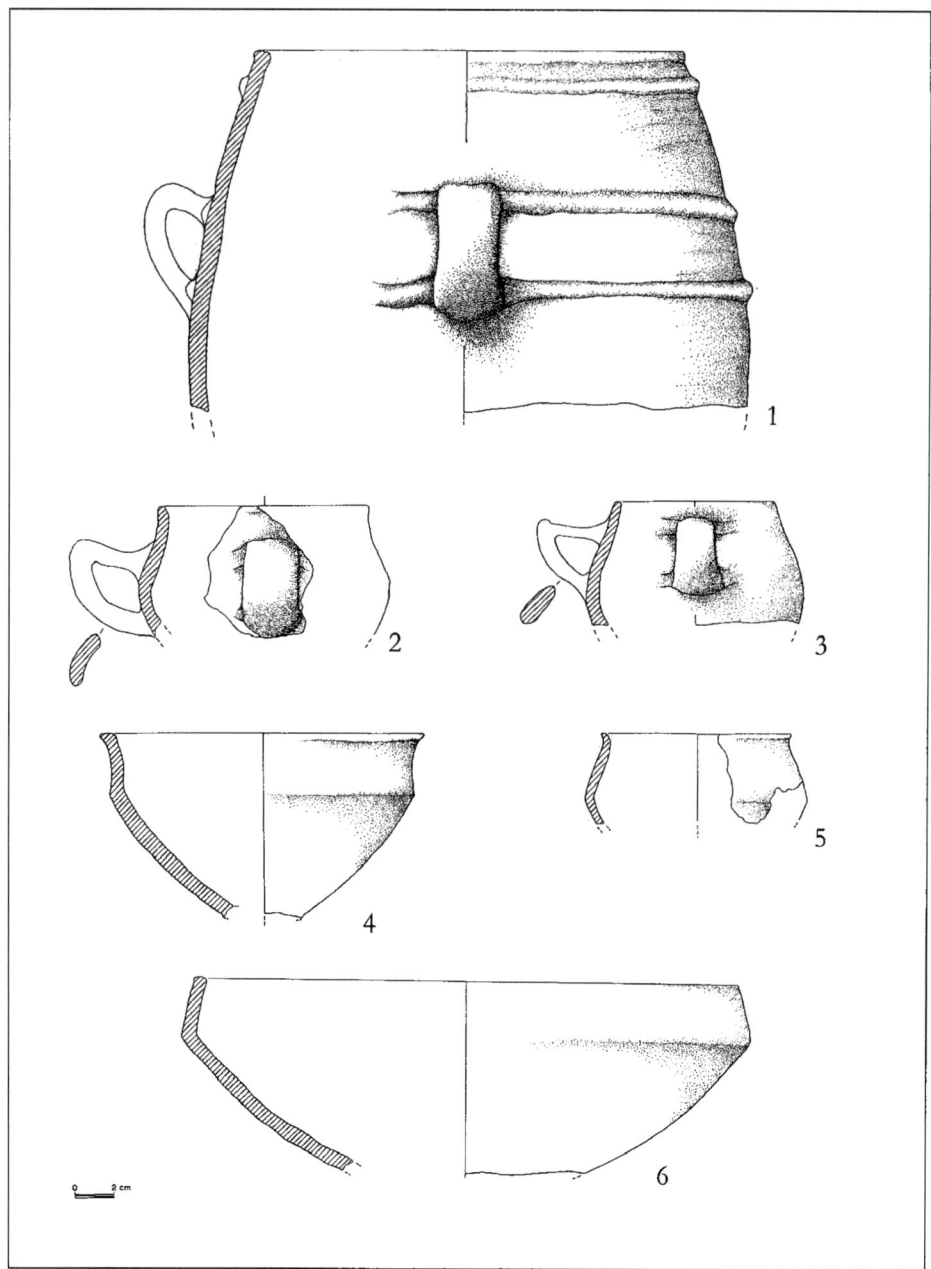

Fig. 7.　Céramique de la phase 2: Madonna del Piano, couche 7.

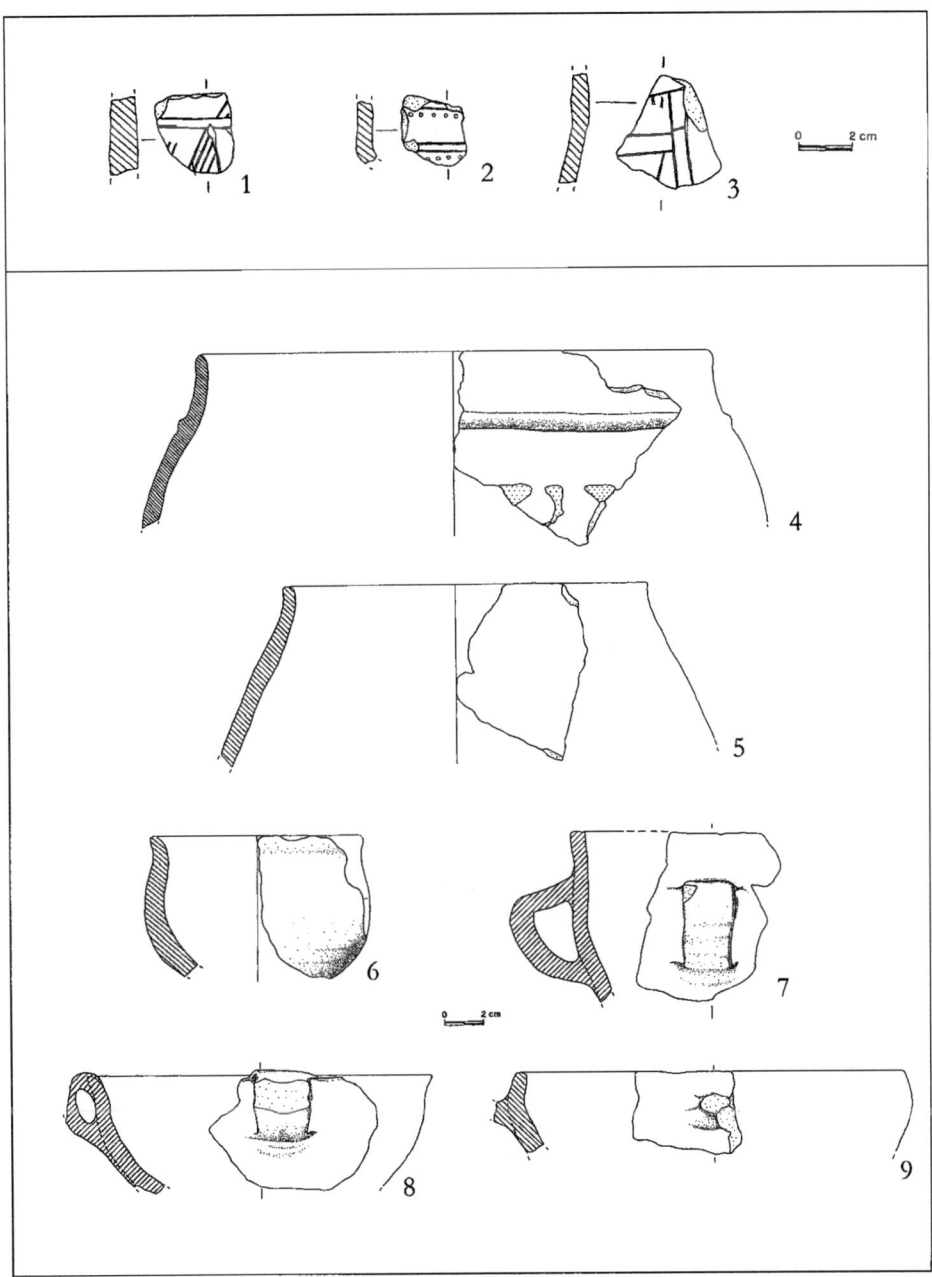

Fig. 8. Céramique de la phase 3: Lastruccia 3, couche 4.

Similar but Different. Bell Beakers in Europe

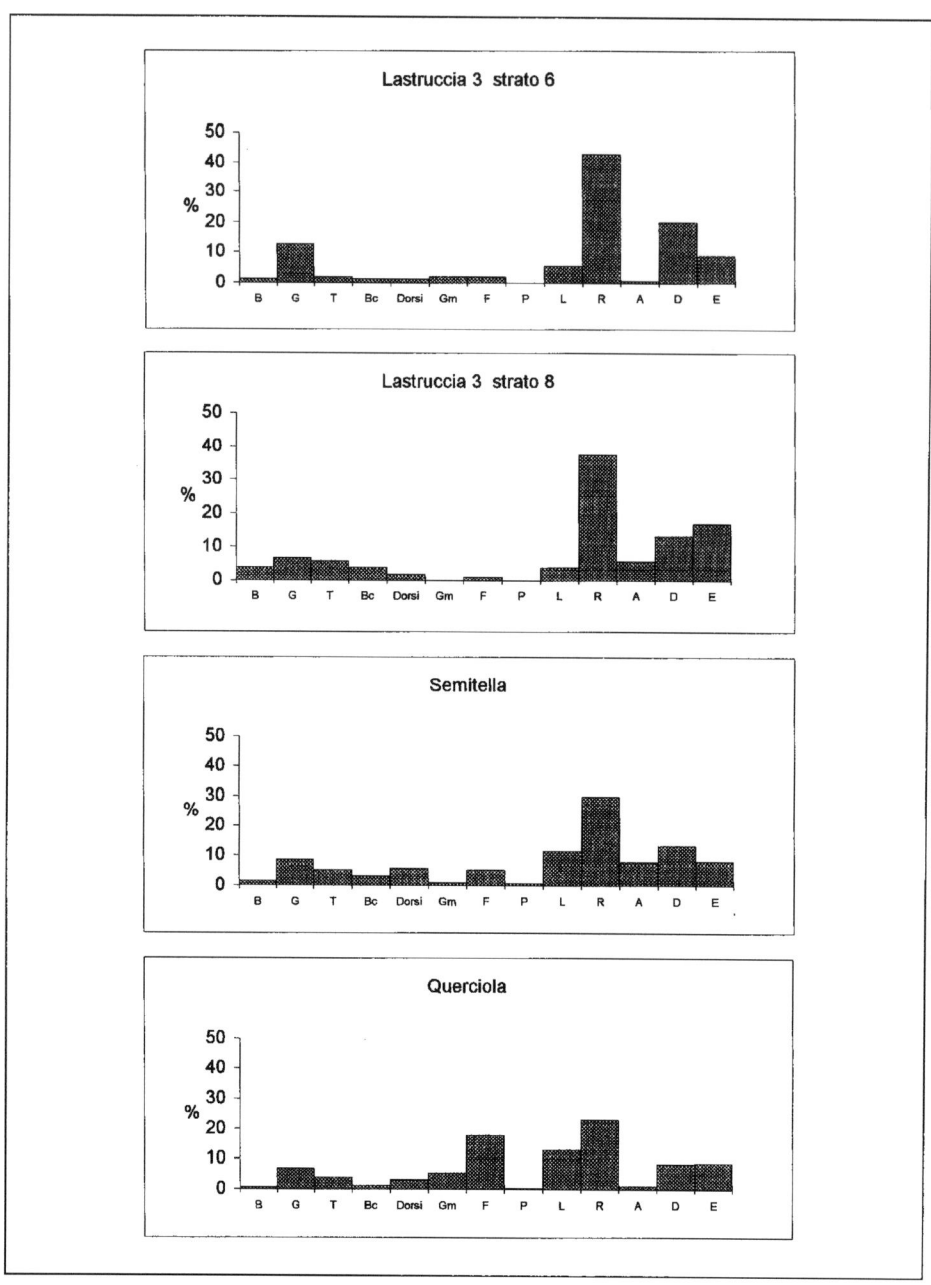

Fig. 9.   Evolution des industries lithiques.

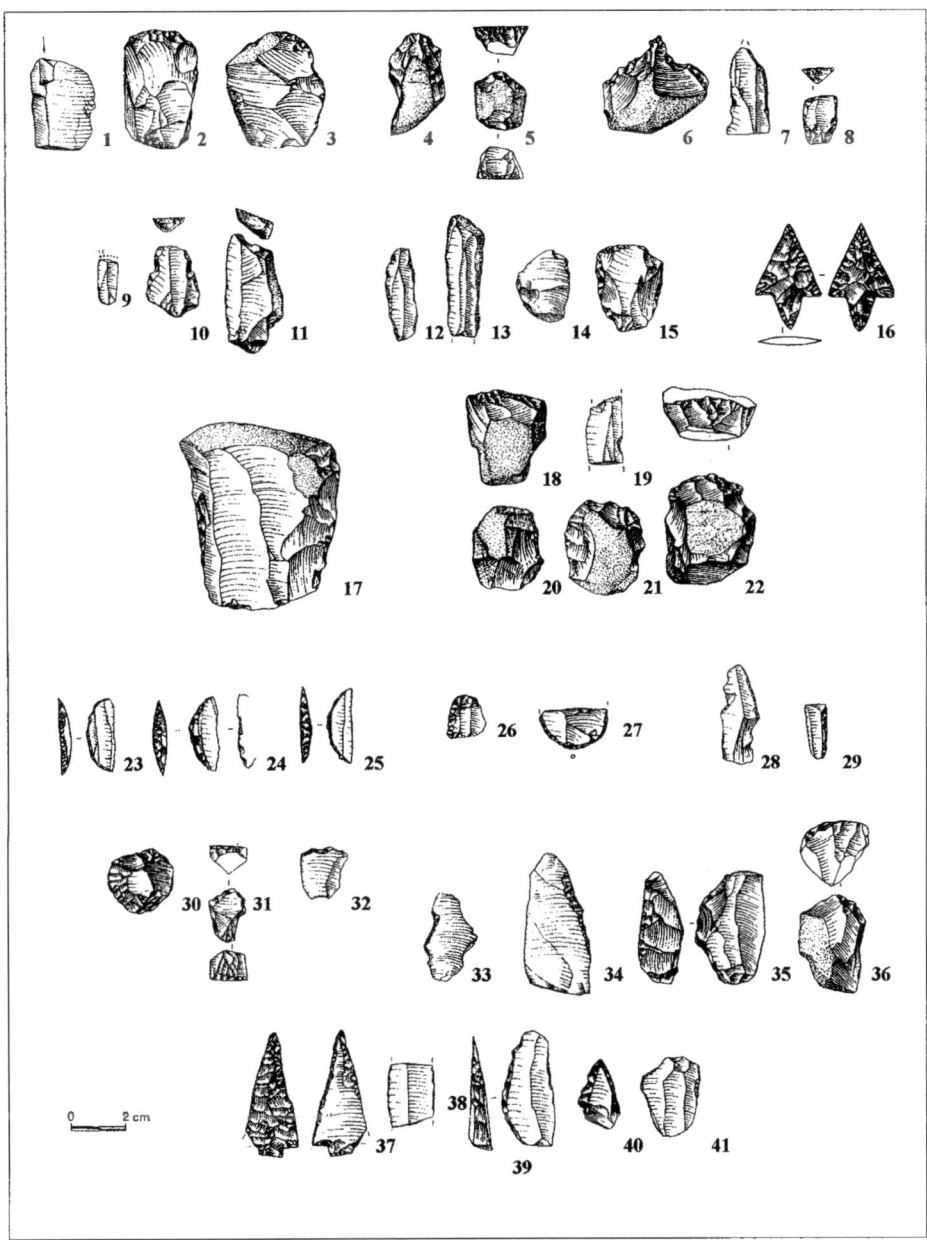

Fig. 10. Industries lithiques de la phase 1: Lastruccia 3, couche 8 (nn. 1–22); Lastruccia 2A couche C2–3 (nn. 23–41).

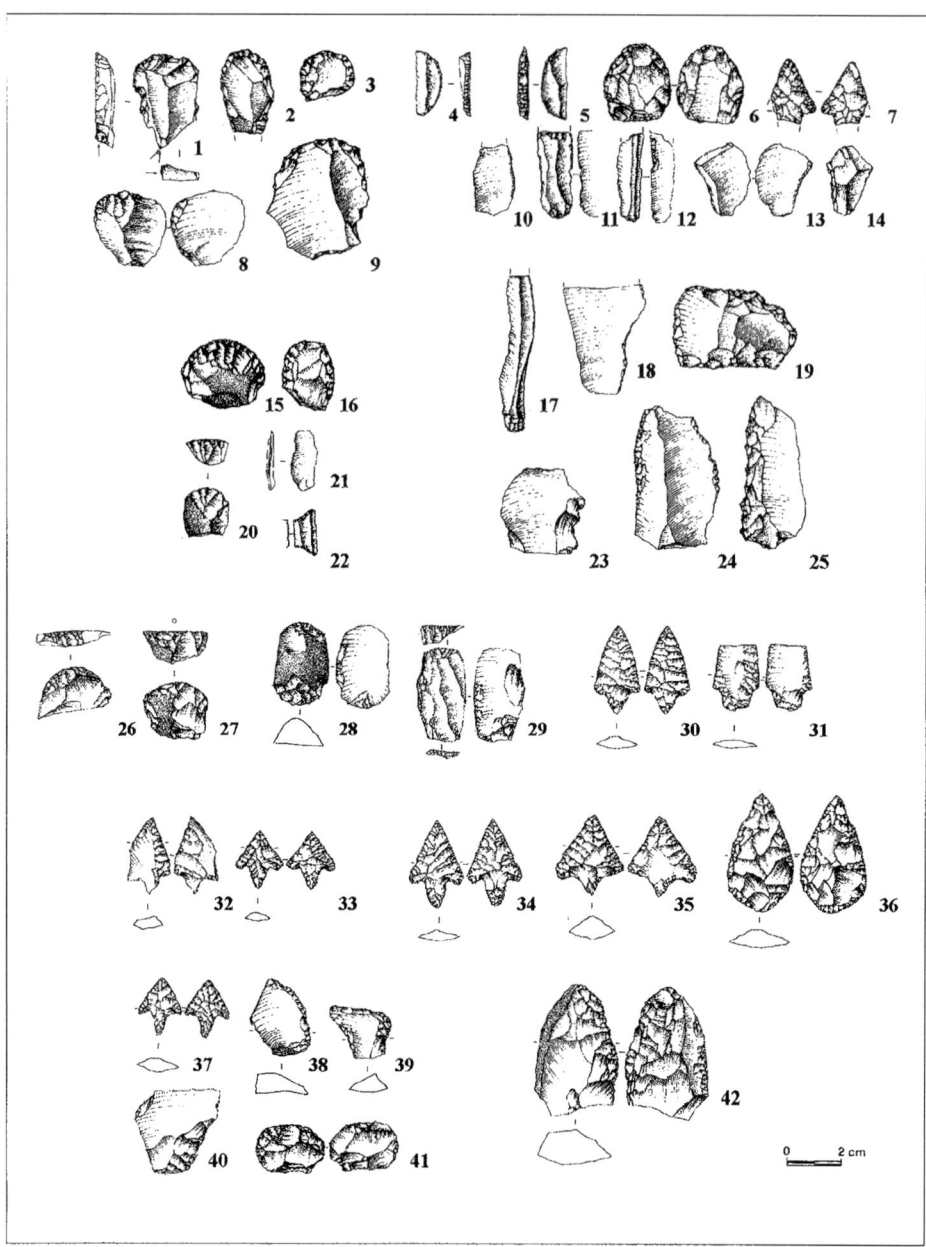

Fig. 11. Industries lithiques de la phase 2: Lastruccia 3, couche 6 (nn. 1–25); Termine Est 2, couche 3E (nn. 26–42).

campaniforme énéolithique, qu'on avait proposé sur la base de l'étude des productions artisanales, est confirmé par une série de datations radiométriques, en particulier celles de Lastruccia 3.

Phase 1

Site	Datation	Non calibrée b.p.	Calibrée B.C. 1 σ	Calibrée B.C. 2 σ	Centrales B.C.
Lastruccia 2A/C2–3	Beta-106578	3840 ±60	2400 – 2190	2465 – 2125 2065 – 2060	2290
Lastruccia 2B/B	Beta-106576	3850 ±80	2455 – 2175	2490 – 2035	2300
Lastruccia 3/8	Beta-106582	3780 ±70	2300 – 2120 2080 – 2050	2450 – 1975	2190
Lastruccia 1/N	Beta - 84136	3760 ±80	2290 – 2030	2450 – 1935	2145

Phase 2

Site	Datation	Non calibrée b.p.	Calibrée B.C. 1 σ	Calibrée B.C. 2 σ	Centrales B.C.
Lastruccia 3/6	Beta-106580	3880 ±80	2465 – 2205	2570 – 2125 2065 – 2060	2335
Termine Est 2/3E	Beta-106584	3680 ±70	2140 – 1945	2270 – 1885	2030

Bibliographie

SARTI L. 1995-96. Cronostratigrafia del Campaniforme in area fiorentina: dati preliminari dall'insediamento di Lastruccia. *Rivista di Scienze Preistoriche* XLVII (1995-96), 239-260.

SARTI L. (ed.) 1997. *Querciola. Insediamento campaniforme a Sesto Fiorentino*. Firenze.

1998. Aspetti insediativi del Campaniforme nell'Italia centrale. In: Nicolis F. / Mottes E. (eds), *Simbolo ed enigma. Il bicchiere campaniforme e l'Italia nella preistoria europea del III millennio a. C., Catalogo della mostra (Riva del Garda, 12 maggio-30 settembre 1998)*. Trento, 137-201.

SARTI L. / ANASTASIO S. 2001, The ox grave from Semitella (Sesto Fiorentino, Firenze). In: Nicolis F. (ed.), *Bell Beakers today. Pottery, people, culture, symbols in prehistoric Europe. Proceedings of the International Colloquium, Riva del Garda (Trento, Italy) 11-16 may 1998*. Trento, 649-651.

SARTI L. / BIRTOLO R. / FOGGI B. / MAGI M. / MARTINI F. 1987-88, Il tumulo eneolitico di via Bruschi a Sesto Fiorentino. *Rivista di Scienze Preistoriche* XLI, 139-198.

SARTI L. / LEONINI V. 1999-2000, L'Epicampaniforme di Lastruccia 1 a Sesto Fiorentino: il complesso ceramico dell'orizzonte N. *Rivista di Scienze Preistoriche* L, 261-295.

SARTI L. / MARTINI F. (eds.) 2000, *Insediamenti e artigianati dell'età del Bronzo in area fiorentina. Le ricerche archeologiche nei cantieri CONSIAG (1994-1996)*. Firenze.

SARTI L. / MARTINI F. 2001, Strategie insediative del Campaniforme in Italia centrale. In: NICOLIS F. (ed.), *Bell Beakers today. Pottery, people, culture, symbols in prehistoric Europe. Proceedings of the International Colloquium, Riva del Garda (Trento, Italy) 11-16 may 1998*, Trento, 187-198.

Similar but Different. Bell Beakers in Europe
Czebreszuk J. (ed.)
Poznań 2004

BELL BEAKERS: AN OUTLINE OF PRESENT STAGE OF RESEARCH

Janusz Czebreszuk (Poznań, Poland)

Bell Beakers (BB) have aroused controversies and surprised researchers for over 100 years. This was only to be expected. The papers written by some most competent European researchers and included in this volume show how rich and multifaceted phenomenon BB are. I shall enumerate some of their most characteristic traits (CZEBRESZUK 2003):

1. BB spread over western and central Europe (in the history of the Continent a structure of a comparable size has been only the contemporary European Union).
2. The full history of BB covers the period of almost 1000 years (although in individual regions their history was always shorter).
3. BB had their internal dynamics; they emerged in southwestern Europe, spread east and survived the longest on the North European Plain and the British Isles.
4. The central element of BB was a set of objects related to the drinking of special beverages and to war and hunting.
5. The objects were always carefully made, hence they had a significant cultural value for their users; they are most often found in graves where a single person was interred lying on his/her side in a flexed position.
6. The general typological evolution of BB goods is similar in all regions; the phenomenon, originally quite uniform (Maritime beakers), diversified regionally with time.
7. BB are closely related to metallurgy (chiefly of copper and gold); they developed the first stylistic of metal goods in the history of the continent, which spread across the vast expanses of prehistoric Europe and was later continued by other stylistics of the Bronze Age.
8. BB were highly mobile culturally and easily moved from one region to another, however, they concentrated in old settlement centers whose roots usually dated back to the Early Neolithic.
9. Mixed cultural structures with groups traditionally living in individual regions developed rapidly; with the appearance of BB in a given region, no radical break in the process of cultural transformations is observed.
10. Upon the appearance of BB in an area, a period of civilization prosperity began, which continued, after their decline, into the Early Bronze Age.

This unusual 'colorfulness' of BB indicates that something important was going on in Europe at that time. In different local communities, occupying absolutely different ecological niches and having different histories, similar needs began to develop, which is seen in the use of similar sets of objects.

What were BB then? Individual papers in this volume show mechanisms that led to the spread of traits – archaeological identifiers of BB. The papers also propose specific interpretations of archeological data. In the latter, ever more space is given to social factors (cf. Czebreszuk 2003). This line of thinking is followed chiefly by British archeologists. However, the present volume is a proof that it has taken root on the Continent as well. The set of objects (frequently related to the theory of the so-called cultural package, cf. Burgess 1976; Czebreszuk 2003a) indicates the importance of the ritual of libation in which an ornamented bell beaker was used (Sherratt 1987); whereas such goods as archery equipment or a dagger relate to another sphere of life: war and hunting. Thence comes the most popular interpretation of BB according to which they revealed the process (by its nature a prolonged one) of emergence of the stratum of warriors in the societies of prehistoric Europe. The stratum later became the base from which a higher stratum (aristocracy) developed. Hence, it was a process whereby permanent social elites appeared among the inhabitants of Europe for the first time.

From this vantage point, BB would thus mark one of the most important turning points in the social history of Europe. As the Early Neolithic brought the emergence of peasants – the oldest stratum of contemporary society – BB are an archaeological manifestation of the early stages of formation of a next stratum of our society: an upper class (aristocracy). The next so great a change in the structure of our society occurred only in modern times when the strata of bourgeoisie and workers arose.

Bibliography

Burgess C. 1976. The Beaker Phenomenon: Some Suggestions, Part I: General Comments and the British Evidence. In: *Settlement and Economy in the Third and Second Millennium B.C.*, British Archaeological Report 33. Oxford, 306-323.

Czebreszuk J. 2003. Bell Beakers. From West to East. In: P. Bogucki / P.J. Crabtree (eds.) *Ancient Europe 8000 B.C. - A.D. 1000: Encyclopedia of the Barbarian World.* New York, 476-485.

Czebreszuk J. 2003a. Bell Beakers in the Sequence of the Cultural Changes in South-Western Baltic Area. In: J. Czebreszuk / M. Szmyt (eds), *The Northeast Frontier of Bell Beakers. Proceedings of the symposium held at the Adam Mickiewicz University, Poznań (Poland), May 26-29 2002.* British Archaeological Reports, International Series 1155. Oxford, 21-38.

Sherratt A.1987. Cubs that cheered. In: W.H. Waldren / R.C. Kennard (eds.), *Bell Beakers of the West Mediterranean*, British Archaeological Report. International Series 331. Oxford, 81-114.